DEFENDING AMERICA

Politics and Society in Twentieth-Century America

William Chafe, Gary Gerstle, Linda Gordon, and Julian Zelizer

A list of titles in this series appears at the back of the book.

DEFENDING AMERICA

MILITARY CULTURE AND THE
COLD WAR COURT-MARTIAL

ELIZABETH LUTES HILLMAN

PRINCETON UNIVERSITY PRESS

PRINCETON AND OXFORD

Library of Congress Cataloging-in-Publication Data

Hillman, Elizabeth Lutes, 1967–

    Defending America : military culture and the Cold War court-martial / Elizabeth
Lutes Hillman.

      p. cm. — (Politics and society in twentieth-century America)

    Includes bibliographical references and index.

    ISBN-13: 978-0-691-11804-8 (alk. paper)

    ISBN-10: 0-691-11804-3 (alk. paper)

    1. Courts-martial and courts of inquiry—United States—History—20th century.
2. Courts-martial and courts of inquiry—Social aspects—United States—History—
20th century.   3. Sociology, Military—United States—History—20th century.
4. Cold war—Social aspects—United States. I. Title. II. Series.

KF7620.H55 2005

343.73′0143—dc22

                                        2004058962

British Library Cataloging-in-Publication Data is available

For Vivian

CONTENTS

FIGURES AND TABLES

DEFENDING AMERICA

INTRODUCTION

This is a book about the American military, its system of justice, and its criminals. It tells of ordinary mistakes and extraordinary violence, of what happened when things went wrong as the Cold War military defended an anxious nation. The military criminals of the Cold War were deserters, rapists, spies, and bigamists. They included a company commander, one of very few African American officers, sentenced to death by a panel of white officers for refusing to advance on a Korean War battlefield; a much-decorated, long-retired admiral spied upon in his San Diego home and then court-martialed for being gay; a petty officer prosecuted for unauthorized absence after going home to Virginia to care for his ailing mother; a private, angry at his Vietnamese girlfriend for her attentions to other GIs (she was a prostitute), convicted for shooting and killing her.[1] These crimes offer a glimpse into the internal world of military service in the decades after World War II, when a fierce battle to preserve a cherished culture was waged against the encroachment of class, racial, and sexual diversity. Hardship and violence, humor and romance, the harsh reality of military service and the awkward process of enforcing law during war: all were part of American military justice. The court-martial exposes the fault lines of the United States during the Cold War, when demographic change and legal reform made the state of the armed forces a telling echo of the state of the nation.

Yet military justice has been almost completely overlooked by scholars of American history and law.[2] Apart from a handful of courts-martial that attracted media attention, military justice has sustained the interest of only judge advocates and a few historians.[3] Its processes have been portrayed as caricatures of modern criminal procedure, its prosecutions a simple reflection of the quality of troops recruited into military service.[4] As a body of law and as a source of history, military justice has been doubly neglected.

This book remedies that neglect. It uses court-martial records to deepen our understanding of how criminal justice worked, how servicemembers lived, and why legal reform mattered in the post–World War II United States. This is a study of "Cold War" military justice not because it covers every year of the conflict or because it details every shift in foreign and military policy.[5] "Cold War" refers instead to the atmosphere of political and cultural anxiety that reshaped the U.S. military and American society more generally. The U.S. military was in a state of transition after World War II, when victory brought glory but also new challenges.[6] The personnel needs of World War II had broadened the spectrum of Americans from which servicemembers were drawn, making the military a more accurate mirror of American society but lowering its exclusivity, and, in the eyes of many, downgrading its social status.[7] Meanwhile, civil rights, feminism, open homosexuality, and political dissent posed fundamental challenges to military authority. The political and social changes of the Cold War rippled through the armed forces with special intensity because of the racial hierarchies, class distinctions, and models of masculinity that had distinguished military culture in the past.[8] The social orders that had regulated American military life were suddenly fragile.

The court-martial registers the insecurity of the Cold War years in especially vivid fashion. A key part of that insecurity was the conflict between legal and political principles in the governance of the armed forces, apparent throughout the process of military justice. Asked to preserve the freedom of American citizens, the armed forces were starkly undemocratic, composed of many nonvolunteers and governed in authoritarian fashion. If the great political divide of the Cold War years was the Soviets' dependence on coercion versus the Americans' emphasis on consent, then the mere existence of the U.S. military disrupted a simple narrative of West versus East. Nowhere was the tension between military tradition and liberal democratic values more apparent than at court-martial, where the Cold War armed forces punished the gravest violations of military rules and regulations. The military prosecuted men who refused to defer to superiors, who spoke out against the war in Vietnam or in favor of communism, who got married without permission or had homosexual affairs. The military's separate criminal justice system, improved but preserved by post–World War II reforms, put those who fought to protect the U.S. Constitution beyond the reach of some of its most basic protections. And until the end of the draft in 1973, many Americans in uniform served reluctantly, compelled to join the military not by a sense of duty but by force of law.

This book traces the ways in which legal reform progressed—and faltered—in a particularly telling arena of criminal justice and social control. Its chapters explore the conflicts that divided the armed forces, and the nation, during the Cold War. The tension between the authority granted commanding officers and the process due at court-martial, along with the clash between the military's increasing heterogeneity and its commitment to an exclusive, archaic culture, tested the very structure of the American military. Protecting individual rights, both in the United States and around the world, became a higher priority in the 1950s and 1960s, colliding with the military practice of enforcing conformity and imposing involuntary service.[9] In this era of political strife, conscription, and war, legal reformers tried to standardize the definition of military crime and regularize its prosecution. They hoped to bring justice to American citizens in uniform much like those uniformed troops hoped to bring freedom and prosperity to the United States' allies around the world.

From the advent of a reformed military justice system in 1951 until the end of the Vietnam War, millions of Americans stood accused before military courts, charged with crimes defined by their commanders and tried according to special procedures set out in the Uniform Code of Military Justice (UCMJ).[10] The greatest reform in the history of American military law, the UCMJ granted accused servicemembers for the first time basic procedural rights, including access to counsel and the opportunity to appeal their cases to a court of civilian judges.[11] The previous regime of military law had been attacked as harsh and unfair during World War II, leading veterans and politicians to demand change. As a result, Cold War troops, whether charged with going AWOL, disobeying orders, or frequenting gay bars, had greater legal protections than had earlier generations of American soldiers. But because the UCMJ granted commanding officers broad discretion to define crime and control its prosecution, the success of its reforms was sharply limited by the military culture in which courts-martial took place.

At the same time that statutory reform brought new standards of justice to military criminal procedure, the military itself grew in authority, significance, and visibility. Until after World War II, the United States military was small and isolated except in times of war.[12] Although most Americans accepted the necessity of a well-prepared, disciplined armed force, they were uncomfortable with the implications of a standing professionalized military establishment. Yet the Cold War made the armed forces a central and permanent element of American society, and military culture took on a prominent role in many Americans' self-definition. Military spending quadrupled between 1948 and 1953.[13] As military operations attracted more funding, personnel, and scrutiny, the armed forces promoted American culture as they protected U.S. interests overseas.[14] The military itself became increasingly politicized. Commanding officers were well versed in public relations, ready to contest efforts to cut military spending and likely to blame others for failures of policy or tactics.[15] Washington, D.C., became a hub of American military activity, with Capitol Hill as attuned to military issues as military officers were to the nation's political climate.[16] In 1950, President Truman declared an "Armed Forces Day" of parades, fly-bys, and exhibits to celebrate the recently unified services.[17] Military displays like the F-84 Thunderjet in New York's City Hall Plaza in 1956 appeared around the country.[18] Enthusiasm for such public displays waned relatively quickly after the late 1950s, but a military presence remained at the center of American culture throughout this period.[19] Television shows brought servicemen into American living rooms as heroes in popular series and in documentaries. Consumers bought $16.9 million worth of "G.I. Joe" dolls and equipment in the first year after their 1964 release.[20]

This convergence of American and military culture was also reflected in the diminishing gap between military and civilian justice during the Cold

War.[21] Because postwar legal reform edged military law closer to civilian law and procedure, the history of the court-martial helps to illuminate the path of civilian criminal law. The UCMJ moved military criminal procedure in the same direction as other systems of American criminal justice after World War II by recognizing the rights of accused persons and articulating the elements of military crimes.[22] Both changes echoed the shift toward specified crimes and higher procedural standards that occurred in many civilian criminal jurisdictions.

But procedure could not keep cultural norms from influencing the outcomes of either military or civilian criminal trials and appeals. Military criminal records document the continuing impact of racial prejudice, socioeconomic distinctions, and assumptions about gender roles and sexual behavior on the process and outcomes of American criminal justice after World War II. The court-martial reveals that defending America involved not just fighting wars, but policing the political ideologies, sexual intimacies, and social interactions of the nation's citizen-soldiers. Official pronouncements declared equality of treatment across race lines, but racism in personnel policies, criminal justice outcomes, and portrayals of enemy forces continued. Recruiters were desperate to find competent troops but ignored women as a viable resource. The military forbade homosexuality but mandated same-sex environments, lionized sexual vigor but touted sexual restraint. The armed forces also participated in the widespread political repression that characterized American political culture during this period. The need to identify and eliminate communists was of paramount importance within the armed forces, where disloyalty could directly undermine national security interests.[23] The possibility of subversion from within the ranks of the military was a particularly galling thought to citizens already wary of the burgeoning Department of Defense. Military courts struggled to balance demands for reform and democratization against a long-standing culture of masculine privilege, racial exclusivity, and authoritarian leadership. Military justice reveals the power and depth of that struggle. It demonstrates not only how judges and judge advocates resolved legal issues and how politics and culture influenced military leaders, but also how soldiers on the ground lived out the conflicts created by the United States' role in fighting the ideological and actual battles of the Cold War.

By seeking insight into military life and American values through the court-martial, *Defending America* argues for the importance of servicemembers' chaotic, disparate lives, and the policies and culture of the military itself, to broader narratives of twentieth-century American and Cold War history. Court-martial records prove that military policies mattered. They also prove that prejudice and discrimination tainted criminal justice even when courts enforced procedural norms, and that living and working in the Cold War military was often brutalizing and frustrating even as it opened new doors of opportunity to so many young Americans. These records, however, do not "prove" the guilt or innocence of the persons accused, nor the guilt or innocence of the institution that recruited, trained, deployed, and prosecuted them. Instead, they show the consequences of war and military culture during years in which military service was a life-changing experience for millions of Americans. Courts-martial for rape, cowardice, and collaboration, for example, make the human toll of the often forgotten Korean War painfully apparent; military crimes related to prostitution reveal the damaging secondary effects of military occupation on local communities and families; vague laws and arbitrary enforcement permitted the armed forces' prejudice against homosexuals to destroy the careers of countless dedicated servicemembers. Military judges, judge advocates, and commanding officers were no more, or less, culpable than many civilians in creating a criminal justice system that operated at times in arbitrary, unjust ways. But the exigencies of war and the pressure to conform to military standards of behavior made striking a balance between legal process and cultural norms even more difficult in the ranks of the armed forces than in civilian jurisdictions.

Chapter 1 examines the Cold War military justice system as a whole, exploring the new use of the court-martial as a less common but more stigmatizing tool of military discipline. Subsequent chapters trace the prosecution of military crime and the evolution of legal doctrine, in the context of the sometimes harrowing realities of military life. Chapter 2 focuses on a central dilemma of military crime and society, the difficulty of enforcing discipline in an institution in which the line between "good" and "bad" behavior was not easy to draw. Chapter 3 considers how the Cold War military, charged with defending self-determination and political autonomy, treated dissent and difference within its ranks as not only undesirable, but potentially criminal. Chapter 4 examines the courts-martial that grew out of the tension between family and military responsibilities, revealing how gendered assumptions about behavior clashed with the military's expectations of its troops. Chapter 5 analyzes how commanders' prosecutorial discretion contributed to racial disparities in military justice, especially in the prosecution of sex crimes. Chapter 6 focuses on the often contentious trials of high-ranking officers, revealing how the privileged status of officers made them less likely to be prosecuted for most crimes but especially vulnerable to punishment for acts that tarnished the military's public image. The afterword sketches the post-Vietnam landscape of military justice, highlighting the changes in military justice that have occurred since the mid-1970s and looking beyond the court-martial to another subset of military justice, the new military commissions intended to try suspected terrorists.

Post–World War II American history has lost the story of the modern court-martial, a drama full of global intrigue, personal tragedy, and grim insight into American politics and culture. This book begins to tell that story.

Chapter 1

NEW RIGHTS, OLD HIERARCHIES

Legal Reform in a Changing Military

John Henry Wigmore, dean of American evidence law and an Army judge advocate during World War I, praised military justice for its decisiveness: "The military system can say this for itself: It *knows what it wants*, and it systematically *goes in and gets it*."[1] But the certainty that Wigmore so admired in the World War I–era court-martial was no longer a feature of military justice under the UCMJ. The code's emphasis on due process was at odds with the speed and decisiveness that Wigmore and many other officers expected from military criminal law. As the UCMJ slowed and complicated the process of disciplining troops through the military justice system, commanding officers responded by convening fewer courts-martial, sidestepping the code's procedures, and inventing new ways to enforce discipline. Meanwhile, changes in the missions and demographics of the armed forces muddied the clarity that Wigmore celebrated. The professionalized, standing American armed forces of the Cold War used the court-martial not as an instrument of summary justice but as a public spectacle and a crude, if unpredictable, disciplinary tool.

This chapter examines how the Cold War armed forces developed a distinctive legal culture as demographic change and political anxiety changed the nature of the U.S. military. By placing both the military and its justice system into the broader post–World War American scene, it sets the stage for understanding the categories of military crime explored in the following chapters. First, it identifies the challenges faced by commanding officers who sought to maintain an exclusive culture of military service in a newly integrated, technologically sophisticated, conscripted armed force. As military demographics shifted, the function of the court-martial shifted as well. Next, it explains this shift, arguing that under the UCMJ a military trial became less an act of disciplining an individual and more a demonstration of military values. Finally, it traces the path of criminal justice reform within military legal culture, where commanding officers, fearing that procedural rigor would undermine the strict hierarchies of military life, resisted the new rules, even as judges, intent on protecting the rights of servicemembers with the shield of the UCMJ, insisted on the importance of due process throughout the court-martial process.

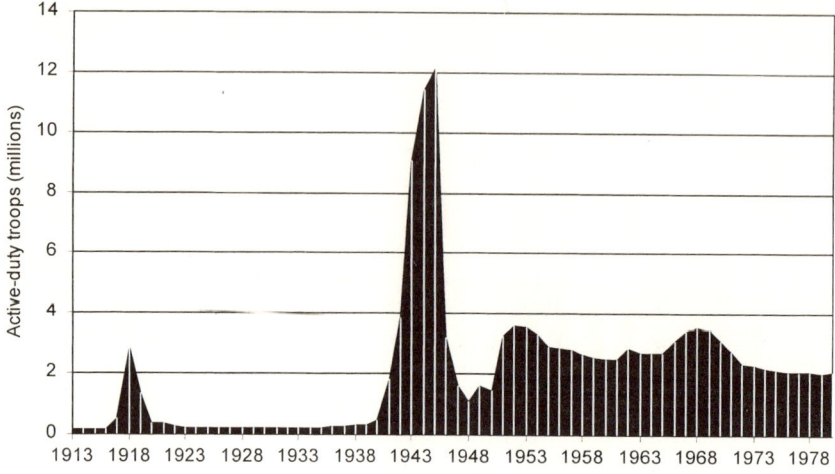

Figure 1.1 U.S. Armed Forces Personnel, 1913–1980

THE NEW MEANING OF MOBILIZATION

As reformers sought to change military justice procedures, the military it-self underwent a massive transition. Mobilizing for the Cold War—the nu-clear, global Cold War—was unlike mobilizing for any other war. Larger, more technically demanding, and more racially diverse than in earlier eras, the Cold War armed forces required new recruiting plans and personnel policies.[2] New civil agencies appeared to address issues of national security alongside the military, which grew into a huge, frequently reorganized bu-reaucracy in the 1950s.[3] The sheer size of the defense establishment was a source of strain on the UCMJ-mandated justice system, which already re-quired more time, training, and paperwork than had military justice in the past.

Though the need for more military personnel heightened in the years of heaviest ground combat in the Korean and Vietnam Wars, the armed forces remained sizable even in times of relative peace (see figure 1.1). During the Korean conflict, more than 3 million servicemembers per year were on ac-tive duty. The Army was the largest branch of service, with about 40 per-cent of the active-duty force, followed by the Air Force around 30 percent, the Navy near 20, and the Marine Corps with less than 10 percent of total military personnel. After the Korean ceasefire in 1953, the number of troops dropped below 3 million and then stayed relatively constant until 1966, when the demands of the war in Vietnam pushed the number higher (see figure 1.2). Troop strength peaked again in 1968 with 3.5 million ser-

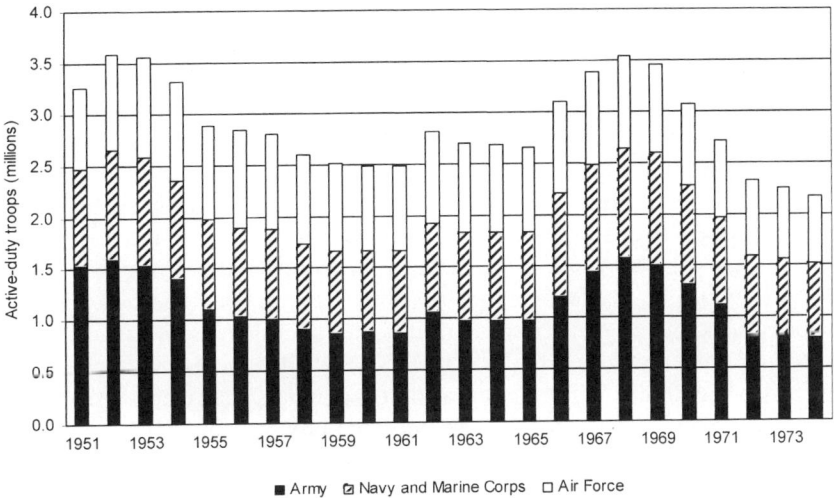

Figure 1.2 U.S. Armed Forces Personnel, 1951–1974

vicemembers, and then began another decline, falling to 3 million by 1970 and 2.25 million in 1973.[4]

Government officials fought a constant battle to meet recruiting goals. Moving the paperwork generated by such a large force required more people in administration in addition to the greater number of troops performing more traditional military roles in support of American deployments. But even with the aid of conscription to supplement volunteers, attracting enough qualified recruits from a war-weary population in a booming economy was no easy task.[5] The era's prosperity hindered recruiting and retention, even after the military instituted policies more conducive to family life and raised the pay scales of officers in an effort to keep pace with civilian salaries.[6] Americans were apprehensive about the future of warfare in an age of nuclear weapons.[7] Waning public confidence jeopardized the positive image of the armed forces that the services relied upon for recruiting and political support.

Changes in the demographics of servicemembers also posed new problems of discipline for leaders of the Army, Navy, Air Force, and Marine Corps, with each branch of service trying to populate its ranks with qualified, orderly troops. In addition to worrying about the number of soldiers in uniform, officials fretted over the quality of servicemembers, as measured by aptitude tests and educational achievement.[8] The military complained often of recruits who entered the service with poor educational backgrounds. These young men were considered disciplinary problems from the start of their military careers, and were in fact more likely to end up facing courts-martial. Indicators of quality in the male enlisted forces dropped precipitously after World War II as recruits became younger, poorer, and less educated.[9] Concerns about this achievement gap helped bring about two 1948 "manpower" reforms: the Women's Armed Forces Integration Act, which allowed for the possibility of military careers for at least a few servicewomen, and President Truman's order to desegregate the armed forces. Despite having little immediate impact on the make-up of the armed forces, these reforms were powerful symbols of the United States' intent to widen the range of Americans to whom the honor and prestige of military service would be available. High tensions accompanied the possibility as well as the actual implementation of racial and gender desegregation. Both veterans and active-duty military officers responded to the changes; as one historian remarked, "[T]he integration of women and blacks further upset the undermanned, marginally effective armed forces."[10] At the same time, government repression targeted gay and lesbian government employees and servicemembers.[11] Fear of homosexual servicemembers intruding into its ranks added urgency to the military's campaigns to identify and eliminate suspected gay and lesbian troops in the 1950s.[12]

Technological change and demographic shifts complicated the task of training and organizing troops, who were no longer best managed with the coercive methods that had characterized military leadership in the past. The younger generation of Americans upon whom the military relied were seen as increasingly rebellious, frustrating those who would control them, whether parents or military officers.[13] Meeting the military's personnel needs was made more difficult by the bureaucratic intricacies of managing conscription, volunteering, deferments, and guard and reserve forces all at one time.[14] As a new psychology of management took hold of the post–World War II military bureaucracy, the unique quality of military discipline as distinct from civilian corporate culture seemed to be dissolving.[15] Military leaders sought new ways to ensure orderly troops at the same time they tried to protect the armed forces' integrity in the eyes of a skeptical public.

Each branch of service devised a recruiting strategy to remedy low reenlistment rates and counter the impression of low-quality recruits.[16] The Air Force stressed both the availability of high-tech training and the attractiveness of an Air Force career.[17] The other services used recruiting slogans that played to their own strengths, the Army focusing on "patriotism and vocational education" and the Navy on "tradition and travel."[18] Concerns that the Air Force was hoarding the brightest recruits prompted then-Secretary of Defense George C. Marshall to adopt a "qualitative distribution policy" that created a system of service quotas based on the mental aptitude of personnel. Adopted in May 1951 and effective until 1958, this distribution of talent plan forced the Air Force to accept recruits in lower classifications, presumably freeing up the "better" recruits to sign with the other services.[19]

Marshall's plan to share the recruiting wealth among the services fore-shadowed Project 100,000, the brainchild of Secretary of Defense Robert McNamara. Project 100,000 was a Great Society program intended to aug-ment the armed forces with recruits previously rejected because of low scores on preadmission intelligence tests.[20] This plan, which Senator Daniel Patrick Moynihan viewed as a means of rescuing young African American men from a destructive, matriarchal culture, brought over 400,000 young men, most from poverty, into the service between 1966 and 1972.[21] Moy-nihan's rationale for the program combined two popular perspectives on military service: that it built character and made men and that the modern armed forces could be an instrument of social change. The additional train-ing that was supposed to accompany the induction of these underprepared men did not materialize, and the consequences were dire, as historian Chris-tian Appy has shown in his study of Vietnam soldiers. Half were sent to Vietnam, where they died at a rate twice that of other troops. Although African Americans comprised only 10 percent of the military in the late 1960s, they were 40 percent of the Project 100,000 inductees.[22] A prime reason for the disproportionately high casualty rate among these troops was the high percentage sent into combat occupations, which made up most of the military occupations deemed suitable for "Project 100,000 men."[23] Halfhearted social engineering efforts like Project 100,000, even coupled with sophisticated recruiting campaigns and extensive testing of potential inductees, failed to repair the military's deficit in skilled servicemembers.

In spite of commanders' complaints about the capabilities of recruits and the difficulty of training ill-prepared troops, not all Cold War demographic shifts worked against the "quality" that recruiters sought among potential soldiers. Better-educated, older, and married servicemembers were associ-ated with lower rates of crime and disciplinary incidents. The percentage of high-school graduates among enlistees rose steadily throughout the cy-cles of military build-up and decline in the 1950s and 1960s, reflecting na-tional trends in education. The Department of Defense estimated that over 50 percent of enlisted troops had graduated from high school in 1952, a figure that rose to 62 percent by 1958, 72 by 1962, over 80 by 1965, and near 90 by 1978.[24] The median age of male military personnel rose grad-ually between the buildups for war: In 1956, it stood at 23 years of age, rose to 24.5 by 1960, then began to fall in 1962 to a new low of 22.7 in 1968–69 before rising again with the reduction of troop strength in Viet-nam.[25] By 1966, nearly 80 percent of officers, but only 40 percent of en-listees, were married. Significant differences reflected the cultures of the various service branches; the rate of marriage was lowest in the Marine Corps (74.5 percent of officers and only 22.2 percent of enlisted men mar-ried) and highest in the Air Force (83.2 percent of officers and 59.7 per-cent of enlisted men married).[26] Though less likely to commit the crimes of recklessness and poor judgment that were common among young troops, the larger contingent of married servicemembers were more likely to violate rules restricting marriage and to commit marital crimes such as adultery and bigamy.

There was one group of recruits who were consistently older, more educated, and less prone to disciplinary problems than the average enlisted person during the 1950s and 1960s: women. They were, however, an almost completely overlooked resource during the first decades of the Cold War. At the outbreak of war in Korea, only 22,000 women were serving on active duty, less than half the number that could have been under existing law (see figure 1.3).[27] The 45,000 women on active duty in 1953 amounted to just over 1 percent of the total number of active-duty personnel. By the late 1950s, the number of servicewomen had fallen to about 30,000, where it would stay until a gradual increase began in 1967.

Because attitudes and assignment policies toward servicewomen varied among branches of service, women were distributed unevenly. Only about 2,000 female Marines served on active duty each year of the 1950s and 1960s, while women in the Army numbered between 11,000 and 20,000 per year (see figure 1.3).[28] Women in the Navy hovered at 7,000 to 8,000 between 1951 and the early 1970s, while the number of Air Force servicewomen fluctuated between about 9,000 and 16,000.[29] In 1965, 70 percent of enlisted servicewomen worked in clerical and administrative positions; nearly a quarter more worked in medical positions, most often as nurses.

Even with the limitations placed on servicewomen's occupational specialties during this period, many servicemen performed the same military duties as servicewomen. In fact, many more service*men* than women performed the less-than-martial tasks to which most female soldiers were assigned. During the Vietnam War, nearly 15 percent of the male enlisted force worked in administrative positions, 22 percent in technical or scientific jobs, and 13 percent as "service workers."[30] "Military"-style duties were scarcer for men than in the past because of the high percentage of technically demanding jobs during the Cold War. Military-specific occupational specialties, including "combat" duties, were assigned to only 18 percent of the total enlisted force during Vietnam, down from 38 percent in World War II and 30 percent during the Korean War.[31]

The Cold War military policies that preferred men to women were less a functional imperative than an attempt to preserve a culture that celebrated masculine authority. The decision of the armed forces to implement programs such as Project 100,000 rather than to mobilize more women reserved the duty and privilege of military service for American men. The possibility of women being "masculinized" by military service was disturbing to many female military leaders, who repeatedly sought ways to make women appear more conventionally attractive in their uniforms. But

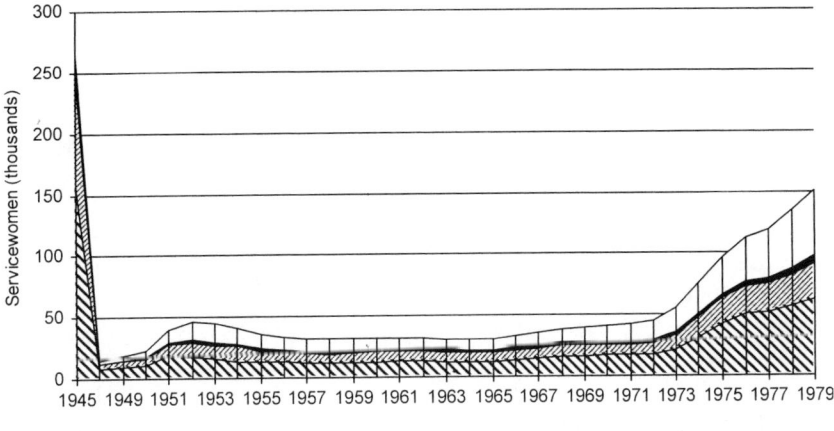

Figure 1.3 Women in the U.S. Armed Forces, 1945–1979

preventing the armed forces from being "feminized" was of greater concern to the military as a whole.[32] The military's increasing rejection of gay
men, at least during times of force reduction, also reflected its desire to promote an image of virile, heterosexual servicemen. With the image of the
soldier as a warrior jeopardized by technology and bureaucracy, putting
more women in uniform was not an acceptable solution to the military's
personnel needs.

Servicewomen were not contemplated as an answer to the military's disciplinary concerns either, though they were court-martialed at extremely
low rates. With the exception of a lower rate of marriage than among servicemen, the demographics of women in the military helped to explain
their good behavior: they were older, better educated, and more likely to
be officers than men.[33] And of course, they were not male, which in civil
as well as military populations made them statistically less likely to be
charged with crimes. Still, women are not absent from court-martial
records. They appear as witnesses, uncharged accomplices, victims, or
lawyers in addition to occasionally as accused persons at courts-martial.[34]

The Vanishing Court-Martial: Spectacle and Military Trials

World War II had highlighted the tension between the nation's professed
role as defender of freedom and democracy and servicemembers' complaints of gross injustice at court-martial.[35] Allegations of incompetent de-

fense counsel, massive discrepancies in punishments for the same offenses, and excessively harsh sentences had plagued the military justice system during the war.[36] Describing a 1948 court-martial as "saturated with tyranny," a federal judge expressed a popular consensus about the undemocratic nature of military justice.[37] James Forrestal, the first secretary of Defense, appointed a committee to draft a code that would modernize military justice.[38] The result was the UCMJ, which established a procedural and substantive criminal law that applied across the Army, Navy, Air Force, Marine Corps, and Coast Guard, each of which had previously operated its own criminal justice system.[39] Trial procedure was dictated by the *Manual for Courts-Martial*, termed "the red book" for its burgundy binding, and the courts-martial of all the services were subject to the authority of the Court of Military Appeals, a civilian court of three judges.[40] The code created a separate system of criminal law that existed alongside but beyond the scope of the Constitution's rules about the investigation and prosecution of civilian crime.[41]

These legal reforms, along with the changing nature of military service and demographics, diminished the number of crimes prosecuted at court-martial.[42] No longer would the court-martial operate as the routine disciplinary tool it had been as recently as World War II, when two million courts-martial were held.[43] During World War II, the Army executed 142 men, including Eddie Slovik, a troubled young Army private put to death for desertion. Slovik's case raised questions about both prosecutorial discretion and the proportionality of court-martial sentences.[44] A leading scholar of courts-martial estimated that one-third of all the criminal cases tried under American jurisdiction during the war occurred in military courts.[45] Yet the rate at which the military court-martialed soldiers was already declining, pushed down by the beginnings of legal reform and by a shift toward less coercive means of enforcing discipline.[46] The first reliable statistics on the annual general court-martial rate show that approximately nineteen general courts took place for every thousand servicemembers during World War I. By the 1970s, the rate had plummeted nearly 90 percent, down to about two courts per thousand servicemembers.[47] The decreasing frequency of courts-martial is easily the most striking feature of twentieth-century military criminal law (see figure 1.4).[48]

The overall court-martial rate declined from nearly 300 per thousand servicemembers in 1920 to less than 30 per thousand by 1970.[49] This decline in criminal trials is unique to the military; although more difficult to document than the court-martial rate, the frequency of civilian criminal trials did not decline appreciably during these decades of the twentieth century. In fact, the rates of criminal trials reported in the FBI's annual crime surveys went up, not down, during many of the years of declining rates of court-martial.[50] Criminal prosecution of civilians actually surged in the

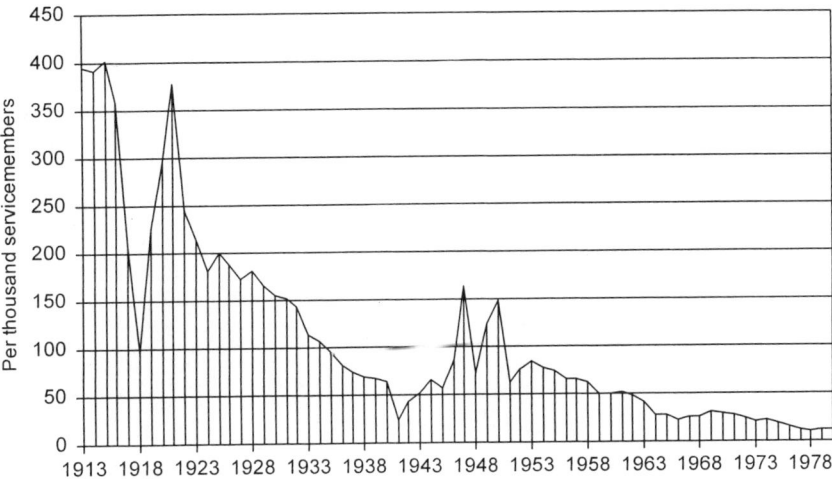

Figure 1.4 U.S. Armed Forces Court-Martial Rate, 1913–1980

post–World War II period with a wave of concern over juvenile delinquency and a sex crime panic.[51] The developing legal culture of the armed forces, with its emphasis on due process, legal representation, and civilian review, led directly to less frequent use of courts-martial.

The downward trend in the court-martial rate was not steady, however; the court-martial rate spiked around the two world wars and the Korean War (see figure 1.4). These departures from the general decline of the court-martial rate were probably caused by the increases in the size of the armed forces that accompanied wars and the disciplinary problems that resulted from rapid increases or decreases in force strength.[52] At the start of a wartime buildup, the legal apparatus of the military grew more slowly than the rest of the armed forces, limiting the resources available to deal formally with disciplinary incidents and temporarily depressing the rate of court-martial.[53] At the end of a war, when getting servicemembers out of uniform became a priority, commanders had new incentives to punish misbehaving troops and greater legal resources to do so. The postwar punishment of servicemembers who had deserted or gone AWOL during war also raised the court-martial rate.[54] Combined, these factors pushed the court-martial rate up after the end of major hostilities.

Despite these wartime aberrations, the court-martial had clearly become a less appealing option to commanders interested in correcting lapses in military discipline. Legal reform made military courts more public, more difficult to control, and more expensive. The new code also made criminal trials more likely to become embarrassing exposés of military folly. As a result, facing court-martial became an increasingly rare fate for wayward soldiers, sailors, airmen, and marines. Newly legalized and administered by officers well aware of the importance of presenting a positive image to the public, military courts could no longer serve as a primary means of enforcing military discipline. Courts-martial instead became a performance of military values for the culture at large, setting the boundaries of deviant behavior for the armed forces, and, to a certain extent, for the American body politic. Criminal censure now occupied the extreme end of commanders' methods of promoting obedience and preserving order among troops. Military criminal prosecutions became a spectacle of the deference to authority, manliness, and heterosexism that the armed forces sought to preserve as fundamental military values even in a new age.

Courts-martial joined other heavy-handed attempts to assert American values during the Cold War. Historian and cultural critic Tom Engelhardt describes how the Pentagon in the 1950s helped to produce television shows and movies that were "war spectacles and spectaculars" for an American public hungry for demonstrations of military power.[55] Engelhardt also characterizes the hearings of the House Un-American Activities Committee as "a traveling road show," a "performance," as "highly stylized and largely ceremonial in nature."[56] The HUAC hearings, like courts-martial, could have profound consequences for those hauled before them. In the larger world of political culture both the hearings and military trials signaled the government's intent to punish those who challenged Cold War political and cultural norms. They marked the gravity of such challenges while advertising the strength and authority of the political and legal institutions that sought to control Americans' behavior. But because the new trials of the UCMJ were so much more difficult to control than earlier versions of courts-martial, Cold War courts-martial did not work well even in this revamped role. Criminal trials, like wars, could be a spectacular means of projecting state decisiveness and power. But both came at great cost.

REFORM AND REACTION UNDER THE UCMJ

As courts-martial became scarcer under the UCMJ, the rules that governed their prosecution multiplied. The legal particulars of courts-martial under the new code show how criminal justice reform culture clashed with the norms of military life, suggesting the resistance to change that also limited progressive reforms in other governmental institutions and criminal jurisdictions. Many of the UCMJ's changes in procedure sought to solve a persistent problem at court-martial: the tendency of commanders to control the outcomes of courts-martial.[57] Commanders themselves often considered the procedural rigors of the UCMJ an impediment to maintaining adequate discipline among troops.[58] By establishing rules for pretrial investigation, requiring that a law officer preside over a general court-martial, recognizing a limited right to counsel, and creating an extensive appellate structure, the UCMJ moved lawyers to the center of a process that had previously kept them on the periphery, edging court-martial procedure closer to a variant of civilian criminal procedure.[59]

There was, however, a limit to how civilian-like or lawyer-dominated court-martial procedure could become. Accused persons appeared in uniform at court-martial, as did judge advocates, law officers, and court reporters. Military rank was apparent in the courtroom; most of the servicemembers who faced trial were junior enlistees only a few months or perhaps a year or two into their enlistments.[60] The crimes charged were more likely to be military than civil in nature.[61] During the first two years under the UCMJ, more than half of court-martial convictions involved military offenses; by the 1970s, the percentage was even higher, reaching 80 percent in one estimate.[62] Courts-martial, then, were not transformed into either civilian criminal courts or models of fairness overnight by the UCMJ. Whether "justice" and "discipline," the oft-articulated twin goals of courts-martial, were inseparable, as advocates argued, or incompatible, as critics claimed, criminal justice in the armed forces pursued different ends from those of civilian criminal justice.[63] Military leaders knew that the perception that courts-martial were "kangaroo courts" could ruin morale and breed defiance among current servicemembers while dissuading potential recruits from joining the service. But they also believed that scrupulous regard for due process was less important than decisive, exemplary punishment for misbehavior.[64]

The court-martial proceeding that an accused soldier faced was more likely to be a special or summary court-martial rather than a full-blown general court-martial. Because the UCMJ's procedural rules were the most onerous at general courts-martial, general courts were the most public, most revealing, and least common of the three types of military courts (see figure 1.5). The UCMJ permitted special and summary courts-martial—which could impose much more limited sentences than general courts—to operate with simpler procedures and fewer appeals.[65] Although the rates of all types of courts-martial were lower under the UCMJ than they had been during earlier periods of military history, commanding officers were most wary of spending precious time and resources on general courts. Because of the high cost of convening general courts, they accounted for fewer than 5 percent of all courts-martial between 1951 and 1973.[66]

Yet general courts saw the most serious crimes, were most affected by legal reform, and left behind the most extensive documentation. Convened to prosecute crimes related to conduct, speech, appearance, and relationships, they offer details of servicemembers' lives as well as proof of the types

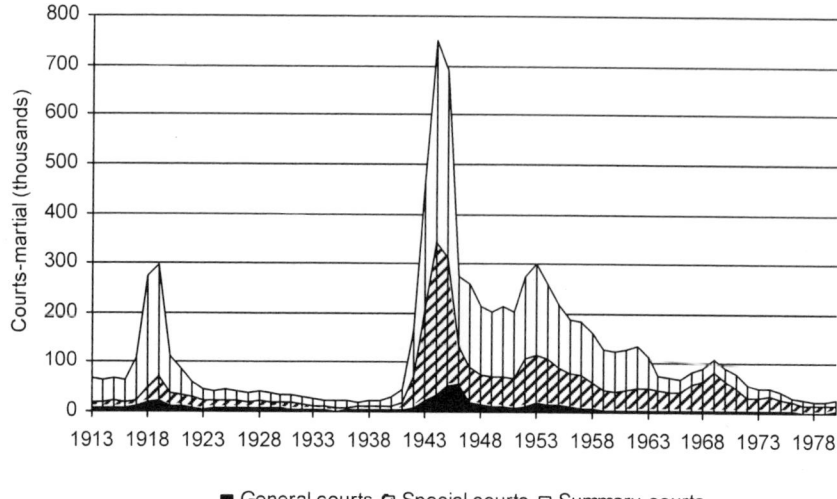

Figure 1.5 Types of Courts-Martial, 1913–1980

of misconduct that commanding officers chose to punish through the harshest means available. Thus these extraordinary courts are the primary focus of this study.[67] The military equivalents of civilian felony trials, general courts were not eliminated by the UCMJ; more than 140,000 were held between 1951 and 1973. At a general court-martial, a servicemember could be prosecuted for any crime and could face any sentence, including death.[68] The UCMJ mandated the presence of a law officer (called a military judge and given greater authority in 1969) and legally trained counsel at general courts and required the preparation of a verbatim transcript and automatic appellate review.[69] A general court also required a panel of at least five members until 1969, when an amendment to the UCMJ permitted an accused servicemember to opt for trial by judge alone.[70] The legal resources invested in general courts are apparent from their predominance among reported opinions of the military's appellate courts: 99 percent of reported military justice cases are from general courts.[71]

Whether general, special, or summary, every Cold War court-martial was likely to result in a conviction. The procedural restrictions imposed by the UCMJ theoretically reduced the control that commanders could exert over the outcome of a trial, but in practice accused servicemembers were convicted as often as they had been under earlier versions of military law.[72] At special and summary courts, conviction rates surpassed 80 percent; at general courts, they approached 95 percent.[73] A convicted soldier most often faced a sentence that included confinement, forfeiture of pay, reduction in rank, or discharge from the service, although general courts could impose death for any of the UCMJ's eight (increased to thirteen during wartime) capital crimes.[74]

Though the UCMJ did not reduce conviction rates or lessen the severity of punishments, it did offer convicted servicemembers new avenues of postconviction appeal. After sentencing, punishments could be mitigated through the several layers of clemency and appeal created by the UCMJ.[75] The first clemency opportunity came from the officers who ordered courts-martial in the first place. These officers, known as convening authorities, could reduce, but not increase, any court-martial sentence. They decided how to proceed with the help of legal staff recommendations. Serious sentences triggered additional appellate processes: Every conviction that imposed a punitive discharge or a sentence to a year or more of confinement went forward to a board of review (later called a court of military review), which could alter the findings of the court-martial and reduce the sentence adjudged.[76] All capital cases, all cases involving flag (general) officers, and all cases forwarded by the judge advocate of each service were then sent to the Court of Military Appeals, which also considered petitions for certiorari in cases that did not qualify for automatic review.[77] The final step in the appellate process was review and approval by a high-ranking official, usually the secretary or the judge advocate general of the applicable service (though the president had to approve all death sentences and any sentence imposed on a flag officer). The UCMJ's reforms produced rates of overturned convictions and reduced sentences (both about 15 percent) similar to those of federal criminal courts during this period.[78]

The declining rate of court-martial reduced the military prison population and altered military policies on restoring convicted servicemembers to active duty. The personnel shortages of the 1950s, 1960s, and 1970s encouraged this trend toward restoring persons to duty whenever possible.[79] The total number of prisoners confined in military stockades and disciplinary barracks dropped under the UCMJ. Between 1949 and 1959, the rate of incarceration among servicemembers fell nearly 75 percent, from nineteen prisoners per thousand soldiers to five.[80] The UCMJ encouraged standardization, but each branch of service continued to set its own policies regarding parole and returning convicted servicemembers to service.[81] The Army's disciplinary barracks and the Navy's retraining commands made "maximum efforts toward effecting rehabilitation" during this period.[82] This emphasis on rehabilitation worked relatively well; recidivism was very low among those restored to duty.[83]

Military justice policies thus reflected personnel needs as well as legal reform. The court-martial was a costly means of eliminating servicemembers, and troops themselves were too valuable to be lost to military service simply because of a conviction at court-martial. The disciplinary spectacle of a military trial was complete long before a convicted servicemember was discharged from the service, permitting military courts to demonstrate values and exert control over current servicemembers even when they did not remove wrongdoers from the ranks.

Legal reform, then, made the military justice system less effective in eliminating "undesirable" soldiers. As a result, military leaders turned to the administrative discharge hearing instead.[84] These hearings replaced courts-martial for a majority of routine disciplinary matters.[85] One senior noncommissioned officer described the disciplinary situation during Vietnam as desperate for more speed and less process: "The Army's got to find a better way [than court-martial] to get rid of people faster who don't want to be here."[86] Administrative separations could eliminate servicemembers quickly and quietly.[87] Discharge boards could order an undesirable discharge "for the good of the service," thus disqualifying a servicemember from receiving any veterans' benefits.[88] These discharges ousted many AWOL (absent without leave) offenders without criminal trials.[89] The number of AWOL and desertion incidents handled through administrative hearings increased further in the early 1970s because of the 1969 military justice reforms and a growing backlog of cases.[90] The services even went so far as to create new categories of discharge to expel unwanted servicemembers.[91] Between 1950 and 1973, the percentage of undesirable discharges issued through administrative, rather than court-martial, proceedings climbed dramatically, from 64 percent in the early 1950s Army to 92 percent by the early 1970s, and from 40 percent in the early 1950s Navy to 66 percent by the early 1970s.[92]

The other alternative to the Cold War court-martial was nonjudicial punishment, permitted by Article 15 of the UCMJ and known as "captain's mast" in the Navy and "office hours" in the Marine Corps. It became another way to avoid the cost and procedural fuss of court-martial.[93] After a 1962 bill raised the maximum punishment available under Article 15 to the level of a summary court-martial, nonjudicial punishment expanded, virtually replacing the summary court-martial entirely.[94] Commanders could now use an Article 15 proceeding to punish a servicemember with partial forfeiture of pay and up to thirty days of correctional custody, an enhancement to their previous authority to impose two weeks of additional duties, restrictions, and limited privileges.[95] These changes in disciplinary tactics effectively circumvented the due process set out in the UCMJ.

The UCMJ's attempt to standardize military criminal law was also limited by social, cultural, and demographic differences among the services. The Army, Navy and Marine Corps, Air Force, and Coast Guard each retained its own intermediate appellate court, corps of military lawyers, and regulations pertaining to legal matters. Judge advocates of the different

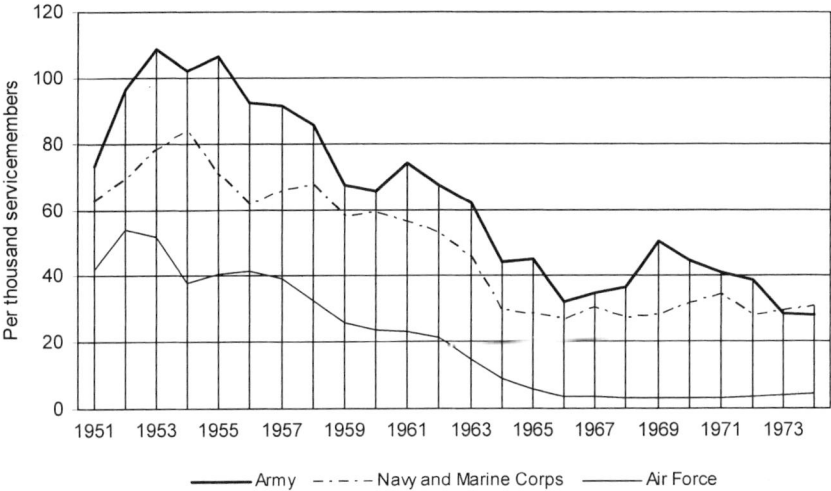

Figure 1.6 Court-Martial Rates of the Service Branches, 1951–1974

branches of service did not frequently interact with their peers in other services, and the opinions of the services' separate appellate courts did not often rely on the decisions of their sister courts for guidance.[96] The services had different missions, types of duty, recruitment patterns, and force structures as well as separate legal institutions. As a result, military criminality varied, and legal reform progressed differently, in each branch of service.

Figure 1.6 depicts the court-martial rates of the services, indicating the Army's relatively high rate of court-martial and the Air Force's relatively low rate. The Army's large number of low-ranking soldiers and its ground-combat mission created disciplinary problems more likely to lead to court-martial than the Air Force's high percentage of officers and more remote, technical mission. The Navy and Marine Corps rate, which falls between the Army and Air Force rates, is reported as a composite rate because a single intermediate appellate court (called the Navy Board of Review and later the Navy–Marine Corps Court of Military Review) heard cases from both services. But the Marine Corps prosecuted crime at a rate that rivaled the Army's for the highest court-martial rate during the 1950s and 1960s.[97] With demographics and a mission similar to that of the Army but with a reputation for stricter discipline, the Marine Corps' high rate of court-martial is not surprising.[98] Leslie Gale's study of comparative crime rates in the services points out that this "service order" of crime corresponded to how "military" each service was, "as indexed by death rates, amount and kind of training, and occupational structure."[99] The most martial of the services, the Army and the Marine Corps, prosecuted significantly more crime than the two least martial, the Coast Guard and the Air Force, with the Navy landing in the middle.[100]

The extent of military criminality, then, correlated to the extent of physical, interpersonal violence involved in various military missions. The Air Force and Navy had a greater number of servicemembers in technically demanding positions than did the infantry-heavy Army and Marine Corps. This distinction helps to explain the higher rates of court-martial in the Army and Marine Corps—both of which valorized physical aggression and issued small arms and other weapons to a higher percentage of their troops. In the Marine Corps and Army, a higher percentage of courts-martial also involved crimes against persons—that is, crimes that caused harm to individuals rather than property—than in the Navy or the Air Force.[101] A study of reported military appellate opinions from 1951 to 1966 revealed that homicide and assault totaled over 60 percent of appealed Army cases, 40 percent of Marine Corps cases, and 30 percent of Navy, Air Force, and Coast Guard cases.[102] These percentages suggest that the training and culture of American ground troops contributed to higher rates of violent crime than did the more bureaucratic cultures of the air and sea services.

The far-flung operations of military law and the difficulty of seeking justice and enforcing discipline through the same system also slowed the pace of change within courts-martial. Even with the ambitious legislation of the UCMJ and many dedicated judge advocates, the code's reforms proved difficult to enforce.[103] Since commanders, not state attorneys general or local district attorneys, decided whether or not to prosecute military crime, the attitudes of individual commanding officers affected the implementation of the code's reforms.[104] Many officers resisted the code's changes, worried that legal culture would supplant military discipline and undermine the obedience and aggressiveness they prized in their troops.

The reformers who drafted the UCMJ were not unsympathetic to such concerns, and they preserved many special features of military criminal law in the code. It gave commanders a central role by granting them discretionary power throughout the legal process, from deciding whether to investigate an alleged infraction to selecting which servicemembers would serve on court-martial panels.[105] To discourage commanders who might be tempted to bully court-martial panels, the code made improper "command influence" a crime, but this offense was almost never prosecuted.[106] Commanders who felt that criminal sanction should be available for violations of military tradition were reassured by the articles of the UCMJ that specified military crimes such as "disrespect toward a superior officer," "failure to obey an order or regulation," and "misbehavior before the enemy," and by the vaguely defined catch-all clauses that made nearly any conduct potentially criminal.[107] The UCMJ struck a tenuous balance between protecting servicemembers' rights and preserving the integrity and authority of military hierarchy.

Servicemembers were conditioned to obey orders and to defer to superiors, a practice difficult to leave behind when a court-martial was convened. After all, it was a crime to disobey under the UCMJ, even for officers. Samuel P. Huntington, a leading scholar of military life in the 1950s and 1960s, described obedience as the cardinal virtue of the commissioned officer.[108] The effects of military hierarchy were even stronger when, as in most courts-martial, the accused person was of low rank and little experience, accused by a commanding officer of high grade and long experience, and judged by persons selected by that commander. Reformers of military criminal justice could depend on legal actors who would follow the rules, but they also faced a social system stacked against those of inferior rank.

The UCMJ sought to minimize the disadvantages faced by those of inferior rank, but it was not an easy task. The armed forces' emphasis upon hierarchy permeated the atmosphere of all courts-martial. During a trial, law officers, judge advocates, accused servicemembers, court reporters, and members of a court-martial panel appeared in uniform, replete with the stripes, bars and other insignia of military grade.[109] In the courtroom, military courtesies were observed along with the rules of military criminal procedure. The UCMJ required that an accused soldier be tried by court-martial members of equal or higher rank whenever possible, a rule intended to prevent a member from both being intimidated by the accused and from deciding the fate of a superior.[110] The highest-ranking officer on a court-martial panel was made president of the court-martial, akin to the foreperson of a jury but with greater authority. In an effort to keep those of higher rank from influencing a junior member to vote with them, the *Manual for Courts-Martial* specified that courts-martial vote by secret written ballot, to be counted by the junior member of the court.[111] Article 31 of the UCMJ recognized the coercive nature of military hierarchy by requiring warnings against self-incrimination long before the Warren Court similarly protected accused civilians.[112] Servicemembers were deemed in need of protection because their habit of obedience and deference to authority made them more likely to respond to questioning against their own interests.

The UCMJ recognized the military's cherished hierarchy, but it also muddied the clarity of the chain of command with procedural reforms such as the requirement for a judicial figure at certain courts-martial. The law officer, renamed a military judge and endowed with greater authority in 1969, acted as a judge might in a civilian criminal trial by managing the trial and deciding issues of law. The law officer had to be both a member of the bar and certified by the Judge Advocate General of his or her service.[113] But the law officer did not always outrank the president of a general court-martial panel, and during a special court-martial, at which no law officer was required, the president exercised judicial powers by ruling on interlocutory challenges and instructing the panel on key legal issues such as the elements of offense, the presumption of innocence, the standard of reasonable doubt, and the burden of proof.[114] Many instances of inappropriate conduct by law officers stemmed from their struggle with the presidents of courts for control of legal authority.[115] The Court of Military Appeals did not always reverse convictions when the law officer so deferred, relying instead on less radical means to remedy the procedural error, including the many opportunities for clemency that were built into the UCMJ's sentence review procedures.[116] But the court recognized, as did judge advocates and accused servicemembers, that military hierarchy influenced criminal procedure even after the UCMJ legalized military justice.

Senior officers did not welcome the lesson that rank had but limited privileges during a court-martial.[117] Naval officers were perhaps the most undone by the new procedural requirements because they were imbued with a sense of privilege derived from the aristocratic traditions of the Navy's officer corps. The Navy's legal system was altered most by the UCMJ, which had been modeled on the Army's Articles of War rather than the relatively archaic Navy rules for courts-martial. The requirements of the new code angered senior naval officers who were accustomed to deference; one naval officer referred to the *Manual for Courts-Martial* as the "pussy-footing red book."[118] Captain Jay Siegel's history of the Navy's Judge Advocate General's Corps relates the disbelief of admirals at being told they could be dismissed from a court-martial—for no cause, by "any young defense counsel"—because the UCMJ allowed the defense counsel to make a peremptory challenge to one member of a court.[119] Later reforms inspired similar complaints. The commandant of the Marine Corps referred to the Military Justice Act of 1968's separation of trial and defense counsel from the same chain of command that ordered a court-martial as "a great change, and a culture shock for [commanders], because no longer were you the man in charge."[120] Legal reform made military courts weaker extensions of a commander's authority.

Senior officers were reluctant to cede authority to lawyers in part because they relied on what an admiral in 1956 termed the "largely paternal" powers of commanders to redeem, encourage, and cajole—as well as to coerce.[121] The centralized authority that military officers sought to preserve was not necessarily wielded in malevolent fashion; commanders could use their discretion to excuse as well as to punish. After a court-martial concluded, the UCMJ permitted the officer who ordered the trial to unilaterally reduce, but not enhance, the sentence of a convicted servicemember. An accused person who had served in combat, performed well in an elite unit, or had a long record of meritorious service was likely to benefit from the intervention of a senior officer, even if convicted of a crime under the UCMJ. Hierarchy, then, did not work exclusively to the detriment of servicemembers who were accused or convicted of crimes. Its impact on the process of military justice was complicated, not extinguished, by legal reform.

The legal institution created by the UCMJ that caused military leaders the most frustration during the 1950s was a new addition to military justice: the civilian Court of Military Appeals.[122] With both the power and will to overturn decisions of the military's intermediate appellate courts, the Court of Military Appeals compelled changes in military policy and court-martial procedure, much to the chagrin of commanders accustomed to deference from civil institutions.[123] In one of its first important doctrinal tasks, the court explained what process was due an accused servicemember under the standards of the UCMJ. Earlier versions of military criminal law had made due process an internal military issue, defined by each branch of service and not subject to judicial oversight.[124] The new term "military due process" was introduced in the first volume of the court's opinions with *United States v. Clay*, a 1951 case involving a Navy hospitalman charged with improperly wearing his uniform and "disorder" for his role in a Friday night street fight in Pusan, Korea.[125] Under the new code, the court-martial panel, akin to a civilian jury, had to be instructed on the elements of the offense, the burden of proof, and the presumption of innocence.[126] Because no such instructions were issued at Clay's court-martial, the Court of Military Appeals reversed his conviction. The court's opinion described the procedural protections required at court-martial, including the right to be informed of the charges, to confront and cross-examine witnesses, to be represented by counsel, to avoid self-incrimination, and to appeal a conviction.[127]

The familiar right of civilians to due process of law in American criminal trials had a different history in military courts. The Court of Military Appeals relied on the UCMJ rather than the Constitution in elaborating servicemembers' rights because courts-martial were considered outside the reach of the Bill of Rights.[128] The court-martial did not lack for constitutional legitimacy, however. Its authority rested in three separate parts of the Constitution: the power of Congress to declare war, raise armies, regulate land and naval forces, and discipline militias; the executive's power to command the armed forces, commission officers, and execute the laws; and the Fifth Amendment's exception to the requirement of a grand jury indictment for those "in actual service in a time of war or public danger."[129] As a result, court-martial procedure was guided by congressional statute and executive order and largely exempt from the constitutional constraints that would reshape civilian criminal procedure in the post–World War II era.[130]

Following the court's opinion in *Clay*, the lawyers and judges of the military justice system turned not to the Constitution or civilian courts but to the UCMJ, and then to the president's *Manual for Courts-Martial*, in order to discern what protections were due servicemembers charged at court-martial.[131] The court was generally quick to recognize technical error during a court-martial, such as the failure to instruct the members properly about the applicable law, but often reluctant to find prejudice in such cases, choosing to admonish trial counsel and law officers for their failures but electing not to overturn each case in which such failures appeared.[132]

Errors were to be expected during the implementation of new procedures, particularly when the demand for experienced lawyers far outstripped the supply of judge advocates. The high turnover among military lawyers and the armed forces' reluctance to spend resources developing legal expertise made judge advocates a scarce resource.[133] The Navy and the Marine Corps in particular had a very hard time retaining lawyers. As Admiral Chester Ward explained the shortage of Navy lawyers to Congress in 1958, "[v]irtually every young lawyer gets out of the service as soon as his military obligation is fulfilled."[134] The Court of Military Appeals even addressed the issue in a 1957 per curiam opinion reversing a conviction because of cumulative errors at trial—errors that had been noted but deemed not prejudicial by the previous reviewing authorities. In chastising the officers who had permitted the case to reach the military's highest court, the court remarked that "[i]t is quite possible that the shortage of legally trained personnel, particularly in the Navy, is so great that the few are just physically unable to carry the heavy burden."[135] Efforts to get incentive pay for Department of Defense lawyers failed during the 1960s, and the Navy and the Marine Corps found that they could not promise young attorneys enough to keep them.[136]

The danger and dislocation of war also made implementing legal reform more difficult. Judge advocates in the field and onboard ships sometimes lacked such basic resources as legal reference books, court-reporting equipment, translators, and law clerks. An Army major dedicated his 1956 primer, *Military Trial Techniques*, to "the many officers in the United States Army, who at one time or another may stand in silence before a military court-martial because they did not know what to say or how to say it."[137] High turnover among officers increased the difficulty of building and keeping corporate knowledge about court-martial procedure.[138] The Navy addressed the problem of lawyer shortages and occasional surges in the number of criminal trials by sending teams of law specialists onto ships that were in port. The "Dockside Court Program," complete with trial and defense counsel, law officer, and court reporter, functioned like a circuit-riding court, and was first used at Norfolk and then expanded to other locations.[139] Such measures helped, but they did not eliminate the practical problems that made meeting the standards of the UCMJ so difficult.

The UCMJ was not the end of efforts to rework military justice. Disagreements over the scope and advisability of legal reform continued into the 1970s as veterans' organizations and bar associations sought further protections for servicemembers while military leaders proposed ways to streamline the new system.[140] Between 1951 and 1973, military justice was the focus of dozens of congressional hearings and the subject of countless official reports from government agencies.[141] Public criticism of the system tended to peak during and immediately after war, when celebrated cases attracted significant media attention. In addition to complaints from those outside the military, criticism from within the services was almost constant, particularly from commanders who felt that the civilianized criminal procedure itself was contributing to disciplinary problems.

Despite concerns about the efficacy of military justice, neither public debate nor internal criticism led to immediate statutory change. Congress was slow to revise the UCMJ, delayed by conflict among the services, the judges of the Court of Military Appeals, and legislators on what sorts of changes were warranted.[142] Minor revisions were enacted in a 1962 bill that increased commanders' ability to punish minor transgressions without recourse to court-martial, a change long sought by military leaders frustrated with the original UCMJ's sharp limits on the punishment that could be imposed short of court-martial.[143] The Judge Advocate General of the Air Force characterized these limits as an undue restriction on "corrective powers of commanders" and blamed the UCMJ for poor morale and disciplinary problems.[144] The regularized procedures of the new military justice system forced the armed forces to refashion military courts and to create alternatives to criminal prosecution. Troublemakers in the ranks could be eliminated more quickly and efficiently through noncriminal, bureaucratic processes.

Not until 1968, at the height of U.S. involvement in Vietnam, did the first major change in the UCMJ become law. The Military Justice Act of 1968 granted greater authority to the military judge, broadened the right of an accused to counsel, established procedures for pretrial release (a military version of bail), and enhanced appellate review opportunities.[145] As a result of these procedural changes, the *Manual for Courts-Martial* was transformed from "a rather slender volume" in 1951 into a massive tome by 1969.[146] Although there were a few calls for more radical reform in the late 1960s and early 1970s, such as the Birch-Bennet Bill to abolish court-martial jurisdiction over all but military offenses, no measure passed that altered the basic legal infrastructure created by the UCMJ.[147]

Military justice under the UCMJ continued to "go in" and "get" many things, but it no longer acted as a the simple tool of military discipline that it had when Major Wigmore was a judge advocate during World War I. The Cold War court-martial became an increasingly rare spectacle as military officers struggled to balance the new requirement for legal process against the time-honored need for obedient troops. Resistance to the changes imposed by the UCMJ, combined with the military's efforts to maintain an exclusive culture even in the face of massive demographic change and an increasingly rebellious civil society, led to new methods of discipline. The turn toward bureaucratic solutions rather than criminal prosecutions, however, was not the end of the line for the American court-martial. The next chapters follow military justice along the track laid by the UCMJ, analyzing how the demands of war, politics, family, sexuality, and class shaped the lives and military service of American servicemembers during the Cold War.

Chapter 2

DISCIPLINING THE ARMED FORCES

Paradoxes of Military Crime

Military service, especially during wartime, required so many deviations from acceptable civilian conduct that enforcing strict standards of behavior through criminal prosecution sometimes seemed unrealistic, if not impossible. The uncomfortable proximity between criminal acts and the work of a soldier, and between the intense bonding of men under fire and homosexual love, made distinguishing crime from military duty a task fraught with tension. Military training fostered physical aggressiveness and promoted the use of violence, creating a belligerent culture that led to criminal excess, both on and off duty. Likewise, the military required same-sex intimacy but criminalized many expressions of homosexuality. This not only left gay men, lesbians, bisexuals, and transgender people vulnerable to exploitation but also denied them even the basic protections of law set out in the UCMJ.

The legal culture created by the UCMJ limited commanders' ability to punish servicemembers at court-martial, but the military trials and appeals that took place still had to negotiate the contradictions raised by the military's embrace of violence, heterosexual aggression, and homophobia. The startling cases explored below demonstrate the sometimes tragic consequences of that lethal mix. This chapter begins to fill in the outlines of military justice sketched in chapter 1, analyzing the conflicts of military life that led to some of the most dramatic Cold War courts-martial. In order to succeed, the military needed its servicemen to feel comfortable living at close quarters in an all-male environment and to overcome their aversions to violence. These aspects of military culture, however, unleashed aggression and sexual desire that neither commanding officers nor individual soldiers could always control.

Prosecuting crime remained the most powerful and public way for commanding officers to mark the distinction between acceptable and unacceptable behavior. But this distinction was especially hard to draw in the realms of violence and sex, where the elemental acts that the military sometimes encouraged could lead to crime. Even the expense and uncertainty created by the UCMJ was not enough to dissuade commanders from using courts-martial in some cases; bureaucratic efficiency was no substitute for the demonstration of military values that a criminal trial provided. Military society, forged in the pressure of war and characterized by intimate, homo-social worlds, forced commanders to send their soldiers complex mes-sages: Be violent, but not too violent; live with, defend, and even love your fellow troops, but do not be homosexual. The expressive function of Cold War courts-martial and the conflicts created by the UCMJ's legalization of military justice were especially clear in prosecutions that involved wartime atrocities and homosexuality.

"THEY TOOK A GOOD BOY AND MADE HIM A MURDERER"

Perhaps the most fundamental barrier to military legal reform was the vi-olence and disorder of armed conflict. Attending to the niceties of due process during the heat of combat seemed misguided, if not ridiculous, to many commanders.[1] Summary justice—written out of legal practice by the UCMJ—rarely seemed more appropriate than in punishing crime in the midst of war, especially crime that rose to the level of wartime atrocities. Like other modern legal systems, procedural justice under the UCMJ did not make exceptions for crimes of war. Commanding officers and military lawyers had to abide by the rules of procedure set out in the UCMJ any time a court-martial was convened, even in theaters of combat. The ten-sion between war and law—between battlefield necessity and due process, between the order to kill and the act of murder, between the serial use of a prostitute and a gang rape—structured the military's attempts to mark the fine line that separated crime from duty.

The demands of war made upholding the standards of military due process more difficult for both judge advocates and commanding officers. War itself was a prominent part of many Americans' military service dur-ing the "Cold" War: close to two million American troops served in Korea between June 1950 and July 1953, sustaining over 150,000 casualties; American forces in Vietnam approached three million and suffered over 350,000 casualties.[2] Combat units faced the most pressure to conserve re-sources, but finding the time and effort required to follow legal procedures was difficult even for units far from the front lines. Shortages of personnel and materiel, rapid increases in troop strength, and the stress and danger of war competed with the UCMJ's emphasis on legal counsel, record-keeping, and other accoutrements of procedural justice.

The chaos of wartime also created disciplinary problems that were diffi-cult to address with criminal prosecution. For example, a staggering crimi-nal docket overwhelmed the brand-new military justice system during the Korean War.[3] In an exception to the general decline in the use of courts-martial under the UCMJ, the military's lack of preparation and rapid buildup for the Korean conflict resulted in many military trials. Nearly one million courts-martial were held between 1950 and 1953, including 48,000 general courts.[4] During wartime, recruits were more likely to lack military experience and more likely to face extreme stress, both of which created more disciplinary problems. The deprivations and indignities of war led to unauthorized absence, alcohol and drug abuse, and minor disciplinary offenses. Crimes as well as tragic accidents occurred when soldiers, bored and lonely, fought among themselves.[5] Although courts-martial during the Vietnam War never reached the levels of the early 1950s, courts-martial continued to address some disciplinary problems, including new forms of misbehavior related to soldiers' disenchantment with the war and with American politics.[6] As awkward as criminal prosecution could become during war, it was more needed than ever. Commanding officers struggled to maintain control over their troops during combat operations, at staging bases, and upon their return to the United States. Military leaders were not about to consign the court-martial, however limited its use, to the annals of military history.

Commanders of ground combat units had to police the line between the lethal aggressiveness that they asked of their troops and the outbursts of violence that constituted crime. The worst military crimes crossed this boundary. Motivated by malice, not recklessness, they occurred when the ordinary violence of war turned into the extraordinary violence of war crime. When soldiers murdered, raped, or tortured enemies or civilians they crossed a line that military leaders depended on to justify military actions and to control their troops. Because the military required its members to act outside the usual boundaries of acceptable social behavior, identifying transgressions against established standards was not always an easy task. Yet the problem could not be ignored. Indiscriminate violence wreaked havoc on both military and civilian communities. It harmed innocents, undermined the relationship between the military forces and local populace, and tarnished the image of American soldiers. Because of its significance as a moral, political, and legal issue, the prosecution of wartime atrocity has received ample attention from journalists, legal scholars, and military historians.[7] I mention it here because the legal management of war crimes demonstrates so clearly the contradictions of prosecuting military crime and enforcing legal reform during war.

Atrocity has been a feature of virtually every war, but not until the Vietnam War did atrocities committed by Americans against foreign civilians enter American popular consciousness, appearing almost immediately in the writings of journalists, soldiers, and scholars.[8] Most infamously, because of its scale and the publicity that attended the one court-martial conviction that resulted, was the My Lai massacre on March 16, 1968.[9] In the course of a combat assault on a Vietnamese village, American soldiers killed several hundred unarmed Vietnamese, raped dozens of women and girls, and destroyed villagers' homes and other property. Criminal charges were eventually brought against eighteen officers, seventeen of whom were either acquitted or had the charges against them dismissed prior to trial.

Lieutenant William Laws Calley was the lone exception.[10] Convicted for killing twenty-two civilians and sentenced to life imprisonment, Calley was paroled after three and a half years of house arrest.

No one was happy with the results of the Calley court-martial. The distraught mother of one of the other soldiers accused of taking part in the massacre told the press that the Army "took a good boy and made him a murderer."[11] In her angst, she exposed an aspect of military life that made it more difficult to hold soldiers criminally responsible for violent acts. Military culture cultivated men's relationship to violence, socializing them to fulfill aggressive, violent roles. Incidents like the My Lai massacre were made possible by the military's arming and training of young men. The military justice system could not deal with the consequences of military service gone so horrifyingly wrong any better than commanding officers could solve the political, social, and cultural dilemmas that made it impossible for American troops to win the Vietnam War.

The villains and the victims were not easy to distinguish even in cases of atrocious violence, nor was blame easy to assign.[12] Superior officers were sometimes prosecuted for murders and rapes committed under their command, but the process of assigning criminal culpability beyond those who actually committed offenses devolved into a legal and political quagmire. Individual accountability, a fundamental premise of criminal law, was hard to apply in cases of war crimes. The importance of obedience in military culture created a special defense most often used in cases of violent crime in combat areas. Servicemen could defend against criminal charges by arguing that they were simply following orders.[13] Under the UCMJ, the "superior orders" defense was accepted as a valid defense to any crime unless the order was "manifestly illegal," meaning that "a man of ordinary sense and understanding would, under the circumstances, know [it] to be unlawful."[14] A valiant effort to allocate blame for situations that defied logic in their inhumanity, this legal standard failed to answer the question of who was ultimately responsible for the violent crimes and other consequences of soldiers' wartime duties. Commanding officers and judge advocates had little choice but to keep trying to articulate and enforce norms of behavior that could guide servicemembers through the legal thickets and mortal dangers of service in combat zones. Courts-martial were both necessary and destined to fail in the effort to identify, punish, and ultimately suppress crimes of war.

SODOMY, SEXUAL PLAY, AND MILITARY CULTURE

The military attempted to channel servicemembers' sexual drives much the same way it tried to control the violence unleashed by military training and war. The armed forces mandated same-sex working environments and encouraged aggressive physicality and sexualized banter among men, yet made homosexuality a serious crime. Courts-martial involving homosexuality reveal how difficult it was to distinguish the male bonding that military leaders counted on from the homoeroticism they hoped to keep at bay. Officially nonexistent yet inescapably present, homosexual intimacy was a fundamental part of military culture. The military justice system was as hard pressed to distinguish acceptable homosocial companionship from unacceptable homosexual behavior as it was to separate "good" from "bad" fighting.

Servicemembers' same-sex activity and the anxieties it provoked led to courts-martial for homosexuality, where investigators' zeal for uncovering and punishing homosexuals collided with the legal rights that the military justice system was designed to protect. Homosexuality was considered a sign of unreliability, a mark of untrustworthiness.[15] Gay servicemen were assumed to be too weak and effeminate to fulfill the duties of soldiers and, because of the stigma of homosexuality, vulnerable to blackmail. The armed forces' administrative regulations regarding homosexuality and the virulent prejudice against homosexuals that pervaded military culture could not be reconciled with the procedural justice advanced by the UCMJ. Even the outcomes of trials for offenses unrelated to sexual orientation were affected by attitudes about homosexuality. Stereotypes of gay men and lesbians undermined the credibility of allegedly homosexual witnesses, prejudiced accused persons who were suspected of being gay but not explicitly charged with homosexual acts, and distorted evidentiary standards.[16]

The tactics used by military prosecutors and investigators to bring gay servicemembers to trial were much the same as the campaigns waged against suspected homosexuals by civilian law enforcement officials.[17] Because of the overlap between many civilian and military communities, much of servicemen's sexual activity—homosexual as well as heterosexual—involved both civilians and servicemembers. Though sodomy was decriminalized in many civilian jurisdictions after the mid-1950s, it remained a military crime under Article 125 of the UCMJ, with a maximum punishment of five years confinement and a dishonorable discharge.[18] *The Manual for Courts-Martial* defined sodomy as "unnatural carnal copulation, either with another person of the same or opposite sex, or with an animal," which was interpreted by military courts to include oral or anal sexual penetration, regardless of either consent or the sex of the persons involved.[19]

Sodomy was a uniquely reviled crime in the Cold War armed forces. A 1963 opinion described sodomy as loathsome, revolting, obscene, abominable, and detestable in the space of a few lines.[20] Consensual homosexual acts were termed "repelling,"[21] "disgusting and repulsive misconduct,"[22] and behavior of a "despicable nature"[23] by military courts. At trial and on appeal, military lawyers and judges described it as "a morbid sexual passion"[24] and perversion, and repeatedly termed homosexuals "perverts."[25] Consent was not a defense to charges of homosexual sodomy.[26] In short, testimony about homosexuality was extremely prejudicial at court-martial.[27] A person accused of same-sex sodomy was prejudiced at court-martial by both the military's generic condemnation of homosexuality and by the specific act charged, perceived by military courts as "a degradation of the virile organ and vicious insult to . . . manhood."[28] The specter of sodomy loomed over all courts-martial for allegedly homosexual conduct and of suspected homosexuals, even if the crime itself was not charged.

As horrifying as sodomy was in the language of the military appellate courts, it was far from unspoken within military culture. Court-martial records suggest broad acceptance of sexual language that included explicit references to sodomy and sexual contact among servicemembers of the same sex. For example, in 1953, Greenie L. Jackson, an Army lieutenant serving in a combat zone in Korea, was dismissed for two crimes: uttering sexually charged remarks to an enlisted man (which he explained as the usual vulgar teasing directed at young enlistees) and making sexual overtures by unzipping the private's sleeping bag and touching him.[29] In upholding the first charge on appeal, an Army board of review accepted the lieutenant's explanation for his remarks, describing the words as "made in jest and accepted as such by all listeners" and noting that such comments, while sometimes inappropriate, were to be expected when servicemen teased each other to relieve the stress of combat situations.[30] The vulgarity and hazing that was considered unavoidable, if not necessary, during the military's indoctrination of young men frequently referenced homosexual acts, including the unspeakable act of sodomy.

Like service in a combat zone, remote tours of duty and extended deployments at sea created conditions of isolation and deprivation that men sought to relieve through sexualized teasing and physical contact. In January 1963, Engineman Third Class Edgar F. Moore was serving onboard a Coast Guard cutter that spent about seven and a half months of each year away from Boston, its home port.[31] After chow one day during a stint in the ice at McMurdo Sound, Antarctica, some of the sailors decided to have some fun at the expense of a young man named Ellis in the aviation repair shop, "a small compartment on the main deck." "Purely as horseplay," they grabbed Ellis and took off his dungarees, initiating about fifteen minutes of sexual teasing and roughhousing.[32] The sailors then sent for Engineman Moore. When he arrived in the repair shop, four men were holding Ellis, clad only in his thermal underwear, down on the deck. Moore proceeded to expose himself, make "some indelicate remarks and gestures" and pretend to write something on Ellis's backside. "All but the victim were laughing" when Ellis was released. Because a Navy lieutenant entered the compartment just as Ellis was pulling up his trousers, this "skylarking," as a Coast Guard board of review termed it, resulted in Moore's court-martial. Moore was no stranger to military justice; three times before he had been convicted at summary courts-martial for minor offenses. Charged with indecent exposure and committing "an indecent and lewd act," Moore was initially sentenced to a bad-conduct discharge. On appeal, however, his sentence was reduced to a loss of grade. The board of review considered Moore's offense "quite different" from the sort of conduct contemplated by the *Manual for Courts-Martial*'s description of "lewd acts," which could by punished by a dishonorable discharge and five years confinement.[33] Moore's act was "a touching in jest," "a mere joke" on Ellis, not a "homosexual touching." To the board of review, "horseplay" was distinct from consensual "homosexual play" and "acts of lust or lechery"; the latter were military crimes, while horseplay was simply part of military life.[34]

The board's decision attempted to draw a line that could be easily erased in the sexual and physical culture of military life. Trying to separate sexualized play from homoerotic conduct was virtually impossible, especially among socially and sexually deprived men. However much military leaders sought to distinguish horseplay from sex and soldiers sought to conceal the homosexual content of their interactions, case after case revealed how fragile such distinctions were.[35] Sexualized teasing could evolve into intercourse, sometimes consensual, sometimes not. In 1958, two privates described their joint sexual assault on a sleeping serviceman as "just the usual rough, vulgar horseplay" involving nudity and physical abuse that was typical of servicemen's behavior.[36]

Sometimes horseplay was simply too rough to dismiss as typical behavior. Although underreporting of male-male sexual assaults hinders any effort to gauge the full extent of sexual exploitation among servicemen, military leaders recognized that servicemen were sometimes assaulted by other soldiers and sailors, most of whom considered themselves heterosexual. Like servicemembers' heterosexual encounters, same-sex intimacy was the trigger for a significant number of violent crimes. Servicemen were sometimes convicted at court-martial for forcible sodomy against other servicemen.[37] Of particular note was a steady stream of cases that reached the appellate courts that involved assaults on sleeping servicemen.[38] The preponderance of cases involving men who were assaulted in their sleep may have been due to a greater likelihood that such victims would report the assault. A soldier who was unconscious when a sexual act commenced was better protected against the impression that he consented to the sex act, in addition to the fact that the group sleeping arrangements in military barracks provided potential witnesses to corroborate the victim's account of the crime.[39]

Although homosexual acts were officially despised in the armed forces, some servicemen sought to prove their manhood through sexual aggression directed at other men, particularly in military prisons. There, soldiers' gang rapes targeted male, rather than female, victims.[40] The facts of these cases are not often clear in the appellate reports, but servicemen thought to be gay appear to be at much greater risk of sexual assault.[41] The emphasis on sexual performance and masculinity that shaped military culture was exaggerated in the isolated, all-male environment of stockades and brigs. In one of a series of courts-martial that resulted from what the Court of Military Appeals described as "a bizarre and sordid incident," Private William G. Miasel was convicted for assault with intent to commit sodomy for a May 1956 gang-rape in the Fort Polk, Louisiana, stockade.[42] Seven men, including Miasel, tied down a prisoner on a bed in what the eighteen year-old Miasel termed "a joke." Miasel testified that he was afraid of one of the prisoners in the group, a man who had been "bullying" and physically intimidating him. In order to avoid a fight, Miasel pretended to commit sodomy on the victim, thinking his act would make him appear a "big shot" and would protect him from sharing the fate of the prisoner being assaulted.[43]

Miasel's effort to portray the incident as the usual teasing that occurs among young men was contradicted by his own statements. Aware of the hierarchy of the stockade and cognizant of the threat of rape, he responded to the situation as a person who took the threat of forcible sodomy seriously, not as a man being teased. Miasel knew that becoming a sexual aggressor was a practical way to adapt and survive in the culture of the stockade. That the assault targeted another man, rather than a woman, signaled strength, not weakness. Despite the military's assumption that homosexuality implied weakness, homosexual acts established informal hierarchies among men in both prisons and isolated military units.

Another environmental factor that increased the likelihood of sexual assault was the heavy drinking that military culture often encouraged. Alcohol lessened servicemembers' inhibitions and corroded their judgment, leading to more consensual and nonconsensual homosexual encounters. Excessive drinking was a hallmark of military culture, an accepted means for servicemen to cope with stress and loss and to entertain themselves in the absence of alternative recreation. Similar to the manner in which prisoners might adopt a different sexual identity during confinement in a same-sex environment, being under the influence of alcohol and drugs could alter servicemen's sexual behavior and desires.[44] At Fort Benning, Georgia, in 1956, a group of soldiers—some of whom were thought by others to be homosexual—were drinking beer at the Patio Beer Garden.[45] When the beer garden closed, the men walked home, pausing on the way to engage in a series of sexual interactions, some consensual, others apparently not. At least one of the privates involved was convicted of aggravated assault and lewd acts for his drunken behavior. Nearly a decade later, a specialist in the Army at Fort Riley, Kansas, pled guilty to sodomy after a similar evening of drinking with fellow troops.[46] The military justice system had to sort out cases like those of the men at the Patio Beer Garden at Fort Benning, in which the heavy-drinking, close-quarters environment of military service created sexual tension and led to physical intimacy among men.

Although men suspected of being gay made up the overwhelming majority of servicemembers court-martialed for homosexuality, military courts denounced lesbian sexuality in terms almost as strong as those used to condemn male homosexuality.[47] The reasons were different, however. Male homosexuality threatened the legitimacy of the male camaraderie that military culture fostered, while lesbians undermined the respectability of military service for women and signaled the sexual unavailability of women for military men. Because so few women served in uniform, criminal prosecutions and administrative discharges of suspected lesbians were rare. Yet the military worried about the tendency of both media coverage and male soldiers to sexualize women in uniform, who wanted legitimacy and respect, not leers and snide comments. It was difficult to recruit servicewomen in the midst of rumors that women in uniform were there for the sexual benefit of military men. The military responded by trying to present servicewomen as sexually respectable, a program that included more warnings about the consequences of female homosexuality and limits on servicewomen's social lives than courts-martial.[48] As historians of women in the Navy explained, "until the early 1970s the Navy dealt with lesbians quietly, chiefly to protect its ladylike image."[49]

In the 1970s, the military's strategy of keeping quiet about lesbians in uniform became less effective as gay liberation arrived, even in the armed forces, and the number of women in the service rose. An occasional court-martial of a suspected lesbian indicated the military's discomfort with female, as well as male, homosexuality. By 1972, however, when such a case finally reached a military appellate court, military judges were divided about whether private, consensual sex acts could constitute a military crime. In October 1970, at Fort Hood, Texas, Private First Class Carmen G. Ortega was court-martialed for "wrongfully committing an indecent, lewd, and lascivious act."[50] Ortega was sentenced to a bad-conduct discharge for sexually touching another WAC private in a barracks room with the door closed. The Army appellate court, which reversed Ortega's conviction because of several errors at trial, referred to Ortega's sexual partner as the "victim," self-consciously using quotation marks to indicate its doubt about whether any party could be considered a victim in the case. At the beginning of Ortega's court-martial, the military judge had instructed the court-martial panel that consent was not a defense to the charge of "lewd acts." But on appeal, the Army court suggested that consent did in fact matter, explaining that recent decisions of the Court of Military Appeals suggested that "in the absence of any aggravating circumstances," "homosexual activity" was not a military crime.[51] Aggravating circumstances were defined as public or nonconsensual sexual activity, or sex between an officer and an enlisted man, an adult and a minor, or an officer and a subordinate civilian in a foreign country. None of these circumstances were present in Ortega's case. The court does not suggest that homosexuals should be retained, but that administrative discharge is the proper remedy rather than court-martial—which is, of course, how the military was already dealing with most allegations of homosexuality.[52]

GAY AND LESBIAN VICTIMS OF CRIME AND THE HOMOPHOBIC DEFENSES

Military law was supposed to defend order within ranks, to contain the consequences of the violent acts that soldiers were socialized into, even to protect servicemembers from themselves and others. Yet it often failed to protect those whom military culture put at greatest risk of harm, including civilian targets of soldiers' atrocities and gay and lesbian soldiers and civilians. In fact, homophobic defenses, in which a defense counsel sought to convince a court-martial that violent conduct was warranted because of an accused soldier's fear of homosexuality, often won the day at courts-martial when a victim was thought to be gay. In perhaps the most troubling consequence of the armed forces' hostility to homosexuality, anti-gay prejudice justified the mistreatment and brutalizing of gay and lesbian servicemembers and civilians by military personnel.

Because the military made being a lesbian criminal, and because lesbianism was often equated with promiscuity in military culture, it was more difficult for judge advocates to prosecute a rape charge that involved a lesbian victim. In 1963, the Court of Military Appeals ordered a new trial for a serviceman convicted of rape because his victim turned out to be a lesbian.[53] The court identifies the Women's Army Corps (WAC) private who brought the charges only as "A" and refers to her as "the alleged victim."[54] In April 1961, two weeks after arriving at Fort Monmouth, New Jersey, A encountered Charles D. Chadd, a master sergeant in the Army, at a club on the post. Chadd asked A to join him for a drink. After initially demurring, she agreed, and moved away from her friends to converse with Chadd over coffee. When A was ready to leave, she realized that her friends had left, and accepted Chadd's offer that they go for a drive together. At this point, the accounts of Chadd and A diverge sharply, as in so many date-rape trials. According to A, Chadd drove her to a secluded area and assaulted her, prompting her to scream, sound the car horn, and bite him in defense; he then desisted and apologized only to renew the assault a short time later, when he finally overcame her resistance and raped her. According to Chadd, A had "engaged in provocative behavior" that led to consensual intercourse in his automobile.[55] When A returned to the WAC barracks on post, she complained immediately of the attack to the private in charge of quarters, who testified at trial that A was "in a state of half shock and her mouth was bleeding," and that she had disheveled clothes and facial bruises. Other servicewomen corroborated this testimony of her condition, and a doctor who examined her afterward noted her injuries and agitated state of mind.[56] The following morning, Chadd was apprehended in his quarters and advised of the charges; later that day, he went AWOL. He was caught, court-martialed, and convicted of rape and unauthorized absence in August 1961, and received an approved sentence of three years confinement and a dishonorable discharge.

Three months later, Army investigators began an inquiry into allegations of A's homosexual conduct. For her part, A denied that she was a lesbian and refuted the charges against her. The investigation was apparently initiated by a jealous former lover of A, whose testimony about A's homosexuality was corroborated by other servicewomen, some of whom were themselves discharged for homosexuality. A WAC lieutenant who had testified briefly in support of A's rape allegation was also administratively discharged for her suspected role as "a ringleader in the WAC homosexual group."[57]

The investigation into A's sexual orientation changed the Court of Military Appeals' view of the April evening that had resulted in Sergeant Chadd's conviction for raping A. In ordering a new trial for Chadd, the court held that an "extraordinary remedy" was required because of the discovery of new evidence and the possibility that a fraud had been perpetrated at Chadd's court-martial.[58] Until reaching the military's highest court, Chadd's petition had been denied on the grounds that proof of A's lesbian tendencies made it even less likely that she had consented to intercourse with Chadd. The Court of Military Appeals rejected that argument, holding that evidence of homosexuality was relevant and admissible on the issues of A's credibility and consent, citing the *Manual for Courts-Martial*'s rule that "evidence of [an alleged rape victim's] lewd repute, habits, ways of life, or associations, and of her specific acts of illicit sexual intercourse or other lascivious acts with the accused or others, is material."[59] The court did not agree with the government's contention that A's homosexual conduct made her less likely to consent to sexual intercourse with Chadd, calling attention instead to A's recent marriage and testimony that she had engaged in sexual relations with her husband. "Moreover, while we do not pretend to psychiatric expertise," the court continued, "we call counsel's attention to the fact that many persons so afflicted are bisexual in their practices."[60] Pointing out that the posttrial investigation portrayed the WAC unit to which A belonged as a "close-knit group of 'gay' girls," the court inferred, without further comment, that A's corroborating witnesses were either lovers or otherwise biased in her favor.[61]

Despite A's convincing testimony, her fresh complaint, and the testimony of both a doctor and criminal investigator about her injuries, the court assumed that A would not have been believed at court-martial if her homosexuality, and that of other witnesses, had been presented to the members.[62] When servicewomen appeared as witnesses at courts-martial, their credibility could be challenged by the insinuation that they were gay.[63] Military judges could, and sometimes did, put an end to such questioning when they deemed it irrelevant or too prejudicial to an accused servicemember.[64] But often the prejudice ran too deep in the minds of judge advocates, court-martial panels, and commanding officers to be controlled even by a diligent military judge or law officer.

Lesbians were not the only victims of crimes deemed less worthy of protection at court-martial. By arguing that gay victims deserved little respect or that the victims had provoked the violence with sexual overtures or assaults, accused servicemen could employ defenses at trial that exploited the military's hostility toward homosexuality. Most of these homophobic defenses involved violent crimes, but the perceived severity of nearly any crime could be lessened if the victim were portrayed as homosexual.[65] Murders and assaults against men who made sexual advances were not uncommon among the violent crimes prosecuted at court-martial.[66]

These cases could be difficult to sort out, given the complex terrain of sexual interaction and the sexual aggressiveness accepted in military life. Servicemen sometimes had violent reactions to the mere suggestion of homosexual acts, while others reacted violently only after consensual sex had taken place or when the sex took a turn that made them uncomfortable. As the forcible assaults recounted above make clear, servicemen were aware of the possibility that they could be sexually assaulted by other men. Neither commanding officers nor military courts wished to undermine their ability to defend themselves against such assaults. It seems safe to conclude, then, that most of the cases that reached the appellate courts involved only doubtful claims of self-defense. A clear case of defending against forcible sodomy would almost certainly not be prosecuted, much less result in a conviction and sentence harsh enough to warrant appellate review. As a result, most instances of gay-bashing were unlikely to appear in the appellate reports.

The military justice system could not overlook servicemen who were killed after a sexual encounter with another serviceman, however.[67] Not only servicemen, but gay civilians who engaged in sexual encounters with servicemen sometimes suffered brutal assaults.[68] The appellate records of many of these cases lack sufficient detail to permit much understanding of the events surrounding the crimes charged. But the *Mathis* case, involving an Army sergeant whose seduction turned to murder, is especially provocative and well documented. Its many appearances in the appellate record provide a wealth of information about the military's efforts to deal with the difficult issues of sanity and culpability that often influenced trials for antigay violence as well as the factual scenario that led one soldier to murder another.[69] Despite its detailed record, however, the truth behind the *Mathis* case is not entirely clear. The only witnesses to the crime were the accused, whose story was preserved during his trials, and the victim, whose account was buried with him.

Around 9 P.M. on a Sunday in August 1963, Sergeant John P. Mathis was drinking beer in the N.C.O. Club in Wildflecken, Germany. A man identified only as "Plater" in the record, was "very intoxicated," and sat down at Mathis's table.[70] Plater told Mathis that he "liked" him, and the two men finished their drinks together.[71] When Mathis rose to leave, he accepted Plater's offer to walk back to Mathis's billet with him. En route, Plater put his arm around Mathis's shoulders and again expressed how much he liked Mathis. Mathis testified that this made him suspicious, but said that he was uncertain of Plater's intent "because so many times I could be wrong," implying that he had been mistaken with respect to other men's sexual overtures in the past.[72] When the men arrived at Mathis's billet, Plater stopped on the street, and Mathis entered alone. But Plater did not go away, and eventually convinced Mathis to return to the club. During their walk, which passed through dark pathways and wooded areas, Plater continued to tell Mathis how much he liked him while Mathis deflected his compliments. Finally, Plater stopped Mathis on the path and made a pass: he talked about sex, kissed Mathis, and touched Mathis's erection. After this, Mathis testified, Plater "began to sound more confident," and told Mathis that "he wanted to love me."[73] Plater "coaxed" Mathis into the bushes, where Mathis did not object to oral sodomy.[74] When Plater's interests turned to anal sodomy, Mathis "resisted weakly at first," then said "God ought to kill us both," and attacked Plater.[75]

The epic fight between the two men receives blow-by-blow coverage in the appellate reports, culminating with Mathis repeatedly smashing Plater's head with a thirty-five-pound rock until, as Mathis himself explained to the court, Plater's skull "caved in."[76] Mathis then dragged Plater's body into the woods, covered it, hid the rock, retrieved his hat and pieces of a knife that had broken during the fight, and returned to his billet.

Mathis was court-martialed twice for killing Plater, first in Frankfurt, Germany, and later at Fort Leavenworth, Kansas, in a retrial ordered by the Court of Military Appeals because of errors in the way the trial court had handled the question of Mathis's mental responsibility.[77] Both times, he was convicted of premeditated murder and sentenced to a dishonorable discharge and confinement for life. Mathis conceded the killing, but defended the murder charge with the claim that he harbored an "intensive hate" for homosexuals, "stronger than any human force," that led him to kill Plater.[78] Mathis's defense counsel supported this insanity defense with evidence of uncharged acts of homosexuality that Mathis had committed in the past, and a psychologist testified that the act of sodomy between Plater and Mathis "precipitated a psychotic episode" that led to the murder.[79] Mathis's testimony did not suggest that he welcomed Plater's advances, but even in his words, he acquiesced with no signs of resistance to their initial sexual contact.

After his second conviction, the Court of Military Appeals ruled that the law officer at trial had erred again, this time by failing to instruct the court-martial on good character after the defense had requested such an instruction. Two witnesses had testified that Mathis was "an efficient, well-trained, outstanding soldier and noncommissioned officer who had never been a disciplinary problem."[80] The instruction requested by the defense included the statement that character evidence "may indicate to you [the court-martial members] that it is impossible that a person of good character would commit the crime charged."[81] The law officer did not give this instruction because, as Chief Judge Quinn pointed out in dissenting from the court's opinion, the good character defense was "a mere abstraction" in light of the admissions that Mathis made concerning his crimes.[82] It was clear that that Mathis committed the act from his confession to the murder and evidence of his conduct preceding the crime. But the Court of Military Appeals held that while there was no doubt that Mathis killed his victim, the act may not have been criminal if he was defending himself. The court also rejected the law officer's instruction on the applicability of the legal defense of justifiable homicide as too weak. The rejected instruction read as follows:

> [Y]ou are advised that the accused was under a duty to exhaust all available means of preventing the act of sodomy upon himself, by a warning or a show of force or use of such force short of killing before he would be justified in killing Plater. In addition, if you find that the killing took place after the completion of the offense of sodomy and was not necessary to prevent repetition or continuation of the offense, then the killing was not or would not be justified. You are advised that a killing reasonably appearing to be necessary to prevent the commission of a violent, atrocious offense such as nonconsensual sodomy, is justified and excusable and, if you so find, the accused must be acquitted.[83]

Though the law officer's charge to the court-martial panel made clear that nonconsensual sodomy was an "atrocious offense" that Mathis could legally use lethal force to avoid, it was not enough for the Court of Military Appeals. It held that Mathis's act was excused if he felt "apparent necessity, nothing more" to kill in order to prevent a sodomitical assault.[84]

This brutal case is made more tragic by Mathis's psychiatric history, revealed in lengthy evaluations of his competency by the many appellate judges who heard his case. Seven weeks before killing Plater, Mathis had visited an Army medical doctor at Fort Riley, Kansas, voluntarily seeking help for his "history of homosexuality."[85] The doctor referred him to a psychiatrist and recommended treatment before Mathis was transferred overseas. Mathis told the medical doctor that his "desire to kill" was getting stronger and that he might "give in" in the future, which led an Army psychiatrist to diagnose Mathis with as a probable "pathological personality type."[86] But the psychiatrist did not delay Mathis's departure, instead releasing him for transfer to Germany with the recommendation that he seek treatment while overseas. Mathis did not receive any additional medical or psychiatric attention after leaving Fort Riley.[87] Like military legal reforms, psychiatric evaluations like Mathis's conflicted with military personnel needs, deployment patterns, and recruiting. As a result, accommodating the mental health needs of servicemembers was not a priority for military leaders. Neither military legal reform nor the Army itself did anything to address the fear and desire that caught men like Mathis and Plater in its grip.

Military criminal justice reveals both the crimes that resulted from the horrors of war and the military culture that existed to prepare servicemembers to survive them. Whether violent excess was an inescapable part of waging war or a frightful consequence of too little discipline and too much power, it could not be remedied at court-martial. Nor could criminal justice reconcile the armed forces' formally hostile posture toward gay men and lesbians with the informal reality that homosexual desire and sexual acts were an all but inescapable part of military culture. As the reforms of the UCMJ changed the function of courts-martial and opened up new avenues of disciplinary action for commanding officers, courts-martial continued to wrestle with the fundamental paradoxes of military service. The hypermasculinity, physical aggression, and homosocial intimacy of the armed forces took its toll on servicemembers and civilians, creating circumstances that could turn men into murderers and courts-martial into caricatures of justice.

Chapter 3

THREATS TO "THE VERY SURVIVAL
OF THIS NATION"

Political and Sexual Dissent

Government leaders and military recruiters wanted soldiers to be viewed as strong, free-thinking men who accepted the constraints of military life as one of the burdens of democracy. The armed forces expected service-members to be staunchly anticommunist and to engage in only limited types of sexual activity lest they corrupt the armed forces with vulnerability and weakness. Cold War military law and regulations denied to servicemembers many of the freedoms most cherished in American democratic culture—speech, association, travel, privacy—in order to protect democracy itself. These restraints, so at odds with political notions of equality and freedom, were considered a necessary concession in the battle to prove American democracy superior to communism.[1] Through persuasion, coercion, and, as a last resort, criminal prosecution, the United States' standing armed forces curtailed individualism in favor of molding obedient troops.

Because of Cold War politics, dissent posed a new threat to the American military at the same time that soldiers' sexual and political opportunities blossomed. National security concerns and the new sexual cultures of the 1950s, 1960s, and 1970s were more than a backdrop to military criminal justice.[2] They defined military crime and shaped its prosecution. Enforcing ideological and behavioral norms became more important as doubts grew about servicemembers' ability to resist communist seduction. Soldiers expected, and sometimes challenged, restrictions on appearance, speech, and conduct long before the rise of the Soviet Union or the spread of communism in Asia. But on the battlefields of the Cold War, servicemembers who violated military rules and regulations about politics and sex did more than embarrass military leaders. Servicemembers' mistakes in judgment seemed to undermine the very standards of the American culture that the armed forces sought to defend.

A military appellate court described the crimes of an Air Force captain who was convicted for socializing with communist agents as a threat to the "very survival of the nation."[3] This sort of rhetoric about the impact of political crimes against the United States echoed similar exhortations about the dire consequences of sexual crimes against the military. Such doom-saying, however, obscured the trivial nature of most political and sexual acts that were actually prosecuted as military crimes. The servicemembers court-martialed for challenging the military's political and sexual norms appear to have posed little danger to the political viability or on-the-ground effectiveness of the armed forces. Nonetheless, military leaders' and government officials' fear that the rapidly expanding armed forces could be undone from within was powerful enough to inspire the prosecution of even insignificant breaches of conduct.

The military's efforts to uncover and punish dissent during the Cold War were a critical part of the nation's effort to eliminate internal threats while fighting the forces of communism abroad. Although neither anticommunist fervor nor efforts to repress extramarital or same-sex sexual behavior were limited to the armed forces, dissidents in uniform were an especially frightening prospect.[4] They could subvert military values from within, operating from trusted positions with access to classified information. Although fear of spying was a standard feature of Cold War political culture, the possibility of military spies was of special concern.

However important it was to eliminate dissidents in uniform, even the most hard-nosed anticommunists realized that aggressive pursuit of suspects threatened the procedural guarantees of the newly adopted UCMJ and, more broadly, the promises of democratic culture. Identifying spies and subversives was no simpler in the military than in civil society, where the communist was a "frighteningly indistinct creature," unmarked by race, ethnicity, "dress, custom, language, or religion."[5] Military leaders who sought to uncover "reds" could not rely on simple visual cues. Instead, they tried to ferret out treasonous intent through constant surveillance and aggressive investigation. Such all-out efforts to find closet communists threatened to transform the United States government into an oppressive authoritarian regime, frightening those wary of totalitarianism as well communism.[6] To many observers, military institutions' mechanisms of enforcing conformity, including courts-martial, bore a troubling resemblance to the tools by which a totalitarian government controlled its body politic. Worse yet, at least for those concerned with the impartiality of the military's new criminal justice system, high-ranking officers seemed able to influence the outcomes of courts-martial that targeted dissenting behavior.[7]

Reforming military criminal procedure while chasing communist sympathizers and other threats to national security created legal dilemmas that military judges and judge advocates could not easily resolve.[8] Judges at the Court of Military Appeals found themselves defending the new system of courts-martial against critics who doubted that the UCMJ, and the new bureaucratic style of the armed forces, could guarantee soldiers' performance under fire.[9] The national imperative for a trustworthy armed force ran up against a growing sense that American servicemembers deserved protection from arbitrary prosecution, unwarranted searches, and the prejudice of commanding officers.

The legalized spectacle of criminal prosecution under the UCMJ was a crude tool for managing dissent in the ranks. It could send a powerful message to citizens and soldiers, but it was fraught with the potential for public embarrassment and too slow to satisfy many commanders. As a result, allegedly disloyal acts were rarely prosecuted in the Cold War armed forces, notwithstanding the publicity that attended many apparently "political" courts-martial. Even rarer were trials of genuine rebels whose primary intent was to undermine military effectiveness. Every servicemember who tested the limits of the military's standards of behavior risked court-martial, whether motivated by outright disloyalty or by fear, carelessness, or passion. Yet most potentially criminal acts led to disciplinary action short of court-martial. Commanders could deal quietly with potentially embarrassing or relatively inconsequential misconduct through less public and less expensive means than court-martial. But if a servicemember's wrongdoing was already known to the public, and if it was of a sort that undermined faith in American military strength or in the moral and political authority of military institutions, the court-martial was available to demonstrate military authority to civilian and military observers alike.

This chapter studies some of the most striking courts-martial of the Cold War era, trials that sought to protect the military's political viability, distinctive culture, and public legitimacy through the ups and downs of wars in Asia and political changes at home. Sexual dissenters, more frequently prosecuted than political dissenters, did not often attract the publicity that followed suspected spies, defectors, and collaborators. But crime involving consensual adult sexual activity was censured for much the same reason as political crime: to warn servicemembers of the potential consequences of transgressive acts and to protect the cultural standards of the increasingly expensive armed forces. These acts of "dissent" injured the military by tarnishing its image and undermining its authority. Their gravamen—that is, their material wrongfulness, the reason they were criminal—were the same. Political conviction, conscious rejection of military norms, and sexual desire were but a few strands within the web of social, emotional, and economic need in which these crimes took place. However disparate the motives behind these acts were, the crimes themselves were prosecuted to insulate the armed forces from criticism that they were not strong enough to win the Cold War.

The following pages analyze how courts-martial for dissent responded to the Cold War imperative to defend America, and how the UCMJ's success in standardizing criminal justice limited the role of courts-martial in controlling servicemembers' politics and sexuality. The courts-martial of repatriated prisoners of war for alleged collaboration with the enemy established an impossibly high standard of ideological loyalty that was unevenly enforced. The difference between the military's treatment of Korean and Vietnam War POW's also demonstrates how shifts in the domestic political climate altered patterns of military prosecution. The trials of suspected spies and defectors reveal that the servicemembers most likely to be prosecuted did not pose the greatest threats, but seemed instead to have the fewest intellectual, emotional, and financial resources among potential subversives. The overlap between political and sexual deviance is clearest in the presumptive homosexuality of spies and the portrayal of homosexuals as politically corrupt—and more likely to be "soft" on communism. Finally, the military's decision to manage the political protesters and drug users of the Vietnam era through largely noncriminal processes exemplified commanding officers' efforts to find ways to punish dissent that avoided the costs and publicity of legalized courts-martial.

Failing to "Stand Firm" against Communist Seduction: The Korean War POW's

The American prisoners of war court-martialed after being released from POW camps were among the most unlikely military criminals of the twentieth century. After the Korean War, fourteen POWs were tried for allegedly collaborating with the enemy in Chinese and North Korean prison camps.[10] Three decades later, a single late-returning prisoner was court-martialed for similar charges at the end of the Vietnam War.[11] These trials captured the attention of the nation, bringing communist "brainwashing" into American popular culture and prompting government officials to invest millions in studies of ideological conversion and mental health.[12] Defending America during the Cold War meant not only bearing arms on behalf of the nation, but also protecting American ideological superiority by spurning communist indoctrination—even under the duress and deprivation of a remote POW camp. The Army's decision to court-martial only an unlucky few among the hundreds of Korean War POW's who failed to resist their captors' inducements confirmed that even under the UCMJ, military justice could still be arbitrary. The legal records of the collaboration trials also show that Americans tried to rationalize the actions of apparent communist sympathizers by ignoring the potential appeal of communist doctrines. Instead, they blamed incidents of collaboration on individual and cultural weakness, the military's failure to prepare soldiers for imprisonment, and the coercive methods of prison camp guards.

Although some of the soldiers who returned from Korean War POW camps were derided as weak, the fact that they survived the experience suggests that the survivors were stronger, more fortunate, and perhaps more pliable than many others. Official figures from the Department of Defense reported a fatality rate of 38 percent among American POW's, with close to 3,000 deaths among 7,190 captives.[13] Korean War prisoners died at a much higher rate than prisoners in other modern wars. In Vietnam, for example, the death rate among the 766 captured Americans was 14 percent.[14] Korean War POWs were physically and mentally abused in overcrowded camps and on long forced marches, especially during the first few months of the war.[15] Summary executions and extreme brutality exacerbated the lack of adequate food, housing, sanitary facilities, and medical care. Under such conditions, separating acts of disloyalty from behavior essential to survival was all but impossible. Most POWs gradually capitulated to demands that they study communism, espouse its principles, and denounce the United States.[16] FBI investigations discovered that many prisoners signed peace petitions and wrote to family members urging that they oppose the war.[17] Five hundred prisoners were investigated for alleged misconduct in the camps.[18]

Yet a scant 14 of the 4,000 repatriated POWs were brought to trial, resulting in 11 convictions.[19] Despite the UCMJ's goal of standardizing criminal procedure across the Department of Defense, the absence of a centralized authority to control investigation and prosecution left the Air Force, the Army, and the Navy to make their own decisions about whether or not to pursue courts-martial. Every one of the POWs court-martialed was in the Army, a distinction partly explained by Army troops' disproportionate representation among the prisoners: fewer than 500 of the 4,000 repatriated prisoners were from the other services.[20] POWs convicted for collaborating were punished through dishonorable discharges and prison terms ranging from two years to life, though most were released by parole boards after a few years of confinement in military prisons.[21]

The Air Force, top-heavy with officers and nervous about protecting the secrecy and legitimacy of its programs, was much more reluctant to prosecute returning POWs than the Army. The Air Force even chose not to court-martial any of the 134 officers who embarrassed the military by refusing to fly in 1952.[22] The charges initially brought against 12 officers in April 1952 were dropped when 6 of the pilots went public, alleging maltreatment by the Air Force and claiming that fear had prevented them from fulfilling their military duties. The pilots ended up with administrative discharges rather than punitive dismissals, sparing them the ignominy of courts-martial and the Air Force the spectacle of criminal trials. Later called the "fear of flying" incident, this episode set a precedent that worried military leaders who thought it would enable others to shirk military duty without penalty.

For the Army courts-martial of repatriated prisoners, the cases of Corporals Edward M. Dickenson and Claude J. Batchelor set the tone.[23] Like most of the court-martialed POWs, these young men were of modest enlisted rank; nine of the fourteen Army prosecutions targeted enlisted men.[24] Batchelor and Dickenson were inexperienced troops captured soon after the start of the war. Each led communist indoctrination efforts among fellow troops at a prison camp in Pyoktong, North Korea, refused repatriation with the initial release of prisoners, and only belatedly returned to United States custody. They were charged with similar crimes, convicted, and sentenced to long prison terms. Their cases reveal the mix of individual hardship, global politics, personal enmity, and public relations that shaped the prosecution of collaboration. If the "very survival of the nation" hinged on prosecuting the likes of Batchelor and Dickenson, American democracy during the Cold War stood on shakier ground than military leaders could afford to admit. Court-martialing young enlistees for collaboration did not solve the problem of American servicemembers being drawn toward communism and did nothing to prepare future generations of soldiers for the trauma of POW camps.

Young, uneducated, and poorly trained, neither Batchelor nor Dickenson anticipated the ordeal that the Korean War would bring.[25] Claude Batchelor was the second of eight children born to a poor family in a small town near Waco, Texas.[26] Restless, he quit school and enlisted in the Army at the age of sixteen. Sent to Japan in November 1948, Batchelor was assigned to play trumpet in the first Cavalry Division band and soon married a Japanese woman. When war broke out in July 1950, he found himself en route to Korea as an infantryman in the Eighth Cavalry. In November 1950, after several months of fighting, Batchelor and the other members of his patrol were captured by Chinese forces. Singled out by the Chinese as a leader among the POWs and flattered by the attention (later, after returning to the United States, Batchelor said, "I think the Chinese selected me because of certain leadership abilities that I possessed"),[27] Batchelor chaired a prisoners' "Peace Committee," led discussion groups intended to teach the principles of communism, confessed to alleged wartime atrocities (including "germ warfare") committed by Americans, and lectured on the injustices of the Rosenbergs' trial, Jim Crow laws, and the Ku Klux Klan.[28] An October 1952 letter that Batchelor sent to his hometown newspaper, *The Winkler County News* in Kermit, Texas, detailed the evils of American biological warfare and capitalism.[29] Batchelor also testified that he had intended to continue studying communism upon his return to the United States and that he had made preliminary plans for creating a communist organization of former American POWs.[30]

Like Batchelor, Edward Dickenson was assigned to the overmatched forces of the Eighth Cavalry in the winter of 1950. He also surrendered to North Korean forces in November 1950, shortly after losing contact with his rapidly disintegrating company. One of thirteen children born to a working-class Virginia family, Dickenson completed school through the sixth grade. At twenty, he was two years older than Batchelor when captured but had been in the Army only seven months. While imprisoned, Dickenson led procommunist discussion groups, sent recordings to his parents criticizing the United States, wrote editorials to his hometown newspaper (*The Post* in Big Stone Gap, Virginia), and informed about other prisoners' escape plans.

In the camps, both men seemed willing to speak and write about the shortcomings of the United States and eager to gain the approval of their captors. Their cooperation brought extra food, money, cigarettes, and liquor from guards and may have worsened conditions for other prisoners.[31] Some POWs testified that Batchelor had helped them by sharing food and cigarettes, but others accused him of reporting to camp authorities on the activities of less cooperative soldiers. Dickenson's testimony against Batchelor in the Chinese "trial" of an American POW proved especially damning. According to Dickenson, Batchelor had recommended that an American POW, considered a spy by the camp guards, be shot for his disloyalty to communism.[32]

After their delayed repatriation, Batchelor and Dickenson were interviewed at length by American intelligence officers and psychiatrists who already knew quite a lot about the two men from other POW interrogations. Both men cooperated, with Batchelor providing a 148-page description of his conduct in the camps that was later admitted into evidence—over the strenuous objections of his defense counsel—at his court-martial.[33] Soon after, the corporals became the subjects of pretrial criminal investigations that resulted in massive reports recommending prosecution. Dickenson's court-martial, the first POW trial involving charges of collaboration, took place in late April 1954, while the Army-McCarthy hearings were in session.[34] Despite the military's promise of immunity from prosecution as part of his agreement to return to the United States, and considerable public support in his favor, Dickenson was convicted and sentenced to ten years confinement.[35] The secretary of the Army eventually reduced his sentence to five years, and he was released from Fort Leavenworth after three and a half years.

Batchelor's court-martial followed Dickenson's in September 1954. It took nearly twice as long, provoked more complex judicial rulings on evidentiary standards, and involved testimony from dozens of expert psychiatrists and other POWs. Batchelor chose a civilian attorney to defend him rather than accepting the two experienced judge advocates assigned to act as his defense counsel, reflecting the doubt of many accused servicemembers about the true allegiances of military attorneys. His legal team submitted pretrial discovery requests for thousands of classified government documents (most were denied on grounds that the documents were not relevant to the charges) and pursued a number of aggressive strategies at trial.[36] Dr. Leon Freedom, a psychiatrist, described Batchelor's "political psychosis," a sort of compartmentalized paranoia that prevented him from distinguishing right from wrong "in the political field."[37] Neither Dr. Freedom nor Batchelor himself, however, managed to create a reasonable doubt about the corporal's guilt in the minds of the members of his court-martial. Batchelor was convicted of "aiding the enemy," "misconduct as a prisoner of war," and violating Article 134, the UCMJ's general article. Sentenced to a dishonorable discharge, total forfeiture of pay, and twenty years confinement, Corporal Batchelor spent four and half years—one year longer than Lieutenant Calley served for his role in the My Lai massacre fifteen years later—in military prison before his parole.[38]

Batchelor elicited more than seventy pages of opinions from military appellate courts; it provoked judicial pronouncements on mental competence, jurisdiction, and a host of other legal issues.[39] The military's highest court conceded that evidence of Batchelor's guilt was "overwhelming" but still carefully analyzed procedural issues raised by his attorneys.[40] These included conflicts between the Geneva Conventions and the UCMJ concerning jurisdiction over the offenses of POW's, doubt over whether Batchelor had accepted an offer of amnesty by returning to American custody, and uncertainty about the consequences of the theories of coercion advanced at trial. The Court of Military Appeal's measured tone and exhaustive review of Batchelor's case confirms how seriously the new military courts viewed their responsibility to ensure procedural justice at court-martial—and how important the POW cases were to the development of military legal doctrine.

But the question lurking behind judicial opinions, media coverage, and psychological studies of the POW's was why Batchelor and others had allegedly "weakened when others stood fast."[41] Because the Army refused to acknowledge that most captured soldiers cooperated with communist indoctrination in order to survive in the camps, military and civilian observers sought to understand, and then correct, the situations or traits that made soldiers vulnerable to communist coercion. Newspaper and magazine accounts of the POWs tended to blame the failures of prisoners on the alienation and moral weakness of post–World War II American culture.[42] "Brainwashing" became another popular explanation after American journalist Edward Hunter translated the Chinese *hsi nao* as "wash brain" in a 1951 book entitled *Brain-Washing in Red China*, introducing the expression into American English (and into Chinese, for that matter; there was no Chinese word for the concept).[43] Also called "coercive persuasion" or "menticide," brainwashing included techniques such as isolation, sleep deprivation, inadequate food and sanitation, assignment of repetitive tasks, threats, assaults, and forced acts of betrayal.[44] The brainwashing rationale effectively shifted blame from the American military, and from the United States itself, onto the deceptive tactics of the communist enemy.

Perhaps the simplest explanation of all, that some POW's found communist thought genuinely appealing given their circumstances, was dismissed out of hand. Soldiers in the army of American democracy who embraced communism were either confused by brainwashing or damned for betrayal in the Cold War military. There was no space in the embattled armed forces of the early Cold War for political dissent based on sympathy toward communism. Yet communist doctrine had intrinsic appeal to young men captured in a war that had gone very badly for the United States and who had firsthand experience with the inequities of American society. Claude Batchelor himself explained that three years of reading communist literature had changed his beliefs, though he was quick to add that returning to the United States had led him to reconsider his new political ideology.[45] The communist syllabus learned and then taught by POWs like Batchelor and Dickenson included substantive critiques of the United State's racial inequality and uneven distribution of wealth. Most captured servicemembers were not the sons of privilege. Often, they joined the Army to escape the social and economic limitations of their families and communities. The FBI investigated and reported on "any pertinent derogatory information" discovered about the POWs who were investigated for collaboration, including at least a few who had connections to the Communist Party in the United States.[46] But both military leaders and the social scientists who so exhaustively studied the POWs ignored the class and racial tensions that shaped military culture as well as American society during the post-World War II period.[47] They focused instead on soldiers' purportedly feeble mental state.

Instead of accepting servicemembers' "weakness" in the face of communist indoctrination as a sign of potential flaws in American society, military officials, social scientists, and journalists turned to more elaborate explanations for POW vulnerability. Batchelor's defense counsel tried to portray his client as mentally incompetent by virtue of "political psychosis," hoping that his court-martial would see an addled young soldier rather than a bright, dedicated communist. Neither, of course, was an entirely accurate image. The unfortunate Batchelor was a trumpet player pressed into service as an infantryman, an undistinguished student happy to finally impress his schoolteachers, even if they were communist guards in a POW camp. But to the United States army, he was a symbol of American vulnerability who had to be punished.

By the end of the Vietnam War, the Army's attitude toward using the military justice system to punish collaborating POW's had shifted closer to the Air Force's perspective in the "fear of flying" episode. The courts-martial of Korean War POWs had been costly, painful, and embarrassing to virtually everyone involved. Afterward, criminal prosecution was considered an inappropriate and overly punitive means of dealing with the issue of delayed repatriates and prisoners who cooperated with their captors.

But there was one court-martial of a Vietnam War prisoner-collaborator: Private First Class Robert R. Garwood, the only Vietnam War POW tried for collaborating with the enemy.[48] Although the geopolitical and military situation of the Vietnam War was not the same as that of the Korean War—the protests of the Vietnam era had no parallels in the 1950s, and the Vietnam War resulted in some seven hundred, not seven thousand, POWs—Garwood's preservice life and wartime experience echoed that of Batchelor and Dickenson. Frequently in trouble as a teenager and anxious to escape an unsteady home life, Garwood enlisted in the Marine Corps in 1963 as an alternative to an Indianapolis juvenile detention center.[49] He was captured in Vietnam in 1965, a young, inexperienced soldier much like Batchelor and Dickenson. Garwood lived with North Vietnamese and Chinese forces until 1979, refusing repatriation and adopting Vietnamese language, dress, and customs. The Marine Corps tracked his activities from 1966 until he returned to United States custody. Two years after his voluntary return, Garwood was court-martialed in a trial extending over eleven months, including ninety-two days of trial, and resulting in sixteen volumes of trial record and exhibits.[50] Garwood countered the testimony of other POW's about his preferential treatment by introducing testimony challenging his mental competence and suggesting a possible brain injury.[51]

Like that of Batchelor and Dickenson, the military's treatment of Garwood was the exception; most returning POW's, even those who had joined peace committees and signed confessions of misconduct while imprisoned, were not prosecuted for military crimes. Garwood was singled out for punishment because he manifested little resistance to communist indoctrination, spurned repatriation with other prisoners in 1973, and because other POWs "hated him while they were in the camps" and were willing to testify against him.[52] The Marine Corps had not pursued courts-martial against any of the Marines who cooperated in Korean War prison camps. But after the public relations disaster of the Vietnam War, the Corps was unwilling to excuse the highly publicized behavior of a troubled soldier.

The crimes of Batchelor, Dickenson, Garwood, and other court-martialed POWs were caused by the combination of communist coercion and the servicemen's lack of education, poor training, and personalities. These young men were blamed for the military's cultural and institutional failures in Cold War even when other servicemembers with apparently greater culpability and whose cases attracted comparable publicity—such as the Air Force's fearful pilots—escaped without criminal censure. Military courts handled the complex legal issues of these cases with diligence and gravity, but the seemingly arbitrary and harsh results of the POW courts-martial did not fulfill the UCMJ's promise of standardized justice and procedural fairness. Batchelor's and Dickenson's courts-martial were attentive to legal process, and clemency mitigated their sentences. But neither the military nor its justice system allowed for the possibility of political dissent among soldiers, inevitable as it might have been during the ideological battles of the Cold War.

SPIES AND DEFECTORS: OUSTING MORE "TURNCOAT GIs"

Not all "turncoat GIs" were unlucky prisoners coerced into denouncing American government and policy.[53] Defectors and spies were a more dangerous, active, and empowered type of political dissenter than collaborating POWs. Wayward POWs called into the question the superiority of American democracy as a political system, but servicemembers who became spies or defected to the United States' communist enemies rejected that system altogether. They contributed to an image of cultural weakness and political corruption in the ranks while adding to commanders' insecurity about their ability to identify and eliminate potential security risks.[54] Defectors exposed lapses in security, spoke out against American policies, and provided data to antimilitary groups, making recruiting more difficult and embarrassing military leaders.

Worse yet, the act of spying was rife with unsoldierly connotations. Disloyal, deceitful and feminized in popular representations, spies relied on cunning rather than physical strength and valued material gain over collective well-being.[55] But spying servicemen, not women, were the primary concern of the Cold War military. There are no cases in the appellate record of servicewomen convicted for spying. Women outside the military— wives, prostitutes and other civilian women who lived near military bases— were considered the more potent threat to soldiers' loyalty and national security than women in uniform.[56] Still, concerns about gender influenced the courts-martial of servicemembers for both political and sexual dissent. After the Korean War POW courts-martial, promoting an image of strong, masculine American soldiers was a key goal of military policy and strategy. Not only might defectors and spies undermine American foreign policy and military strategy, they might threaten the legitimacy of the growing American defense establishment.

Like the collaborating POWs, military spies and political deserters acted out of self-interest and complex motives rather than simply for ideological reasons. But they were prosecuted because of the active political dissent suggested by collaboration, spying, and defection. The Cold War military could not tolerate soldiers so disaffected by military life or so distracted by personal concerns that they gave away secrets or fled their military duties for communist enticements.

The politics that delayed the repatriation of Korean War POWs and affected the trials of collaborating POWs also influenced the handling of spying and defection cases. Defectors to both sides of the Iron Curtain were vital to the Cold War effort as both public relations opportunities and sources of information.[57] The public nature and legal process of courts-martial made criminal trials a poor means of controlling the flow of information, a key goal of American military and foreign policy. Debriefing, negotiation, administrative action, and other means of collecting information and coercing compliance were cheaper and quieter methods of dealing with soldiers suspected of compromising security than criminal prosecution.

Although some of the men accused at court-martial probably did release sensitive government information, the very few courts-martial for spying and political desertion that took place reveal hapless efforts to transfer information for personal gain, not devious schemes to bring down the U.S. government. Servicemembers were sometimes court-martialed for making contact, or trying to make contact, with agents of communist governments, but none appear to be communist ideologues or sophisticated double agents. Instead, the Cold War military's convicted spies and defectors were a motley collection of opportunistic, foolish, and troubled young men.[58] Presumably the more intrepid of American communists in military uniforms either operated without detection or were handled through less public, less procedurally restricted means than the military justice system. The record suggests that only servicemembers who so bungled their attempts to make contact with communist agents that they could not be ignored were court-martialed for their crimes.

Private Robert D. Blevens, termed an "East German defector" by military officials for his unauthorized forays across the Iron Curtain in 1953, was typical of the malcontented soldier without explicitly political motives who was court-martialed for political crimes.[59] The fickle Private Blevens was a bit player in the tense drama of post–World War II Berlin.[60] His story reveals the harsh consequences risked by servicemembers who disregarded rules prohibiting contact with communist agents, as well as the difficulty of prosecuting suspected spies through newly legalized courts-martial.[61]

Private Blevens arrived in Germany in January 1953 and quickly got into trouble. After less than a month in Berlin, he landed in the Army stockade for fighting and drinking. Upon hearing that his commander had recommended court-martial, Blevens flew into a rage, screaming "that he might as well be in the Russian Army as in an American stockade."[62] Unwisely, the impulsive Blevens translated his angry words into action. He located the "Russian Headquarters" in the East Zone of Berlin and sent Ingrid

Jonek, his German girlfriend, to investigate. After Jonek reported that "he would be treated like a king" if he joined the Russians, Blevens arranged an escape to East Berlin.[63] Greeted with champagne and hotel accommodations by East German secret agents, Blevens received civilian clothes, a free apartment, an identification card, and "a great number of 'Communistic books' to read."[64] The East Germans noticed that Blevens had a "Public Information" card that he had picked up while stationed in Japan and mistakenly assumed he was a journalist. Soon after, Blevens was asked to write articles that would "follow the Communist line."[65] Pleased with the attention, Blevens readily agreed and was praised for his efforts, which involved signing his name to political tracts that he copied from documents the agents provided him.

After three months, a "boss" from the East German police visited the private and explained that it was "time to get to work."[66] The boss told Blevens that he would now be talking to American soldiers in order to convince them to defect. At this, Private Blevens balked. He returned to the West Zone of Berlin and was taken into military custody.

During his second confinement in the Army's Berlin stockade, however, Blevens had second thoughts. He stayed in contact with the Russians through Jonek and soon decided to try to escape again and return to East Germany. Advised by Russian agents that Blevens could break out of the stockade by using a saw, Jonek visited Blevens and managed to slip him the tool. Blevens used it to escape and returned to East Berlin, where he was kept busy copying American documents at a communist compound. After yet another change of heart, he stole some papers from a filing cabinet to turn over to American authorities. Caught almost immediately by East German police, Blevens was jailed in Dresden, where he was beaten and coerced into signing a confession about his counterintelligence work for the United States. After being sent to a political school, Blevens again escaped and returned to West Berlin, where he was arrested once more, this time by the French police, who turned him over to American authorities.

Now securely in the custody of the U.S. Army, Blevens was tried and convicted for deserting (twice), escaping from confinement, and violating the general article of the UCMJ.[67] On December 21, 1953, he was sentenced to be dishonorably discharged, forfeit all pay, and serve thirteen years in confinement, a sentence upheld by military appellate courts.

On appeal, Blevens's defense counsel argued that his court-martial had erred by imputing the intent of the East German organization with which Blevens was affiliated to Blevens himself. Conceding that the communist group promoted "the violent overthrow of the United States Government," Blevens's counsel explained that there was no proof that Blevens himself advocated the use of violence against the United States.[68] The Court of Military Appeals quickly dispensed with this claim, stressing the special loyalty required of military personnel and pointing out that Blevens knew communists sought to overthrow the U.S. government and that the East German group was a communist organization.[69] The court lingered over the question of whether Blevens was actually "affiliated" with the communist group, but eventually upheld that conclusion, relying on his willingness to write articles for the East Germans and his claim to have recognized the secret "Communist handshake" of one of his visitors. This flimsy evidence was enough to convince both a court-martial and an appellate court that Blevens was a substantive threat to the U.S. government.

Private Blevens's harsh sentence resulted from both his cavalier disregard for the requirements of military service and the fear of communism that pervaded American culture and politics during the 1950s. The judges of the Court of Military Appeals, like other judges of the day, felt obliged to defend the nation against communism. In rejecting Blevens's appeal, the court stressed the "special trust" granted servicemembers and the "unqualified loyalty" demanded in return, condemning Blevens's offenses as "conduct of a most reprehensible nature."[70] Suggesting that Blevens could have been convicted of the capital crime of aiding the enemy under Article 104 of the UCMJ—one of the charges that earned POW Batchelor a twenty-year sentence—the court implied that Blevens was fortunate to have escaped with only thirteen years confinement.[71] Yet it seems unlikely that Blevens had much to offer the Soviets, given his low rank and the short time he had spent in Berlin. Plied with flattery and material gifts by Russian agents who probably cultivated him more as a means of embarrassing the United States than as an actual source of information, Blevens hardly qualifies as the sort of sly operative implied by the term "defector."

Nor did most of the other Cold War soldiers who defected, even those who made conscious decisions to establish residences in foreign countries as signs of protest against American policies. As American involvement in Vietnam escalated in the mid-1960s, soldiers who objected to the war and their role in it left military service for personal and political reasons. In 1967, Roy Ray Jones, a twenty-one year-old private from Detroit, became the first American soldier to flee to Sweden.[72] Hundreds of others followed, helping to push the military's desertion rates to record levels toward the end of the war in Vietnam.[73] Servicemen were willing to desert, a capital crime under the UCMJ during times of war, because of their frustration at U.S. involvement in Vietnam, the constraints of military life, and the racism that continued to shape military policy and culture. Vietnam-era deserters were disproportionately both racial minorities and from impoverished families. They were likely to have volunteered for military service and were almost all low-ranking enlisted men who served—like the majority of American servicemembers—in noncombat military occupations.[74] The case of Ray Jones, an African American, was relatively typical:

He was involved in an interracial, international romantic relationship that the Army discouraged, angry at the racism he encountered in the service, and willing to follow the lead of antiwar and civil rights activists who helped him escape and then made him a spokesman for their cause.[75] Like many deserters, Jones's motivations for escaping the Army were complex. He became overtly politicized after, not before, leaving the service.[76] Only 10 to 15 percent of Vietnam-era deserters named political reasons as their motive for leaving.[77] Most deserters—like most collaborators and most spies—were not politically motivated, even during the height of antiwar protest.

The court-martial continued to be used with restraint by military leaders and government officials, who did not choose to punish most deserters at court-martial.[78] At first glance, this decision seems curious, particularly since the majority of deserters eventually returned to U.S. custody and were therefore subject to military jurisdiction. Desertion posed a direct threat to the military's effectiveness and a public affront to military authority. But, as we have already seen, sometimes the risks of a disciplinary spectacle could outweigh the potential gains. The armed forces feared creating more opportunities for servicemembers like Dr. Howard B. Levy, whose court-martial became a platform for denouncing American policies in Vietnam.[79] A staunch opponent of the war who was one of many medical doctors drafted into service, Levy refused to teach medicine to the Army's elite Green Berets and openly condemned American involvement in Vietnam, American racism, and the Green Berets themselves, calling them killers of women, children, and the impoverished Vietnamese.[80] Drawing public attention to the plight of dissidents in uniform was an undesirable by-product of military criminal prosecution that could be avoided by the use of administrative and bureaucratic, rather than criminal, procedures.

The UCMJ itself, which limited investigative tactics and required at least some disclosure of information by prosecutors, also made courts-martial for desertion and spying a less appealing option. The Code interfered with the military's efforts to control information and protect its public image, forcing military courts to balance individual rights against collective security. The military's no-holds-barred investigations of suspected political crimes conflicted with the protections guaranteed by the UCMJ. The April 1962 court-martial of an Air Force captain at Wiesbaden Air Base, Germany, who was wooed by communist operatives is a case in point.[81] Joseph P. Kauffmann was convicted of compromising national security by meeting with East German agents after an investigation and trial marked by what an Air Force Board of Review called "massive and deliberate violations of [Kaufmann's] constitutional rights."[82] These violations included eavesdropping on conversations between Kauffman and his defense counsel, four separate searches, described by the court as "illegal nocturnal prowl-ings," of Kauffman's off-base home, and, during Kauffman's trial, a system of handkerchief signaling between the trial counsel (the military prosecu-tor) and a witness on the stand in an attempt to protect classified informa-tion.[83] After the final judicial review of his case, Kauffman stood convicted of a single charge: violating a regulation by not reporting his contacts with a foreign government. For this offense, Kauffman was resentenced to ten years of confinement, a harsh punishment for a relatively minor crime. Even the evidence admitted at trial and later excluded proved only that Kauff-man had danced, sung, ate, drank, and talked at length to communist agents, not that he had turned over sensitive information. In the eyes of the Cold War military justice system, severe penalties were warranted de-spite procedural irregularities and limited evidence because "[t]he very survival of this nation" depended upon "strict compliance" with security regulations.[84] Like Private Blevens's indiscretions in Berlin, Captain Kauff-man's socializing hardly seems threatening enough to warrant such apoc-alyptic predictions. But Kauffman was court-martialed nonetheless, proof that military leaders would not yet relinquish criminal prosecution as one of their weapons at the ideological front of the Cold War.

ISOLATING THE "SEX PERVERT": HOMOSEXUALITY AS DISSENT

Uncovering homosexuality was nearly as high a priority as ferreting out spies in the Cold War military. The two threats were closely linked. Ho-mosexual soldiers were seen as more vulnerable to communist conversion because of their psychological weakness and more likely to be coerced into disloyal acts because of shame at the prospect of being exposed as gay. Ser-vicemen suspected of being gay were more closely scrutinized by military police and special agents, and suspected spies could expect inferences at trial that they were gay simply because of the association between homo-sexuality and dissipation. Even the collaborating Korean War POWs were linked to homosexuality. In the POW encampments, the all-male prison culture created opportunities for sexual commerce and intimate relation-ships among men; prisoners themselves spread rumors of widespread ho-mosexuality in some Korean War camps.[85] Throughout this period, ho-mosexuals, spies, and collaborators were all deemed aberrant and weak, an affront to the image of masculine strength that the armed forces hoped to project. Spies and gay troops were especially troubling because of their ap-parent invisibility. It was as hard to tell from looking at soldiers whether they were gay as it was to gauge whether they might be security risks.

Like courts-martial for collaboration, espionage, and political desertion, prosecutions for homosexuality expose military leaders' assumptions about who was likely to succumb to temptation. The case of Herbert Lee Northrup, a communications specialist court-martialed at Ramstein Air Force Base in Germany in 1960, makes explicit the overlap between the crimes of homosexuality and political treachery. Several times, Airman Northup set out to defect to East Germany with a stolen "top secret" document. Each time, he lost his nerve and returned to West Berlin without having contacted Soviet agents.[86] Despite his failure to transfer any information at all, Northup was court-martialed, convicted, and sentenced to twenty years confinement and a dishonorable discharge. In this case, as in most Cold War courts-martial of suspected spies, defense attorneys raised alternatives to disloyalty as explanations for their client's actions, suggesting that family, money, and sexual problems—not a desire to betray his country—had led a young and inexperienced airman into grave error. But this defense tactic backfired when the issue of Northup's sexual orientation entered the minds of court-martial members.[87] Blaming Northrup's actions on "personal problems created by his alcoholic mother, his debts, and his concern over his latent homosexual tendencies" was a gamble, given the strong association between being gay and being a traitor. The two were not even clearly separable identities in the Cold War United States; homosexuals were seen by many as no less threatening to American culture and democracy than political deserters or double agents.

In cases of suspected homosexuality, just as in cases of apparently political crimes, legal reform came into conflict with Cold War military culture. Because the armed forces' extreme prejudice against homosexuals made impartiality nearly impossible to achieve, procedural errors and reversals on appeal were common in trials for alleged homosexual acts. Military appellate courts were forced to admonish judge advocates, law officers, and military judges who introduced and admitted prejudicial evidence against accused servicemen or who conspired together to win convictions at court-martial.[88] The military's zealous pursuit of lesbian and gay servicemembers compelled rebuke from those dedicated to the integrity of military criminal procedure.

Legal reform and the need for military personnel, combined with the increasing tolerance of the nation for nontraditional sexual behavior as the 1960s progressed, made the disciplinary spectacle of courts-martial less appealing than other, noncriminal means of punishing homosexuality. But courts-martial for alleged homosexuality were not so rare as those for outright political dissent. Like prosecutions for spying, they created a thicket of complex legal issues for military and civilian judges to resolve. Perhaps most crucial was the question of what evidence—of specific acts, of past behavior, of the accused's character, of his or her associations—should be admitted in order to prove sexual acts and orientation. As the Court of Military Appeals explained in a 1953 opinion, because most sex crime prosecutions focused on the only two people who knew the details of an alleged crime, corroborating evidence was difficult to come by.[89] As a result, courts-martial for sodomy and other crimes of homosexuality were often swearing contests in which prosecutors struggled to prove the crime "beyond a reasonable doubt" and servicemembers defended against the allegations with a character defense, often "the best, if not the only, defense" available.[90] Under the UCMJ, evidence of good military character could be introduced to create doubt about whether the accused servicemember was guilty, despite criminal trials' usual focus on specific acts of misconduct rather than an accused person's character or disposition. Law officers' and military judges' decisions regarding whether and what kind of character evidence would be admitted were often determinative at trial and then carefully scrutinized on appeal.[91] As an Army board of review explained in 1957, character evidence could be "compelling," especially if "given by comrades-in-arms who lived with the accused and served with him for lengthy periods at remote posts where homosexual tendencies, if they existed, would be most apt to manifest themselves."[92] Even when a servicemember was convicted of consensual homosexual sodomy at trial, character evidence could turn the tide on appeal.[93] Character evidence could sway members of a court-martial, appellate judges, and commanding officers by suggesting that long, successful military careers and "normal" family and sexual relationships should outweigh the moral failing of implied homosexuality. Accused soldiers strove to present themselves to the court as able and willing to conform to expected norms of sexual behavior and family roles.

Military precedents conflicted on whether an accused servicemember's sexual history could be admitted as a means of proving a particular act of misconduct charged at court-martial. For example, in 1955 the Court of Military Appeals made an effort to clarify at what point evidence of past sexual activity became so remote in time and circumstance from the crime alleged that it should be excluded from consideration.[94] The court held that the only uncharged acts of homosexual behavior that could be properly admitted at trial for a particular homosexual act were those that occurred between the parties accused of committing the charged offense.[95] This legal interpretation would have dramatically limited the humiliating testimony that accused gay servicemembers faced at court-martial. In 1958, however, the Court of Military Appeals shifted course, this time holding that evidence of past homosexual acts was indeed admissible as proof of an accused's intent to commit sodomy.[96] The court elected to treat consensual and forcible sodomy as closely related crimes, terming "specious" the argument that homosexuality had little to do with forcible assaults: "Certainly, a person who practices homosexuality is likely to assault for the purpose of satisfying his perverted sexual cravings, and proof of previous deviations from the sexual norm is a valuable ingredient in establishing specific intent in subsequent offenses of the same kind."[97] If one believed that gay men were likely to assault other men in order to gratify their lust (akin to the argument that straight men denied the opportunity for sex with prostitutes were likely to rape women), then admitting evidence of sexual orientation at court-martial could be justified despite evidentiary doctrines that prohibited it. In 1963, twenty year-old Richard R. Kindler, an airman since the age of eighteen, was convicted for committing "indecent acts" upon a sleeping fellow airman.[98] Kindler denied the allegation, testifying: "I'm just as normal as anybody else around here. I hope to get married some day and have a family just like anybody else. I'm not a homosexual. I'm not a queer."[99] Because the prosecuting attorney had cross-examined Kindler about his homosexual experiences between the ages of twelve and fourteen, an Air Force board of review ordered a rehearing on the grounds that such questioning went too far in prejudicing Kindler before the court-martial. But the Court of Military Appeals disagreed, holding that Kindler had opened the door to his sexual background by claiming to be "perfectly normal" sexually. The court explained that Kindler's early homosexual conduct increased the likelihood that he was lying about his current sexual behavior. Recognizing that public policy favored the protection of juveniles and that evidentiary principles counseled against the admission of acts remote in time or place from the charged crime, the court nonetheless held that evidence of Kindler's behavior as a young adolescent was admissible. Because Kindler had engaged in a regular course of homosexual activity over a two-year period, and because the evidence showed him to have "apparent judgment and discretion" in this early adolescence, the court found the prosecution's cross-examination on his past sexual behavior appropriate to impeach his claim of a "normal" sexual orientation.

Prejudice against homosexuality also undermined procedural safeguards when government agents conducted humiliating and invasive searches reminiscent of the illegal searches conducted by military spy-catchers. Military courts had to address the legal ramifications of agents who disregarded basic standards of privacy and reasonableness in their zeal to identify and collect evidence against servicemembers thought to be gay. Illegally seized evidence might, and often did, convince a commander to administratively discharge a servicemember accused of homosexuality. But when admitted at court-martial, it threatened the integrity of the military justice system. In extreme cases of commanding officers and military police ignoring the constraints of the UCMJ, judges tried to reassert control by reversing convictions.[100]

Law enforcement agents in search of gay servicemen often focused their efforts on civilian establishments near military bases, a tactic that created many opportunities for illegal searches. In the summer of 1957, Radarman Seaman Clifford C. Hillan was convicted of committing a "lewd and lascivious act" with another man in a room at the Norfolk, Virginia, YMCA.[101] Hillan was nabbed by the Navy Shore Patrol in a witchhunt so outrageous that a Navy board of the review swiftly overturned his conviction on appeal. The Shore Patrol's nightly routine began with Chief Thames of the Patrol checking the YMCA room register to see which rooms were rented to civilians. Those rooms were considered off-limits to the Navy's searches. All other rooms, however, were considered "public domain" and therefore subject to warrantless searches based only on the suspicion of patrolmen. Chief Thames and his assistant used "peep holes," which were masked with chewing gum when not in use, to peer through the walls and closets into the locked rooms occupied by servicemen. Thames testified that he became suspicious when he saw men touching themselves and each other, "running around the 'Y' from floor to floor," heard bedsprings creaking (which had alerted him to Hillan's activities), or noticed two men together in a single room.[102] Chief Thames claimed that he had caught 231 men during just over two years of operating the Norfolk YMCA dragnet.[103] In considering Hillan's appeal, a Navy court pointed out that the Shore Patrol's activities did not prevent homosexual activity but instead caught those "who were unfortunate enough to be found in embarrassing and compromising attitudes after surprise and forced entry into private rooms."[104] Rejecting these searches as obviously illegal, the Navy board explained that no legal doctrine supported the searches of private hotel rooms by military officers who burst in unannounced, without the consent of the occupants and without a warrant. Not all servicemembers who were caught had the benefit of military legal reforms, but at least some did find protection from punishment, if not from social approbation, in the UCMJ.

Even when homosexual acts or orientation were not part of the charges before a court-martial, evidence that the accused might be gay could affect his or her fate. Because homosexuality was considered a sign of moral corruption, it was often considered probative in assessing the credibility of witnesses and the trustworthiness of an accused. In 1955, Chief Judge Quinn of the Court of Military Appeals, dissenting from the court's decision to permit a prosecutor to ask about "homosexual tendencies" at a trial for unrelated charges, pointed out that "the mere suggestion" of homosexual acts was "likely to overcome the presumption of innocence."[105] Assumptions about the corrupt nature of homosexuals prejudiced servicemembers at courts-martial whenever unrelated charges were prosecuted alongside charges of homosexual conduct and during trials for nonsexual crimes, such as larceny, desertion, and arson, in which testimony about the accused's alleged homosexual inclinations or acts was admitted.[106] Military prosecutors who had obtained convictions in these cases often found their work undone by appellate judges who tried to hold the line against admitting prejudicial testimony about homosexuality when it was not germane to the crimes charged. Even when evidence of homosexual conduct was excluded at trial, however, it could surface in the sentencing reports that influenced commanders' decisions about clemency. For example, a sentencing report in the case of a nineteen-year-old seaman recruit convicted of several charges unrelated to sex in 1957 noted the accused's "probable . . . homosexual tendencies."[107] A Coast Guard Board of Review considered the information appropriate despite its potential for inciting prejudice, pointing out that the accused could have rebutted any false information in the report by submitting a brief to the board of review.[108] Gay or straight, servicemembers accused of crimes sometimes successfully invoked the protections of the UCMJ. But so long as homosexual acts were themselves military crimes, due process could not eliminate the substantive prejudice against lesbian and gay servicemembers at court-martial.

BREAKDOWN AND REBELLION: COURTS-MARTIAL FOR DISSENT DURING THE VIETNAM WAR

Worries about spying and homosexuality did not disappear during the Vietnam War, but new forms of dissent and insubordination diverted the attention of military leaders.[109] Efforts to repress unwanted sexual and political behavior by individual soldiers became less important to military leaders than preventing widespread rebellion and propping up disintegrating morale. Soldiers joined protest organizations, held demonstrations, spoke out in coffeehouses, and published and distributed underground newspapers. Servicemembers' resistance to military authority reached unprecedented levels during Vietnam, spurred by the same factors that triggered protest outside the armed forces but compounded by the military's emphasis on obedience among troops and by soldiers' access to weapons.

The draft guaranteed a significant subset of nonvolunteers among American forces, virtually ensuring that political dissenters would be a part of the Vietnam-era military.[110] Increasing pressure for racial and economic justice in the United States magnified antiwar sentiment, and the civil rights movement emboldened African Americans frustrated at both the race typing that persisted in military assignments and the social segregation enforced in and around military bases and posts. Sexual, social, and racial hierarchies were also challenged by the antipoverty movement, the rise of the counterculture, increasing drug use, and gay liberation. At least one among the many underground GI newspapers focused on gay and lesbian issues.[111] Group, as well as individual, resistance grew during this period, and new associations emphasized the importance of understanding law and policy to their members. The Black Brothers United, an underground GI organization, trained its members in military law and regulations, following the lead of other dissident groups.[112] During Vietnam, even the UCMJ became a tool of rebellion, used by resisters to develop strategies of protest in a new climate of dissent.

Finding ways to restore morale and to renovate the image of the armed forces was a task of military criminal justice as well as of recruiting and public affairs offices. Alcohol use had long been a problem among servicemen, but drug use and addiction undercut military discipline and public relations during and after Vietnam.[113] Servicemembers were court-martialed for drug use and for the incidents of "indiscipline" that became more common in combat situations as the war continued.[114] Though most soldiers did not come out openly as opponents of the war, "the level of resistance within the military by the late 1960s was extraordinary," and disciplinary problems, including a rising desertion rate, resulted.[115]

The practice of flushing out silent communist sympathizers, who might sell information to foreign agents, through aggressive investigation and prosecution gave way to attempts to quiet rebellious servicemembers through administrative action and occasional courts-martial. With a culture rooted in deference to authority and with responsibility for prosecuting the very war that so many Americans were protesting, the armed forces could not avoid becoming a site of political and social unrest, regardless of the measures military leaders took to screen or eliminate dissidents.[116] Public dissent such as speaking out against American policies and organizing opposition became increasingly common.[117] Because the military could not easily ignore servicemembers who chose to make their views known—as it might have overlooked defectors who did not seek publicity—these cases were more likely to result in courts-martial.[118]

Most of those punished for speaking out during Vietnam were enlisted men rather than officers, and many were men of color. Racial politics influenced the prosecution of political dissent as well as courts-martial for racially motivated violence, which also increased in the late 1960s and early 1970s.[119] The 1966 courts-martial of the "Fort Hood 3," an African American, Italian American, and Puerto Rican American who refused orders to report to Vietnam, attracted widespread media attention.[120] Other enlisted personnel were prosecuted for similar offenses, whether or not they were motivated by political conviction. For example, Private Victor McNeal Bell was convicted of disloyalty and AWOL at court-martial after speaking out against the Vietnam War in Saint Chrysostem's Church in Chicago, on August 28, 1968.[121] After being introduced by a group of clergymen, Bell read a statement encouraging others to follow him in rejecting military conscription and the "war machine" of the United States.[122] For promoting "disloyalty and disaffection among the troops" and going AWOL, Bell was sentenced to a year confinement (reduced from the three and a half years adjudged at his court-martial) and a bad-conduct discharge.[123] On appeal, an Army board of review carefully considered, and dispensed with, the arguments of Bell's defense counsel regarding his client's rights. The army court did not stop there, however. Its judges used Bell's appeal to make their own case for the legitimacy and fairness of trial under the UCMJ. The board noted that the acquittal rate at general courts-martial was higher than in U.S. District Court trials (6 percent compared to 3.9 percent) and added that military defendants enjoyed benefits not available to civilian defendants, such as "the right to free legal representation by an appointed qualified lawyer," "an automatic right to appeal, at no cost," and "a full and complete disclosure of all relevant evidence at every stage of the case."[124] The court responded directly to its rising chorus of critics by detailing the procedural protections available to accused servicemembers. Like the armed forces in general, military justice was under siege by the end of the Vietnam War. Judges as well as generals felt obliged to defend themselves and their institutions against from attacks without and within the military itself.

The military's defensiveness about racial and procedural justice could help servicemembers convicted of political crimes. In Bell's case, the Army board set aside his conviction on the charge of uttering disloyal statements, leaving a single conviction for AWOL, because the trial judge had not inquired sufficiently into the circumstances surrounding Bell's guilty plea. Bell told the court that in trying to get away from the Army he had become involved with antiwar protesters. With nowhere else to go, he joined the protesters and read a statement that the group had written for him. Coerced by peace activists rather than communists, Bell's case elicited a more sympathetic hearing from the military courts than did Batchelor's and Dickenson's cases fifteen years earlier.

Addressing the deeper sources of dissent and disobedience, including the racial, economic, and sexual inequities embedded in the military's infrastructure, was again left for another day by military leaders. But the Vietnam-era armed forces tackled the problem of illegal drug use head-on. Using illegal drugs was another means of dissent for servicemembers disillusioned with military life and culture. Drug and alcohol abuse had long been a disciplinary issue for commanding officers, who recognized that substance abuse contributed to minor disciplinary infractions as well as serious crimes.[125] Political vulnerability was also linked to drug use, particularly after some of the Korean War POWs admitted to smoking marijuana.[126] Heroin addiction was also a problem during the Korean War, leading one Army commander to term drug abuse "the number-one transgression in the Eighth Army in the spring of 1950."[127] The Department of Defense concurred, identifying heroin during the mid-1950s as more dangerous and popular among servicemembers stationed in Asia than morphine, opium, or marijuana.[128] The violence of war, the dislocation of foreign service, and the hardships of military life predisposed servicemembers to escape physical and emotional stress with alcohol and illegal drugs.

Although not necessarily a manifestation of political resistance, the dramatic increase in illegal drug use among servicemembers in Vietnam was due in part to the atmosphere of protest and defiance.[129] Poor morale, breakdowns in military authority, and easily accessible drugs created a problem in Vietnam of staggering proportions.[130] Servicemembers' drug use exasperated commanders and triggered congressional investigation.[131] It also confirmed that courts-martial were no longer an effective means of addressing either routine disciplinary issues or political dissent. Although the armed forces initially responded with widespread criminal prosecution—drug-related criminal investigations increased by 80 percent from 1968 to 1969 and another 38 percent from 1969 to 1970—the increase in illegal drug use quickly outstripped the military's ability to criminalize it.[132] An amnesty program was implemented instead to encourage treatment and reduce courts-martial, though it was lined with what one observer termed "punitive booby traps" that permitted commanders to punish servicemembers without adhering to the procedural rules that restricted criminal investigations and trials.[133] Other noncriminal means targeted at drug offenders were massive urinalysis testing, centralized treatment facilities in the Air Force and Navy and decentralized rehabilitation programs in the Army, and the use of "undesirable discharges" to eliminate drug users, which avoided the costs and uncertainty of obtaining conviction and punitive discharges at court-martial.[134]

During the Vietnam War, communism remained a primary threat, but drug abuse had replaced brainwashing as the explanation of choice for the American military's lack of success in Asia. By 1971, the military had shifted the focus of its political education program from anticommunist indoctrination to an antidrug campaign.[135] The military continued to respond to the appearance of dissenters in uniform by discounting explicitly political motives, choosing instead to rely on explanations less threatening to its vision of American democratic and military superiority.

Eliminating ideological weakness was not an appropriate task for the military justice system. It could deal with only the loudest and least capable of dissenters, the defectors, spies, and homosexuals who were unlucky enough to lose their cover and the angry protesters whose public outbursts had to be silenced. Courts-martial failed to solve the problem of rebellious troops during the Vietnam War—in fact, criminal trials provided the very vehicles for publicity that antiwar activists sought. The procedural protections guaranteed under the UCMJ forced the armed forces to look beyond criminal sanction in their quest for conformity. The absurdity of the circumstances that led to these courts-martial and the procedural violations that occurred in so many investigations and trials reveal the tension and uncertainty that legal reform created in military criminal justice. The Cold War court-martial stumbled when it tried to defend the nation against the confusion and doubt sown by dissenting soldiers. It could not protect the rights and freedoms the Constitution promised Americans at the same time it punished soldiers who wavered from the political and sexual convictions that military culture demanded of them.

Chapter 4

CRIME AND THE MILITARY FAMILY

The military justice system was the last resort of commanding officers whose troops refused to meet the expectation that military duty come first among the many responsibilities of their lives. Military folklore reflected the assumption that enlisting in the service replaced an individual's existing family with a new military family, complete with its own rules, traditions, and loyalties. When young recruits shouted in marching cadence, "we like it here, we love it here, we finally found a home!" they were articulating a worldview that embraced military priorities as their own.[1]

But the pressures of family did not cease when soldiers and sailors donned uniforms. Military crime reveals the personal consequences of war and military life on individual servicemembers. Many were prosecuted for going AWOL (absent without leave) to manage family responsibilities, while others ran afoul of military rules about marital status and sexual behavior when they tried to get married or sought out new sexual partners. This chapter analyzes three types of military crime to expose the essential contradictions between military and family life. The first involves the conflicts between the social expectation that men would provide for their families and the military's requirement that they be present for duty. The second concerns crimes such as bigamy, adultery, and violations of marriage regulations, acts that were prosecuted because they undermined military authority and imperiled the image of family life that military recruiters and government leaders sought to project. The final group of courts-martial involves violence within military families. It reveals the aggravating factors that made some incidents of military domestic violence criminal during a time when the armed forces, like the rest of the United States, accepted most domestic violence as a part of family life. During the Cold War, the strength of American families, like the strength of the American military, was celebrated as evidence of U.S. superiority over communist countries. Yet these two institutions did not peacefully coexist. Military duty imposed hardships on family members and threatened domestic stability, while domestic obligations exacted a toll from servicemembers and limited the demands commanding officers could make on their troops. Nowhere was the strain more apparent than at court-martial.

GENDER, CLASS, AND CRIMINAL ABSENCE

Q. Do you like the Army better than you like this woman?
A. Well, I don't know, sir, I wouldn't say that. I don't like the Army at all.[2]

The tension between military and family loyalties was reflected in this 1952 exchange between a military judge and an enlisted man court-martialed for deserting the Army to support the mother of his child ("this woman" in the words of the military judge). During the Cold War, more servicemembers were married, more were deployed overseas for extended periods, and more enlisted to escape poverty. As a result, family responsibilities weighed heavily on soldiers and sailors. The armed forces had to reassert the primacy of military duty in the lives of its members. The responsibilities that attached to marriage, family, and sexual encounters competed with the military for the attention and resources of servicemembers.

The military's claim on the services and loyalty of American men was reinforced by its ability to prosecute those who would substitute their own judgments about where they might be needed for the military's decisions about where they belonged. Unauthorized absence undermined the armed forces' control over its members, even when soldiers went AWOL, as many did, to deal with family medical or financial emergencies. While separating "political" from "personal" motives is not always possible, the vast majority of soldiers who deserted during the Vietnam War—as well as during World War II and the Korean War—were not motivated by political convictions.[3] Servicemembers whose relatives lacked the resources to manage personal problems were more likely to leave without notice than others, making AWOL and desertion crimes of the military's lower classes. The military was supposed to supplant a soldier's family in many respects; it is no coincidence that the most common legal use of the term "desertion" outside military circles involved husbands, and sometimes wives, who abandoned their mates.

Crimes of absence underscored the distinction between military and civilian culture. A young civilian who quit work, slept in late, or stayed a few extra days on vacation might suffer economic loss or social approbation, but could not be prosecuted for committing a crime. But a serviceman who "quit his unit" or "absented himself" could be—and often was—court-martialed.[4] The military crime of absence dominated the court-martial docket during this period. An Army report showed that desertion and AWOL were charged at 76 percent of all courts-martial held between 1951 and 1953.[5] In the early 1970s, AWOL offenses accounted for between 65 and 90 percent of courts-martial reported in studies of three separate Army posts.[6] Criminal trials for unauthorized absence had long been intended to control the soldier's urge to shirk military duty by making examples of those who abandoned their stations.[7] Severe and public punishment of a few absence offenders was supposed to deter others and help to protect the social stability and mission effectiveness of military forces.[8] Although there is little proof that this approach worked very well—during the Vietnam War, for example, the Marine Corps policy of treating absence offenders far more harshly than the other services did not reduce its desertion rate[9]—the strategy of exemplary justice remained an important part of the armed forces' response to absenteeism during the Cold War. Even when they failed to deter other absences, courts-martial for AWOL and desertion signaled the special demands of military life to soldiers and civilians alike.

The legal doctrines that governed courts-martial for criminal absence had no corollaries in the jurisprudence of civilian crime. In fact, the military's need to deter crimes of absence was one of the most convincing rationales for the continued existence of a separate military justice system under the UCMJ. Public sympathy for deserters after the Civil War was the primary motivation for the construction of Fort Leavenworth's military prison, which isolated convicted soldiers from civilian criminals and communities.[10] The swelling case law of criminal absence during the 1950s created a unique body of doctrine influenced by civilian law but insulated from direct intervention by civilian courts.[11] The Supreme Court declined to rule on the legal questions of unauthorized absence, leaving the law that governed this military-specific crime to be worked out by military appellate courts, commanders, and judge advocates.[12] The history of absence crimes suggests one of the reasons for this divide. Although unauthorized absence was a serious offense under virtually every military code in history, civilians did not always share the perspective of military leaders about the wrongfulness of absence without leave.[13] The bulk of courts-martial involved charges that could not have been prosecuted in civilian criminal courts.

The UCMJ set out an array of offenses to classify the different types of criminal absence.[14] Because unauthorized absences varied in severity, the code established a graduated series of absence crimes. Within this hierarchy, desertion was the most serious, a dire threat to the military's effectiveness and an affront to soldierly loyalty, a basic tenet of military culture. It was punishable by death during wartime and by up to five years of confinement and a dishonorable discharge during times of peace.[15] AWOL offenses, which could be punished with a maximum of six months confinement and a dishonorable discharge, were distinguished from desertion by the servicemember's intent.[16] To convict for desertion, the military had to prove beyond a reasonable doubt that the accused servicemember intended to avoid duty *permanently*. AWOL, on the other hand, was a strict liability crime, requiring no proof of the offender's state of mind. Mere proof of absence was sufficient for to convict for AWOL.[17] Commanding officers considered the length, circumstances, and manner of termination of servicemembers' absences as well as any evidence of intent in deciding what sorts of charges—if any—to bring against them at court-martial.

The servicemembers most often prosecuted for criminal absence occupied the bottom of the military's hierarchy of rank, education, and race. Detailed studies of Vietnam-era deserters are especially helpful in understanding these demographics because the type of soldier most likely to desert stayed relatively constant from World War II through the Vietnam War.[18] Studies of Vietnam absence offenders show that military personnel who were poorly educated or from underprivileged economic backgrounds, both often correlated to minority racial status, were more likely to be prosecuted for AWOL and desertion.[19] The servicemembers whose families lived below the poverty line—numbering at least 70,000 during the Vietnam War—were much more likely to be drawn away from their military responsibilities than those with the resources to solve family problems from a distance.[20] Three-quarters of absence offenders came from "economically unstable" homes.[21] Three-fourths of deserters had not finished high school;[22] a deserter was three times more likely to be without a high school diploma than the average enlisted man.[23] Nonwhite servicemembers were more likely to be prosecuted for absence crimes than were white personnel.[24] Twenty-one percent of military absence offenders in Vietnam were African American, about double the percentage of black troops.[25] The armed forces did not collect data on other racial minorities, but the number of Spanish-speaking absentees was also disproportionately high compared to their percentage of the military population.[26] Rank mattered as well as race in determining the likelihood that a soldier would be court-martialed for criminal absence; junior enlisted personnel committed the great majority of unauthorized absence offenses.[27] Most Vietnam-era absence offenders were under twenty-two years of age, unmarried, had less than two years of service, and occupied one of the two lowest enlisted pay grades (E-1 and E-2).[28]

Deserters and other absence offenders have been described as generic failures in some studies, which point out that a failure to succeed in the military often paralleled failure in civilian life.[29] But simply labeling these men misfits obscures the social and cultural barriers to integration into military life faced by those who lacked strong educational backgrounds, well-developed social skills, or financial security. Poverty frequently precipitated unauthorized absence, evidenced by both the statistics and the reasons for leaving that servicemembers themselves provided. Personal problems, especially those involving family and economic troubles and an inability to adjust to military life, were the most common motivations for unauthorized absences.[30]

Although a lack of resources lay behind many absence crimes, the trials and appeals of absence offenders often centered on how trouble with women, not money, drew servicemen away from their posts. Crimes of absence were prosecuted under a regime of gender relations that posed essential contradictions for servicemen who were also husbands, lovers, fathers, and sons. The armed forces were central in the reconstructions of gender that occurred during the Cold War, and the emphasis on male authority and responsibility that shaped American law and culture during the 1950s was in full force within the ranks of military service.[31] As nuclear families were defined and women were urged to accept domestic responsibilities, men were encouraged to provide for their families.[32] This dominant vision of masculinity did not go unchallenged. Some women and men rejected its constraints while others struggled to meet its demands. As one scholar recently described it, during the Cold War "[m]anliness did not go away; manliness was put on trial."[33] The gender crises of the 1950s intensified as the civil rights movement and Vietnam War moved to center stage in the 1960s. The uncertainty and frustrations of the Vietnam era sparked a new set of social and cultural disruptions, within and without the military.[34] It was against this background of challenges to gender roles that courts-martial for AWOL and desertion attempted to reinstate the importance of loyalty and sacrifice to American servicemembers.

Men were the culprits in the overwhelming majority of AWOL and desertion cases. Only a handful of servicewomen were prosecuted for criminal absence during this period.[35] But women are far from absent in the case law of AWOL and desertion.[36] As the wives, lovers, mothers, and sisters of servicemen, women appear at courts-martial as rivals to the military for the fidelity of men. In criminal absence cases, servicemen often appear caught between the demands of women and the demands of military service, a space filled with female-inspired desire, distraction, and need.

The military was close to an all-male force during this period, but women were part of virtually every aspect of military service, even the legalized arena of courts-martial. Female family members testified about the states of mind of accused servicemembers during courts-martial, providing information that could be critical in determining whether the intent required for desertion was present.[37] The wives of servicemembers were often witnesses during sentencing hearings, hoping to mitigate the punishments imposed on their husbands.[38] Women who socialized around military bases also appeared at courts-martial to testify on the whereabouts and drinking habits of accused men.[39] AWOL servicemen sometimes committed crimes against women during their absences, as in the case of an Army private who strangled and robbed two civilian women while AWOL from Fort Meade in 1966,[40] or a soldier who assaulted a German girl during a four-hour unauthorized absence in 1961.[41] Women also appear as coconspirators of accused servicemen in absence cases involving crimes such as theft,[42] fraud,[43] and even felony murder.[44] Women also appeared in courts-martial in a professional capacity, as expert witnesses,[45] attorneys,[46] and by the 1970s, as military judges in rare instances.[47]

Women played a crucial role in the narratives of criminal absence constructed by servicemen at trial, then interpreted by military judges in appellate opinions. They appear as the bodily antithesis of the honor, strength, and sacrifice that military culture valorized. In the newly bureaucratized, race- and gender-integrated military, women were particularly threatening to the norms of masculinity, aggressiveness, and physicality that were already being undermined by increasingly technical military missions. Like other government institutions during the Cold War, the armed forces pointed toward the inadequacies of American women as an explanation for many social, moral, and cultural problems, including recruiting shortfalls and the negative impression of the armed forces among some youth.[48] Social commentary and popular culture represented the "softness" and corruption of American men as the result of excessive mothering and increasing female authority (sometimes termed "Momism"), blaming the emasculating effects of an organizational society and the displacement of male authority by mothers and other female figures.[49]

Military leaders could be quite explicit about the danger women posed to men in uniform. Consider the rules that governed convicted absence offenders who were released on parole in the 1950s at Lackland Air Force Base, Texas. Parolees were admonished to perform their work, to limit their talking and smoking, to avoid alcoholic beverages, and to "have no contact or dealings with women."[50] Such regulations treated women as both a reward to be denied men who were still being punished and a threat to the continued good behavior of rehabilitating convicts. Sometimes men left military service to seek out sexual companionship from women or to protect female family members from other men.[51] Both actions were understood to be normal, if not essential, within military as well as American culture. Nonetheless, they resulted in court-martial convictions. The armed forces tried to make clear that servicemen owed their primary loyalty to fellow troops, not to women.

That the military considered women dangerous rivals is obvious in court-martial records, where women appear as a primary cause of servicemen's criminal absence. In a particularly bald statement of the conflict between a woman and military duty, the Army Board of Review related in a 1956 opinion how one soldier's wife "constantly demanded that he choose her or the Army"; the fact that he "chose her on two occasions" led directly to two convictions for absence without leave.[52] Some servicemen's wives felt an "aversion to Army life" and encouraged their husbands to abandon their duties.[53] The Army Board described a soldier's plight in

1953: "He was torn between returning to duty and remaining with his wife. The wife was reluctant to let him go. The accused's mother tried to talk him into returning but she could not compete with his wife."[54] The claim of a wife over her husband was considered so strong that even another powerful female presence, in this case the mother of a serviceman, could not dislodge her control over his actions.

Mothers sometimes testified on behalf of their sons at court-martial, hoping that evidence of their sons' good character would mitigate the punishment imposed.[55] But the presence of a mother was not always salutary for an accused serviceman; sometimes, a maternal figure could highlight the weakness of an accused and contribute to the impression that he did not belong in the armed forces. For example, in reviewing the case of an airman tried for desertion in 1963, the board of review noted that "[a]t the time of apprehension, accused was trying to hide under a bed in his mother's house,"[56] an image that could not have positioned him well in the eyes of the court-martial members who judged him.[57] Some mothers supported their sons' efforts to escape military service; one testified about her son's allegedly fraudulent enlistment, while another advised her son—incorrectly—that he could rely on a medical discharge to avoid further service.[58] Another mother failed to tell her son that she had received a letter from Army officers about his AWOL status.[59]

Wives, even more than mothers, seemed to interfere with military priorities at every turn. Servicemen abandoned their military duties to be with wives who needed help with pregnancy,[60] childbirth,[61] miscarriage,[62] and illness.[63] Many men chose to live with their spouses during their unauthorized absences.[64] The enlistment contract of a serviceman was in clear competition with his marriage contract. Military and civilian courts analogized military status to marital status, recognizing the similarity between the two.[65]

Of course, not all wayward servicemen left to be with women who were their wives. In January 1970, an Army private left Fort Carson, Colorado to see a newborn son born out of wedlock;[66] a seaman apprentice in the Coast Guard went AWOL from San Diego in 1968 to help his seventeen-year-old pregnant girlfriend, who had traveled from Philadelphia to Los Angeles in search of his help.[67] Others also left to be with women who were pregnant with their children,[68] and many men left to be with their female lovers.[69]

Women were not only sexual or romantic distractions from military duties. They were also part of the families left behind when servicemen joined the military. Sometimes women struggled to make ends meet while the men of their family served in uniform. Servicemen frequently went AWOL to provide for families, including their wives and lovers.[70] Many young enlisted men, with meager paychecks and little financial flexibility, found themselves, and their families, in precarious financial and emotional situations. In 1959, the Army Board of Review described a private's six-month AWOL as resulting from the "panic" created by "seemingly insoluble home conditions" and "limited income."[71] Servicemen convicted of absence offenses often described impoverished families who were desperate for help; as another private explained at his 1964 court-martial, he and his wife couldn't "make it in the Army."[72] A private, one of six brothers in the service in 1952, went AWOL from Fort Jay, New York, to help his parents, who were both in desperate need of medical care, and to care for the three young children at home.[73] Another enlistee explained at his court-martial that he knew it was wrong to go AWOL but thought that "being a man" required that he also "look out" for his family.[74] An Army private left to help his "drunk and destitute" mother; an airman basic left Chanute Air Force Base, Illinois, in 1956 to travel to California, where his mother had been deserted by his father, leaving several small children whom he felt obliged to try to help.[75] A petty officer in the Navy ignored orders to report to Norfolk and instead went to his home in Roxbury, Virginia, where his father had recently suffered a stroke and was unable to care for his ailing mother and their two children.[76] In each of these cases, the responsibility that men felt to alleviate female poverty was a direct cause of unauthorized absence.

Servicemen's efforts to provide for their families were not the only gendered reason for criminal absence. Courts-martial also reveal absences caused by servicemen's anger at the behavior of their female intimates. Many men introduced mitigating evidence of their distress at the disloyalty of their wives, while others pointed to female betrayal as the reason for their absences. A specialist in the Army went AWOL in Honolulu in 1966 "to check up on his wife's activities," which included a liaison with another man.[77] In a 1958 case involving a staff sergeant who went AWOL from Offutt Air Force Base in Nebraska, the Air Force Board of Review contrasted the man's "seventeen and a half years of almost continuous service" with the infidelity of his wife, who "had been running around and drinking" and "going with" another man, all of which prompted the sergeant's decision to "get away from it all" by going AWOL.[78] Other servicemen described to courts-martial how their "disloyal" wives drove them to desert the military and forced them to spend their time solving family problems.[79]

Female intransigence often seemed to frustrate servicemen who felt entitled to obedience and deference from female companions. In 1968, an Army lieutenant explained to a court-martial "that he went AWOL because his girl had refused his proposal of marriage."[80] Others went AWOL after their wives told them they were filing for divorce.[81] Many unauthorized absences were prompted by marital problems, as soldiers left their duty stations to mend broken relationships or seek divorces to escape them.[82]

When servicemen seemed to lose control of themselves because of their wives' infidelity, military courts reacted with unusual sensitivity.[83] In the case of a petty officer court-martialed for a 1961 unauthorized absence, a Navy board's sympathetic opinion described a rampaging wife who led the petty officer not only to desert the Navy, but to attempt suicide. His wife had threatened "to place their children in an orphanage if he did not send her more money" in addition to becoming pregnant by another man.[84] Even seemingly perfect soldiers could be driven to abandon their fellow servicemen by the actions of their wives. A Marine lieutenant was convicted of desertion in 1960 but spared harsh penalties because of his wife's betrayal. A Navy board described the events leading up to the lieutenant's absence as "an emotion-upsetting development" that caused an otherwise "excellent" officer to desert.[85] When questioned at trial, however, the lieutenant explained his wife's infidelity, which he discovered shortly before he deserted, as follows: "I have two children. My wife presented me with a third one while I was overseas, however, that she managed on her own."[86] Based on this wry description of his predicament, the board of review found that "the shocking impact of such a disclosure was a major factor" in the lieutenant's desertion, implying that his bad judgment resulted from a reasonable response to such horrifying information.[87] Perhaps other evidence appeared in the record of trial that supported the "shocking impact" of his wife's behavior on the lieutenant, but the Navy board does not reference it. Instead, the board imputes outrage to the lieutenant that his own testimony—quoted in the board's opinion—contradicts.

Another 1960 case of an officer gone AWOL warrants special attention for the insight it offers into the class and gender dynamics of criminal absence. It reveals how servicemen could try to excuse an unauthorized absence by blaming women and how class differences between male soldiers and their female companions could influence the reasoning of military judges.[88] The Court of Military Appeals heard the case of Air Force Second Lieutenant Frank K. Carey, a "very outstanding" soldier, a "distinguished graduate" from the Officer Candidate School, and the "best student" in a training course at Keesler Air Force Base, Mississippi, who was convicted and dismissed from the service for an unauthorized ten-day jaunt with a woman not his wife.[89] The lieutenant's conviction was upheld, but the case prompted an unusually detailed opinion for the court as well as an impassioned dissent. *Carey* exposes the military's tendency to demonize women in order to shift the culpability for an unauthorized absence in especially clear fashion.

Relying on the "good soldier" defense, which permitted servicemembers to present evidence of their good character at court-martial, Carey's defense counsel presented evidence that he was a "very conscientious NCO" during a tour of duty in Morocco that took place before he was commissioned, that he was both "quiet" and "serious about the moral aspects of life," and that he impressed superiors as an outstanding student of impeccable character.[90] Character witnesses professed shock at learning of Carey's behavior, and concluded that he must have been under "extreme stress" to commit such an offense.[91] The defense counsel then put two civilian psychiatrists on the stand to testify about the "acute dissociative reaction" that had afflicted Carey at the time of his absence, when his "capacity for rational judgment left him" and he risked "a complete break with reality" if he had not gone AWOL.[92]

What had caused such a reaction? One Eleanor Marie Davis, a "barmaid" who had met Carey in November of 1958.[93] Both were married to others at the time; both lied to each other about their marital status. They began a relationship that led to a brief, and for Lieutenant Carey, unauthorized, trip to California, after which they returned to Biloxi, Mississippi. Carey's defense counsel argued that this trip, which resulted in a conviction for the strict liability crime of AWOL, "was so incongruous with his normal behavior" that it raised sufficient doubt about Carey's sanity to make his conviction invalid.[94] Unable to convince the court-martial of his innocence, Carey's claim of insanity also failed to persuade the military appellate judges who heard his case.

Despite the failure of his appeals, the lieutenant's defense struck a chord among the men who heard it. The majority opinion goes to great lengths to explain the decision, lingering over the nuances of proof and evidence in what was a straightforward case. In dissent, Judge Ferguson castigates the majority for ignoring the expert testimony of the two psychiatrists in favor of "the medical expertise of a barmaid."[95] Miss Davis had testified for the government, rebutting the experts' statements of mental disorder with her own observations that nothing in Carey's behavior seemed out of the ordinary to her. The dissent attacks Miss Davis as an incompetent witness "whose experience is directed toward affording companionship to lonely males."[96] Judge Ferguson sums up his opinion of the case rather neatly in one sentence: "The evidence . . . paints a factual picture of a young, brilliant, overconscientious, and religiously oriented officer whose amoral entanglement and contemporaneous absence without leave so shocked his confederates that explanation for his dereliction seemingly must be found in a disordered mind."[97]

Lieutenant Carey was not the only person whose character was at issue, however. Miss Davis is described with contempt throughout the court's opinions in this case. Twice the majority quotes her ungrammatical English (referring to their travel plans, "she 'didn't think no more of it,'" and in reference to a conversation about the possibility of his divorce, "'there wasn't no further plans made of it'") in summarizing her testimony, effectively highlighting the lack of education that accompanied her position as "barmaid."[98] Because the question of an accused's sanity could be raised by the defense at any point in court-martial proceedings, the Court of Military Appeals could rely on a legal doctrine to justify the attention they granted to Carey's insanity defense on appeal.[99] However, its treatment of Miss Davis as a threat to Carey's welfare, and thus to the military itself, better explains the judicial reasoning of the opinions than the criminal law of insanity. Davis's Eve-like temptation of the lieutenant is the entire basis for the dissent, while the majority opinion is clearly reluctant to privilege her testimony over that of experts brought out by the esteemed Lieutenant Carey.

In vilifying Eleanor Davis, the Court of Military Appeals protected the status of the officer corps by displacing blame for Carey's bad judgment onto his lower-class female consort. This rhetorical switch echoed throughout prosecutions for criminal absence, which the military used to enforce its entitlement to the bodies of men in uniform. Unauthorized absence reveals a hallmark of military culture: that those at the bottom of the military hierarchy struggled more than those positioned above them, and that the military sometimes obscured that struggle by blaming women for soldiers' mistakes. Young, poor, low-ranking, and nonwhite servicemen bore a disproportionate burden in the military's enforcement of crimes of absence, reflecting the greater difficulty that these groups of servicemen had in both managing external commitments and conforming to the style of life the military demanded of them. Women became markers of the conflict between civilian and military life, appearing in court-martial records as symbols of domestic responsibility and sexual temptation. Unauthorized absences were literal connections between the lives of servicemembers and the civilian communities from which they came and in which they worked. Courts-martial for AWOL and desertion proved that civilian life and military duty were neither entirely separate nor without conflict. By prosecuting crimes like unauthorized absence, commanders asserted the unique demands of military service against the "civilianization" of military justice and the bureaucratization of military missions.

CRIMES AGAINST MARRIAGE: IMAGES OF RACE AND NATION

Cold War military leaders grudgingly accepted the increasing number of married servicemen as part of the cost of maintaining a large standing force of skilled personnel. Commanders did not, however, concede their authority to regulate servicemembers' marital choices through policy and law.[100] Beginning in World War II, servicemen's ability to marry was restricted by rules that required those stationed overseas to get official approval before getting married.[101] Violations of marriage regulations were prosecuted at court-martial under Article 92 of the UCMJ, which penalized disobeying orders, in each branch of service during the 1950s and 1960s.[102] In addition to helping to protect the military's image within the United States, courts-martial for violations of marriage rules tried to discourage servicemen from fathering children out of wedlock. Such relationships competed with military duty for soldiers' attention and created friction in the communities around military bases.[103]

The regulations limiting marriage sometimes made it more difficult for well-intentioned servicemen to legitimize their relationships with foreign women. This dynamic appears in the case of Paul S. Nation, Jr., a seaman apprentice in the Navy, who applied to marry a Filipina in July 1956.[104] Nation followed the onerous procedures for approval that were set out in an April 1955 order promulgated by the commander of naval forces in the Philippines. He secured the assistance of the naval chaplain and the endorsement of his commanding officer, obtained parental affidavits of consent and birth certificates, and submitted an application complete with supporting documents. Then, Nation and his fiancée observed a six-month waiting period, mandatory under the regulation unless "exceptional circumstances" existed.[105] At the end of the six months, the couple reaffirmed their desire to marry, as required under the regulation, and eagerly awaited approval. But Nation's commander still refused to sanction the marriage. When the seaman married his betrothed anyway, he was promptly court-martialed and sentenced to a bad-conduct discharge and six months confinement at hard labor.

Nation successfully appealed his conviction, however, by persuading the Court of Military Appeals that the six-month waiting period was an unlawful order because it imposed an unreasonable restriction on the right to marry. The court declined to comment on the details of the regulation. But if it had, the "exceptional circumstances" clause of the rule would have been exposed as unfair and unreasonable. The clause defined three circumstances in which the customary waiting period could be waived: when the intended wife was pregnant, when the applicant was the father of an out-of-wedlock child, or when "both prospective spouses [were] of the same race and nationality."[106] Though consistent with the military's assertion that the regulations were intended to encourage servicemen to take responsibility for their out-of-wedlock progeny, the waiver clause makes explicit the Navy's discomfort with cross-racial marriage. If Nation had been Filipino instead of white, he would not have been forced to wait six months to marry.

Cross-racial marriages like the one that Nation entered into threatened the racially homogenous family that Cold War America embraced—and that the military itself undermined by enabling social and cultural interaction across lines of race and nation.[107] Servicemembers who had sexual relations or who chose to marry outside of their race faced the possibility of official legal censure as well the pressure of unofficial discrimination and disapproval.[108] Their families were also challenged by immigration laws that restricted the entry of some aliens into the United States and by state laws that prohibited interracial marriage—until the Supreme Court declared miscegenation laws unconstitutional in 1967.[109]

The armed forces assumed that servicemen would become sexually involved with the women who surrounded military bases.[110] But when those women were not American, and especially when they were not white, the military placed legal barriers between them and servicemen. When asked why he went AWOL several times in 1950 and 1951, a private in the Army testified during his court-martial about his commanding officer's refusal to permit him to marry a Korean woman: "he said, 'No. There is a war on in Korea and we didn't come over here to marry women.'"[111] This problem was not limited to Asia; servicemen stationed in Europe also left their posts after being denied permission to marry foreign women.[112] Balancing the tension between military duty and family responsibilities was doubly challenging for those whose romantic and sexual lives took place outside the boundaries of American culture.

Though not their primary intention, military leaders who enforced restrictions on marriage could make it harder for servicemen to care for their female companions and children. Enforcing the UCMJ's prohibition on bigamy sometimes had a similar effect. Military personnel were a mobile labor force, often stationed in locations far from home for extended periods of time.[113] Servicemen moved from duty station to duty station, culture to culture, and, sometimes, from one woman and family to another.[114] Bigamy, defined in the 1951 *Manual for Courts-Martial* as marrying while a "lawful wife" was still living, was a predictable consequence of servicemembers' way of life.[115] Its prosecution marked the conflict between a military culture that constantly uprooted servicemembers and the renewed American emphasis on stable, married, family life.

Bigamists made commanding officers anxious about both the military's public image and fraud against the government. Despite these concerns, criminal prosecution of bigamy was unusual, especially after the mid-1950s.[116] Still, members of every service, across a wide range of military grades, were convicted of bigamy at court-martial.[117] Few bigamists were prosecuted in the Navy and Marine Corps, probably because most sailors and marines had fewer opportunities to get married than land-based Army and Air Force personnel.[118] Military courts considered bigamy a "service-connected" crime because it could involve fraud if more than one wife of a serviceman tried to obtain military benefits.[119]

The usual bigamy court-martial involved an airman who failed to extricate himself from a hastily arranged first marriage before entering into a second marriage, usually in a different geographic location. In 1956, an Army board of review characterized the facts in one such case as "neither complex nor, we regret, unique."[120] Army Specialist Second Class Willie Guidry had married his pregnant girlfriend, Mary Carey, the daughter of an American serviceman and a Filipina, in the Philippines in 1954. Soon thereafter, Guidry left his wife behind when he was reassigned first to Okinawa, and then to White Sands Proving Ground, New Mexico. In 1955, Guidry married again, this time in Las Cruces, New Mexico. When his first wife wrote to Guidry's commanding officer to request help in contacting Guidry, who refused to respond to her entreaties, the Army investigated, and Guidry was court-martialed for bigamy. In this case, the military treated bigamy as a serious crime. Guidry was convicted and sentenced to a dishonorable discharge, total forfeiture of pay, and nine months confinement at hard labor. The fate of Mary Carey, the wife he left behind in the Philippines, is not clear from the records. It is unlikely that Guidry was required to support her—or their child—since he lost his military job and paycheck.

Guidry's case, however, was not quite typical. His prosecution was one of only two bigamy prosecutions among the thirty-nine reported appellate cases that involved marriage to an alien.[121] Given the services' disapproval of interracial and overseas marriages, servicemen probably bypassed the formalities of marriage, or else failed to notify the military of their married status, more frequently when they engaged in relationships with non-Americans than when they became involved with U.S. citizens. Because investigations for bigamy were often initiated when servicemen tried to claim benefits for their latest wives or when the wife of a soldier contacted his commanding officer, servicemen were insulated from prosecution when their female companions were unlikely—because of language, culture, or distance—to demand support from the military itself.

Trying to evade the responsibilities of marriage could be more difficult when a serviceman married an American woman. In 1955, a private in the Marine Corps who went to Reno for the weekend returned a married man, to his immediate regret.[122] In order to protect his assignment to aviation cadet training, which did not accept married servicemen, the young man wrote a letter announcing his death in a car accident, attached a false signature, and mailed it to his brand-new wife, hoping that she would accept his demise—and his letter's assertion that she was not entitled to death benefits—quietly. She did not. With the help of her mother, his new wife contacted his military unit to find out what had happened. The marine was court-martialed for forgery and mail fraud, caught trying to mitigate a conflict between married life and military service.[123]

Adultery and wrongful cohabitation, also marriage-related crimes, were less serious charges than bigamy. The 1951 *Manual* set one year as the maximum penalty for adultery, which military judges also applied to wrongful cohabitation sentences, compared to the two years that a bigamy conviction could bring.[124] Formality and ritual, so important in military culture, were both challenged by soldiers' bigamy. Hence it was a graver offense than simply engaging in sexual intercourse considered unlawful by a commanding officer. Bigamy undermined community standards of marriage more deeply than extramarital sexuality or nonmarital living arrangements.[125] Convictions for any of the three charges, however, could result in a punitive discharge, the rough equivalent of a civilian felony conviction.

A much-cited 1956 opinion established a definition of criminal cohabitation that encompassed a wide variety of heterosocial living arrangements.[126] The Court of Military Appeals held that public knowledge of a cohabiting couple was not an element of the crime, explaining that so long as a serviceman lived with a woman who was "neither wife, nor sister, nor mother," the arrangement discredited the military and could be prosecuted as a crime.[127] Despite this remarkably broad definition, cases of wrongful cohabitation were even less common than bigamy cases, and almost always included additional charges such as larceny or fraud.[128]

Like bigamy prosecutions, most prosecutions for unlawful cohabitation took place in the United States rather than overseas, despite the thousands of servicemen who lived with women who were not their wives while posted in other countries.[129] An Air Force captain who lived with a woman not his wife in Great Falls, Montana, in 1952 was considered more likely to damage the military's reputation than servicemen who similarly cohabited in Korea or Japan.[130] Like bigamy prosecutions, more cases arose in the Army and Air Force, both of which assigned personnel to longer terms of land-based duty, and thus provided greater opportunity for cohabitation, than in the Navy or Marine Corps.[131] Many cohabitation cases involved fact patterns nearly indistinguishable from bigamy prosecutions. For example, in 1972 Wesley G. Parker, an Army staff sergeant, was court-martialed after trying to obtain benefits for a woman to whom he was not legally married.[132] In 1956, Parker married an American woman in the United States, then "heard" that she'd divorced him a year later. In 1962, he married a Korean woman in Seoul (illegally, since he had not received approval of his official request to marry). In 1969, he married a third woman in Seattle, having tried but failed to divorce his Korean wife while he was stationed in Vietnam in 1967. Parker's court-martial was unusual in the Cold War military. But the trail of women he left behind was not. Ironically enough, the mistake that led to his court-martial was trying to provide for his wife, something that men were told was an essential part of manliness in post–World War II America.

Adultery, by itself, was not as potentially damaging to the military's reputation as wrongful cohabitation. Instances of adultery were infrequently prosecuted under the UCMJ, a practice consistent with the treatment of adultery under earlier versions of military law.[133] The 1951 *Manual for Courts-Martial* included a sample specification for the charge of adultery, but the crime was hardly mentioned in military legal treatises and guidebooks.[134] Adultery prosecutions were suppressed in part by the storm of negative publicity that could accompany the decision to prosecute. Courts-martial for sex offenses like adultery could expose intimate and embarrassing aspects of military life to a critical public, diminishing the status associated with military service and causing Americans to doubt the wisdom of military criminal prosecutions.[135] For example, in a widely publicized 1972 court-martial at the Naval Air Station at Cecil Field, Florida, a Navy chaplain was acquitted of adultery charges that were based on his relationships with the wives of servicemen who were away on duty.[136] The Navy's prosecution called attention to a fear of many deployed servicemen: that a disloyal comrade would take up with an unfaithful wife. The Navy chaplain's court-martial unsettled military personnel and even angered the American Baptist Convention, which rejected the military's authority to punish a chaplain for offenses related to his religious vocation. However, unlike the other American jurisdictions that leaned away from criminalizing adultery during this period, the armed forces did not decriminalize extramarital sex.[137] Commanding officers retained the authority to prosecute servicemembers who engaged in extramarital relationships even though adultery was normalized into the world of overseas military service.

Adultery appears as the primary charge only in cases involving cross-racial sex, sex with a woman married to another serviceman, or sex in violation of an explicit order forbidding it. The first case of adultery-only prosecution under the UCMJ was the court-martial of Lieutenant Melvin Butler, an African American in the 371st Armored Infantry stationed in Nurnberg, Germany in 1952. Convicted of "wrongfully occupying a bed with a German female," Butler was court-martialed after the duty officer found him in his room in the company of a German woman during a 1:00 A.M. search of the officers' quarters.[138] The politics of race and gender influenced civil as well as military crime during this period; "white slavery" charges under the Mann Act, which made transporting a woman across state lines for immoral purposes a federal crime, sometimes supplemented charges of adultery against servicemen whose adulterous relationships included interstate travel.[139] The only other cases in which adultery was the primary charge appear motivated not by racism, but by efforts to enforce the loyalty that servicemen were supposed to demonstrate toward each other and the deference owed their superiors.[140] Many servicemen feared that their wives would not be faithful, prompting military leaders to enforce a code of sexual ethics that might—at a minimum—keep servicemen away from the wives of their brothers-in-arms.

Military sexual ethics tried to preserve a public impression of service-members as not only faithfully married, but affirmedly heterosexual. The 1961 court-martial of Herbert W. Parker, an Army private, for alleged homosexuality depicts the legal convolutions that could result from the interaction of marital status and the stigma associated with male homosexuality.[141] The accused private's former wife, referred to only as "Miss Gluck" in the record, was a civilian employee of the Army in Japan who married Parker, then a twenty-four-year-old enlistee, in December 1959. After Parker was transferred to Fort Benning, Georgia, their marriage ran into trouble. Late one night, after a Saturday evening party at the couple's Columbus, Georgia, home, Gluck found her husband having sex with another man. Gluck testified that when her husband realized she had seen him, he said: "Now you know. Get the hell out of here."[142] Parker disputed his wife's account of the evening, but her story had an immediate impact on his military life. When Parker arrived at work on Monday morning, the news had preceded him. His officemates stared and shook their heads, and he was told he could not work there any longer. Feeling that he "had nothing left," Parker went AWOL, for which he was convicted in a separate court-martial.[143] Convicted of sodomy on the basis of his former wife's testimony, Parker was sentenced to a dishonorable discharge and two years confinement.

On appeal, the Court of Military Appeals focused on whether Gluck's testimony against Parker should have been admitted at trial. She was the government's key witness, the only person who would testify about the alleged act of sodomy.[144] But Gluck was also Parker's wife at the time of the incident. Parker argued that her testimony violated the marital privilege that prevented one spouse from testifying against another, a privilege rooted in the common law doctrine of coverture, which subsumed a woman into her husband's legal person when they married.[145] Under military law at the time, a wife could testify against her husband's wishes only if she was injured by the offense that her testimony concerned.[146] Holding that a husband's sodomy with a third person did not constitute an offense against the wife, the court rejected Gluck's testimony as contrary to the public policy behind marital privilege, which was intended "to foster peace in the family and to preserve the marital relationship."[147] The court regarded the "despicable nature" of sodomy as reason enough to prohibit a wife from testifying against her husband, since any public revelation of such an act would be very likely to end a marriage—as it apparently had in the case at hand.[148] The court reversed Parker's conviction for sodomy, certain that he was the party harmed by his wife's testimony of such "reprehensible" behavior.[149]

Here, the military's interest in preserving marriage conflicted with its prejudice against homosexuals. It was silly to deny that Parker's wife was harmed by his extramarital sexual behavior; it effectively ended her mar-

riage, denied her sexual companionship, and exposed her to public embarrassment. Yet denying that harm enabled the court to enlist Miss Gluck
in repressing her husband's homosexual desire. The evidentiary doctrine
of marital privilege became a means of asserting the military's heteronor-
mativity: It prevented disclosure of homosexual acts even as it silenced the
voice of a woman who sought justice at court-martial.[150]

Courts-martial reflected servicemembers' struggle to reconcile Cold
War notions of domesticity and sexuality with the demands and opportunities of military service. Soldiers were expected to support their families
only if those families fit into the framework of racial homogeneity and gender relations that the armed forces tried to defend as essential to American
politics and culture. The military expected, even encouraged, its members
to engage in consensual heterosexual activity. But the relationships, and
children, that resulted often drew soldiers' attention away from their military duties. Military life, which exposed many servicemembers to persons
of different races and cultures and required frequent moves from one post-
ing to another, was at odds with the segregated, stable families that Cold
War America sought to produce. Defying the armed forces' rules about
marital status and sexual behavior was one of soldiers' responses to this
conflict.

DOMESTIC VIOLENCE

The model of military family life that ascended during the Cold War was
also home to domestic violence.[151] The legal rules and fact patterns of military domestic violence prosecutions reveal how the military's culture of
male authority and female deference influenced courts-martial and altered
the intimate lives of servicemembers. The danger, lengthy separation, and
economic need that military duty could impose on servicemembers'
spouses and children created a climate in which family violence was a grave
problem. Servicemen shot and stabbed their wives, girlfriends, and sexual
partners to death near military bases around the world.[152] Easy access to
weapons converted bad judgment into deadly negligence, especially when
combined with anger, frustration, or the effects of drugs or alcohol.[153] As
in civil society, instances of fatal domestic violence in the armed forces often
culminated an escalating pattern of abuse.[154]

During the 1950s, 1960s, and early 1970s, however, domestic violence
was only rarely prosecuted in either civilian or military jurisdictions. In
1964, the Court of Military Appeals articulated a view of marriage that
helped to discourage prosecutions of domestic violence. In reviewing the
case of an airman who was convicted of assault and battery for having

"slapped" and "struck" his wife, the court explained that public policy favored the preservation of marriage so long as only "occasional or sporadic injury to one spouse by the act of the other" took place.[155] The court observed that "it is certainly much more desirable, especially if there are children, that [the wife] remain in a united household with her husband, in spite of any passing injury to her, if the husband otherwise fulfills his marital responsibilities and obligations."[156] With a justice system so willing to accept women's vulnerability to abuse because of their economic dependence on men, it is no surprise that domestic violence rarely appeared at court-martial. Commanding officers and military judges, like their civilian counterparts, were reluctant to protect wives from their husbands because that protection could end marital relationships.

Court-martial records reveal only the most extreme cases, those in which the military's interest in preserving good order and discipline made it impossible to ignore incidents of violence. The military appellate record includes mostly cases from overseas, where there was no American civilian alternative to court-martial jurisdiction over these crimes. Neither civilian nor military law-enforcement agencies kept records of most wife beatings that did not result in death, leaving the family murder rate as the most reliable historical indicator of relative levels of domestic violence.[157] Wife killings during the twentieth century have generally peaked during wartime, but they began to rise more steadily in the 1960s along with American rates of other types of violent crime.[158] From 1951 to 1973, seven cases of nonlethal domestic violence and eighteen cases of domestic murder appear in the appellate record.[159] Though too small to support broad conclusions, this sample suggests if the victim survived the incident, only very public fights or assaults that were accompanied by other crimes were likely to trigger courts-martial.[160]

Domestic violence occurred among servicemembers from all ranks of military service. The full range of military grades, from airman to colonel, was represented among those convicted, though the majority of offenders were noncommissioned officers. The Air Force and the Army prosecuted nearly all the military's domestic violence, each accounting for about half of the murders and assaults. The Air Force prosecuted the highest number of domestic violence incidents despite having the lowest overall crime rate among the services, probably because it also possessed the highest percentage of married servicemembers and thus included a larger number of likely offenders. The Navy and Marine Corps, neither of which was as accommodating to family concerns as the Army and Air Force, were vastly underrepresented in this arena of crime. Only one wife murder, by a Marine corporal, and one domestic assault, by a Marine gunnery sergeant, appear in appeals from the sea services.

The precise charges varied, depending on the nature of the crime and the status of the offender. For example, one officer was charged under the "conduct unbecoming an officer and a gentleman" article of the UCMJ for a fight with his wife that took place in a base parking lot.[161] Late one May evening in 1951, after a cocktail party at the Fort Monroe Officers' Beach Mess near Langley Field, Virginia, Army officer Donald E. Downard grew angry at his wife's attentions to another man. In the parking lot outside the Beach Mess he shouted obscenities, accusing his wife of flirting with a higher-ranking officer during the party. When she responded with a tirade of her own and a slap across his face, the couple's fight attracted a number of onlookers, including other servicemembers and their wives. For kicking and striking his wife, pulling her hair, and "using profane, abusive, obscene, and insulting speech" toward her, Lieutenant Colonel Downard was charged with and convicted of "conduct unbecoming an officer and a gentleman."[162] Downard was one of only four officers, two of whom had killed their wives, convicted of domestic violence during this period. This suggests that the public nature of the fight, and the manner in which he handled the dispute, made Downard's conduct more worthy of censure than other, less visible domestic abuse.

Military courts seemed to punish domestic violence with sentences significantly lighter than the maximum punishments available under the UCMJ.[163] However, generalizing about the severity of punishment at courts-martial for domestic violence is difficult. Appellate courts did not always publish their opinions, and opinions that did appear did not always include details on sentencing.[164] Reductions in sentences were often made after trial, when convening authorities could lessen the severity of sentences in order to compensate for errors at trial or mitigating circumstances.[165] The military's tendency to punish offenders with relatively mild sentences reflected much the same attitude that civilian criminal courts had toward domestic violence. Considered a problem best left to private, rather than public, solutions, violence against a spouse was not punished as harshly as other types of interpersonal violence.

A 1963 court-martial for attempted murder at Whiteman Air Force Base, Missouri, suggests the pattern of events that could lead to court-martial as well as the light sentence that could result from a conviction for domestic violence.[166] Technical Sergeant Vaughn E. Riska and his wife had separated on New Year's Eve 1962. After several unsuccessful attempts to reconcile over a period of weeks, Riska suspected infidelity and became angry after "peeking through a window" and observing his wife in the company of another airman on Sunday, February 17, 1963.[167] Riska followed his wife and the airman as they drove to a store on base. While the airman entered the store and left Riska's wife in the car, the sergeant made his move. Climbing into the front seat of the car despite his wife's attempts to lock the doors, Riska said, "Irene, this time I'm going to kill you," and stabbed her in the throat with a pocketknife.[168] The airman, however, returned to the car and intervened, and Mrs. Riska survived the attack. A court-martial found the sergeant not guilty of attempted murder but guilty of a lesser charge, assault with a deadly weapon, and sentenced him to three months confinement and a bad-conduct discharge. Yet Riska's words (*"this time I'm going to kill you"*) and his wife's frightened reaction to his approach point toward prior violence in their relationship. Riska was prosecuted at court-martial because the assault took place on base, in public, and was complicated by the involvement of another servicemember. Nonetheless, his sentence was slight given the severity of his assault and the fact that part of his sentence punished him for an unrelated charge—stealing a television set from another airman—for which he was also convicted.

Servicemen could defend against charges of domestic violence by blaming their wives for provoking them, hoping that testimony of the soldiers' mental distress would convince courts-martial to either acquit or impose light sentences.[169] As a result, psychiatric testimony became an increasingly important part of domestic murder prosecutions.[170] This trend reflected the growing use of psychiatrists in civilian criminal courts during the 1960s, particularly in cases involving alleged sexual abnormality or violent sexuality.[171] It also fit into widespread social commentary blaming the apparent increase in family discord after World War II on married women and their sexual maladjustment.[172] While such defenses seemed to mitigate punishment for family violence, they were not always accepted by court-martial panels. In fact, a court-martial imposed the only death sentence in a Cold War domestic violence case on an Army warrant officer who argued unsuccessfully that his wife's "continuous carping had driven him insane temporarily."[173] In May 1952, he had twice hit his wife in the head with a pickaxe before staging a car wreck to disguise the murder. There were limits to the blame that courts-martial were willing to place on the wives of discontented servicemen.

As we saw in chapter 2's discussion of the tragic *Mathis* case, soldiers who had serious psychiatric disorders often found getting help from the military medical establishment difficult because of the stigma associated with mental illness, military culture's emphasis on male strength and toughness, and the pressure on doctors to return troops to duty, especially when they were stationed overseas. Servicemen who recognized their own mental instability sometimes sought out assistance before losing control and harming others. For example, an Air Force sergeant was hospitalized for psychiatric treatment in November 1958 after telling a chaplain that he had been on the verge of killing his wife and committing suicide several times during the previous two weeks.[174] Diagnosed with manic depression, schizophrenia, and "personality disturbance," he was medicated and discharged.[175] Several weeks later, he stabbed his wife to death with a kitchen knife.[176] Dealing with the hardships of mental illness was especially difficult in the stressful confines of military service.

Psychiatric disorders also appeared in the most celebrated military domestic violence cases of the Cold War era: those involving women who killed their servicemen-husbands. Because of popular fascination with female violence, women who kill have often garnered more attention than their more numerous male counterparts. Only two of the eighteen domestic murders prosecuted at court-martial during this period were committed by women, yet only the cases of husband-killing became a recognized part of the legal-historical record. The notoriety of military wives who murdered their husbands while stationed outside the United States was partly due to their special legal status. Not members of the military and yet subjected to military criminal law, these women were tried and convicted by courts-martial because no other American jurisdiction had the legal authority to prosecute their crimes. Commanding officers worried that without court-martial jurisdiction, civilians who committed crimes while accompanying military forces overseas would escape prosecution entirely.[177]

In 1957, the U.S. Supreme Court decided that the disciplinary concerns of military leaders did not outweigh the rights of individuals to be tried by civilian, rather than military, criminal courts. These issues reached the Court in *Reid v. Covert*, the habeas corpus challenge of two military wives who had been court-martialed for murdering their husbands.[178] The Court held that persons accompanying the armed forces overseas during times of peace could not be tried at court-martial for capital offenses. The lead case in this challenge to military jurisdiction involved Clarice Covert, the wife of an Air Force master sergeant who killed her husband in March 1953 at an air base in England. Covert confessed to the murder during an appointment with an Air Force psychiatrist that took place the day after the murder. She had been in treatment for some months because of anxiety over her husband's gambling and drinking and her family's perilous financial situation. Doctors had prescribed sedatives but recommended against hospitalization. Covert led investigators to her husband's body, which lay on a bed under a pile of blankets, and admitted to using a hand axe to hit him in the head the night before. At trial and on appeal, Covert's sanity was the primary issue. Her psychiatric defenses failed to sway her Air Force court-martial, and she was sentenced to life imprisonment.[179]

In an effort to preserve court-martial jurisdiction over military dependents, the Air Force fought each adverse ruling in Covert's case with a vengeance.[180] But judge advocates could not prevent her unconditional release on order of the Supreme Court. After *Reid v. Covert*, civilians were largely removed from court-martial jurisdiction, leaving commanding officers frustrated and demonstrating civilian judges' doubt about the fairness of military justice under the UCMJ.

The courts-martial that resulted from conflicts between family and military responsibilities show how servicemembers and commanding officers struggled to fit military policies to the contours of a new American society. Military families coexisted with deployment patterns that kept men away from the constraints of home and community for long periods of time, creating economic and sexual tension for both civilian women and military men. The commitment to racial homogeneity that many Americans still prized, especially in intimate relationships, was weakened by the global travel and interracial context of military life. The military's proximity to violence further complicated the prosecution of sex- and marriage-related crimes, as the armed forces asked its troops to distinguish between situations in which violent aggression was absolutely required and those in which it was forbidden. In short, the military sought to protect family models and sexual norms that did not fit into the changing demographics and lifestyles of late-twentieth-century Americans. Courts-martial exposed the contradictions of criminal laws that attempted to preserve a military society of orderliness and male dominance while demographic and cultural changes made that society increasingly obsolete.

Chapter 5

COMMANDING DISCRETION

Race, Sex, and Military Crime

Many servicemembers and civilian observers of twentieth-century military justice assumed that racism was as endemic to courts-martial as it was to American civilian criminal courts. African Americans in particular considered racial prejudice a fundamental part of military justice, notwithstanding the armed forces' official commitment to racial equality. Discriminatory assignment policies, the limited off-post housing and social activities available to nonwhite servicemembers, and prosecutions that took place in the wake of race riots and civil rights protests contributed to racial tension in the Cold War military. But perhaps most damaging to the court-martial's image as an impartial instrument of discipline and justice was the basic structure of military justice, which permitted thousands of individual officers to decide which cases ought to be prosecuted and which sentences deserved to be mitigated. That discretion, wielded by an almost exclusively white corps of commanding officers who were advised by almost exclusively white judge advocates, exacerbated the perception of systemic injustice. Despite its procedural reforms, the UCMJ left the military justice system open to allegations of racism by leaving command discretion, and a racially exclusive officer corps, intact.

This chapter explores the racial consequences of the command discretion that shaped the process and outcomes of military justice during the Cold War. It begins with a study of African American servicemembers under the UCMJ, pointing out that black troops were overrepresented among those prosecuted for minor offenses, more harshly punished for crimes of sexual coercion and assault, and more likely to be executed for capital crimes. The second section turns to a racially charged subset of military crime, prosecutions for rape, to examine how race-based ideas about male sexuality and female vulnerability altered legal doctrines and affected the results of courts-martial. The transnational, multiracial world in which most American servicemembers lived and worked was ordered by racial hierarchies more complex than simply white over black. The third section examines these racial complexities through the lens of military prostitution, a venue where crime was never far away and where race so clearly mattered. Servicemen's sense of sexual entitlement, fueled by the military's culture of sexual opportunity, clashed with the military's efforts to limit race mixing and sexual exploits that could damage community relations and distract soldiers from their military duties. Each prostitution-related court-martial that went forward balanced the military's interest in punishing misconduct against its interest in preserving a culture of male sexual entitlement and racial homogeneity.

"EVEN IN MISSISSIPPI A NEGRO GETS A TRIAL LONGER THAN THAT": AFRICAN AMERICANS AT COURT-MARTIAL

Hastened by the personnel needs of the Cold War and the civil rights movement, the successful integration of the armed forces has been celebrated as one of the signal achievements of the United States armed forces.[1] The crucial first step was President Truman's 1948 order, which set the armed forces on course to end segregation and treat servicemembers equally, regardless of race. The military's promise of racial equality did not go unnoticed. Because the armed forces were more visible internationally than any other American organization, the rhetoric and appearance of racial equity in the military was especially important to the United States' effort to claim the moral high ground in the war against communism.[2] Desegregation, along with the economic benefits of military service and the enhanced social status often accorded soldiers, encouraged many African Americans to enlist. The Gesell Committee, appointed by President Kennedy in 1962 to study progress toward racial integration in the armed forces, lauded the military as a "pace setter" in the race to desegregate American workplaces.[3]

The president's committee, however, also pointed out areas of troubling disparity in the military's treatment of soldiers of color, including the low number of black officers in uniform and the military's failure to integrate its police forces and shore patrolmen.[4] Given the military emphasis on deference to those of higher rank, the paucity of nonwhite commissioned officers was an especially notable shortcoming in the military's efforts to integrate. The percentage of African Americans in the total force stayed close to 8 percent through the 1960s, but African American officers remained an anomaly into the 1970s.[5] Black officers accounted for 1.6 percent of the officer corps in 1962; in 1971, their percentage reached 2.3.[6] Presented in absolute numbers instead of percentages, the racial differential is even more striking. The Navy—the most racially exclusive of the services during the Cold War, with only 5 percent African American personnel in 1960—reported 149 African Americans among the 70,000 naval officers on active duty in 1960.[7] Segregated units were abolished by 1954, but it took the federal civil rights legislation of 1964 and 1965 to push the military toward realizing President Truman's stated goal of equitable treatment across race lines.[8] Because each branch of military service established its own methods and timeline for integration, the pace of desegregation varied in different military units.[9] Even when units were integrated, race typing persisted in the assignment of soldiers to occupational specialties. African Americans were more often relegated to menial, arduous jobs than similarly prepared white troops.[10]

Discrimination off base, as well as on post, affected servicemembers of color and became the target of civil rights protests. Efforts to end civilian discrimination around military posts were especially successful when court decisions coincided with civil rights legislation, as they did in the Department of Defense's 1968 push to reduce housing discrimination.[11] The black press kept a close watch on the plight of African Americans in the military throughout this period, but major protests against discriminatory policies did not occur until the escalation of troops in Vietnam. Most inflammatory were revelations that black troops suffered disproportionately high casualty rates during the first years of heavy U.S. fighting in Vietnam, a consequence of the personnel policies that consigned many African Americans to combat duty.[12] Racial tensions climaxed in the early 1970s, echoing the unrest within American civil society, when race riots aboard ships and on military posts forced the armed forces to confront the costs of racism directly.[13] While the military manifested no greater resistance to racial integration than many other segments of American society, it did not acquiesce to political pressure to integrate without protest. Perhaps more important, desegregation left racial inequality embedded in the infrastructure of military society.

As the civil rights movement gradually transformed the armed forces and the rest of the United States, the court-martial became a focus of resentment over ongoing discrimination. One military historian referred to military justice during the Vietnam War as "[t]he greatest source of systemic racism in the armed forces, and the greatest focus of complaints regarding discrimination."[14] Documenting the precise extent of racial discrimination in military justice is a difficult task, even with the volume of data collected by the commanding officers and military researchers in response to criticism of military justice after World War II.[15] Whether racial factors were decisive in legal decision making is not easy to determine; statistics cannot reveal the subjective mindsets of the commanders and judge advocates who determined the course of military justice. Yet the sum of quantitative data and case histories from the 1950s, 1960s, and 1970s make clear that assumptions about race influenced whether a commander decided to prosecute, how a judge advocate chose to defend a client, and how a court-martial panel viewed an accused servicemember.

A long history of courts-martial being used to single out African Americans for punishment formed the backdrop for both the widespread perception and the actual incidence of racism in Cold War military justice.[16] During World War II, the NAACP had assisted hundreds of African American servicemen who faced selective prosecution and excessive punishments at courts-martial.[17] Perhaps most infamous was the Port Chicago incident, when fifty black sailors were court-martialed for refusing orders to load ammunition onto ships docked in San Francisco Bay.[18] Their trials took place in the summer of 1944, just three weeks after 320 men were killed while loading ships. The deadliest homefront accident of the war, the Port Chicago explosions frightened hundreds of sailors, most of them white, into refusing to return to harbor duty. But only African Americans, half of whom were under twenty-one years of age, were court-martialed and sentenced to long prison terms. In the wake of Port Chicago, civil rights leader Adam Clayton Powell titled a 1946 article "The Rape of Justice by Court Martial," an indication of how betrayed many African Americans felt by military justice.[19]

The NAACP's success in challenging sentences imposed at World War II courts-martial led soldiers to write hundreds of letters to NAACP attorneys, alleging that high rates of courts-martial, improper convictions, and disproportionately severe sentences were common among black troops during the Korean War. The records of both the NAACP and the NAACP Legal Defense and Education Fund (LDEF) reveal persistent concerns about racism at court-martial.[20] In what became Thurgood Marshall's most famous capital case, the NAACP convinced President Truman to commute Lieutenant Leon A. Gilbert's death sentence to twenty years at hard labor.[21] Gilbert, a decorated veteran of World War II and one of very few African American officers during the Korean War, was court-martialed in September 1950 for "misbehavior before the enemy."[22] While in retreat from a bloody engagement with North Korean forces, Gilbert disobeyed a superior's order to advance against the enemy. Whether Gilbert was in the state of panic alleged by his superiors or whether he was prudently withdrawing his men after three solid weeks of fighting remains subject to dispute.[23] The Army used Gilbert's court-martial to call attention to the harsh consequences of disobedience to orders as compared to the dangers of combat, attempting to forestall more problems with soldiers "straggling" by making an example of Gilbert. Marshall's investigation of Gilbert's case, however, coupled with the absence of any similar courts-martial of white officers, suggests that it was racism, not cowardice, that placed Gilbert in danger of death by firing squad. Gilbert was tried by a court-martial composed of only white officers and was not permitted to bring his own witnesses forward to testify in person. Furthermore, at the time of his company's retreat he had been without sleep for six days and was suffering from both acute dysentery and what a psychiatric report termed a severe "anxiety reaction." The Gilbert case led Marshall to undertake what he termed at the time "the most important mission of my career," a five-week study of military justice in Korea in 1951.[24] After compiling extensive evidence of procedural injustice, Marshall spoke out across the nation about the Jim Crow policies of the Army, the unsung heroism of African American troops, the brief trials (shorter than in Mississippi, he said), and harsh sentences of military justice.[25] After Marshall's trip, the NAACP LDEF appealed many court-martial convictions on behalf on black soldiers who felt mistreated under the UCMJ.[26] When the NAACP narrowed its focus to school desegregation cases in the mid-1950s, its involvement in military justice declined. But racism at court-martial remained a grave concern of civil rights leaders throughout the 1950s and 1960s.

It did not help the military's efforts to promote an image of racial equality that nearly all of the judge advocates of the Navy and Marine Corps were white until the mid-1970s.[27] Although Army and Air Force lawyers of color served during the 1960s, they too were scarce.[28] A 1971 task force appointed by Secretary of Defense Melvin Laird to study the administration of military justice concluded that both intentional and systemic discrimination influenced the process of military justice.[29] The task force pointed out an example of systemic discrimination in the 66 percent of court-martial defendants who worked in four menial occupational specialties, occupations to which African Americans were more likely to be assigned than other soldiers. It also found that African Americans were more likely to receive formal punishment and more likely to be falsely accused than white servicemembers.[30] With an overwhelmingly white set of military legal decision-makers prosecuting a disproportionately high percentage of nonwhite servicemembers, Cold War courts-martial were bound to be viewed as racist, even if their outcomes had not been demonstrably skewed against African American troops.

Consider, for example, the ways in which race figured in the Korean War POW courts-martial discussed in chapter 3. Most of the POWs court-martialed were charged with a political offense such as collaboration. Only one, a private who was also the only African American among those court-martialed, was charged with general misconduct rather than an explicitly political crime. Private First Class Rothwell B. Floyd was convicted for abusing other prisoners by taking food, medication, and valuables from the sick and the dead and for disregarding the authority of senior officers in the camps.[31] Whether Floyd was treated more harshly than others whose conduct was similarly blameworthy is difficult to establish. But there is little doubt that his insubordination was viewed in a different light by white officers accustomed to deference from persons of color.

The military did not collect comprehensive data on the racial and ethnic identity of the Korean War POWs, but official reports did uncover evidence of racial tension in the camps.[32] The language used by prisoners in the camps referred to enemy troops with racial epithets (Chinks, Chinamen, coloreds), and the groups of POWs who resisted the indoctrination programs were sometimes called the "KKK" for their obstinate defense of American values.[33] Official studies of the POW's overlooked the possible effects of racial hierarchies on servicemembers' behavior in the camps even as they documented the disproportionate number of nonwhite and economically disadvantaged prisoners.[34] Military researchers even placed part of the blame for prisoners' vulnerability to communist seduction on single mothers who raised "dependent" boys, foreshadowing the 1960s debates over Project 100,000 and the Moynihan Report's contentious claims about the detrimental effects of African American mothers on their sons.[35] It is impossible to untangle the stereotypes of race and gender that shaped popular and official perceptions of the collaborating POWs. In August 1953, an *Army Times* columnist challenged the "brainwashing" explanation for the POWs' alleged weakness, preferring to blame women instead: "There are only two things I can think of at the moment for which weak men readily sell their souls—money and women. And China has more women than money."[36] The columnist also felt that African Americans were particularly vulnerable to the promise of Chinese wives. The high politics of fear and anticommunism that motivated the prosecution of repatriated Korean War POW's collaboration did not preclude racist explanations for the misbehavior of servicemen.

During the late 1960s and early 1970s, courts-martial became both a source of unrest and a part of the military's solution to the racial tensions that surfaced in nearly every major incident of soldier rebellion. The armed forces were well aware of the price they paid in morale and public image because of the racial bias in military justice.[37] Efforts to make the court-martial system racially just, however, were complicated by the use of courts-martial to prosecute servicemembers accused of violence and disorder in racially motivated incidents. In most cases, criminal prosecution caused more racial conflict than it resolved.

Racial tensions climaxed in the military between 1967 and 1973, when nearly all of the courts-martial related to racial violence occurred.[38] In 1968, 252 courts-martial for serious resistance such as speaking out, disregarding orders, and fighting took place; 382 such cases were prosecuted in 1970.[39] In the summer of 1969, violent racial incidents took place in all major overseas areas and at many domestic military installations, including Forts Belvoir, Bragg, Carson, Dix, Hood, Jackson, Lee, Sheridan and Sill.[40] Combat refusals in Vietnam, when soldiers ignored the orders of superiors, became more common in 1971 and 1972, reflecting the heightened racial tension within military units.[41] In 1971, a clash between African American soldiers and white troops stationed near Darmstadt, Germany revealed the no-win situation that resulted from outright racial violence.[42]

After criminal charges were filed, political pressure in favor of waiving the charges mounted until the Army capitulated, only to suffer renewed criticism for its failure to prosecute after all. Hundreds of sailors were involved in race riots onboard the *U.S.S. Kitty Hawk* and *U.S.S. Constellation* during 1972. Fragging, the murder of officers by subordinate troops, also became more common late in the Vietnam War. Even the Army's conservative estimates reported hundreds of incidents of officers threatened, injured, or killed by rebellious troops.[43] Although such violence was linked as much to rank and class hierarchies as to racial unrest, its existence indicates the extraordinary upheaval that rent military society during the war.[44] After 1973, race riots no longer captured headlines, but crimes related to racial struggle continued to be prosecuted at court-martial.[45]

The prisons occupied by soldiers convicted of race-related insubordination and other military crimes became cauldrons of resistance during the Vietnam War. Richard Moser's study of soldier protest identifies fifteen major prison uprisings between 1968 and 1972.[46] Twice in 1968, prisoners at the Long Binh jail, a Marine Corps and Navy brig in Da Nang, Vietnam with a population that was nearly 90 percent African American, revolted to protest poor conditions and racial injustice.[47] The most infamous prison riot, the Presidio "mutiny," also occurred in 1968.[48] It was a short-lived protest by twenty-seven servicemen who were confined in a San Francisco stockade.[49] The disturbance was triggered when a guard shot and killed an imprisoned soldier with a history of drug and mental health problems as the prisoner ran away from a work detail. The protesting prisoners demanded relief from overcrowding and inhumane prison conditions. After the riot ended, twenty-two prisoners were convicted of mutiny at court-martial. The armed forces' inability to subdue prisoners was yet another sign that courts-martial were creating more racial problems than they were solving during this period.

Part of the problem the military faced in trying to defend the fairness of the military justice system was the perception that commanding officers prosecuted servicemen of color for misbehavior that would be overlooked if committed by a white serviceman. The prosecutorial discretion that characterized military justice allowed, for instance, a wide range of disciplinary responses to a servicemember's absence. An absence as brief as a single hour could lead to court-martial, while an absence of a few days might lead to only an oral reprimand.[50] Official policies that established guidelines for the treatment of absence offenses sometimes limited commanders' options by requiring specific legal actions, such as harsh punishment for repeat offenders.[51] But the broad discretion that the UCMJ permitted commanders, and the informal nature of so much of military discipline, left plenty of room for allegations of prejudice and second-guessing of commanders' decisions.

As the military shifted away from a procedurally rigorous, criminal system of discipline and into a more bureaucratic mode of managing infractions, discretion became an even more salient aspect of military justice. The overall decrease in the court-martial rate did little to ameliorate the impression that African Americans were more likely than white servicemembers to be censured through administrative as well as criminal punishment.

Because most courts-martial involved charges of criminal absence, the discretion that commanders wielded in disciplining servicemembers for unauthorized absence was a crucial factor in racial disparities at court-martial.[52] AWOL and desertion cases were "the mainstay of the military lawyer's practice" throughout this period.[53] Yet all of those courts-martial for unauthorized absence prosecuted only a small fraction of the total number of servicemembers who deserted or went AWOL during the Cold War. Most wayward soldiers and sailors were never brought to trial. After the Korean War, the armed forces adopted a "basic solution for large-scale desertions" that involved not courts-martial, but screening and administrative elimination of men considered potential deserters.[54] For example, during the 1950s, the Army sought to reduce its AWOL rate by promulgating orders and enforcing regulations that specified categories of AWOL-prone men. Those considered "unfit" included men with records of civil or military crime or misbehavior, "sexual perversion," "drug addiction," "an established pattern for shirking," or a pattern of failing to repay debts.[55] Army regulations authorized the discharge of any servicemember deemed "temperamentally unsuited" for a military unit, hoping that commanders might eliminate those at risk of AWOL before they committed any crime.[56]

For the unauthorized absences that occurred despite these precautionary efforts, the military increasingly turned to administrative discharges and nonjudicial punishment, both more efficient options than courts-martial.[57] During the Vietnam War, fewer than 1 percent of those absent ninety days or more were convicted of desertion at court-martial.[58] Designed to conserve resources, preemptive screening and administrative discharges shifted the focus of absentee prevention from criminal prosecution to near-summary removal of those servicemembers who appeared to possess the traits of future criminals.[59] During a time in which the color of one's skin was still considered a rational predictor of criminal propensity, this meant that servicemembers continued to be sorted by race and treated accordingly, notwithstanding the military's official commitment to racial equity.

"[W]HAT WE KNOW AS MEN": RACE, RAPE, AND WAR

The prosecutorial discretion that shaped the treatment of unauthorized absence was also at work in the handling of other, less frequently prosecuted military crimes. Of these, the most racially charged was rape. Unlike crimes of absence, sexual assault was unmistakably criminal under civilian as well as military law. Because of the link between sexual and military conquest, and because ideas about female sexual availability and male sex drives were so often shaped by racial stereotypes, the military's prosecution of rape is critical in understanding how race influenced courts-martial.

Rape and other acts of violence against women were not limited to times of war, but it is no accident that soldiers' most brutal rapes and murders occurred during war. Rape has long been associated with war in the popular imagination, in government propaganda and through military strategy.[60] The carnage of World War II included two of the best-known modern examples of mass rape during wartime: the rape of over 100,000 German women by Allied troops in Berlin and the 1937 "Rape of Nanjing," when Japanese soldiers assaulted thousands of Chinese women.[61] American servicemen did not escape the modern soldier's propensity to rape. In every war from the Civil War through the Vietnam War, women were brutalized by advancing and occupying U.S. forces.[62] The violence prosecuted as war crime has often included the sexual assault of women.

Racial difference was a component of most American war crime in the late-twentieth century. Almost all of the war crimes prosecuted in the 1950s, 1960s, and 1970s involved violence against women that crossed lines of race and nationality.[63] The military's assumptions about the sexual availability of Asian women influenced both the nature and targets of soldiers' violent excess. Racial violence, excessive brutality, and group action characterized crimes of war. American servicemen's sense of cultural and racial superiority exacerbated their tendency to dehumanize nonwhite enemies.

The interaction of soldiers' sexual entitlement and American racial hierarchies sometimes fostered resentment among American troops of color. Part of this resentment was frustration at being singled out for harsh punishment in sexual assault cases.[64] Replicating the pattern that appeared in adultery prosecutions, African American soldiers were more likely to be tried and more likely to face harsh punishment for rape than were white servicemen.[65] Even apparently neutral legal doctrines were applied in ways that prejudiced accused African Americans. The court-martial of John H. Henderson, an Army corporal convicted of rape in 1952, illustrates how African American defendants were often identified and categorized.[66] In rejecting Henderson's appeal, the Court of Military Appeals wrote that "judicial conscience" required the court to remember "'as judges what we know as men.'"[67] What judges, commanders, and court-martial members "knew as men" included an understanding of gender roles and sexual relations that put African American men at a profound legal disadvantage.

Henderson appealed his conviction on the grounds that his use of force, a common appellate issue in rape cases, had not been proved at trial. The Court of Military Appeals sustained his conviction, explaining that the force required for the crime of rape could be "actual or constructive" and that many factors ought to be considered in determining whether force was used and how much the victim could reasonably have resisted.[68] The court's opinion appears to advocate a sensitive, even feminist, understanding of the realities of sexual coercion—and to foreshadow the late-twentieth-century reforms of rape law that recognized the complexities of proving force and measuring resistance.

But this was not the understanding of rape that appears in other courts-martial for crimes of sexual violence. That Henderson was prosecuted at all marked his case as unusual. Very few rape cases reached the military appellate courts that did not involve extreme violence, very young or very old victims, or a third-party witness who could corroborate the charges. None of these factors were present in Henderson's case. Yet he was not only charged, he was convicted and sentenced to ten years confinement at hard labor, a dishonorable discharge, and total forfeiture of pay. In its opinion, the court identifies Henderson as "a quiet young Negro soldier" and his victim as "a 39 year old French-woman, previously chaste and of a religious disposition and background."[69] Both the sexual history of the woman and the racial identity of the man influenced the court's analysis of whether their sexual intercourse was accomplished by force. The myth of the savage black rapist and vulnerable white victim made it difficult for any African American accused of rape to convince a court-martial, or a panel of appellate judges, of his innocence.[70] Henderson may well have been guilty of the crime charged, but it is extremely doubtful that a white serviceman would have been charged, or could have been convicted, for a similar act.

The imposition of capital punishment at court-martial best demonstrates the unequal treatment of African American servicemen, especially those convicted of sex crimes. The UCMJ did little to change the racial disparities of the military death penalty that were apparent during World War II, when African Americans comprised less than 10 percent of the armed forces but accounted for almost 80 percent of the soldiers executed in Europe during the war.[71] Of the twelve men executed under the UCMJ between 1954 and 1961, eleven were African Americans.[72] In a case that reached the Supreme Court on a habeas corpus appeal in 1954, NAACP attorneys Thurgood Marshall and Robert L. Carter argued to no avail that the death sentence imposed on two soldiers convicted of raping a white woman in Guam was the result of coerced confessions and gross procedural injustice.[73] White servicemen were also sentenced to death at court-martial, but they were granted reprieves far more often than men of color.[74] The last execution under American military law was the 1961 hanging of Army Pri-

vate John A. Bennett for the rape and attempted murder of an eleven year-
old Austrian girl.[75] During the six years between Bennett's conviction and
his execution, eight other servicemen were executed, every one an African
American. In the 1950s, six white men were also on death row in the military, but each was spared execution, two by federal courts, four by President Eisenhower. By themselves, these numbers show only the racial disparities in court-martial results, not the intentions that led to these outcomes.
But the numbers, coupled with the wide discretion that shaped military
justice, made the capital court-martial look like a modern, bureaucratic
lynching.

CRIME IN THE "GI's KINGDOM": RACE, GENDER, AND PROSTITUTION

Prostitution was among the most celebrated aspects of military sexual culture, accepted as a part of military service despite the law-breaking that it
so often entailed. Servicemen's associations with female sex workers created enough crime to trigger a large number of prosecutions. From illegal
drug use to brutal murders, crime pervaded the sex industry that serviced
American troops.[76] The military crime that surrounded prostitution during the Cold War offers a telling glimpse into the racial entitlement and
male privilege that so often defined servicemen's interactions with women.
Court-martial records reveal the racial tensions that shaped the sex industry, showing how servicemen both profited from and contested norms of
sexual commerce.

   The sex trade was rooted in notions of men's right to purchase and control female sexuality, a right that was closely associated with military service and racial hierarchies. The race of prostitutes helped to determine the
prices they might charge, and sex entrepreneurs catered to military customers' prejudices by segregating their services so that white men could
seek sex only in the company of other white men. Integrated sex commerce
risked undermining the sexual entitlement of white men, even though a
primary attraction of commercial sex was the chance it provided for sexual
relations outside the usual constraints of race and class. Sex across the color
line was part of the exotic appeal of commercial sex around military out-
posts. This overseas culture of sexual opportunity ran up against the military's interest in restraining the sexual activity of servicemen in hopes of
decreasing the risk of unnecessary violence and disease, promoting stable
families, and protecting the armed forces' public image.

   The armed forces did not officially embrace the sex trade, but did little
to discourage the commercial sex industry that matured, especially around
overseas bases, after World War II. Despite the nearly limitless reach of the

military's criminal law, merely paying for sex was not prosecuted as a crime under the UCMJ.[77] In fact, there was considerable peer pressure to succumb to the lures of the sex industry in some military units. A study completed by the Eighth Army in 1965 documented the impact of that pressure, reporting that over 80 percent of servicemen said they had been with a prostitute.[78] When U.S. troops were pulled out of Vietnam, they left behind some 500,000 Vietnamese prostitutes.[79] Some military leaders welcomed soldiers' use of prostitutes as a sign of masculine aggressiveness: at least one Marine Corps general believed that the "best Marines" were to be found in the brig, and that beer halls and houses of prostitution should be brought on base.[80] Prostitutes in Japan, Korea, Thailand, and Vietnam multiplied as the sex industry boomed and other Asian economies faltered in the 1950s and 1960s.[81] In Korea, the devastation of the war in the early 1950s and the poverty that followed on its heels pushed many women into prostitution.[82] In the "GI's Kingdom," as the region of camptowns that surrounded the highest concentration of American troops in Korea was known, servicemen could live in relative luxury on very little money.[83] Many soldiers, unaccustomed to the wealth and power their paychecks and weapons lent them in war-torn countries, enjoyed a service economy that catered to every conceivable need.[84] For many servicemen who were stationed overseas, prostitutes served as temporary substitutes or exotic alternatives. As commanding officers tried to build working relationships with the communities surrounding domestic and foreign military installations, they also negotiated a new empire of sexual services and new modes of sexual behavior.[85]

Because of the central role sex workers played in the lives of many servicemen, it can be difficult to distinguish soldiers' relationships with prostitutes from their intimate associations with other women. The alienating effects of military service created a need for emotional support and sexual intimacy that sex workers could meet.[86] Prostitutes comforted men stationed far from home and family in addition to providing sexual release. Some servicemen married current or former sex workers, while others engaged in long-term relationships with prostitutes.[87] On the other hand, the contempt with which some soldiers held female sex workers could endanger women who were not prostitutes. When accused of committing crimes against women and girls, servicemen routinely claimed that they had mistaken their victims for prostitutes. The needs and attitudes of servicemen combined with the exploitation of female sex workers to make all women vulnerable to the disrespect that many men felt for prostitutes.

Commanders' tacit acceptance of prostitution was consistent with the practice of many civilian jurisdictions, where antiprostitution laws remained on the books but were not strictly enforced after World War II. By the late 1960s, most legal scholars and government officials accepted the relaxed attitude of police toward prostitution as an appropriate response to new sexual norms that had taken hold since the war.[88] A parallel shift in sexual attitudes prevailed in the armed forces, but within limits. The Court of Military Appeals characterized the years from the mid-1950s through the late 1960s as a time of "dramatic and drastic changes in overt sexual expression," but nonetheless declined to rule that association with prostitutes no longer constituted a military offense.[89]

The military sex industry created disciplinary problems for military leaders even as it provided a wide range of sexual opportunities to servicemen. In order to keep servicemen out of areas considered especially dangerous, commanding officers periodically declared certain businesses or areas off-limits. Servicemen who violated these restrictions were occasionally prosecuted for disobeying orders, a serious military offense.[90] Still, most of the commercial sex industry remained within easy reach of military personnel, especially in "R&R" areas popular with men on leave. The armed forces also repeatedly warned servicemen about the risks of contracting sexually transmitted diseases from prostitutes, hoping to encourage either abstinence or precautions against infection.[91]

Commanders sought to limit racial conflict as well as health problems by placing limits on the military sex trade. In 1965, an Army private brought women to a motel near Fort Leonard Wood, Missouri, instructed them to charge at least ten dollars per soldier—and told them not to take "colored men."[92] Whether the private/pimp was concerned about depressing prices or mixing races (or both), his race-conscious business decision was made in recognition of the tension that accompanied cross-racial sexual interaction. A 1971 NAACP report noted that African American soldiers in West Germany stayed away from enlisted men's clubs because drunken white soldiers often wanted to fight if they saw black soldiers with German women.[93] The NAACP reported further that "[r]acial polarization appear[ed] most pronounced" among Army troops during off-duty recreation, when social and sexual situations created far more friction than professional working relationships.[94] The same social tensions were present among integrated Marine units in Korea during the 1950s.[95] Even integrated military units that functioned effectively on the job were afflicted by racial prejudice off-duty.

In the sex industries of Asia, where white American servicemen dominated a marketplace of Korean, Japanese, and Vietnamese women, non-white servicemen were often frustrated by overt racial discrimination. In Korea, African American soldiers were excluded from some clubs and denied credit in others, a practice fueled by the prejudices of both Koreans and their white American customers.[96] Although some Korean women catered to African Americans, the discrimination practiced by the bars and clubs angered black servicemen, who finally lashed out in July 1971 with a coordinated attack on the segregated clubs around Camp Humphreys, a major Army post.[97] Although dozens were injured, major property damage sustained, and hundreds of police officers called out to suppress the violence, the military did not press criminal charges against any known rioters, probably because of the potential embarrassment and political ramifications of public trials.[98]

Many crimes committed by servicemen in search of sex did, however, lead to prosecution. For commanding officers, the worst of these crimes was the murder of one serviceman by another. Because murders of military personnel were difficult to overlook—they cost American lives, damaged morale, and posed public relations problems—they were more likely to lead to court-martial than other acts of violence that occurred in the context of commercial sex.[99] Though not a common occurrence, a number of servicemen were court-martialed for assaulting and killing other soldiers in and around houses of prostitution in Korea and Japan.[100]

Many such assaults were motivated by jealousy over prostitutes' involvement with other servicemen, signaling the sexual ownership that soldiers asserted over women, even women whom they knew to be prostitutes. While racial motives were rarely made explicit in court-martial records, racial prejudice could heighten the aggressiveness of servicemen who resented their female sexual partners' involvement with men of other races.[101] In 1965, at an air base in Germany, Airman Second Class Salvador Garza was convicted for the murder of an African American airman who had become involved with Garza's sometime girlfriend. Assigned to the same unit as his victim, who was sitting, unarmed, in an off-post apartment playing with an infant when Garza began shooting at him, Airman Garza explained that he feared the "Negro airman" would ruin his girlfriend, perhaps by turning her into a prostitute.[102] He considered the murder a way to show her that "he was a man."[103] This incident reveals a constellation of social pressures that led to murder: a serviceman with access to weapons and a culture that encouraged their use, a racially integrated military unit corrupted by assumptions about African American sexuality, and a young Latino trying to assert his masculinity against a perceived slight. The conflicting messages that the military sent about the meaning of race and the requirements of manhood were difficult for servicemembers to navigate.

Efforts to assert masculine authority and racial privilege sometimes led to violence against prostitutes as well as other servicemen. The only incidents of prostitute murder that appear in the appellate record occurred outside the United States, probably because much of the crime committed by servicemembers within the United States was prosecuted in state, rather than military, criminal courts, and because much of servicemen's contact with prostitutes occurred overseas.[104] Sex workers' lack of credibility made prosecuting these crimes difficult, but not impossible. In a 1956 case military prosecutors put Okinawan prostitutes on the stand to testify against an Army sergeant charged with the rape and murder of a five year-old girl.[105] The sex workers' help was crucial because the accused had spent the day of the murder in their company. Because of their testimony, the sergeant was convicted and sentenced to death.

Although such horrific crimes could provoke aggressive investigation and prosecution, neither civilian nor military police made reducing crime against prostitutes a priority. In the late 1960s and early 1970s, the Korean public registered outrage at the murders of several young Korean prostitutes who had allegedly been killed by American soldiers.[106] Though many crimes against sex workers went unpunished, the crimes that were prosecuted leave little doubt about the lethal nature of the sex industry. Many girls and women died in this line of work. Servicemen murdered prostitutes after sex that was not to their liking, because the women slept with other men, and in furtherance of robberies. During the Korean War, for example, an Army corporal murdered a Japanese prostitute after their rough sex had made him angry.[107] In Vietnam, a private shot and killed his Vietnamese girlfriend, who was a prostitute, because of her attentions to other GIs.[108] In 1969, an Air Force sergeant robbed a prostitute in Rome at knifepoint, slashing her from throat to ear.[109] Men who worked in the sex business were also at risk of violence at the hands of servicemen, especially in Asia. The early 1950s saw a series of courts-martial involving servicemen who killed Korean and Japanese men during the course of robbing houses of prostitution or in eruptions of apparently unprovoked violence.[110] Most such incidents did not come to the attention of military courts. But when they did, courts-martial could punish soldiers harshly.

Prosecutors' reluctance to investigate and prosecute crime against sex workers had an even greater effect on the number of courts-martial for sexual assault than on courts-martial for nonsexual violence. Because they were assumed to consent to most sexual activity, prostitutes found pressing charges in rape cases very difficult. Still, some servicemen were prosecuted and convicted for rapes of sex workers in both Korea and Germany during this period.[111] Unusually brutal or public assaults on prostitutes could impel commanding officers and military lawyers to bring charges even in cases in which they knew credible witnesses were scarce and success at trial was not assured. Some cases were pursued because of the youthfulness of the victim, which made the crime more egregious in the eyes of both military officers and the local community. For example, three marines were court-martialed at Da Nang for the 1966 rape of a Vietnamese girl whom they said they thought was a prostitute.[112] Military justice did not alter the armed forces' culture of sexual conquest, but courts-martial were used to draw the line against extraordinary misconduct, whether the victim was a prostitute or not.

Servicemen who failed to distinguish between prostitutes and other women committed a significant proportion of the collateral crime that occurred around the sex industry. A soldier's inability to find a prostitute when he wanted one could lead to attempted rape and even murder.[113] In 1952, an Army private who dragged a Japanese girl away from her companion on a Tokyo street and into a public bathroom defended himself against a charge of attempted rape by explaining that he thought the girl was a prostitute when he assaulted her.[114] In 1969, a similar defense was raised by a drunken lance corporal in the Marine Corps. He attempted to rape a woman in her Okinawa home, which he mistakenly thought was a house of prostitution.[115]

There was no single reason that servicemen raped women, nor a unifying rationale behind soldiers' use of prostitutes. But the attitudes toward women and sexuality endorsed by military culture put women at risk of violence if they did not behave in the manner that servicemen expected. In the situations described above, women were harmed when they did not submit to the demands of servicemen. Sex workers were at greatest risk, but frustrated servicemen might direct their rage—whether the result of the losses experienced during war, unfulfilled sexual desire, or martial aggression—at virtually anyone who might cross their path at an inopportune time. A particularly brutal and sexually charged case from Munich in 1954 illustrates the grim consequences of such encounters. An Army private searched for a prostitute just before killing and mutilating a German boy who had somehow offended him. The soldier stabbed the boy with a pocketknife, cut open his abdomen, and cut off his genitals.[116] Cases such as these made military leaders wary of completely eliminating the sex industry around major installations for fear of closing a safety valve that prevented violence from exploding in other directions.[117] In military culture, violence and sex often overlapped, and prostitutes were more acceptable targets for soldiers' excess than others who might be harmed in their absence.

The military's sex culture also made the consumption of sex a fraternal, rather than individual, pursuit. In 1957, several noncommissioned Army officers picked up three prostitutes in Louisville and set them up in a parking lot at Fort Knox, Kentucky, for the benefit of the trainees stationed there—who quickly surrounded the car that held the prostitutes.[118] In the alert facility at K. I. Sawyer Air Force Base, Michigan, a sergeant arranged a strip show in May 1972 and then lined up airmen in a corridor outside a room where two prostitutes entertained customers.[119] Much like gang rape, its not so distant cousin, serial use of a prostitute was more about male bonding and shared experience than it was about heterosexual intimacy or release.[120] The sex trade in which so many servicemen indulged broadcast norms of female sexual availability and male sexual aggression. Americans who served in the Cold War military could not help but hear the message.

Prosecutions for crime related to sex commerce and sexual assault reveal that the military could not command its soldiers to exercise discretion in their sexual affairs any more than it could issue an order eliminating the racial hierarchies of American society during the Cold War. The racial and sexual attitudes adopted by the armed forces shaped soldiers' sexual activity and defined the targets of the violence that sometimes accompanied it. Courts-martial provide telling evidence of the difficulty of controlling soldiers who were first socialized into violent behavior, then stationed far from a community that might help to constrain their aggression. Military culture assumed that nonwhite women were sexually available to white men, that African American men were more likely to commit crimes of sexual violence, and that all servicemen required outlets for their sexual aggression.

Legal reform failed to extinguish the prejudice that many servicemembers brought with them into military service, and evolving legal doctrines could not change the perspectives of judges and commanding officers on the essential attributes of race and sex. Prosecutions for nonsexual types of military crime, particularly for criminal absence, were also marked by assumptions about racial difference. Criminal justice reform in the military, like similar civilian efforts, tried to substitute procedural values for individual judgment. But the UCMJ preserved the prosecutorial discretion of commanding officers and failed to challenge military sexual culture, ensuring that the Cold War court-martial would remain a site of racial injustice.

Chapter 6

"GENTLEMEN UNDER ALL CONDITIONS"

Officers on Trial

Military custom and law bestowed privileges on commissioned officers that made courts-martial a different experience for officers than for enlisted servicemembers. Servicemembers greeted officers of higher rank by saluting and addressed them as "sir" or "ma'am." To disobey an officer's order violated the UCMJ, as did assaulting or disrespecting an officer.[1] The UCMJ also made it more difficult to impose penalties on misbehaving officers than on enlistees.[2] Moreover, the privacy and autonomy of high rank insulated officers from criminal prosecution. Officers were not subject to the same surveillance as enlisted personnel, who often lived in military housing, where their belongings—and personal lives—were open to the scrutiny of superiors.

Nor were officers as likely to be intimidated by the military's disciplinary system. When accused of wrongdoing, their money and education helped them negotiate the bureaucracy of the military and its justice system more effectively than most enlisted troops. Court-martialed officers were more likely to pay for civilian attorneys, to mobilize political support, and to attract media coverage. They could sometimes avoid prosecution altogether, as in the 1969 case of Green Beret officers who were implicated in the murder of an alleged Vietnamese double agent.[3] The Green Berets escaped court-martial partly because they managed to portray their treatment as politically motivated and their actions as approved by Army intelligence officers. On the rare occasions when officers were convicted at courts-martial, their political and legal skills could pay off with more lenient punishment than their crimes seemed to warrant. Given the many opportunities for clemency that followed a court-martial conviction, persistent, well-connected officers could negotiate more favorable outcomes than their less resourceful brethren. The best-known court-martial of the Vietnam War was the trial of Lieutenant William Calley, convicted for his central role in the My Lai massacre.[4] Calley, who depicted himself as a victim of the way the United States fought the war in Vietnam, served only three and a half years under house arrest despite being sentenced to life imprisonment.[5]

Yet officers' special status was double-edged. It imposed duties and set expectations that separated the military's elite from its rank-and-file and made officers targets for prosecution when military operations went awry.

Officers and noncommissioned officers alike were expected to look out for lower-ranking soldiers, particularly at training bases, where experienced servicemembers tutored impressionable new troops. The "Ribbon Creek incident," a fatal 1956 training accident for which a Marine Corps drill instructor was court-martialed, demonstrates the criminal culpability that could attach to servicemembers who failed to protect the soldiers charged to their care.[6] The armed forces also expected officers, especially those at the military's highest ranks, to protect sources of revenue and to enhance the military's prestige. As role models, leaders, and representatives of the armed forces to the public, officers' mistakes damaged the military's reputation more than the mistakes of privates or corporals.

The UCMJ even specified an officers-only crime in Article 133, the "conduct unbecoming an officer and a gentleman" clause, giving military leaders a special criminal statute for use in patrolling the boundaries of officers' behavior.[7] The lieutenant colonel who raged out of control and beat up his wife in the parking lot of an officers' club—an incident discussed in chapter 4—humiliated the Army in a way that a corporal's similar misconduct would not.[8] The charge against the lieutenant colonel ("conduct unbecoming an officer and a gentleman") and the location of his crime (the officers' club) were reserved to persons of his status. His acts were not criminal because of the physical harm they imposed but because of the social disgrace they brought. Wayward officers cast doubt on the legitimacy of the institution that had commissioned and promoted them. Worse yet, they undermined the trust in the judgment of superior officers that the military counted on. The errors of officers, especially those of high rank, could not be shrugged off as the youthful indiscretions of inexperienced enlistees. They were effectively the errors of the military itself.

This chapter explores the domain of officers' crime for insight into the legal consequences of military rank. Courts-martial of officers were politicized by their higher public profiles and the high stakes of the Cold War, which subjected officers' loyalties and competence to heightened scrutiny. Restrictions on officers' conduct were defined by the geopolitics of fighting communism and the importance of maintaining domestic support for the mushrooming defense budget. Still, courts-martial of officers were unusual, partly because officers made up such a small fraction of servicemembers. They comprised only 10 to 14 percent of the American military between 1951 and 1975.[10] This remained true even as the number of officers gradually increased, driven by the Cold War's need for more educated, and thus higher ranking, military personnel.[11] Fewer in number, better paid, and often older than enlisted troops, officers were much less likely to be court-martialed than the troops they commanded. But when officers were prosecuted, the military's need to protect its political viability—to defend itself, not only the nation—took center stage. Trials of officers threatened the military's image nearly as much as commanders' errors compromised its missions. The courts-martial of officers could undermine the faith of both the American public and foreign allies in the U.S. military.

Distinguishing the crimes of officers from the rest of military crime is not a neat task, however. The Cold War military was a graduated hierarchy, composed not just of commissioned officers and junior enlistees, but many levels of status and privilege. Not all officers were treated similarly, nor were officers the only military personnel burdened with the duty to protect subordinates and promote a positive image of military service. Noncommissioned officers, or NCOs, shared some of the privileges and incurred many of the responsibilities of commissioned officers.[11] The perks of being a junior officer paled in comparison to the benefits that came with the military's highest grades. The clout and visibility of generals and admirals gave the military's highest-ranking officers unique vulnerability to—and protection from—criminal prosecution. Despite these differences, commissioned officers constitute a legally recognized, culturally significant subgroup of the military. Analyzing the courts-martial of officers reveals the legal consequences of the deference and obedience that the armed forces demanded while highlighting the political dimensions of military justice.

This chapter's first section canvasses the categories of crime discussed in earlier chapters, revealing how the military's expectations of its officers influenced prosecutions for virtually every type of military crime. The rest of the chapter focuses on an arena of criminal prosecution in which politics played an especially large role: military investigations of homosexuality. The armed forces' desire to promote a respectable public image and to prevent abuses of military authority made officers a frequent target of efforts to uncover alleged homosexuals. The second section analyzes the 1958 court-martial of a retired naval officer and the final section documents the wide array of Cold War prosecutions for homosexual crimes that were influenced by the status of the officers involved. Taken as a whole, the courts-martial of Cold War officers reveal the criminal consequences of the military's expectation that officers be—or at least appear to be—unimpeachably loyal and unmistakably heterosexual.

THE POLITICS OF OFFICERSHIP

The overall pattern of officers' crime was similar to that of enlisted servicemembers. With the important exception of criminal absence, which was the most common crime of enlistees but was almost never prosecuted against officers, commissioned officers were accused of nearly every military crime. Officers were convicted for sexual assault, for murdering their wives, for marrying too many women, for being gay, for spying and defecting, for collaborating as POWs, and for wartime atrocities.[12] Like enlistees, officers got into legal trouble because their mistakes came to light in a manner that a commanding officer could not ignore.

Few commanders chose to overlook the public political dissent of their officers. The armed forces wanted its servicemembers to appear invulnerable to possible communist indoctrination, able to resist ideological seduction and to defend American superiority. Officers who criticized American policies were a liability serious enough to be worth the expense and negative publicity of criminal trials. For example, five officers who spoke out against the United States while in captivity were among the Korean War POWs court-martialed for collaborating.[13] One of the court-martialed officers, forty-three year old Lieutenant Colonel Harry Fleming, had been an American adviser to the Republic of Korea for just one month before his capture in October 1950.[14] Imprisoned by North Korean and Chinese forces until August 1953, Fleming was a leader in the camps because of his rank and willingness to take on the responsibility, notwithstanding the camp guards' efforts to undermine the chain of command among POWs. Over time, Fleming became more cooperative with the camp guards, leading indoctrination classes and participating in anti-American propaganda. But he continued to resist in subtle ways. When guards were not listening, Fleming tried to interject criticism of communism into his classroom teaching.[15] Moreover, Fleming explained that he cooperated in hopes of helping other prisoners, not because he believed any "malarkey" about the evils of capitalism.[16] Imprisoned officers realized that encouraging resistance and helping POWs survive were important but sometimes incompatible goals. Fleming and his fellow officers defended their actions as reasonable, but they failed to convince either the Army officials who ordered their prosecution or the court-martial panels that convicted them.[17] Two later courts-martial of outspoken Army officers, the prosecutions of Howard Levy and Henry Howe, suggest how much the armed forces wanted to deter officers from criticizing the military during the Vietnam War, when the efficacy of military operations was again being doubted.[18] POW or not, an officer who seemed to take advantage of his military rank to challenge American policies was a threat to the political legitimacy of the American armed forces.

Bungled military operations also threatened the legitimacy of the Cold War military. When military failures came to light, courts-martial of officers could shift attention away from the military's shortcomings in training and execution to the ineptitude and poor judgment of individual officers. The Korean War court-martial of Lieutenant Leon Gilbert, noted in chapter 5's analysis of racial disparities in military justice, is one example. Gilbert was punished more harshly than others in his retreating unit because he was the officer in charge. With the war going badly for the Army, he was an easy target to blame. Commander Lloyd "Pete" Bucher, the captain of the *U.S.S. Pueblo* during the Vietnam War, was another appealing target. Similarly excoriated for acting cowardly after North Korean gunboats overpowered his dilapidated surveillance ship in January 1968, Bucher escaped court-martial only when the secretary of the Navy disregarded a naval court of inquiry's recommendation that the *Pueblo* skipper be court-martialed.[19] When unsuccessful missions were exposed to public scrutiny, officers who were involved could be singled out for their inadequate performance under fire.

Sometimes the authority granted officers put them at risk of being blamed for the military's institutional failures; other times, that authority tempted them to exploit military units and civilian communities for their own purposes. Officers who took advantage of their positions for personal and financial gain could face court-martial. Among the most enterprising of those was Navy Captain Archie Kunze, dubbed the "American mayor of Saigon" for his control of illegal commerce and flamboyant lifestyle.[20] The eventual charges brought against Kunze focused on the government supplies and transportation he provided for a Chinese woman with whom he was having an affair. Kunze's rank could not protect him from punishment for such brazen disregard of both military regulations and norms of civil conduct.

Military justice records also reveal commanders' intolerance for officers and NCOs who attempted to profit from sexual commerce, notwithstanding the normalized nature of prostitution in military culture. Courts-martial of soldiers-turned-sex-entrepreneurs appeared at regular intervals in the appellate record from 1951 through the early 1970s. Under the UCMJ, servicemen could be prosecuted for "pandering" when they directly encouraged or profited from the work of a prostitute.[21] Pandering prosecutions sought to discourage servicemen from flaunting their relationships with prostitutes and to prevent illicit financial gain.[22] The typical pandering case involved an officer or NCO who brought a woman onto a military installation and then arranged for, advertised, and profited from her sexual acts with other servicemen.[23] Pandering prosecutions included sexual commerce transacted both on and off military installations. A Marine Corps staff sergeant spent a June 1951 afternoon at Camp Lejeune soliciting fellow noncommissioned officers to have sex with a young woman he had brought with him;[24] several noncommissioned Army officers picked up three prostitutes in Louisville and set them up in a parking lot at Fort Knox, Kentucky, in 1957;[25] an Air Force sergeant at K. I. Sawyer Air Force Base, Michigan, arranged a strip show in May 1972 then charged airmen to have sexual intercourse with the dancers in a nearby barracks.[26] The profit-seeking motives of panderers made them suspect, since military culture frowned on the exploitation of fellow soldiers even as it winked at sexual conquest.

It is important to keep in mind that most officers—even those whose conduct was improper—did not end up facing court-martial. Military leaders could deal with recalcitrant or incompetent officers the same way they dealt with most errant enlistees, by resorting to administrative discharges and nonjudicial punishment. Moreover, the Cold War armed forces were full of politically savvy officers.[27] It took great political skill to navigate the military—a complex, high stakes bureaucracy—successfully. High-ranking officers learned to work within the system, to express their dissenting views carefully, and to maintain control of the information and images that the public could access.[28] Only those officers whose personal lives or political allegiances put their interests at odds with the interests of their service risked criminal censure. The American military was anxious to present a unified, coherent message to Americans, and to observers around the world, not to air its internal problems before a critical public.

THE CRIMES OF ADMIRAL HOOPER

In April 1957, Navy officials informed retired Rear Admiral Selden G. Hooper that criminal charges were being filed against him. Three weeks later, he stood accused before a court-martial at the U.S. Naval Station in San Diego, listening as witnesses testified about his sexual activities and intimate relationships. Convicted of sodomy, conduct unbecoming an officer and a gentleman, and conduct that discredited the armed forces, Admiral Hooper was dismissed from the Navy and stripped of the veterans' benefits and retirement pay that he had earned during twenty-five years of active-duty service.[29]

Because of his retired status and military grade, Hooper's prosecution was unusual, even in the antigay environment of the armed forces during the late 1950s.[30] Until Hooper, no retired servicemember had been prosecuted under the UCMJ, and only a handful of retired veterans had been prosecuted under prior regimes of military law.[31] The Cold War brought a massive increase, however, in the number and visibility of retired military personnel. The number of military retirees rose rapidly, from just over 133,000 in 1951 to over 200,000 in 1958, 300,000 in 1962, 400,000 in 1964, and 500,000 in 1966.[32] Retirement aside, officers of Hooper's rank rarely faced court-martial; most flag officers who had been tried for military crimes in the past had been involved in high-level political disagreements or blatant criminal activity.[33] Neither were courts-martial the norm for servicemembers accused of being gay during the Cold War. Administrative discharge hearings could oust suspected lesbians and gay men without the time and expense of a formal legal proceeding under the UCMJ.

Some cases, however, still warranted criminal action in the eyes of military leaders concerned about the threat of homosexuality. The case of Admiral Hooper reveals how much military rank affected the policing of homosexuality among servicemembers—even servicemembers who were long retired from active service. Hooper's court-martial makes sense only when his high military grade is taken into account. His behavior would have embarrassed the Navy had it been well known, but few outside his circle of friends knew he was gay.[34] Yet Hooper's involvement with young sailors so troubled the commandant of the California-based Eleventh Naval District that he ordered Hooper's court-martial and then appeared personally in the courtroom during the trial. Admiral Hooper's story, absent from post World War II histories of military and gay life, deserves notice for its vivid depiction of how the status of officers could put them at greater risk of punishment for sexual nonconformity.

Hooper's background reveals a man dedicated to the military since childhood and proud of his service to his country. He was born in Chicago on Christmas Day, 1904, to Rosa Hooper Lyon, an artist.[35] An only child, Selden became interested in military service during frequent moves around the country with his mother.[36] He attended military preparatory schools in Palo Alto, San Francisco, and Washington, D.C., en route to a 1923 appointment to the United States Naval Academy. Tall and thin, Midshipman Hooper ran track, fenced, and excelled in theater productions.[37] A senior yearbook picture reveals fine features on a handsome, narrow face; his classmates described him as a "gentleman under all conditions and a friend to be welcomed."[38]

Hooper's military record after graduation was exemplary. From his early duty assignments through his tours in the Philippines during World War II, he was rated by dozens of superior officers, all of whom lauded his performance and integrity as a naval officer.[39] Hooper's naval career was spent on submarines as well as surface ships, and included a tour as an instructor at the Naval Academy in 1935. Later, he requested and received an assignment to the Naval Reserve Officers' Training Corps at Marquette University in Milwaukee, Wisconsin. Lieutenant Hooper arrived at Marquette in October 1940, intending to work on a graduate degree and enthusiastic about the opportunity to train young officers.[40] But his plans, like those of countless others, were interrupted with the events of the following year. The outbreak of World War II sent Hooper to the Western Pacific, where he commanded first a single destroyer and later a destroyer division. Hooper returned from the war a decorated combat veteran. His highest award was the Silver Star, for "conspicuous gallantry and intrepidity . . . during operations against enemy Japanese forces" in 1944.[41] After the war, Captain Hooper was assigned to the Commandant's Office of the Eleventh Naval District, where he served as director of the Naval Reserve.

Once he retired from the Navy, Hooper lived in Coronado, California, where he became interested in civic affairs and continued to be invested in his military status. Held in high regard at the time of his retirement, Hooper had been part of the military since enlisting in the California National Guard at age seventeen. Well aware of the privileges that accompanied high rank, Hooper planned his 1948 retirement with the knowledge that he would be promoted to rear admiral upon the close of his active-duty career.[42] Three years after retiring, he was still corresponding with the Bureau of the Naval Personnel about which medals and ribbons he was authorized to wear, indicating his interest in maintaining a military appearance.[43] No longer absorbed with military duties, Hooper joined the Lions International, Kiwanis Club, the Chamber of Commerce, and Red Cross.[44] "[A]ctive in social service work devoted to attempts to help wayward boys," he wrote to the Naval Academy in 1949 about plans to open "a military school for boys" in the San Diego area.[45]

Hooper's public life of civic engagement took place alongside a private world of homosocial and homoerotic encounters. Although he was neither out to the most of the San Diego community nor active in the largely secret homophile movements of the 1950s, Hooper participated in a gay subculture that included many current and former servicemen.[46] With both financial resources and extensive military experience, Hooper served as a mentor to young sailors and a conduit into a gay male world. Hooper explained how to obtain favorable Navy assignments as well as how to communicate surreptitiously with other gay sailors through codewords. He invited men to his home for dinners, companionship, and sex.[47] Even when he faced court-martial, he supported his young friends, advising them to tell the truth to investigators but warning of the potential consequences. The former lovers who testified at Hooper's court-martial said that they knew they were homosexual before they met Hooper, but that he introduced them to other men and explained the language and culture of the gay community.

This was not a role that the Navy wanted its retired flag officers to play. Gay mentoring aside, Hooper's sexual behavior pushed the boundaries of convention, exacerbating his crimes in the eyes of the military. The charges brought against him included a "lewd and lascivious act" with a seaman, allegations that he had hosted a party at which male guests engaged in sodomy, and a charge of public association "with persons known to be sexual deviates."[48] His preferred sexual partners were men in their teens and early twenties, all either interested in joining the Navy or already enlisted in the service. His parties and relationships with multiple men made Hooper appear promiscuous. At least two of his lovers were the sons of military officers, an Air Force colonel and a Navy lieutenant commander.

The youth of Hooper's lovers suggests his sexual preference for much younger men and boys; their inexperience and limited resources point toward a difference in power that made his relationships suspect as potentially exploitative. Hooper was fifty-two years old at the time of his court-martial. The young men who testified against him ranged in age from eighteen to twenty-two. He met some of his eventual sexual partners while they were high school students as young as fifteen. But Hooper's age alone did not account for his court-martial. Sexual connection between older men of means and younger, physically attractive partners was far from unusual in military circles. It was the gender of Hooper's lovers, not simply their age, that made Hooper vulnerable to court-martial.

The gay admiral was the prime target of the Navy's investigation. Although other servicemembers were accused of being gay because of their association with him, only Hooper was court-martialed. During his trial, Navy prosecutors depended on the testimony of two sets of witnesses.[49] The first were members of Hooper's social circle, including at least three enlisted sailors with whom he had sexual relations.[50] Testifying against Hooper could not have been an easy task for these young men.[51] Junior enlisted sailors facing a court-martial panel of senior military officers, they were asked to betray their friends and risk public humiliation by revealing intimate details of their sexual relationships.[52] At least one, Roscoe "Duke" Braddock, who another witness said had entered into a "gay marriage" with Hooper, chose not to cooperate with prosecutors;[53] another wavered during the investigation and court-martial, changing his testimony to implicate Hooper after initially denying the allegations.[54] Two men testified to committing sodomy with Hooper, and one described the most scandalous accusation against the admiral: a 1953 strip poker party in Hooper's garage apartment that was a prelude to many acts of sodomy.[55] Witnesses recounted intimacies that took place within Hooper's home, including the admiral's embrace of another man and two men kissing.[56]

The Navy's case against Hooper depended heavily on the testimony of "admitted" homosexuals, who were not considered credible witnesses to many military officers. As a result, the evidence gathered through surveillance of Hooper's home was crucial in meeting the standard of proof (beyond a reasonable doubt, as in civilian criminal courts) required for conviction. That evidence was provided by a second set of witnesses, the Office of Naval Intelligence agents who had staked out Hooper's house for several weeks in the winter of 1957.[57] Armed with binoculars and periscopes, four agents peered into Hooper's home out of a neighbor's second-story window and through the fence around his yard.[58] Late one March evening, after watching Hooper and his male friends hold a "drinking session," the agents testified that they had observed Hooper and Braddock dance, undress, kiss—and then turn off the lights in Hooper's garage apartment, effectively ending the surveillance.[59] Less than a week later, Braddock and John Peter Schmidt, another enlisted sailor, went to Hooper's home for dinner. The intelligence agents again watched through binoculars as the three men dined and talked, after which Braddock departed. Hooper and Schmidt then walked Hooper's dogs, had a few more drinks, and watched television. Once again, the evening of surveillance ended when Hooper turned off the lights—this time after he and Schmidt had kissed, danced, and disrobed.[60]

A decorated combat veteran and a civic-minded retiree, Hooper was a prime candidate for the "good soldier" defense, which allowed him to present evidence of his good military character to create reasonable doubt as to his guilt in the minds of the court-martial members.[61] Admiral Hooper's best chance of acquittal was to convince the court-martial that he was not the sort of man that the military associated with the crimes alleged. He called several character witnesses, including his mother, who lived with him and testified that her son was not a homosexual. A psychiatrist from San Diego County Hospital also testified that, in his expert opinion, Hooper was not a homosexual. But Hooper had reasons beyond his good character to hope for a positive resolution of the case on appeal. Just six days before denying Hooper's first appeal, the Court of Military Appeals had dismissed the conviction of an Army private for sodomy because the law officer had helped to coerce a reluctant witness into testifying.[62] Under the UCMJ, military courts routinely overturned egregious violations of procedural justice at court-martial.

Hooper also had a strong legal claim that he was not subject to court-martial jurisdiction for acts committed after retirement and within his own home. Retired officers had been vulnerable to court-martial under prior versions of military law, and the UCMJ had a provision that seemed to bring retirees within the reach of court-martial. But the Supreme Court appeared ready to limit, not extend, the jurisdiction of courts-martial under the UCMJ.[63] The judicial trend toward restricting the jurisdiction of courts-martial over persons not in active military service boded well for Hooper's defense.

But neither Hooper's twenty-five years of honorable service nor trends in legal doctrine helped him recover his status as a military veteran. The audacity of an admiral who chose to live at the center of a gay male world and who drew young sailors into that world with him was too much for the Navy to overlook. His case reveals the tenacity of military justice in pursuing persons of high rank whose conduct might ruin the Navy's public image. The reforms of the UCMJ and Hooper's commitment to defend himself against the Navy's charges failed to prevent the military from pursuing its long-retired gay admiral.

HOMOSEXUAL CRIME AND OFFICERS

Hooper's case was singular; even the most homophobic of commanding officers rarely pursued gay suspects past retirement. Yet after World War II the increased visibility of homosexuality in popular culture, political movements, and public spaces sparked anxiety about sexual orientation in many quarters of American society.[64] The military's investigations and prosecutions of suspected homosexuals reflected this fear. Afraid that homosexuals, increasingly visible and pathologized in Cold War culture, would corrupt young men and women in uniform, the armed forces prosecuted officers for both consensual and coercive relationships with enlisted servicemembers.[65] The prosecutions of officers for homosexual relationships with enlistees reveals how distinctions of class and rank put officers at greater risk of formal and informal censure if they were thought to be gay.

Some of the court-martial narratives that resulted from officers' prosecutions read like Admiral Hooper's tale. Older, experienced servicemen could attract harsh sanctions if they became sexually involved with younger men. A large age difference between consensual sexual partners increased the likelihood of criminal censure, even if the younger partner was not a minor.[66] Commanding officers faced with an incident of consensual sex between a male officer and a male enlistee were likely to charge the officer with a crime and process the enlisted man for an administrative discharge. Coercing the cooperation of young servicemembers, whose testimony was essential at the courts-martial of more senior officers, was often easy for military investigators and prosecutors.[67]

The case of Jack Bennington, court-martialed in 1961, was relatively typical. It involved excessive drinking, male bonding, and an officer who denied committing a sexual act with an enlistee. An Army lieutenant, Bennington was convicted and sentenced to dismissal after an alleged incident of homosexual fellatio took place after a "beer bust" at Fort Knox, Kentucky.[68] Married with two children, Bennington had a spotless eleven-year military record.[69] He seemed in good position to win a swearing contest against his accuser, who was an Army private with a record of past misconduct, including homosexual acts, and who had been granted immunity from prosecution for testifying against Bennington. But Bennington lost his battles in court until he reached his last resort, the Court of Military Appeals, which finally reversed his conviction. The military's highest court rejected the evidence against Bennington as insufficient and lamented the unsavory character of his accuser. The damage to Bennington's reputation and career, however, could not be undone.

Investigations of suspected homosexuals targeted officers partly because they were considered the "ringleaders"—like Admiral Hooper in San

Diego—of homosexual subgroups in the service.[70] Careers could be destroyed by charges of homosexuality, regardless of whether the allegations were proved at trial. Those who felt wronged by accusations of homosexuality were sometimes successful in pressing libel charges against their accusers.[71] Still, restoring the reputation of an officer accused of a crime as reviled as sodomy was no easy task. Enlisted men as well as officers tried, often without success, to protect themselves against the costs of being revealed as gay. Those costs included not only court-martial or administrative discharge, but coercive or violent responses by fellow servicemembers.[72] This pressure could give rise to the blackmail against homosexuals that the military feared. For example, in 1955 the Court of Military Appeals considered the case of an Army lieutenant charged with possession of marijuana. The lieutenant, who had homosexual "tendencies" according to his own testimony, explained that he had obtained the drugs for a corporal so that the corporal would not expose him as gay.[73] Fear of public exposure could invert the usual hierarchies of military rank, exposing officers to intimidation by those with less official power.

While some officers were court-martialed for ill-advised but consensual sexual interactions with enlisted men, others willfully abused their authority in pursuit of sex. Officers who used their rank and influence in efforts to coerce sex from lesser-ranking servicemen were of grave concern to military leaders.[74] In 1965, in a case involving an Air Force major accused of exposing airmen to gay male erotica, a board of review articulated the need to protect recruits from homosexual superiors: "We do not doubt for a moment that perusal of the scandalous homosexual literature and the nude photographs . . . would tend to debauch and corrupt the morals of an immature, inexperienced airman."[75] Certain that homosexuals posed a threat, even in print, commanding officers felt justified in taking aggressive action to stop them.

The military's fear of sexual predators in its ranks of officers was not entirely misplaced. Some courts-martial involved egregious same-sex coercion and assault. In 1955, a Navy ROTC instructor sexually assaulted a student while both were drunk. The student immediately complained, and the instructor was court-martialed for sodomy.[76] In 1963, a lieutenant in the Naval Reserve, while serving as a dentist on active duty in Japan, drugged several patients, photographed them nude, and then sexually assaulted them.[77] Sexual harassment and assault, then, were features of the military landscape, and were punished under military law, long before the numbers of women in uniform increased in the 1970s. Abusive officers were a threat to the integrity of the officer corps and to the morale and welfare of enlisted servicemembers, and the military justice system treated them as such. It is worth noting the irony that the military's extensive experience in policing same-sex sexual harassment did not pave the way for similarly rigorous policing of opposite-sex harassment, which plagued the armed forces after women entered the ranks in larger numbers in the late 1970s.

Sexual exploitation was not only the province of commissioned officers in the military hierarchy, of course. Others in positions of military authority were also punished for initiating inappropriate sexual contact with male subordinates. In 1956, an enlisted instructor was court-martialed for enticing basic trainees to accompany him on a drunken spree and then committing oral sodomy on one of them; a decade later, an Air Force technical sergeant was tried and convicted for drinking to excess with a subordinate and then persisting in unwanted sexual advances.[78] Like the officers who were prosecuted for similar acts, these men undermined the stability of the military's hierarchy by exploiting their positions of authority in relationships with junior servicemembers.

Courts-martial, however, were not the harshest of punishments that officers faced during the Cold War. They could be informally held responsible for alleged misconduct as well, and were vulnerable to vigilante justice. Angry troops could resort to organized resistance such as mutiny or to more covert action, including fragging, as the murder of superior officers by their own men became known during the Vietnam War.[79] Allegations of homosexual inclinations could result in not just courts-martial, but physical violence. As Admiral Hooper discovered, the military's antigay policies could turn the military rank structure upside down.

In 1966, Commander Walter J. Whitley, aide to the president of the Naval War College, experienced that inversion firsthand when he was convicted and dismissed from the Navy for "wrongfully behaving in an indecent, lewd and lascivious manner" after being beaten up by an enlisted sailor.[80] Two seamen were involved in the plot that led to Whitley's court-martial. The first testified that he had a consensual sexual relationship with the commander. The second said that Whitley had picked him up with the intent of having sex. Whitley took the second seaman home, unaware that the enlistee had stolen a billy club from the police earlier that evening, intending to "roll queers."[81] The seaman struck Whitley on the head and chest, injuring him severely enough that he sought treatment from a Navy doctor the next day. Because Whitley lied to the doctor about the source of his injuries, he was also charged at his court-martial with making a false statement.[82] Outed by gay bashers, Whitley's experience suggests the extent of the violence against homosexuals that was tolerated, if not encouraged, in military culture. It also confirms the physical vulnerability of officers who were gay.

Whitley's ultimate fate, however, points out the conflict between the Navy's desire to uncover homosexuals, especially those who held positions of authority, and the legal constraints imposed by the UCMJ. Convicted at trial, Whitley won a resounding victory on appeal when the Court of

Military Appeals denounced his investigation and trial as "a dismal picture of deceitful and capricious actions by high ranking Navy officers."[83] Investigators had questioned Whitley outside the presence of his counsel, locked him in the psychiatric ward of a Navy hospital and forbade his counsel from visiting him (apparently under guise of a suicide watch), and searched an off-base building that Whitley owned without his consent. The court reversed his conviction for a multitude of errors and remanded his case to the JAG of the Navy.[84] In cases that targeted alleged homosexuals, overzealous military police, prosecutors and commanders were sometimes stymied by the procedural rules that governed at court-martial. Though courts-martial for homosexuality continued throughout the Cold War, it is no surprise that savvy commanders so often turned to administrative action when allegations of homosexuality surfaced.

Major Lloyd E. Yeast, convicted for his association with several Columbus, Ohio, gay establishments and their employees during the spring of 1965, also managed to find relief on appeal. Though Yeast's court-martial conviction was upheld, his one-year sentence was cut in half.[85] Yeast was prosecuted for allegedly frequenting gay bars in the company of two airmen, one of whom the major asked to spend the night in an apartment owned by Paul Rawson, a bartender at the Kismet Café, which was known for its gay clientele. Yeast's close relationship with Rawson, who had both "a homosexual reputation" and an apartment full of "photographs of nude and seminude males and homosexual type literature," did not help his chances at court-martial.[86] Like Hooper and most other officers accused of homosexuality, Yeast relied on a character defense at trial. He had an "impressive combat record," over twenty years of service, was held in "high regard" by his military associates, and had fulfilled his "parental responsibilities" (though there is no mention of a wife in the appellate report).[87] But this was not enough to persuade his court-martial to acquit.

On appeal, however, Yeast won a partial victory. He lost his challenge to the admission at court-martial of photographs and other materials that had been seized from Rawson's residence without a warrant after the Columbus police intimidated Rawson, who was apparently under the influence of alcohol or drugs, into consenting to the search.[88] But Yeast won his challenge to one of the charges against him, the allegation that he had committed a crime by visiting a bar that catered to gay men. In an astonishing policy analysis, given the military's hostility toward homosexuals, the court held that taking airmen to a gay bar did not constitute a crime. The court pointed out that merely socializing with enlisted men was not criminal, and the Kismet Café's "sizable 'tourist' or non-homosexual patronage" was proof that not all its customers were gay.[89] It termed "common knowledge" that "some establishments frequented by sexual deviates become widely-known tourist attractions innocently patronized by large numbers of non-deviates."[90] The court decided that simply going to a gay bar, even in the company of junior enlistees, could not constitute a crime under the far-reaching general article of the UCMJ. By 1965, military courts accepted homosexuality as part of the social world in which servicemembers lived. Even if the armed forces were unwilling to accept that some of their officers might be homosexual themselves, the court's recognition marked a significant shift.

Regardless of its grudging acknowledgement of a gay social world, the military considered the sort of close relationships that Yeast and Whitley had developed with enlisted men a threat to good order and discipline. Officers were expected to avoid becoming so intimate with persons of inferior rank that their judgment or impartiality might be questioned. Whitley's case suggests that the risk of exploitation in a relationship among unequals could run in either direction. Officers risked their careers and their reputations when they became too close to enlistees. Excessive familiarity between officers and enlistees, sexual or not, was of such concern that it was given a special name, fraternization, and prosecuted as a military crime.

But rare were the cases so egregious they triggered criminal prosecution in this era of administrative, rather than criminal, sanction. The *Manual for Courts-Martial* did not specify fraternization as a separate offense under the general article until 1984, and the services did not promulgate regulations to clarify its definition until the 1970s.[91] The first official Army policy on fraternization was not drafted until 1974, when the Army responded to a female officer's relationship with an enlisted man by issuing a regulation defining their relationship as improper.[92] Part of the military's reluctance to specify fraternization as a crime was its inherent murkiness. Men were expected to be brothers-in-arms when they became part of the military family; the bonds of friendship between servicemembers, forged in times of hardship and need, were often powerful. Drawing a line between such intense relationships and the improper associations that could be prosecuted as criminal threatened to undermine the morale of troops and the customs of the service. Clarity about the boundaries of fraternization eluded commanders and judge advocates despite the volumes of official guidance that were issued to try to standardize interpretations of the law from the 1970s through the 1990s.[93]

Complicating the issue after World War II were demographic shifts that reduced the social distance between officers and enlisted personnel, making the parameters of acceptable interaction even less clear. The 1946 Doolittle report, prepared in response to "[c]omplaints and comments on the lack of democracy in the Army, instances of incompetent leadership, and the abuse of privileges," recommended that official policies be refined to permit more open relationships between officers and enlistees.[94] But its recommendations were largely ignored by service leaders who were uncertain that good order and discipline could survive such a sea change in military culture.[95] The social distance between officers and enlisted personnel was challenged, but not erased, during the Cold War.

Uncertainty about the contours of fraternization reduced prosecutions for the crime and resulted in tentative opinions from military courts. Rarely charged at court-martial, fraternization appears in only three opinions of military appellate courts between 1951 and 1973.[96] All three were prompted by same-sex relationships. During this period, when women were but a small minority of servicemembers, fraternization was a gay crime. Its prosecution was triggered by fear that homosexual officers would take advantage of their positions and seduce junior servicemembers, discrediting the armed forces and corrupting the chain of command in the process.

Edgar Dauphin Free, a captain in the Marine Corps Reserve, was the appellee in the first fraternization case to reach the Court of Military Appeals.[97] The court's 1953 opinion tries to establish a legal standard by which to gauge potentially improper relationships but declines to articulate any rule to divide appropriate from inappropriate conduct. The opinion is light on facts, and it does not mention homosexuality explicitly. But its description of the conduct that led to the charges reads like an account of an officer on a date. Free drove his companion around while they talked, bought dinner and drinks, and afterward asked his friend to spend the night. The evening apparently ended when Free climbed into bed with his friend, who was an enlisted man. The court tried to clarify the boundaries of social interaction in the Cold War military, carefully noting that Free's actions might have demonstrated innocent camaraderie rather than criminal familiarity under different circumstances. Though it accepted that "democratic concepts of social relations" had lessened the social divide between officers and enlistees, the court explicitly rejected the Doolittle report's recommendations, insisting that fraternization remained a cognizable military crime and that the military's "standards of honor and conduct" were at stake.[98] Refusing to specify a definition for the crime, the court listed examples of what sort of conduct might, or might not be, fraternization—and defended the ability of officers to discern acceptable from unacceptable behavior.

After Captain Free's case, fraternization disappeared from the appellate reports until the 1970s, when two other cases of alleged homosexuality were prosecuted as fraternization. Like Free, Lieutenant Junior Grade Carl R. Pitasi was court-martialed because of the allegations of an enlisted man.[99] This enlistee, referred to only as "Schultz" in the record, became disenchanted with the Navy during a tour of duty at Great Lakes Naval Station in Illinois, where Pitasi was also stationed. Emboldened by liquor,

Schultz decided to renounce his American citizenship in hopes of being discharged. He "attempted to burn his white hat and, being unsuccessful, burned his ID card, liberty card, and chow pass."[100] Pitasi, who was the officer on duty, sent Schultz to the brig. The next day, Pitasi spoke to Schultz at length about his frustrations with the Navy, the first of a series of conversations that culminated in Schultz spending the night in Pitasi's quarters. Schultz testified that Pitasi indecently assaulted him that night, that the assaults continued over several weeks, and that he reported Pitasi to authorities yet continued to see the lieutenant because he hoped his association with Pitasi would "enhance his chances of getting out of the Navy."[101] To Schultz, the junior officer was a "get out of jail free" card; to Pitasi, the troubled enlistee was an object of desire.

Consistent with the pattern of "victim" testimony in other prosecutions of officers for consensual homosexual acts, Schultz's willingness to testify against Pitasi and his account of the consensual nature of the sex wavered during the investigation and court-martial. Eventually, naval prosecutors granted Schultz immunity in return for his testimony, and he was administratively discharged "through association as a homosexual" after the trial.[102] Pitasi was court-martialed because he crossed the line that separated the conduct expected of officers, which included both paternal counseling and fraternal support, from conduct that threatened to undermine the privileges and authority of the officer corps. But in this case, Pitasi was not the only wrongdoer whose sexual activity and military status was influenced by the antigay posture of armed forces. Schultz took advantage of the situation, using the Navy's condemnation of homosexuality and Pitasi's vulnerability as an officer—which made Schultz's testimony against him valuable to military authorities—to achieve his goal of discharge from the service. Whether or not Schultz considered himself gay, he found the escape that he wanted so desperately in the military's policies and laws regarding homosexuality.

Lieutenant John William Lovejoy, like Pitasi, was court-martialed for a homosexual relationship with an enlisted man.[103] And as in Pitasi's case, the facts leave open the question of whether the relationship was consensual or coerced. Lovejoy's relationship with Seaman Paul A. Niebank began on the *U.S.S. Henry Clay*, a submarine based in Charleston, South Carolina, where Lovejoy was serving as a supply officer when Niebank reported onboard in April 1967. At the time, Niebank was twenty years old, Lovejoy nine years his senior. At Lovejoy's court-martial, Niebank testified that he approached the officer first by asking Lovejoy for advice about travel and sightseeing in the British Isles. When Lovejoy responded that he and a Midshipman Surplus (no given name appears in the reports) were planning a trip to England during an upcoming leave period, Niebank asked if he might join them. Lovejoy agreed, and the three men shared transportation and lodging costs during the trip. Soon thereafter, the aptly named Surplus departed, and Niebank and Lovejoy stayed on together in London, later visiting Niebank's relatives in England.[104] After their European vacation, they flew back to New York, spent a night in New York City, and then flew home. In Charleston, Niebank stayed with Lovejoy in his apartment until the end of their mutual leave period.

At trial, crew members from the *Henry Clay* testified that despite their difference in military grade, Lovejoy and Niebank addressed each other by their first names, a gesture of familiarity considered inappropriate between officers and enlisted personnel. The two men did not hide their living arrangements and appeared to be very close: they cooked and ate together, drove each other around in Lovejoy's car, and went water-skiing with other crew members. Had Lovejoy been an enlistee, their relationship might not have concerned their commanding officer. But Lovejoy was a lieutenant in the Navy, and such intimacy with a young sailor was not what the Navy expected of its officers.

Lovejoy's court-martial focused on his sexual relationship with Niebank as much as their social familiarity, again portraying fraternization as a crime of homosexuality. Granted immunity for his testimony, Niebank described sexual touching and acts of oral sodomy that took place at Lovejoy's initiative and against Niebank's wishes. Niebank testified that he objected to Lovejoy's sexual overtures, which occurred regularly, but he continued to share meals and housing with the lieutenant. Lovejoy's account of their relationship was quite different: He denied that any sexual acts had taken place between them, provided no explanation for Niebank's accusations, and claimed to have "normal heterosexual relationships" with no predilection for homosexuality.[105] Lovejoy called other officers and shipmates from the *Henry Clay* to testify about his "excellent character both as an individual and as a Naval Officer."[106] Despite this vigorous character defense, Lovejoy was convicted and dismissed from the Navy after a four-day trial at which thirteen witnesses testified. The military's intolerance for gay men made any homosexual acts, regardless of consent, grounds for criminal charges. Lovejoy—like Admiral Hooper—was reduced to debating the quality of his character rather than challenging Niebank's portrayal of their relationship as coercive.

Prosecution of enlisted men for AWOL was the most common military crime, but the prosecution of officers for crimes of sex and privilege consumed significant military legal resources as well. The privileges enjoyed by those at the top of the military's rank structure granted both additional protection from and special vulnerability to criminal prosecution. As the class distinctions that had separated officers from enlisted personnel in the military's past eroded after World War II, the armed forces struggled to deal with the disorder of a more democratic armed force. Appearances of propriety were ever more important as the officer corps became less exclusive. Because the power and class dynamics of military service were played out in a nearly all-male milieu, especially onboard ships and during extended deployments, homosexual intimacy was seen as a primary threat to the military fraternity. Courts-martial were wielded in spirited defense of the military's impressionable youth; even gay retirees were perceived as menacing. Unfortunately, this intense concern with regulating the sexual abuse of power would not apply to the treatment of the young women whose entry into military service would pose the next great challenge to American military culture.

AFTERWORD

The end of the draft in 1973 signaled a new era in the history of the American armed forces and in military justice. Young men were no longer impressed into service, and commanding officers no longer had to answer the daunting question of how to control reluctant, rebellious servicemen.[1] Americans chose to enter military service for economic, professional, and ideological reasons, not because their government forced a duty of citizenship upon them. The conflict between coerced service and individual liberty receded, even though draft registration continued to be a requirement of male citizenship.

But the advent of the all-volunteer force did not alter the basic makeup of the military or its justice system. The class and racial demographics of the military changed only slightly. The military remained an important source of economic opportunity for those from less privileged backgrounds, and the percentage of women rose but then stalled at around 15 percent.[2] The self-selected group of Americans drawn to military service lent military culture an increasingly reactionary bent, helping to preserve a masculinist military tradition even in the presence of larger numbers of servicewomen.[3] Likewise, the structure of military justice did not change dramatically after the Vietnam War. The UCMJ continued to protect the authority of commanding officers to prosecute at will.[4] Military judges remained marginally independent at best.[5] Commanders both ordered prosecutions and selected the court-martial panels that adjudged guilt or innocence.[6] Individualized sentencing, unrestricted by the guidelines that so altered the civilian criminal sentencing process, continued to be the rule at court-martial.[7]

Military criminal law and procedure changed relatively little in the late-twentieth century.[8] The rules of evidence were codified in 1980 to resemble the federal rules; the *Manual for Courts-Martial* doubled in size; and the benchbook distributed to military judges grew longer and more complex. The path to the Supreme Court was made more direct in 1983, when Congress amended the UCMJ to permit petitions for a writ of certiorari to the Supreme Court in cases heard by the military's highest court.[9] While the structure of military justice remained largely intact and the rate of court-martial low, military lawyers were asked to handle increasingly specialized and complex legal duties.[10] As a result, judge advocates spent less time on courts-martial and garnered less experience in criminal justice matters than their predecessors.

While the internal practice of military justice stagnated, the U.S. civilian judiciary grew increasingly deferential to the armed forces, beginning in the 1980s.[11] This trend made military leaders bolder in asserting jurisdiction and limited servicemembers' opportunities for legal remedies. In the 1950s and 1960s, the Supreme Court had restricted court-martial jurisdiction, holding that the Constitution did not permit courts-martial to try civilians or to try crimes unrelated to military service.[12] The Court reversed itself in 1969 and did not look back; by the 1980s, military crimes no longer had to be "service-connected" and both the UCMJ's sweeping "catch-all" statutes and the policy of registering only men for the draft were granted constitutional legitimacy.[13] The frequent hearings that Congress held during the 1960s and early 1970s on military justice matters disappeared, and congressional leaders did not reassess the military justice system after the early 1980s.[14]

The military-legal establishment became more insulated from civilian scrutiny as the all volunteer, professionalized armed force matured.[15] Courts-martial fell out of the public eye, with scholars, like Congress, paying little attention to military justice. In the 1970s, military justice had attracted criticism from a number of high-profile observers: a highly respected judge advocate general, Kenneth J. Hodson, wrote a series of scholarly articles advocating reform of the military justice system; Yale Law School professor Joseph W. Bishop, Jr., published a study recommending major procedural changes; and Robert Sherrill authored a widely read critique of courts-martial.[16] By the end of the twentieth century, such critics had faded from public view, leaving the nonprofit National Institute of Military Justice and bar association committees as nearly the only organizations outside of the military paying attention to courts-martial.[17] Public involvement in court-martial reform became very limited, although the Joint Service Committee on Military Justice now publishes a notice of proposed changes to court-martial rules in the Federal Register and holds a public meeting to consider possible changes.[18] Together, these developments left commanders and judge advocates free to shape court-martial rules and practice as they see fit.

This public and private neglect of military justice contributed to the scandals that dogged the armed forces and its criminal justice system at the turn of the twenty-first century. The list of embarrassing incidents is long and grim: the groping of women by naval aviators at the annual Tailhook convention in 1991; the 1992 death of Allen Schindler, a seaman bludgeoned to death by fellow troops because he was gay; the mock rapes enacted at an Air Force Academy survival school until legal challenges ended the practice in 1995; the Aberdeen Proving Ground drill sergeants court-martialed for sexually assaulting female trainees in 1996; the brutal 1999 murder of Private First Class Barry Winchell, a gay soldier at Fort

Campbell, Kentucky, by fellow troops.[19] It is no accident that so many scandals involved sexual misconduct, given the military's celebration of hypermasculine behavior, the sexual harassment that has become routine in the lives of many servicewomen, and the armed forces' reluctance to recognize the contributions of lesbian and gay servicemembers.[20] Commanding officers use their own discretion in deciding whether to investigate or ignore allegations of inappropriate sexual activity involving servicemembers. Sometimes castigated for not prosecuting aggressively enough, other times criticized for unfairly singling out individuals for punishment, military officers rarely seem able to strike a balance between military necessity and individual rights in cases that mix military crime and questionable sexual conduct.

The current practice of military criminal law is also complicated by efforts to extend military criminal jurisdiction over the civilian and government personnel who help the military with the peacekeeping and nation-building tasks that now constitute the majority of military operations. In an effort to reduce the cost associated with these new missions, the military has grown more dependent on civilian contractors.[21] Duties that used to be performed by servicemembers are now assigned to civilians and government employees, and contract employees staff critical parts of military organizations, making it more difficult for commanding officers to exert control over some of their personnel.[22] Civilians, after all, cannot be prosecuted at court-martial for going AWOL, challenging the authority of a superior, or acting in a manner "unbecoming" to "an officer and a gentleman." Responding to the entreaties of those who sought greater federal control over the persons who accompany military forces overseas, Congress acted in 2000 to extend federal criminal jurisdiction over the civilians who accompany military forces overseas.[23] Defense Department employees, defense contractors, and dependents of servicemembers or civilian employees are now subject to prosecution in a federal district court for any act committed outside the United States that would be "punishable by imprisonment for more than one year if the conduct had been engaged in within the special maritime and territories jurisdiction of the United States."[24] Previously, the United States could exert only limited jurisdiction outside its borders except through military tribunals, which left only foreign courts to try and punish most crimes of American civilians committed outside the U.S. This change in the federal criminal code might be used to extend the possible jurisdiction of military tribunals over civilians; one provision states that it will not "deprive a court-martial, military commission, provost court, or other military tribunal of concurrent jurisdiction with respect to offenders or offenses that by statute or by the law of war may be tried by a court-martial, military commission, provost court, or other military tribunal."[25] Thus civilians accompanying military forces overseas may eventually be subject to court-martial for alleged criminal acts—even though they do not receive the benefits, preferences, and prestige that their colleagues in uniform can look forward to as veterans.

As much as court-martial jurisdiction grew in the last decades of the twentieth century, the most dramatic expansion of military jurisdiction was President George W. Bush's November 2001 military order sweeping all "suspected terrorists" under the veil of military commissions.[26] The order established military commissions as the exclusive authority to try any person suspected of engaging in terrorist acts or conspiracies against the United States. Military commissions are a more convenient forum in which to prosecute enemies of the state because they are not limited by the same procedural rules as other American courts.[27] They can be convened outside the United States and can prosecute any crime of war. They can be held in secret, defense counsel must be approved by the government, and no appeals are permitted to any civil court. There are no limits on the length of pretrial detention allowed. Some six hundred prisoners held by American forces in Afghanistan and at Guantánamo Bay, Cuba, await release or trial by military commission. Their treatment will become the exemplar of American due process to observers around the world. Now, more than ever, the legacy of the Cold War court-martial has global implications. The military justice system created by the UCMJ and tested in the Korean and Vietnam Wars is now the framework for prosecutions that will likely be among the most hotly contested, intensely scrutinized American criminal trials of the new century.

The extent of military commissions' jurisdiction and legal authority were not clear when President Bush's military order in 2001 resuscitated a legal forum that had fallen into disuse after the 1940s. But there was little doubt that the new military commissions would share the same political and cultural terrain as courts-martial. Military commissions seek to punish foreign war criminals, not American servicemembers, but both criminal courts are freed from the constitutional and practical limitations that constrain civilian courts. Their jurisdiction overlaps; any crime that can by tried by a commission may also be prosecuted at a court-martial.[28] They share a common culture, since the same judge advocates who will prosecute, defend, and preside over commissions were trained at courts-martial. Rules prescribed by the president govern both types of trials.[29] Like the modern court-martial, the new military commissions are rooted in the earlier practice of military law. The United States has relied on military commissions to prosecute suspected spies, terrorists, and other lawbreakers during wars and national emergencies.[30] During the Civil War, military tribunals were used to punish crimes of political revolt and acts of war; after the war, they were a means of swiftly punishing crimes that threatened the newly reconstituted Union.[31] World War II brought military commissions to center stage with the imposition of martial law in Hawai'i and the prosecution of German saboteurs and Japanese officers before American military courts.[32] American military involvement in Korea, Vietnam, Grenada, Panama, the Persian Gulf, Somalia, Haiti, Afghanistan, and Iraq during the last half of the twentieth century did not result in military commissions because the fighting took place outside of American borders, and because local and international criminal tribunals were available to prosecute crimes of war.[33] But amendments to the UCMJ and scholars of military law sought to preserve the nation's authority to convene military commissions into the twenty-first century.[34]

American law has recognized the legal authority of military commissions but has restricted their reach with constitutional and statutory law. Military commissions are manifestations of the war power, the inherent authority of a commanding officer to control a battlefield and keep the peace in occupied territories. Constitutional authority for regulating military commissions is derived from the clauses related to war-making and military governance. Article I of the Constitution grants Congress the power to make the rules that govern the armed forces as well as the power to declare war.[35] But congressional regulation of military tribunals has been incomplete, leaving the executive branch to make most decisions regarding military justice matters. The president's authority to order prosecution by military commissions and to prescribe the rules for both commissions and courts-martial stem from his role as commander-in-chief of the armed forces.[36]

The Constitution is less explicit about the role of the judicial branch in military justice matters, but civilian courts have passed judgment on issues of military justice through petitions for writs of habeas corpus (appeals on the grounds of unlawful detention) and through direct appeal to federal courts. The Supreme Court has permitted military courts wide latitude during times of war, but has imposed some restrictions. During the Civil War, the Court allowed military commissions to operate virtually unchecked. After the war, the Court found its voice, setting sharp new limits on the authority of military courts by holding that a commission lacked the authority to try persons outside a theater of war when the civil courts were open and available.[37] During World War II, however, the Court permitted the execution of Nazi saboteurs convicted by a secret military commission, and after the war, the Court upheld the authority of military commissions to prosecute crimes of war committed by foreign soldiers.[38]

In 2001, when the United States enlisted military commissions in the war on terrorism, the Supreme Court's role in shaping the new tribunals was uncertain. The Bush administration faced questions about the commissions' legitimacy almost immediately, drawing attention to the rules of the commissions, which do not offer the procedural protections guaranteed by the U.S. Constitution, the Geneva Conventions, or the UCMJ.[39] In particular, advocates of international human rights opposed the indefinite detention of uncharged prisoners and the limited access of prisoners to legal counsel. In three cases decided at the end of the Supreme Court's 2004 term, the Court signaled that its deference to military courts, and to executive authority during wartime, may have limits after all. In *Rasul v. Bush*, the Court ruled that federal courts have jurisdiction to hear writs of habeas corpus filed by detained foreign enemy combatants; in *Hamdi v. Rumsfeld*, that detainees have a right to challenge their detentions as "enemy combatants" before a "neutral decision-maker."[40] While the Court declined to reach the merits of the third case, *Rumsfeld v. Padilla*, the trio of Guantánamo Bay cases made clear that the civilian judiciary would help to define military due process in the future.[41]

Just as courts-martial in the Cold War asserted U.S. dominance, resolve, and authority, the new military commissions will project American power and values. The paradoxes of the Cold War court-martial, which sometimes defended the nation at the cost of individual rights, will again be on display in the military commissions of the war on terrorism. The United States has demonstrated great faith in its uniformed lawyers by entrusting them with the responsibility to exact justice from the legal and political chaos of terrorism. Experience tells us that this faith is not misplaced, but that we ought to watch closely if justice is to result. Judge advocates and commanding officers will fare better if civilian oversight, scholarly debate, and public engagement return to American military affairs. Balancing the defense of the nation, the rule of law, and the violence of war will be no easier in twenty-first-century military commissions than it was at Cold War courts-martial.

ACKNOWLEDGMENTS

My journey through twentieth-century military justice was made possible by the support of many archivists, teachers, friends, and colleagues. Librarians at Yale, Columbia, and Rutgers, and many government libraries guided my research with skill and patience. I am especially grateful to Adrienne Cannon at the Library of Congress, Geir Gundersen and Helmi Raaska at the Gerald R. Ford Library, David Haight at the Dwight D. Eisenhower Presidential Library, Gary W. LaValley at the United States Naval Academy, Daniel C. Lavering at the Judge Advocate General's Library in Charlottesville, and Mike Parrish at the Lyndon Baines Johnson Library and Museum. I was able to take advantage of these library collections because of generous support from many sources. At Yale University, these included the Center for the Study of Race, Inequality, and Politics, the Fund for Lesbian and Gay Studies, the International Security Studies Program, and the Olin Center for Law, Economics, and Public Policy. Additional support came from the American Historical Association's Littleton-Griswold grant in legal history and research grants from the Dwight D. Eisenhower Foundation, the Gerald R. Ford Foundation, and the LBJ Foundation. For sharing their memories and records of military justice, I appreciate the cooperation of the Honorable Robert L. Carter, the Honorable Herbert M. Donaldson, Kristin Booth Glen, and Victor Rabinowitz.

Rutgers School Law School in Camden supported my work in many ways, none more crucial than the sabbatical that I used to complete this manuscript. Rutgers also provided research funds, engaged colleagues, interested students, and a collegial atmosphere in which to work. I am grateful to Debbie Carr, Angela Forte, Celia Hazel, Kaeko Jackson, MaryAnn Purvenas and the rest of the Rutgers staff for their indispensable help; to Nicole Papanier and Harshal Purohit for research assistance; and to Perry Dane, Jay Feinman, Dennis Patterson, Ray Solomon, and the junior faculty colloquium for improving the substance of my work.

My understanding of military justice and its role in American history and law grew as I presented parts of this book to various groups. For their encouragement and insight, I am indebted to audiences at the North Carolina Law Review Symposium on Treason and Loyalty, the "Sexual Worlds, Political Cultures" conference sponsored by the Social Science Research Council, the Center for the Study of Sexual Minorities in the Military at the University of California at Santa Barbara, faculty workshops at Benjamin N. Cardozo School of Law and Villanova Law School, and many other scholarly conferences. I am grateful to Judith Reppy, Mary Katzenstein, Carol Burke, Cynthia Enloe, and many other scholars of military life whom I met through a Peace Studies Program at Cornell University sponsored by the Ford Foundation; to my colleagues at the University of Pennsylvania, the United States Air Force Academy, Yale University and Law School, and Rutgers School of Law at Camden; to the Honorable Andrew S. Effron, Robert C. Mueller, and Stephen D. Smith at the United States Court of Appeals for the Armed Forces, who introduced me to military justice; to Jean-Christophe Agnew, Jon Butler, John Demos, William N. Eskridge, Jr., Abraham S. Goldstein, Robert W. Gordon, David Montgomery, Gaddis Smith, Vicki Schultz, Reva Siegel, and Stuart Schwartz, who saw me through the intellectual and practical complexities of a joint degree program.

Nancy F. Cott guided my dissertation with grace and insight; I could not have found a more generous or thoughtful adviser. Other friends and scholars also provided critical help, including Aaron Belkin, Margot Canaday, George Chauncey, Skip Delano, Mary Dudziak, Drew Faust, Lorry Fenner, Eugene R. Fidell, Laura Kalman, Alice Kaplan, Alexander Keyssar, Jonathan Lurie, Wendell Pritchett, Charles Rosenberg, Barbara Savage, Michael Sherry, Ed Stein, Bob Strassfeld, Barbara Welke, and Marilyn Young. The generosity and support of Linda K. Kerber and Leisa Meyer, historians of American military policy and law themselves who took time to push my arguments further, were especially important to the development of this work. Brigitta van Rheinberg at Princeton University Press shepherded the manuscript through a process that made it a far better book. I am grateful to Brigitta, Alison Kalett, the Press's anonymous readers, and the series editors, especially Julian Zelizer, for their astute comments and patience.

For their love and support, I wish to thank my family and friends, old and new, especially Robert Blaine Lutes, Mary O'Neil Lutes, Jean Marie Lutes, the Baden-Lasars, Nick Simon, and the many Duekers who have enriched my life, especially Alice, Elena, and Vivian. Jean Marie has been my first, fastest, and best reader; I could not have written this book without her, and I cannot thank her enough. Alice gave me more than I can say—in fact, she gave me everything not mentioned above that I needed to finish this book. For the joy and wonder they brought into our lives, I thank Elena and Vivian. This book is dedicated to Vivian, who is now fast asleep in her crib next door, oblivious to the clicking of my keyboard and, I hope, having dreams of things far happier and less complicated than the stories told in these pages.

APPENDIX A

ABBREVIATIONS IN CITATIONS

A.B.R.	Army Board of Review
A.C.M.R.	Army Court of Military Review
A.F.B.R.	Air Force Board of Review
A.F.C.M.R.	Air Force Court of Military Review
C.G.B.R.	Coast Guard Board of Review
C.G.C.M.R.	Coast Guard Court of Military Review
C.M.A.	Court of Military Appeals
C.M.R.	*Court-Martial Reports*, volumes of published military appellate opinions from 1951 through 1975
MCM	*Manual for Courts-Martial*, first published in 1951, revised edition in 1969
M.J.	*Military Justice Reporter*, volumes of published military appellate opinions after 1975
N.B.R.	Navy-Marine Corps Board of Review
N.C.M.R.	Navy-Marine Corps Court of Military Review

APPENDIX B

TABLE B.1
U.S. Armed Forces Personnel and Courts-Martial, 1913–1980

	Personnel				Courts			
Year	Total	Army	Navy and Marine Corps	Air Force	General	Special	Summary	Total
1913	175,305	92,756	82,549		6,876	12,817	49,563	69,256
1914	159,854	98,544	61,310		6,285	11,577	44,601	62,463
1915	170,901	106,754	64,147		7,032	13,655	48,004	68,691
1916	175,308	108,399	66,909		6,290	12,283	44,172	62,745
1917	526,174	421,467	104,707		9,612	13,906	85,075	108,593
1918	2,833,251	2,395,742	437,509		17,297	31,681	224,979	273,957
1919	1,320,450	851,624	468,826		22,237	47,662	227,420	297,319
1920	383,485	204,292	179,193		10,635	28,563	74,797	113,995
1921	230,725	230,725	140,000		10,605	24,410	52,178	87,193
1922	247,709	148,763	98,946		8,092	21,247	31,352	60,691
1923	216,428	133,243	83,185		5,464	16,934	23,947	46,345
1924	228,276	142,673	85,603		6,875	15,593	19,008	41,476
1925	222,993	137,048	85,945		7,355	16,891	20,174	44,420
1926	217,066	134,938	82,128		6,900	15,047	18,897	40,844
1927	217,761	134,829	82,932		6,704	13,715	17,141	37,560
1928	220,094	136,084	84,010		7,355	14,815	17,551	39,721
1929	223,561	139,118	84,443		6,130	13,463	17,443	37,036
1930	224,648	139,378	85,270		6,090	11,708	17,006	34,804
1931	223,080	140,516	82,564		4,908	12,057	16,800	33,765
1932	215,668	134,957	80,711		3,646	11,360	15,807	30,813
1933	217,282	136,547	80,735		2,138	9,176	13,518	24,832
1934	216,724	138,464	78,260		1,983	8,452	12,836	23,271
1935	220,996	139,486	81,510		1,668	7,150	12,030	20,848
1936	254,390	167,816	86,574		1,965	7,115	11,589	20,669
1937	276,328	179,968	96,360		2,451	7,137	11,057	20,645

(continued)

TABLE B.1 (*Continued*)
U.S. Armed Forces Personnel and Courts-Martial, 1913–1980

Year	Personnel				Courts			
	Total	Army	Navy and Marine Corps	Air Force	General	Special	Summary	Total
1938	322,488	185,488	137,000		3,057	7,869	11,442	22,368
1939	333,839	189,839	144,000		2,310	7,692	12,159	22,161
1940	457,023	269,023	188,000		2,151	8,131	18,641	28,923
1941	1,093,000	1,462,315	338,000		3,688	13,626	26,298	43,612
1942	2,775,183	3,075,608	783,183		7,935	63,510	93,530	164,975
1943	7,274,273	6,994,472	2,050,273		22,939	183,799	259,383	466,121
1944	10,963,969	7,994,750	3,456,969		34,914	307,376	407,011	749,301
1945	11,986,497	8,267,958	3,855,497		52,604	260,380	376,922	689,906
1946	6,110,756	1,891,011	1,294,756		55,839	79,759	140,200	275,798
1947	2,008,714	991,285	591,714		18,575	73,085	168,321	259,981
1948	1,058,180	554,030	504,150		15,141	60,854	137,068	75,995
1949	1,611,887	660,473	535,540	419,347	12,520	57,004	131,812	201,336
1950	1,499,094	593,167	455,817	411,277	9,759	60,132	146,020	215,911
1951	2,807,681	1,531,774	929,300	788,381	8,463	59,597	135,026	203,086
1952	3,591,493	1,596,419	1,056,232	938,261	12,767	94,890	165,370	273,027
1953	3,557,252	1,533,815	1,043,659	977,593	17,121	98,506	183,677	299,304
1954	3,386,534	1,404,598	949,588	959,946	16,074	91,902	151,930	259,906
1955	2,885,119	1,109,296	865,865	909,958	14,148	76,868	125,299	216,315
1956	2,844,401	1,025,778	870,705	947,918	12,177	65,990	109,417	187,584
1957	2,795,798	997,994	877,969	919,835	9,078	64,741	111,144	184,963
1958	2,600,581	898,925	830,500	871,156	6,741	54,333	100,341	161,415
1959	2,504,310	861,964	801,911	840,435	4,318	39,584	82,220	126,122
1960	2,476,435	873,078	788,605	814,752	3,288	39,260	80,270	122,818
1961	2,483,771	858,622	803,998	821,151	2,786	42,534	82,153	127,473
1962	2,807,819	1,066,404	857,390	884,025	2,667	45,415	88,311	136,393
1963	2,697,689	975,155	853,890	868,644	2,888	44,981	64,621	112,490

1964	2,728,003	972,445	856,914	855,802	2,717	40,850	32,134	75,701
1965	2,704,661	968,313	864,196	823,633	2,298	40,274	30,270	72,842
1966	2,991,077	1,199,784	1,006,921	887,353	2,089	39,593	27,182	68,864
1967	3,364,391	1,442,498	1,036,888	897,494	2,746	54,129	27,608	84,483
1968	3,487,653	1,570,343	1,072,709	904,850	3,498	61,435	24,626	89,559
1969	3,476,700	1,512,169	1,085,640	862,353	3,712	77,659	28,074	109,445
1970	3,216,540	1,322,000	952,000	791,349	4,173	58,615	28,794	91,582
1971	2,869,857	1,124,000	835,000	755,000	4,053	43,611	29,403	77,067
1972	2,505,587	811,000	786,000	726,000	3,109	28,654	24,462	56,225
1973	2,303,098	801,000	760,000	691,000	2,676	26,344	18,767	47,787
1974	2,178,301	783,000	735,000	644,000	2,718	30,319	14,372	47,409
1975	2,133,741	784,000	731,000	612,000	2,527	25,427	12,899	40,853
1976	2,091,741	779,000	716,000	585,000	2,344	18,770	9,654	30,768
1977	2,071,181	782,246	722,000	570,000	1,713	14,040	8,959	24,712
1978	2,060,708	771,000	721,000	569,000	1,495	13,036	7,467	21,998
1979	2,024,000	758,000	707,000	559,000	1,684	12,204	9,270	23,158
1980	2,050,000	777,000	715,000	558,000	1,967	13,803	10,516	26,291

Source: Annual Reports of the Judge Advocates General (Washington, DC: Department of Defense, 1913 to 1980), supplemented by additional figures collected in Leslie Gervaise Gale, "Crime and Military Organization: A Service Comparison of Rates of Adjudicated Crime in the Armed Forces of the United States" (Ph.D. diss., State University of New York-Buffalo, 1969); Louis Ephriam Hicks, "The Effect of Technology on Social Control in U.S. Military Organizations: Trends in Court-Martial Rates from 1917 to 1991" (Ph.D. diss., University of Maryland, 1994); and Daniel Aloysius Lennon, "Naked Power and Dressed Judges: A Sociological Description of the U.S. Army Legal System, 1917–1984" (Ph.D. diss., Northeastern University, 1988).

Note: Because of limitations in the precision of these statistics, the tables should be viewed as guides to the number of courts-martial rather than exact figures. Court-martial statistics were collected for fiscal years rather than calendar years in most of the annual reports, but some calendar years totals are included. The Army reported only the total number of courts-martial that took place ir 1960 rather than the number of each type, so the data in table B.1 reflects my estimates (based on the average of the 1959 and 1961 rates, applied tc the total number of courts-martial in 1960) of the number of general, special, and summary courts that took place in 1960. Likewise, from 1934 to 1938 I interpolated the number of special and summary courts-martial in the Army, since only the number of general courts-martial was reported. Data is unavailable for courts-martial in the Navy and Marine Corps during the years 1921, 1940, and 1941. Only the total number of general courts convened in fiscal year 1952 was reported; I interpolated the values for summary and special courts for those years in order to represent them on the charts and in the tables. In the Navy and Marine Corps tables, the statistics prior to 1951 count "deck" courts-martial as summary and "summary" as special courts-martial. This categorization permits rough comparison of the pre-UCMJ naval rates of courts-martial with both the Army courts held before the UCMJ and the post-UCMJ courts held in all of the services.

TABLE B.2
Court-Martial Rates of the Armed Forces and Service Branches, 1913–1980

Year	Armed Forces General	Armed Forces Special	Armed Forces Summary	Armed Forces Total	Army General	Army Special	Army Summary	Army Total	Navy-Marine Corps General	Navy-Marine Corps Special	Navy-Marine Corps Summary	Navy-Marine Corps Total	Air Force General	Air Force Special	Air Force Summary	Air Force Total
1913	39.2	73.1	282.7	395.1	64.1	4.3	520.3	588.6	20.2	150.6	118.3	289.1				
1914	39.3	72.4	279.0	390.8	45.8	2.5	393.2	441.5	27.9	157.0	126.3	311.2				
1915	41.2	79.9	280.9	401.9	48.1	2.7	405.1	455.9	26.4	173.5	110.7	310.6				
1916	35.9	70.1	252.0	357.9	56.2	4.1	429.0	489.3	23.1	151.4	93.9	268.5				
1917	18.3	26.4	161.7	206.4	46.4	19.8	374.0	440.2	17.9	95.3	57.1	170.3				
1918	6.1	11.2	79.4	96.7	50.0	23.6	383.2	456.8	11.3	38.7	29.9	79.9				
1919	16.8	36.1	172.2	225.2	43.8	19.9	349.5	413.1	12.1	49.5	38.3	100.0				
1920	27.7	74.5	195.1	297.3	18.4	9.3	187.7	215.4	21.6	126.8	82.8	231.2				
1921	46.0	105.8	226.2	377.9	5.2	6.2	88.5	99.8	18.0	127.0	90.0	235.0				
1922	32.7	85.8	126.6	245.0	19.4	28.7	245.9	294.1	16.4	128.4	101.0	245.8				
1923	25.3	78.2	110.7	214.1	33.1	28.6	293.5	355.2	13.9	117.7	85.8	217.4				
1924	30.1	68.3	83.3	181.7	34.3	32.1	174.1	240.5	25.7	105.8	63.7	195.2				
1925	33.0	75.8	90.5	199.2	43.5	57.4	143.6	244.5	21.9	109.2	70.3	201.4				
1926	31.8	69.3	87.1	188.2	32.3	53.6	126.2	212.1	15.9	104.9	64.9	185.8				
1927	30.8	63.0	78.7	172.5	32.7	45.8	95.0	173.6	17.9	99.2	64.4	181.5				
1928	33.4	67.3	79.7	180.5	39.9	54.8	103.1	197.8	19.2	102.8	58.9	180.9				
1929	27.4	60.2	78.0	165.7	41.4	47.6	100.5	189.6	15.0	91.4	55.6	162.0				
1930	27.1	52.1	75.7	154.9	38.7	40.7	87.5	166.9	13.9	71.0	48.1	133.0				
1931	22.0	54.1	75.3	151.4	42.2	45.4	92.6	180.2	10.5	75.7	45.2	131.4				
1932	16.9	52.7	73.3	142.9	34.9	41.3	91.6	167.9	8.6	66.7	43.1	118.4				
1933	9.8	42.2	62.2	114.3	35.2	40.5	92.6	168.4	5.7	62.5	39.2	107.4				
1934	9.2	39.0	59.2	107.4	28.8	41.3	93.0	163.1	5.0	55.6	36.2	96.9				
1935	7.6	32.4	54.4	94.3	21.9	44.3	91.4	157.5	3.2	38.0	30.1	71.4				
1936	7.7	28.0	45.6	81.3	12.3	30.2	75.8	118.3	2.6	35.7	23.6	61.8				
1937	8.9	25.8	40.0	74.7	11.5	28.0	70.0	113.3	2.4	32.5	21.3	56.2				
1938	9.5	24.4	35.5	69.4	10.1	26.0	65.0	107.8	2.6	28.2	17.8	48.6				
1939	6.9	23.0	36.4	66.4	10.4	24.0	60.0	91.3	1.8	25.5	18.4	45.8				
1940	4.7	17.8	40.8	63.3	12.4	23.0	57.0	84.6	1.6	19.7	13.3	34.6				
1941	3.4	12.5	24.1	39.9	14.6	22.0	53.0	84.7	0.9	10.9	7.4	19.2				
1942	2.9	22.9	33.7	59.5	10.8	21.1	50.1	82.0	5.3	32.0	35.4	72.7				
1943	3.2	25.3	35.7	64.1	6.9	16.5	60.0	83.3	4.0	32.3	33.5	69.8				

Year																
1944	3.2	28.0	37.1	68.3	4.5	13.1	31.5	49.2	3.5	29.9	33.2	66.6				
1945	4.4	21.7	31.5	57.6	1.9	19.3	33.0	54.2	7.0	22.0	26.4	55.4				
1946	9.1	13.1	22.9	45.1	2.8	22.5	36.5	61.8	15.3	22.7	29.8	67.8				
1947	9.3	36.4	83.8	129.4	3.0	27.2	38.9	69.1	14.5	48.9	120.4	183.8				
1948	14.3	57.5	129.5	71.8	3.2	21.6	33.8	58.6	11.1	47.2	109.6	167.9				
1949	7.8	35.4	81.8	124.9	7.5	10.5	21.1	39.0	10.3	47.3	107.4	165.0	3.5	15.6	51.7	70.9
1950	6.5	40.1	97.4	144.0	7.0	31.1	68.5	106.7	8.7	53.0	121.4	183.1	2.6	13.7	54.9	71.1
1951	3.0	21.2	48.1	72.3	17.2	66.9	147.6	231.8	2.1	26.2	34.1	62.5	1.6	9.9	30.5	42.0
1952	3.6	26.4	46.0	76.0	8.4	38.2	80.1	126.7	3.0	26.0	38.0	69.0	1.6	14.7	37.7	54.1
1953	4.8	27.7	51.6	84.1	7.5	48.0	107.8	163.3	3.7	27.7	46.6	77.9	2.2	14.4	35.3	51.9
1954	4.8	27.1	44.9	76.8	4.8	25.1	72.7	102.7	4.2	29.3	50.2	83.8	2.0	10.3	25.8	38.1
1955	4.9	26.6	43.4	75.0	5.1	34.5	57.0	96.5	2.9	25.0	42.5	70.4	1.9	10.3	28.5	40.7
1956	4.3	23.2	38.5	66.0	7.3	36.2	65.5	108.9	2.9	23.0	35.6	61.5	2.0	10.0	29.3	41.3
1957	3.3	23.2	39.8	66.2	6.9	36.7	53.8	97.4	2.4	24.4	38.8	65.6	1.5	9.3	28.3	39.1
1958	2.6	20.9	38.6	62.1	8.9	41.3	56.4	106.7	1.9	24.4	41.3	67.5	1.6	6.9	24.0	32.5
1959	1.7	15.8	32.8	50.4	7.6	35.5	49.4	92.5	1.3	18.4	38.4	58.1	1.0	5.4	19.3	25.8
1960	1.3	15.9	32.4	49.6	5.6	34.8	51.2	91.6	1.0	20.1	37.6	58.7	0.7	5.1	18.1	23.8
1961	1.1	17.1	33.1	51.3	4.2	31.3	50.2	85.7	0.6	19.4	36.0	56.0	0.5	4.2	18.5	23.2
1962	1.0	16.2	31.5	48.6	2.8	23.5	40.9	67.2	0.6	18.4	34.1	53.1	0.3	3.4	17.6	21.3
1963	1.1	16.7	24.0	41.7	2.2	22.1	41.1	65.4	0.6	18.4	26.6	45.7	0.6	3.2	11.0	14.8
1964	1.0	15.0	11.8	27.8	2.2	27.3	44.3	73.9	0.5	16.1	12.6	29.2	0.5	3.2	5.2	8.8
1965	0.9	14.9	11.2	26.9	1.8	25.0	40.8	67.5	0.4	15.2	12.8	28.4	0.5	2.8	2.6	5.9
1966	0.7	13.2	9.1	23.0	1.9	27.1	33.1	62.2	0.4	14.5	11.9	26.8	0.3	2.1	1.4	3.7
1967	0.8	16.1	8.2	25.1	1.8	24.0	16.7	42.5	0.5	16.9	12.9	30.3	0.3	2.1	1.1	3.5
1968	1.0	17.6	7.1	25.7	1.5	24.4	16.8	42.7	0.8	14.9	11.4	27.0	0.3	2.0	1.0	3.3
1969	1.1	22.3	8.1	31.5	1.3	21.1	12.8	35.2	0.9	15.0	12.0	27.9	0.4	2.0	0.9	3.2
1970	1.3	18.2	9.0	28.5	1.3	24.3	9.3	34.9	1.4	16.1	14.0	31.5	0.3	2.4	0.6	3.3
1971	1.4	15.2	10.3	26.9	1.6	28.9	7.6	38.1	1.1	16.4	16.9	34.4	0.3	2.5	0.4	3.2
1972	1.2	11.4	9.8	22.4	1.6	39.0	9.3	49.9	1.1	12.5	14.4	28.0	0.3	3.1	0.3	3.7
1973	1.2	11.4	8.2	20.8	1.8	28.1	10.2	40.0	1.0	13.5	14.9	29.4	0.4	3.3	0.2	3.8
1974	1.3	13.9	6.6	21.8	2.3	21.9	11.7	35.9	0.8	17.6	12.2	30.6	0.4	4.0	0.2	4.6
1975	1.2	11.9	6.1	19.2	2.1	16.7	13.0	31.8	0.9	18.3	11.9	31.1	0.3	2.5	0.1	3.0
1976	1.1	9.0	4.6	14.7	1.9	16.3	8.6	26.8	0.9	15.0	10.6	26.5	0.4	1.9	0.1	2.4
1977	0.8	6.8	4.3	11.9	2.3	18.5	6.7	27.5	0.5	11.3	9.6	21.5	0.3	1.4	0.0	1.8
1978	0.7	6.3	3.6	10.7	2.1	13.3	5.2	20.6	0.5	10.2	7.8	18.5	0.2	1.6	0.0	1.8
1979	0.8	6.0	4.6	11.4	1.9	8.8	2.5	13.2	0.4	10.3	9.8	20.5	0.3	1.7	0.1	2.1
1980	1.0	6.7	5.1	12.8	1.5	6.5	2.5	10.5	0.5	11.3	9.8	21.6	0.5	2.3	0.1	2.8

Source: Calculated from the data collected in Table B.1.

TABLE B.3
Women in the United States Armed Forces, 1945–1979

Year	Officers	Enlistees and Officer Candidates	Army	Navy	Marine Corps	Air Force
1945	82,772	183,484	155,870	92,021	18,365	
1948	7,982	6,476	8,095	4,030	167	2,166
1949	8,536	9,545	9,277	5,131	353	3,320
1950	8,455	13,614	10,982	5,193	580	5,314
1951	13,958	25,667	17,853	9,458	2,065	10,249
1952	15,174	30,760	17,434	11,268	2,462	14,770
1953	14,436	31,049	15,261	11,644	2,662	15,918
1954	12,801	25,799	12,594	13,218	2,502	13,286
1955	11,373	23,818	12,938	8,643	2,248	11,362
1956	11,175	22,471	12,646	8,066	1,747	11,187
1957	11,212	20,961	11,730	7,668	1,617	11,158
1958	10,809	20,367	11,464	7,247	1,645	10,820
1959	10,822	20,896	12,168	7,723	1,826	10,001
1960	10,772	20,778	12,542	8,071	1,611	9,326
1961	10,784	21,287	12,811	8,672	1,612	8,976
1962	11,168	21,045	13,074	8,666	1,697	8,776
1963	10,556	20,215	12,144	8,216	1,698	8,713
1964	10,609	19,186	11,730	7,741	1,448	8,876
1965	10,647	19,963	12,236	7,862	1,581	8,841
1966	11,293	21,296	13,322	8,196	1,832	9,239
1967	12,619	22,554	14,483	8,521	2,311	9,858
1968	13,344	25,053	15,807	8,696	2,780	11,114
1969	13,183	26,323	15,878	8,636	2,727	12,265
1970	13,102	28,377	16,724	8,683	2,418	13,654
1971	12,907	29,868	16,865	8,801	2,259	14,850
1972	12,636	32,397	16,771	9,442	2,359	16,491
1973	12,775	42,627	20,736	12,628	2,288	19,750
1974	13,140	61,575	30,715	17,030	2,738	24,232
1975	13,596	83,272	42,295	21,174	3,186	30,213
1976	14,169	97,584	49,611	23,004	3,452	35,686
1977	15,292	103,674	51,790	23,255	3,928	39,993
1978	16,715	117,597	56,841	25,292	5,085	47,094
1979	18,959	132,123	62,017	29,402	5,960	53,703

Source: Selected Manpower Statistics, FY 1979 (Washington, DC: Department of Defense, 1979). Note that this table follows the military practice of including officer candidates in the enlisted force total.

NOTES

INTRODUCTION

1. For the Korean War case, see William T. Bowers, William M. Hammond, and George L. MacGarrigle, *Black Soldier, White Army: The 24th Infantry Regiment in Korea* (Washington, DC: Center for Military History, U.S. Army, 1996), 185–86. The other cases described are *United States v. Hooper*, 26 C.M.R. 417 (1958); *United States v. Charity*, 11 C.M.R. 621 (N.B.R. 1953); *United States v. England*, 44 C.M.R. 142 (1971).

2. On the need for scholarly study of substantive military criminal law in the twentieth century, see Andrew S. Effron, "Military Justice: The Continuing Importance of Historical Perspective," *Army Lawyer* (June 2000): 1–10; on how the practice of segregating court-martial opinions from those of civilian courts in legal publications contributes to an unnecessary gulf between military and civilian law, see Eugene R. Fidell, "If a Tree Falls in the Forest . . . : Publication and Digesting Policies and the Potential Contribution of Military Courts to American Law," *JAG Journal* 32 (1982): 1–29.

3. The articles of the *Military Law Review* (1958–1975), the *Naval JAG Journal* (1951–1975), the *U.S.A.F. JAG Bulletin* (1959–1964), later named the *U.S.A.F. JAG Law Review* (1964–1975), and the *Army Lawyer* focus primarily on issues of legal doctrine and practice, with nearly all articles written by practicing military attorneys. For the historians who have studied military justice, see the works of Jonathan Lurie and William T. Generous, Jr., cited below, and the scholars cited in chapter 1, infra.

4. For harsh criticism of the military justice system, see, e.g., Robert Sherrill, *Military Justice Is to Justice as Military Music Is to Music* (New York: Harper and Row, 1970); Luther C. West, *They Call It Justice: Command Influence and the Court-Martial System* (New York: Viking, 1977); Michael I. Spak, "Military Justice: The Oxymoron of the 1980s," *California Western Law Review* 20 (1984): 436–65.

5. Bipolar politics were the order of the day throughout this period, but as historian John Lewis Gaddis has pointed out, the Cold War is best viewed not as a single historical moment but as a global conflict with a start, a middle, and an end. John Lewis Gaddis, *We Now Know: Rethinking Cold War History* (New York: Oxford University Press, 1997). The post–World War II legal reforms that set the tone for military crime and punishment during the Cold War did not stagnate through the challenges that the Korean War, the uncertain peace that followed, and the Vietnam War posed to the military justice system.

6. The Cold War continued after the Vietnam War, but the armed forces took on a different role in the political and social climate of the last decades of the twentieth century. On Americans' failed efforts to sustain the "victory culture" of World War II, see Tom Engelhart, *The End of Victory Culture: Cold War America and the Disillusioning of a Generation* (New York: BasicBooks, 1995). On the military service of Americans during World War II, see, e.g., Samuel Andrew Stouffer et al.,

eds., *The American Soldier*, 2 vols, (New York: J. Wiley, 1949); Martin L. van Creveld, *Fighting Power: German and U.S. Army Performance, 1939–1945* (Westport, CT: Greenwood Press, 1982); Leisa D. Meyer, *Creating G.I. Jane: Power and Sexuality in the Women's Army Corps during World War II* (New York: Columbia University Press, 1996).

7. See, e.g., Morris Janowitz, *The Professional Soldier: A Social and Political Portrait* (Glencoe, IL: Free Press, 1960), 15, focusing on the demographics of the officer corps in particular.

8. On post–World War II culture and politics, see generally John P. Diggins, *The Proud Decades: America in War and Peace, 1941–1960* (New York: Norton, 1988); David Halberstam, *The Fifties* (New York: Villard, 1993); Taylor Branch, *Parting the Waters: America in the King Years, 1954–1963* (New York: Simon and Schuster, 1988); Mary L. Dudziak, *Cold War Civil Rights: Race and the Image of American Democracy* (Princeton: Princeton University Press, 2000); Elaine Tyler May, *Homeward Bound: American Families in the Cold War Era* (New York: BasicBooks, 1988); David Savran, *Taking It Like a Man: White Masculinity, Masochism, and Contemporary American Culture* (Princeton: Princeton University Press, 1998).

9. See, infra, afterword for an overview of military law and justice between 1973 and 2001, when terrorist attacks on the World Trade Centers and the Pentagon led to new prominence for military courts as a means of trying suspected terrorists.

10. Approximately three million courts-martial were held between 1951 and 1973, when the draft ended and a largely conscript military gave way to an all-volunteer force. The Uniform Code of Military Justice, 64 Stat. 108 (1950), became effective on May 31, 1951; the last serviceman to be drafted in the final draft call of the twentieth century began service on June 30, 1973. See Janice H. Laurence and Peter F. Ramsberger, *Low-Aptitude Men in the Military: Who Profits, Who Pays?* (New York: Praeger, 1991), 63. For my calculations of the number of courts-martial, see appendix B.

11. The best single study of the UCMJ itself is William T. Generous, Jr., *Swords and Scales: The Development of the Uniform Code of Military Justice* (Port Washington, NY: Kennikat Press, 1973). See also Jonathan Lurie, *Arming Military Justice: The Origins of the United States Court of Military Appeals, 1775–1950* (Princeton: Princeton University Press, 1992), 127–49; Walter T. Cox III, "The Army, the Courts, and the Constitution: The Evolution of Military Justice," *Military Law Review* 118 (1987): 1–30; Edmund M. Morgan, "The Background of the Uniform Code of Military Justice," *Vanderbilt Law Review* 6 (1953): 169–85. The official documentation surrounding the adoption of the code has also been published; see *Index and Legislative History: Uniform Code of Military Justice* (Washington, DC: 1950) and *Report of Committee on a Uniform Code of Military Justice to the Secretary of Defense* (Washington, DC: 1949).

12. That is, during the Civil War, 1861–65; World War I, 1917–18; and World War II, 1941–45.

13. Engelhardt, *The End of Victory Culture*, 75.

14. See generally Michael S. Sherry, *In the Shadow of War: America since the 1930s* (New Haven: Yale University Press, 1995); and James Patterson, *Grand Ex-*

pectations: The United States, 1945–1975 (New York: Oxford University Press, 1996).

15. Robert Buzzanco, *Masters of War: Military Dissent and Politics in the Vietnam Era* (New York: Cambridge University Press, 1996), 13–19.

16. Engelhardt, *The End of Victory Culture*, 78–79.

17. Flag Day and Loyalty Day were other militaristic holidays; see Richard M. Fried, *The Russians are Coming! The Russians are Coming! Pageantry and Patriotism in Cold-War America* (New York: Oxford University Press, 1998), ix and 88–89.

18. Ibid., 90.

19. Ibid.

20. See Engelhardt, *The End of Victory Culture*, 75, on the military's influence on television; see 175–77 on G.I. Joe.

21. On the militarization of the United States in the twentieth century, see Sherry, *In the Shadow of War.*

22. On civilian criminal law, see generally Lawrence M. Friedman, *Crime and Punishment in American History* (New York: BasicBooks, 1993); Eric M. Monkkonen, *Crime, Justice, and History* (Columbus: Ohio State University Press, 2002).

23. On the domestic war against communism, see, e.g., Stanley Kutler, *The American Inquisition: Justice and Injustice in the Cold War* (New York: Hill and Wang, 1982); Ron Robin, *The Making of the Cold War Enemy: Culture and Politics in the Military-Intellectual Complex* (Princeton: Princeton University Press, 2001); Stephen J. Whitfield, *The Culture of the Cold War*, 2nd ed. (Baltimore: Johns Hopkins University Press, 1996); Ellen Schrecker, *Many Are The Crimes: McCarthyism in America* (Boston: Little, Brown, 1998); Engelhardt, *The End of Victory Culture*, 69–174.

CHAPTER 1
NEW RIGHTS, OLD HIERARCHIES

1. "The military system can say this for itself: It *knows what it wants*, and it systematically *goes in and gets it.* Civilian criminal justice does not even know what it wants; much less does it resolutely go in and get anything. Military justice wants *discipline*—that is, action in obedience to regulations and orders; this being absolutely necessary for prompt, competent, and decisive handling of masses of men." John Henry Wigmore, "Lessons from Military Justice," *Journal of the American Juridical Society* 4 (1921): 151, quoted in Charles M. Schiesser and Daniel H. Benson, "Modern Military Justice," *Catholic University Law Review* 19 (1970): 489–519. Italics appear in the quotation.

2. For an analysis of post–World War II recruiting strategies, see Mark R. Grandstaff, "Making the Military American: Advertising, Reform, and the Demise of an Antistanding Military Tradition, 1945–1955," *Journal of Military History* 60 (1996): 299–323.

3. See, e.g., Kenneth Allard, *Command, Control, and the Common Defense*, rev. ed. (Washington, DC: National Defense University, 1996), 125–39.

4. Source of troop strength figures is *Selected Manpower Statistics*, published annually by the Department of Defense.

5. See e.g., Allan R. Millett and Peter Maslowski, *For the Common Defense: A Military History of the United States of America*, rev. ed. (New York: Free Press, 1994), 494–569; see also Clay Blair, *The Forgotten War: America in Korea, 1950–1953* (New York: Times Books, 1987).

6. Morris Janowitz, *The Professional Soldier: A Social and Political Portrait* (Glencoe, IL: Free Press, 1960), 182.

7. See, e.g., Margot A. Henriksen, *Dr. Strangelove's America: Society and Culture in the Atomic Age* (Berkeley and Los Angeles: University of California Press, 1997), 36.

8. The military's interest in testing its recruits was crucial in the rise of standardized testing in the United States. See Nicholas Lemann, *The Big Test: The Secret History of the American Meritocracy* (New York: Farrar, Straus, and Giroux, 1999), 70–80.

9. Millett and Maslowski, *For the Common Defense*, 506.

10. Ibid.

11. See John D'Emilio, "The Homosexual Menace: The Politics of Sexuality in Cold War America," in Kathy Peiss and Christina Simmons, eds., *Passion and Power: Sexuality and History* (Philadelphia: Temple University Press, 1989), 226–40.

12. See Allan Berubé, *Coming Out under Fire: The History of Gay Men and Women in World War Two* (New York: Plume, 1990), 228–54; Rhonda R. Rivera, "Our Straight-Laced Judges: The Legal Position of Homosexual Persons in the United States," *Hastings Law Journal* 30 (1979): 799–955, 837–55; William N. Eskridge, Jr., "Privacy Jurisprudence and the Apartheid of the Closet, 1946–1961," *Florida State University Law Review* 24 (1997): 703–838. See also Robinson O. Everett, *Military Justice in the Armed Forces of the United States* (Harrisburg, PA: Military Service Publishing, 1956), 4 (explaining the similar security threats that drug addicts and homosexuals posed to youth).

13. On attempts to assert parental control, see James Gilbert, *A Cycle of Outrage: America's Reaction to the Juvenile Delinquent in the 1950s* (New York: Oxford University Press, 1986); William Graebner, *Coming of Age in Buffalo: Youth and Authority in the Postwar Age* (Philadelphia: Temple University Press, 1989).

14. See George Q. Flynn, *The Draft, 1940–1973* (Lawrence: University of Kansas Press, 1993), 110–33 and 164; see also John O'Sullivan and Alan M. Meckler, comps., *The Draft and Its Enemies: A Documentary History* (Urbana: University of Illinois Press, 1974), 156–219.

15. See, e.g., Janowitz, *The Professional Soldier*, 38–40; Paul R. Schratz, ed., *Evolution of the American Military Establishment since World War II* (Lexington, VA: George C. Marshall Research Foundation, 1978).

16. On conscription and military personnel policies in general, see Flynn, *The Draft*; Charles C. Moskos, Jr., *The American Enlisted Man: Rank and File in Today's Military* (New York: Russell Sage Foundation, 1970); Robert K. Fullinwider, ed., *Conscripts and Volunteers: Military Requirements, Social Justice, and the All-Volunteer Force* (Totowa, NJ: Rowman and Allanheld, 1983).

17. See Mark R. Grandstaff, *Foundation of the Force: Air Force Enlisted Personnel Policy, 1907–1956* (Washington, DC: Air Force History and Museums Program, 1997), chapter 3. For an analysis of Air Force recruiting patterns and the merits

of an all-volunteer force, see Douglas A. Patterson and James A. Hoskins, *The Air Force, Conscription, and the All-Volunteer Force* (Maxwell Air Force Base, AL: Air University Press, 1987).

18. Grandstaff, *Foundation of the Force*, 99.

19. Ibid., 108. The distribution plan ended up distributing recruits by race, as well as educational background, among the services, which may have been its intention in the first place. See Morris J. MacGregor, Jr., *Integration of the Armed Forces, 1940–1965* (Washington, DC: Center for Military History, U.S. Army, 1981), 395, quoting observers who believed that the plan was a racial redistribution operation and noting that statistics supported that conclusion, since the plan spread African American troops among the Navy and the Air Force as well as the Army. The Army's difficulty in recruiting compared to the other services continued after the end of the Vietnam War. In 2004, the *New York Times* reported that the personnel demands of the war in Iraq had led the Army to offer financial incentives to servicemembers about to leave the Navy and Air Force in an effort to attract more qualified persons into the Army. The plan was called "Operation Blue to Green" for the change in the colors of the uniforms that it entailed. See Eric Schmitt, "Other Services Eyed by Army for Recruiting," *New York Times*, July 9, 2004.

20. See Christian G. Appy, *Working-Class War: American Combat Soldiers and Vietnam* (Chapel Hill: University of North Carolina Press, 1993), 32–33.

21. Ibid.; see also Marilyn B. Young, *The Vietnam Wars, 1945–1990* (New York: HarperCollins, 1991), 320, quoting Moynihan.

22. Appy, *Working-Class War*, 33.

23. Thirty-seven percent were sent into combat positions. See Paul Starr, with James Henry and Raymond Bonner, *The Discarded Army: Veterans after Vietnam* (New York: Charterhouse, 1973), 192. See also Janice H. Laurence and Peter F. Ramsberger, *Low-Aptitude Men in the Military: Who Profits, Who Pays?* (New York: Praeger, 1991) which concludes that the military did little to help two groups of underprivileged men: the Project 100,000 men (1966–1971) and the "ASVAB Misnorming" men, who were admitted to the Army between 1976 and 1980 because of an error in scoring an Army aptitude test. See also Thomas G. Sticht, William B. Armstrong, Daniel T. Hickey, and John S. Caylor, *Cast-off Youth: Policy and Training Methods from the Military Experience* (New York: Praeger, 1987).

24. See table P25.5, *Selected Manpower Statistics* (Washington, DC: 1967), 37; table P25.5, *Selected Manpower Statistics FY 1979* (Washington, DC: 1979), 107–8.

25. The Department of Defense data does not begin reporting age until 1956; see table P25.1, *Selected Manpower Statistics, FY 1979*, 100–101.

26. See table P25.3, *Selected Manpower Statistics* (1967), 39. Women were not included in these figures.

27. See Jeanne Holm, *Women in the Military: An Unfinished Revolution*, rev. ed. (Novato, CA: Presidio Press, 1992), 149–53.

28. For statistics, see tables P25.62 through P25.65, *Selected Manpower Statistics, FY 1979*, 115–21. On women in the Marine Corps, see Mary V. Stremlow, *A History of Women Marines, 1946–1977* (Washington, DC: History and Museums Division, U. S. Marine Corps, 1986).

29. See tables P25.62 through P25.65, *Selected Manpower Statistics, FY 1979*, 115–21.

30. Robert J. Stevenson, "The Officer-Enlisted Distinction and Patterns of Organizational Reaction to Social Deviance in the U.S. Military," *Social Forces* 68 (1990): 1191–1210, 1197.

31. Ibid.

32. See, for example, Susan Jeffords's argument about the stress that Vietnam placed on the desired masculine authority of the military in *The Remasculinization of America: Gender and the Vietnam War* (Bloomington: Indiana University Press, 1989).

33. Until the late 1960s, military policies prevented women from remaining in the service if they married. See, e.g., Jean Ebbert and Marie-Beth Hall, *Crossed Currents: Navy Women from WWI to Tailhook* (Washington, DC: Brassey's, 1993), 175–77.

34. A concerted effort to integrate women into the military legal corps did not begin until the 1970s, although there were a handful of female judge advocates and law specialists during the 1950s and 1960s. The first Judge Advocate General of the Navy, Rear Admiral Ira H. Nunn, spurned women as potential judge advocates, following earlier naval leaders who had rejected qualified women who volunteered for their legal training programs in 1950. The first woman to serve as a Navy lawyer was Mary McDowell, a WAVE (the acronym for female Navy officers: Women Accepted for Volunteer Emergency Service) who had served in legal billets during World War II and eventually became a law specialist in 1952. McDowell was the first woman general court-martial law officer and the first female captain in the Navy JAG corps. See Jay M. Siegel, *Origins of the Navy Judge Advocate General's Corps: A History of Legal Administration in the United States Navy, 1775–1967* (Washington, DC: 1997), 525 and appendix O, "Women in the Navy Judge Advocate General's Corps," A-153 to A-160.

35. For a summary of the injustices catalogued after World War II, see Robert J. White, "The Uniform Code of Military Justice—Its Promise and Performance, the First Decade, 1951–1961: A Symposium, the Background and the Problem," *St. John's Law Review* 35 (1961): 197–214.

36. In recognition of these injustices, and in response to adverse publicity, the War Department appointed a Clemency Board headed by Supreme Court Justice Roberts to examine all World War II general courts-martial. See Herman L. Goldberg and Frederick A. C. Hoefer, "The Army Parole System," *Journal of Criminal Law and Criminology* 40 (1949): 158–69; "Collateral Attack on Courts-Martial in Federal Courts," *Yale Law Journal* 57 (1948): 483–89, 488.

37. Quotation is from *Beets v. Hunter*, 75 F. Supp. 825 (1948), cited in George A. Spiegelberg, "Special Committee on Military Justice," *American Bar Association Journal* (January 1949). This case involved a soldier in the Third Armored Division in Europe who was convicted of raping a German girl; the opinion quoted above granted the soldier's habeas corpus petition on due process grounds, freeing him from imprisonment at the United States Disciplinary Barracks at Fort Leavenworth, Kansas.

38. The impetus behind the UCMJ is not entirely clear in existing accounts of its adoption, largely because most historians of military justice have been more in-

terested in the insider story of military-legal change than the larger historical framework. William T. Generous, for example, credits the individuals who championed the new code, while Frederick Bernays Wiener—an accomplished historian of military justice, a staunch defender of most things military, and ardent critic of the UCMJ—dismisses the reforms of the UCMJ as "a manifestation of the urge to unify that was then widespread." See William T. Generous, Jr., *Swords and Scales: The Development of the Uniform Code of Military Justice* (Port Washington, NY: Kennikat Press, 1973); Frederick Bernays Wiener, "American Military Law in the Light of the First Mutiny Act's Tricentennial," *Military Law Review* 126 (1989): 1–43, 35. Personalities, and even the "urge to unify" to which Wiener attributed the UCMJ, were keys to the reform effort, but the impulse to curb the abuses of arbitrary justice, both perceived and actual, also had deeper roots in American society and culture.

39. The Navy and Marine Corps had been governed by the Articles for the Government of the Navy (AGN), which Siegel's history of Navy judge advocates points out had not changed "since Cromwell's time" (Siegel, *Origins of the Navy Judge Advocate General's Corps*, 504), as had the Coast Guard during times of war. The Army and Air Force had used the Articles of War. See Jonathan Lurie, *Arming Military Justice: The Origins of the United States Court of Military Appeals, 1775–1950* (Princeton: Princeton University Press, 1992), for a thorough review of the pre-UCMJ systems of criminal law.

40. See 64 Stat. 108 (1950) for the UCMJ itself. President Truman signed the code into law on May 5, 1950, and it became effective one year later, on May 31, 1951. The *Manual for Courts-Martial*, 1951, was the responsibility of the executive branch of government. The Court of Military Appeals was not an Article III court under the Constitution, but a creation of statute (the UCMJ). Its judges were appointed by the president, subject to congressional approval, for terms of fifteen years. See Lurie's two-volume history of the court, *Arming Military Justice* and *Pursuing Military Justice: The History of the United States Court of Appeals for the Armed Forces, 1951–1980* (Princeton: Princeton University Press, 1998); see also John T. Willis, "The United States Court of Military Appeals: Its Origins, Operation, and Future," *Military Law Review* 55 (1972): 39–93.

41. For example, the constitutional right to specificity in criminal statutes, based on the presumption that an act cannot be criminal unless clearly stated in a statute prior to its commission, did not affect crime under the UCMJ, nor did the emphasis on a mental element in civilian crimes alter military definitions of criminal conduct. On these developments in civilian courts, see Henry M. Hart, Jr., "The Aims of the Criminal Law," *Law and Contemporary Problems* 23 (1958): 401–41; Herbert L. Packer, "Mens Rea and the Supreme Court," *Supreme Court Review* (1962): 107–52; "The Void-for-Vagueness Doctrine in the Supreme Court," *University of Pennsylvania Law Review* 109 (1960): 67–116; Forrest W. Lacey, "Vagrancy and Other Crimes of Personal Condition," *Harvard Law Review* 66 (1953): 1203–26; Caleb Foote, "Vagrancy-Type Law and Its Administration," *University of Pennsylvania Law Review* 104 (1956): 603–50; Gary V. Dubin and Richard H. Robinson, "The Vagrancy Concept Reconsidered: Problems and Abuses of Status Criminality," *New York University Law Review* 37 (1962): 102–36; Herbert L. Packer, *The Limits of the Criminal Sanction* (Stanford, CA: Stanford University Press, 1968). For recent scholarly assessments, see Louis D. Bilionis, "Process, the

Constitution, and Substantive Criminal Law," *Michigan Law Review* 96 (1998): 1269–1334; John Calvin Jeffries, Jr., "Legality, Vagueness, and the Construction of Penal Statutes," *Virginia Law Review* 71 (1985): 189–245. The civilian judges of the Court of Military Appeals did, however, develop military versions of many civilian legal doctrines. See, e.g., Walter T. Cox III, "The Army, the Courts, and the Constitution: The Evolution of Military Justice," *Military Law Review* 118 (1987): 1–30. The extent of servicemembers' civil rights has been a popular topic of debate among legal scholars; for one important rumination on the civil rights of servicemembers, see Earl Warren, "The Bill of Rights and the Military," *New York University Law Review* 37 (1962): 181–203.

42. Nearly every scholar of military justice has remarked on the dampening effect of legal reform on the court-martial rate, but none have explored the decline in a broader historical context. See, e.g., James B. Jacobs, "Legal Change within the United States Armed Forces since World War II," *Armed Forces and Society* 4 (1978): 391–422; Louis Ephriam Hicks, "The Effect of Technology on Social Control in U.S. Military Organizations: Trends in Court-Martial Rates from 1917 to 1991" (Ph.D. diss., University of Maryland, 1994); Leslie Gervaise Gale, "Crime and Military Organization: A Service Comparison of Rates of Adjudicated Crime in the Armed Forces of the United States," (Ph.D. diss., State University of New York-Buffalo, 1969); William C. Westmoreland and George S. Prugh, "Judges in Command: The Judicialized Uniform Code of Military Justice in Combat," *Harvard Journal of Law and Public Policy* 3 (1980): 1–93.

43. Two million is the most commonly used estimate for the number of World War II courts-martial; another figure often used is 1.7 million. See Lurie, *Arming Military Justice*, 128. Part of the difficulty of finding a precise figure is the question of which years (and months) should be included in the data. For tables of the statistics, see appendix B. I computed a total of 2,070,303 courts-martial from 1942 to 1945. Of that total, the vast majority was the lesser variety of courts-martial that punished relatively minor offenses (special and summary courts-martial and deck courts). Only 118,392 of the 2 million were general courts, the most serious type of military criminal trial. For further data, see Siegel, *Origins of the Navy Judge Advocate General's Corps*, 492, 10–26n; Hicks, "The Effect of Technology"; Gale, "Crime and Military Organization"; and Daniel Aloysius Lennon, "Naked Power and Dressed Judges: A Sociological Description of the U.S. Army Legal System, 1917–1984" (Ph.D. diss., Northeastern University, 1988). The records of the government officials who reviewed petitions of servicemembers convicted at general courts-martial during World War II confirm that a court-martial conviction did not signal the end of a possible military career the way that it came to under the UCMJ. See, e.g., the fifteen boxes of chronologically and alphabetically organized memos in Correspondence Relating to Reviews of General Courts-Martial, Office of the Secretary of the Army, 1947–1952, Record Group 335, National Archives at College Park, MD. Most petitioners were contesting their sentences through the Army Board for Correction of Military Records with the hope of receiving veterans' benefits and erasing the stigma of their dishonorable discharges; most defended their crimes as results of either ill health or youthful indiscretion. Many were repeat offenders who had faced court-martial up to eight times before finally being discharged by a general court.

44. On capital punishment during the war, see Dwight H. Sullivan, "Playing the Numbers: Court-Martial Panel Size and the Military Death Penalty," *Military Law Review* 158 (1998): pp. 1–47, 45n. Slovik, who left his unit repeatedly while it was engaged in combat, remains the only soldier executed for a purely military offense (in his case, desertion) since the Civil War. His case prompted a widely read exposé, William Bradford Huie, *The Execution of Private Slovik: The Hitherto Secret Story of the only American Soldier since 1864 to be Shot for Desertion* (New York: Signet, 1954). For a starkly unsentimental view of this case, see Frederick Bernays Wiener, "Lament for a Skulker," *Combat Forces Journal* 4 (1954): 33.

45. Frederick Bernays Wiener, "The Teaching of Military Law in a University Law School," *Journal of Legal Education* 5 (1953), 475–99.

46. See Generous, *Swords and Scales*, on pre-UCMJ legal reform.

47. From the annual reports of the judge advocates general to Congress and the Department of Defense's annual *Selected Manpower Statistics*; see also Hicks, "The Effect of Technology."

48. See appendix B for figures; see also Gale, "Crime and Military Organizations," fig. 1, 47–48.

49. In 1920, the Army, Navy, and Marine Corps included over 341,000 troops and reported 108,417 courts-martial; in 1980, the Air Force, Army, Navy, and Marine Corps combined for a troop strength of over 2 million yet reported only 26,291 courts-martial. See appendix B for more data.

50. See the annual volumes of *Crime in the United States* (1950–1980); "Developments in the Law: Changes in Prison and Crime Demographics," *Harvard Law Review* 111 (1998): 1875–1904. See also Gale, "Crime and Military Organizations," 89–112, for an extended comparison of civilian and military rates of crime, concluding that the rate in the armed forces has generally been higher than among civilians and attributing the difference to the military's mission of training men to employ violence.

51. On juvenile delinquency during the 1950s, see Gilbert, *A Cycle of Outrage*. For a critique of the emphasis on boys' delinquency rather than girls', see Rachel Devlin, "Female Juvenile Delinquency and the Problem of Sexual Authority in America, 1945–1965," *Yale Journal of Law and the Humanities* 9 (1997): 147–83. On the prosecution of sex crimes after World War II, see George Chauncey, Jr., "The Postwar Sex Crime Panic," in William Graebner, ed., *True Stories from the American Past* (New York: McGraw-Hill, 1993); Estelle B. Freedman, "'Uncontrolled Desires': The Response to the Sexual Psychopath, 1920–1960," in Peiss and Simmons, *Passion and Power*, 199–225; Eskridge, "Privacy Jurisprudence."

52. See Gale, "Crime and Military Organizations," 51–54, for a detailed analysis of the trends around wartime.

53. See, e.g., Hicks, "The Effect of Technology"; see also discussions of the shortages of judge advocates and other legally trained personnel in Siegel, *Origins of the Navy's Judge Advocate General's Corps*; Gary D. Solis, *Marines and Military Law in Vietnam: Trial by Fire* (Washington, DC: History and Museums Division, Headquarters, U.S. Marine Corps, 1989); and *The Army Lawyer: A History of the Judge Advocate General's Corps, 1775–1975* (Washington, DC: 1975).

54. See Westmoreland and Prugh, "Judges in Command."

55. Tom Engelhardt, *The End of Victory Culture: Cold War America and the Disillusioning of a Generation* (New York: Basic, 1995), 76.

56. Ibid., 126.

57. See Generous, *Swords and Scales*, 34–53.

58. See, e.g., Westmoreland and Prugh, "Judges in Command," *Public Policy* 3 (1980): 1–93.

59. For a useful overview of the changes in civilian criminal procedure under the Warren Court, see Morton J. Horwitz, *The Warren Court and the Pursuit of Justice* (New York: Hill and Wang, 1998); for a summary of the most salient distinctions between courts-martial and civilian criminal trials, see Michael I. Spak and Jonathon P. Tomes, "Courts-Martial: Time to Play Taps?" *Southwestern University Law Review* 28 (1999): 481–553, especially 482–511; for the "civilianization" argument, see Edward F. Sherman, "The Civilianization of Military Law," *Maine Law Review* 22 (1970), 3–103.

60. Both anecdotal evidence (virtually all studies of military justice and discipline remark on the youthfulness of offenders) and statistical studies confirm the age and rank profile of most servicemembers tried at court-martial. For example, one study found that 22 percent of Army enlisted men were in the lowest two pay grades in 1969, but that those same pay grades accounted for nearly 70 percent of those charged at special and summary courts. See Paul S. Lermack, "Summary and Special Courts-Martial: An Empirical Investigation," *St. Louis University Law Journal* 18 (1974): 329–79, 336–37. Another study of two major Army posts in the 1970s found that over 70 percent of servicemembers accused at special courts were in the lowest three enlisted grades and over 90 percent of accused persons came from the lowest four enlisted grades. See Patrick J. Mackey, "Exploring the Myths of Military Justice: The Judicial System as It Actually Functions," (Thesis for the Judge Advocate General School, April 1975), 12–13. Theses written for the Army's JAG school are available in the library of the school in Charlottesville, Virginia. Each includes a disclaimer that the views expressed within are the author's alone and do not represent an official statement of policy by the military.

61. See Gale, "Crime and Military Organization," 78–82 for data from 1951 to 1967; see Lermack's figures for 1968–70 at Lermack, "Summary and Special Courts-Martial," 340–41. Though the general trend toward prosecuting military rather than civil offenses is clear, precise categorization of military crime is difficult. Some crimes violated both civil norms and military duties, and some courts-martial involved charges for both civil and military offenses. For an important collection and categorization of military criminal cases and legal process during this period, see Homer E. Moyer, Jr., *Justice and the Military* (Washington, DC: Public Law Education Institute, 1972).

62. Statistics from May 1951 through March 1953 are reported in a joint report of the Judge Advocates General of the Army, Navy, and Air Force and the General Counsel of the Coast Guard. See Report of Board of Officers, Exhibit C, April 2, 1953, Roll 24, Col. Charles L. Decker's Collection of Records Relating to Military Justice and the Revision of Military Law, 1948–1956, Record Group 153, National Archives at College Park, MD. On the 1970s, see Mackey, "Exploring the Myths," 22; Westmoreland and Prugh, "Judges in Command," 1–93.

63. See, for example, David Schlueter's approving quotation of the 1960 Pow-

ell report's description of the discipline/justice conundrum: "It is not proper to say that a military court-martial has a dual function as an instrument of discipline and as an instrument of justice. It is an instrument of justice and in fulfilling this function it will promote discipline." David A. Schlueter, "The Twentieth Annual Kenneth J. Hodson Lecture: Military Justice for the 1990's—A Legal System Looking for Respect," *Military Law Review* 133 (1991): 1–24, 11. For the opposite conclusion, see the many works of Edward F. Sherman including "Military Justice without Military Control," *Yale Law Journal* 82 (1973): 1398–1425.

64. For example, the rules for search and seizure that protected the privacy and property of civilians were not easily applied to servicemembers, whose very persons were subject to intimate inspection. See, e.g., the analysis of the implications of the adoption of the exclusionary rule, which prevents unlawfully obtained evidence from being admitted during a criminal trial, by the military justice system in "Restrictive Developments in the Law of Search and Seizure," *Duke Law Journal* (1960): 275–91.

65. For analysis of the operation of special and summary courts during this period, see my dissertation, Elizabeth Lutes Hillman, "Cold War Crime and American Military Culture" (Ph.D. diss., Yale University, 2001), 79–82.

66. General courts-martial accounted for only 4.4 percent of courts-martial during this period (140,299 out of 3,184,481). Rear Admiral Chester Ward, the Navy's judge advocate general in the late 1950s, sought to eliminate as many general courts as possible, particularly in desertion cases, "where lesser procedures would work better and faster." Siegel, *Origins of the Navy's Judge Advocate General's Corps*, 628. With the help of the Court of Military Appeals, which ruled in 1957 that the offense of desertion required specific intent (thus reducing many charges of desertion to the lesser offense of AWOL), see *United States v. Cothern*, 23 C.M.R. 382 (C.M.A. 1957), "[b]y 1959, Ward had succeeded in reducing the number of general courts by over fifty percent of their 1956 level." Siegel, *Origins of the Navy's Judge Advocate General's Corps*, 628–29. The Powell report, the work of a committee of nine general officers appointed by secretary of the Army Wilber M. Brucker to study military discipline in October 1959, recommended several ways to reduce the court-martial rate. See *Report to Honorable Wilber M. Brucker, Secretary of the Army, by the Committee on the Uniform Code of Military Justice, Good Order and Discipline in the Army* (Washington, DC, January 18, 1960) (hereinafter Powell Report).

67. Lesser military courts such as summary and special courts-martial and alternative disciplinary strategies both deserve scholarly scrutiny as well, but their nuances are beyond my scope.

68. Only general courts and a relatively rare species of the special court-martial could adjudge punitive discharges, which disadvantaged servicemembers after they left the service by denying them veterans' benefits and making employment much more difficult. The rate of general courts-martial increases slightly after 1969 if the number of "BCD-specials," or special courts at which a bad-conduct discharge could be adjudged, are factored in. For such a study, see Westmoreland and Prugh's charts in "Judges in Command," 91–93. Note, however, that the numbers reported as court-martial rates in these charts are the rates per ten thousand servicemembers, not per thousand servicemembers (despite the assertion to the contrary

at 91), which accounts for the order of magnitude difference between my numbers (and those of Hicks and Gale, among others) and those reported by Westmoreland and Prugh.

69. Descriptions of each type of court are set out in the UCMJ, Articles 16 through 20.

70. Soon after, bench trials became the most common form of court-martial. See Solis, *Trial by Fire*, 204; Mackey, "Exploring the Myths," 32, reporting that judge-alone trials were very popular among accused troops in a study of courts-martial during 1972 and 1973 at Fort Knox, where bench trials accounted for 96 percent of courts, and Fort Bragg, where they were 94 percent of the total.

71. See Gale, "Crime and Military Organization," 164, for numerical analysis of the reports from 1951 to 1967. Case reporters published during the years after Gale's study was completed follow the trend, with nearly all reported opinions coming from general courts.

72. See, e.g., Robert J. Stevenson, "The Containment and Expulsion of Wayward Soldiers in the U.S. Military," *Social Science Journal* 25 (2) (1988): 195–210; Gale, "Crime and Military Organization," 43; Edmund M. Morgan, "The Background of the Uniform Code of Military Justice," *Vanderbilt Law Review* 6 (1953): 161–85, 169; Mackey, "Exploring the Myths," 34.

73. Ibid. See also table in Powell Report, 252. A study of AWOL offenders at Fort Meade between 1971 and 1974 reported a conviction rate of 94 percent. See Bruce M. Burchett, "Race and the AWOL Offender: The Effect of the Defendant's Race on the Outcome of Courts-Martial Involving Absence Without Leave" (Ph.D. diss., Carleton University, 1983), 166. Note that these rates were comparable to the conviction rates in some civilian criminal jurisdictions, particularly if guilty pleas are factored into the civil court statistics.

74. There is little disagreement among observers of military justice about common court-martial sentences, but statistics on the sentences imposed at court-martial are hard to come by because of the many opportunities for clemency that were available and because the results of most courts-martial were not reported in published opinions. A joint report of the Judge Advocates General of the Army, Navy, and Air Force and the General Counsel of the Coast Guard stated that from May 1951 through March 1953, 66 percent of all approved Army court-martial sentences involved a punitive discharge and confinement of three years or less. See Report of Board of Officers, Exhibit C, 2 April 1953, Roll 24, Col. Charles L. Decker's Collection of Records Relating to Military Justice and the Revision of Military Law, 1948–1956, Record Group 153, National Archives at College Park, MD. Capital offenses during peacetime were Articles 94 (mutiny or sedition), 99 (misbehavior before the enemy), 100 (subordinate compelling surrender), 102 (forcing a safeguard), 104 (aiding the enemy), 110a (willfully hazarding a vessel), 118 (1) (premeditated murder) and (4) (felony murder), and 120a (rape); during times of war, "escalator" clauses expanded the list to include Articles 85 (desertion), 90 (assaulting or willfully disobeying an officer), 101 (improper use of the countersign), 106 (spying, for which death was mandatory upon conviction), and 113 (misbehavior of a sentinel).

75. See Articles 60 to 76, UCMJ.

76. Article 66, UCMJ.

77. See Article 67, UCMJ. This resulted in about 10 percent of all courts-martial being reviewed by the Court of Military Appeals during the 1950s and 1960s. See George William Jernigan, "The Courts of Military Review: Evolution of Judicial Institutions" (Ph.D. diss., Louisiana State University, 1973), 3.

78. Jernigan's study found very similar rates in the military justice system (85.8 percent of cases of reviewed cases were affirmed) as compared to the federal courts of appeal (82.0 percent affirmed) between 1962 and 1971. He also found that military appellants received sentence reductions at nearly the same rate (14.3 percent of cases) as civilian appellants (15.4 percent). See Jernigan, "The Courts of Military Review," 138.

79. For pre-UCMJ policies, see the records of clemency boards in Folder OSA 334, Clemency Board (1950) and Folder 201-W (1950) in Correspondence Relating to Reviews of General Courts-Martial, Office of the Secretary of the Army, record group 335, National Archives at College Park, MD. On the changes implemented under the UCMJ, see Memorandum from Major General Hubert D. Hoover, USA (ret), Assistant, Office of the Secretary of the Army, June 19, 1952, "Army and Air Force Clemency and Parole Board," explaining the August 1951 policy change (in a Department of the Army letter, dated August 21, 1951, titled "Restoration of Sentenced and Unsentenced Prisoners"), folder 334, Army and Air Force Clemency and Parole, June–December 1952, record group 335, National Archives at College Park, MD. In the same folder, a Memorandum for the Adjutant General of the Army, "Conference on Classification of Prisoners in Disciplinary Barracks," April 30, 1952, notes that "problems encountered in the administration of clemency, restoration, and parole as a result of major changes brought about by the Uniform Code of Military Justice, uniform policies promulgated by the Department of Defense, and the liberalized policy of salvaging all possible manpower through restoration."

80. See Powell Report, 284.

81. See Paul M. Owen, "The Interest of the Armed Forces in Probation and Parole," (Thesis for the Judge Advocate General School, April 1958), 53–57. See Jernigan, "The Courts of Military Review," 141, on Army and Air Force policies; on the other services, see *House of Representatives, Committee on Armed Services, Subcommittee no. 1 Consideration of H.R. 5783 to amend Titles 10, 14, and 37, United States Code, to provide for the confinement and treatment of offenders against the UCMJ* (Washington, DC: May 14, 1968). The bill's "principal purpose . . . [was] to attain uniformity among the Armed Forces in the administration of military correctional facilities and the treatment of persons sentenced to confinement under the UCMJ," 8373.

82. Owen, "The Interest of the Armed Forces," 58 and 124.

83. There are many sets of recidivism and restoration statistics for the Army and Air Force, including monthly reports and comprehensive studies, in Record Group 335, National Archives at College Park, MD. One summary report on recidivism reported that 69 of the 1,837 prisoners who were restored after being sentenced to punitive discharges and confinement between July 1950 and October 1952 were again sentenced to discharge and confinement at court-martial; this computes to a recidivism rate of 3.8 percent. See Memorandum for Brigadier General E. C. McNeil, Special Assistant to the Secretary of the Army, "Recidivism Rate for Army Re-

storees," January 14, 1953, Folder 334, Army and Air Force Clemency and Parole, June–December 1952, Record Group 335, National Archives at College Park, MD.

84. See, for example, Jacobs, "Legal Change," 33n (quoting Major General Reginald C. Harmon, the Judge Advocate General of the Air Force, "who declared that the tremendous increase in undesirable discharges by administrative proceedings was the result of efforts of military commanders to avoid the requirements of the Uniform Code.").

85. An Army judge advocate commenting on the increased use of administrative separations noted the elimination of "[t]he routine cases of ill discipline that clogged courts-martial dockets in the 1950s." See Michael E. Klein, "*United States v. Weasler* and the Bargained Waiver of Unlawful Command Influence Motions: Common Sense or Heresy?" *Army Lawyer* (February 1998): 3–46, 45n. See also Solis, *Trial by Fire*, 132, on the increase in Marine administrative discharges late in the 1960s; Clifford A. Dougherty and Norman B. Lynch, "The Administrative Discharge: Military Justice?" *George Washington Law Review* 33 (1964): 498–528. There were some procedural reforms that affected servicemembers' rights during administrative hearings, including a 1965 Department of Defense regulation that gave those facing an undesirable discharge the right to counsel and gave minority and women servicemembers the right to be judged by at least one member of their own race or sex. See Jacobs, "Legal Change," 394–95. However, these reforms did not satisfy critics of the administrative discharge hearing; see Sam Ervin, "Military Administrative Discharges: Due Process in the Doldrums," *San Diego Law Review* 10 (1972): 9–35.

86. Quoted in Lawrence M. Baskir and William A. Strauss, *Chance and Circumstance: The Draft, the War, and the Vietnam Generation* (New York: Alfred A. Knopf, 1978), 161.

87. See, e.g., Wiener, "Tricentennial," 39–43, especially 43 ("the services were extremely unhappy with what the CMA was doing" by undermining command influence and reducing control of commanders over court-martial results, so they turned to administrative separations: "in actual fact . . . the armed forces were actually on strike against the Uniform Code."); David A. Schlueter, "The Court-Martial: An Historical Survey," *Military Law Review* 87 (1980): 129–66, 161 ("Few commanders are willing to run the risk of an acquitted servicemember returning to the unit and flaunting his 'victory' over the command. . . . The current trend is to use administrative discharges and other remedies rather than a court-martial.").

88. See Starr, *The Discarded Army*, 168–71; see also Bruce M. Burchett, "Race and the AWOL Offender: The Effect of the Defendant's Race on the Outcome of Courts-Martial Involving Absence Without Leave" (Ph.D. diss., Carleton University, 1983), 14–15; Baskir and Strauss, *Chance and Circumstance*, 159–60.

89. See, e.g., Baskir and Strauss, *Chance and Circumstance*, pp. 285–86, 4n, estimating that about 83,000 of over 200,000 "undesirable" discharges issued during the Vietnam War were for unauthorized absences.

90. Lawrence M. Baskir and William A. Strauss, *Reconciliation after Vietnam: A Program of Relief for Vietnam Era Draft and Military Offenders* (Notre Dame, IN: University of Notre Dame Press, 1977), 18; *Chance and Circumstance*, 161; G. David Curry, *Sunshine Patriots: Punishment and the Vietnam Offender* (Notre Dame, IN: University of Notre Dame Press, 1985), 31–33.

91. See Jacobs, "Legal Change," 397, reporting that in July 1966 a new Army regulation created "a discharge for the good of the service," which almost always resulted in an "undesirable" discharge; in 1967, the Army processed 297 of these good-of-the-service discharges; in 1972, it processed 25,465! See Starr, *The Discarded Army*, 167–84; Office of Assistant Secretary of Defense for Manpower and Reserve Affairs, *Types of Discharges Issued to Enlisted Personnel by Fiscal Year, 1950–1972* (Washington, DC, August 31, 1972).

92. See Jacobs, "Legal Change," table 1, 398.

93. See *Hearing Before a Subcommittee of the Committee on Armed Services, U.S. Senate, 87th Cong., 2nd sess. on H.R. 11257, amending sec. 815 (Article 15) of Title 10, U.S. Code, Relating to Nonjudicial Punishment* (Washington, DC, July 17, 1962), 41, noting congressional concern about military leaders' "tendency to circumvent safeguards for the serviceman" established by the UCMJ (hereinafter 1962 nonjudicial punishment hearings); see also Harold L. Miller, "A Long Look at Article 15," *Military Law Review* 27 (1965): 37–108; Jacobs, "Legal Change," 398–99; see generally Generous, *Swords and Scales*.

94. 1962 nonjudicial punishment hearings, 3. Documenting the extent of nonjudicial punishment is difficult because of the records of Article 15 hearings could be removed from a servicemember's personnel file after a period of good behavior. See Miller, "A Long Look at Article 15." The limited statistics reported in Gale's dissertation show an increasing number of Article 15 actions; see also Jacobs's comment in his 1978 article, "Legal Change," 399: "With the increased judicialization of court-martial procedures brought about by the UCMJ, reliance on Article 15 for maintaining good order and discipline is increasing."

95. 1962 nonjudicial punishment hearings, 4897–98.

96. See Lermack, "Summary and Special Courts-Martial," 335–36.

97. See Gale, "Crime and Military Organization," 57, reporting the crime rates of the services in descending order were the Army, Marine Corps, Navy, Air Force, and Coast Guard, and noting that the order is left undisturbed by the addition of figures for nonjudicial punishment for the limited number of years for which that data was available.

98. See Solis, *Trial by Fire*, 231. See also the thoughtful analysis of Marine Corps culture in Thomas E. Ricks, *Making the Corps* (New York: Scribner, 1997), especially 219–27.

99. Gale, "Crime and Military Organization," 135.

100. Gale also makes a related argument about the tendency of more "military" troops to commit a greater number of civil (as opposed to military) offenses, but the data are not as conclusive as in proving the service order of crime. His dissertation asserts that the Army and Marine Corps prosecuted a somewhat higher percentage of civil crimes as compared to military offenses than the other services, and that military crime in general tilted toward civil offenses during the twentieth century. For example, in 1966 and 1967, civil crimes constituted 42 percent of Marine Corps, 44 percent of Navy, and only 17.7 percent of Air Force crimes at court-martial (Gale does not report Army figures for these years). See Gale, "Crime and Military Organization," 82–84. Because the data on the types of crimes punished at special and summary courts are elusive, and because categorizing the types of offenses prosecuted at general courts is so tricky, this argument may be correct, but it has yet to be proven.

101. See Gale's numerical analysis of the Court-Martial Reports from 1951 to 1966 at 108. Gale's compilation of cases reported between 1951 and 1966 reveals that the percentage distribution of crimes against persons (limited to homicide and assault cases) as compared to crimes against property (limited to robbery and larceny cases) was nearly twice as high in the Army as in the Air Force and significantly higher in the Marine Corps than in the Navy. His more detailed analysis of cases for 1966 and 1967 revealed that the Navy and Marine Corps prosecuted larceny, robbery, and burglary at approximately the same rates, but that the Marine Corps prosecuted murder, rape, and assault at rates three to ten times higher than the Navy. See Gale, "Crime and Military Organization," 73–75. Gale's analysis relies on data received in personal correspondence with the Navy, so verifying or expanding the scope of his analysis is not possible. For example, Gale does not include rape and other sexual assaults in the category of crimes against persons; if his analysis were expanded to include those crimes, the percentage of crimes against persons would be even higher as compared to crimes against property. In the introduction to his remarkable dissertation, Gale notes that he compiled the voluminous statistics upon which he relied over a period of many years. Whenever possible, I verified the figures reported in official sources.

102. See Gale, "Crime and Military Organization," Table 7, 75. Similarly, note that burglary was the only crime against property among the four types of civil crimes deemed important enough to note separately in Army and Air Force monthly reports during 1952; the other three were crimes against persons: murder, rape, and aggravated assault. See reports in Army and Air Force Clemency and Parole, January–May 1952, Office of the Secretary of the Army, Folder 334, Record Group 335, National Archives at College Park, MD.

103. On the history of lawyers in uniform, see *The Army Lawyer: A History of the Judge Advocate General's Corps, 1775–1975*; Siegel, *Origins of the Navy Judge Advocate General's Corps*. Siegel's book is a veritable gold mine of information about the leaders and policies of the naval justice system.

104. See Richard B. Cole, "Prosecutorial Discretion in the Military Justice System: Is It Time for a Change?" *American Journal of Criminal Law* 19 (1992): 395–410.

105. UCMJ, Articles 22, 23, and 24 (concerning the authority of a commander to convene a court-martial), 25 (to appoint members of a court-martial), 26 (to appoint the law officer of a general court-martial), 27 (to appoint trial and defense counsel), 28 (to appoint court reporter and interpreter), 32 (to order pretrial investigation and appoint investigating officer), 33 (to forward charges).

106. See Articles 37 and 98, UCMJ. In the code's first three decades of operation, the crime of unlawful command influence was prosecuted only once. See Moyer, *Justice and the Military*, sec. 3–361.

107. UCMJ, Articles 89, 92, and 99; for other military-specific crimes, see Articles 83 (fraudulent enlistment), 84 (unlawful enlistment), 85 (desertion), 86 (AWOL), 87 (missing movement), 88 (contempt toward officials), 90 (assaulting an officer), 94 (mutiny), 98 (noncompliance with procedural rules), 100 (subordinate compelling surrender), 101 (improper use of a countersign), 102 (forcing a safeguard), and 113 (misbehavior of a sentinel). For catch-all articles, see Articles 133 and 134.

108. See Samuel P. Huntington, *The Soldier and the State: The Theory and Politics of Civil-Military Relations* (Cambridge: Harvard University Press, 1957), 74: "The supreme military virtue is obedience." See also Article 92, UCMJ, "Failure to obey order or regulation"; see also Article 90, "Assaulting or willfully disobeying officer," and Article 91, "Insubordinate conduct toward noncommissioned officer."

109. For visual representations of courts-martial, see the training films related to military justice. These films include "General Court Martial," Motion Picture 111-TF-4237, Records of the Office of the Chief Signal Officer, U.S. Army, Record Group 111; "Justice and the Soldier," Motion Picture 111-TF-3294, Records of the Office of the Chief Signal Officer, U.S. Army, Record Group 111; "Nonjudicial Punishment," Motion Picture 342-TF-6789, U.S. Air Force Military Airlift Command, Record Group 342; "Investigation of Narcotic and Dangerous Drug Offenses," Motion Picture 111-TF-4718 (1973), Records of the Office of the Chief Signal Officer, U.S. Army, Record Group 111; "The Code: The U.S Fighting Man's Code of Conduct," Motion Picture 26.228, Record Group 26; "Special Court Martial," Motion Picture 26.607 (1952), Record Group 26; "JAG Corps," Motion Picture 111-LC-40710 (1957), Record Group 111. All films are held in the Motion Pictures, Sound, and Video Unit of the National Archives at College Park, MD. See also the many illustrations in Solis, *Trial by Fire.*

110. See Article 25(d)(1), UCMJ.

111. See Article 51(a), UCMJ.

112. See Article 31, UCMJ. The protections offered by this article, cited approvingly by the Supreme Court in *Miranda v. Arizona*, 384 U.S. 436 (1966), have been much celebrated in military-legal circles. For a cogent account of the history and scope of self-incrimination protection under the UCMJ, see Chief Judge Everett's opinion for the Court of Military Appeals in *United States v. Ravenel*, 26 M.J. 344 (1988). For explanations of the abbreviations used in military court citations, see appendix A.

113. See Article 26(a), UCMJ.

114. See Article 51, UCMJ. On the tension between law officers and the presidents of courts-martial, see the transcript of a 1985 interview, at 119, in the Wilton B. Persons Papers, Senior Officers Oral History Program, Military History Institute, Carlisle Barracks, Carlisle, PA. For background on Persons, see Michael E. Smith, "Major General Wilton Burton Persons, Jr., United States Army (Retired), the Judge Advocate General of the Army (1975–1979)," *Military Law Review* 153 (1996): 177–243.

115. For example, in a 1952 general court-martial of an Army private who had accidentally killed a fellow soldier while on duty in Korea, the Court of Military Appeals ordered a rehearing because the law officer had inappropriately deferred to the president of the court-martial. The president, not the law officer, had ruled on motions at trial, advised the accused of his rights, and taken on an inappropriate judicial role. See *United States v. Berry*, 2 C.M.R. 141 (1952).

116. For example, *United States v. Jones*, 3 C.M.R. 36 (1952) involved an Army private convicted of AWOL at a court-martial in which the president of the court disagreed with the law officer's determination that one of accused's prior convictions was inadmissible. Confusion over the issue hindered the fairness of the trial,

but the court held that any prejudice to the accused was overcome by the reductions in sentence that brought the total years of confinement down from twenty-five years to ten. See Articles 59 to 76, UCMJ, on review of court-martial sentences.

117. For example, Siegel summarizes reaction to the code as follows: "It would be the height of understatement to say only that there was widespread criticism of the Code from the fleet and the field. Commanders thought it was a disaster, that the whole structure of discipline was destroyed. Further, they were being asked to embrace an alien system." Siegel, *Origins of the Navy Judge Advocate General's Corps*, 503. Lurie also points repeatedly to opposition from commanders in the field, characterizing early reaction from senior leadership as "the continued carping of the JAGs about the UCMJ and the USCMA," Lurie, *Pursuing Military Justice*, 64; see also the comments of Air Force and Navy leaders at 93–94. Scholarly criticism of the Court of Military Appeals' decisions abounded as well; see, e.g., William Frachter, "Presidential Power to Regulate Military Justice: A Critical Study of Decisions of the Court of Military Appeals," *New York University Law Review* 34 (1959): 861–90.

118. Joseph Ross, "Military Memoirs: Legal Service in the Navy, Uniform Code of Military Justice," *Experience* 10 (2000): 25, 45–48, at 48, which also notes that the implementation of the code "was a difficult learning experience" for naval officers. Another naval officer reminiscing about courts-martial before the UCMJ remarked that "courts-martial were regarded as an extension of command, and an acquittal was seen as a mark against the disciplinary system for which the senior officers were responsible." Arthur W. Machen, Jr, "Military Memoirs: Legal Service in the Navy, Rocks and Shoals," *Experience* 10 (2000): 24–25, 43–45.

119. See Article 41(b), UCMJ; Siegel, *Origins of the Navy Judge Advocate General's Corps*, 505–06. A peremptory challenge permits counsel to eliminate a potential juror without stating a cause for the dismissal.

120. Quoted in Solis, *Trial by Fire*, 125; for another account of resistance to the Military Justice Act of 1968, see Walter T. Cox, III, "The Twenty-Seventh Annual Kenneth J. Hodson Lecture: Echoes and Expectations; One Judge's View," *Military Law Review* 159 (1999): 183–202, 189.

121. Siegel, *Origins of the Navy Judge Advocate General's Corps*, p. 563, 11–59n.

122. See Lurie's definitive two-volume history of the court, *Arming Military Justice* and *Pursuing Military Justice*.

123. Although military personnel could not be appointed to the Court of Military Appeals, its first judges had extensive military experience, as did nearly all of their successors. As Wiener describes the initial three judges: "Chief Judge Robert E. Quinn had been Governor of Rhode Island and a Judge of its Superior Court; during World War II he had served as a Captain, USNR. Judge George W. Latimer, a Justice of the Supreme Court of Utah when appointed to the CMA, had as a Colonel been Chief of Staff of an Army Infantry Division in the Pacific. Judge Paul W. Brosman, a Professor and Dean at Tulane University Law School, had served as a Lieutenant Colonel in the Army Air Forces." Wiener, "Tricentennial," 236n. For complete information on these and later judges of the court, see Lurie, *Arming Military Justice* and *Pursuing Military Justice*. On the role of the early court, see Lurie; for a judge's well-known assertion of the court's powers, see Paul W. Brosman, "The Court: Freer Than Most," *Vanderbilt Law Review* 6 (1953): 166–68.

124. Disavowing the possibility of imposing external constraints on military procedure, the Supreme Court opined in 1911: "To those in the military or naval service of the United States the military law *is* due process." *Reaves v. Ainsworth*, 219 U.S. 296, 304 (1911).

125. *United States v. Clay*, 1 C.M.R. 74 (1951). Several legal scholars have written on the topic: Seymour Wurfel, "Military Due Process: What Is It?," *Vanderbilt Law Review* 6 (1953): 251–87; Honorable Robert E. Quinn, "The United States Court of Military Appeals and Military Due Process," *St. John's Law Review* 35 (1960–61): 225–54; David A. Schlueter, "The Twentieth Annual Kenneth J. Hodson Lecture: Military Justice for the 1990s—A Legal System Looking for Respect," *Military Law Review* 133 (1991): 1–29, 13–14; Thomas G. Becker, "Games Lawyers Play: Pre-preferral Delay, Due Process, and the Myth of Speedy Trial in the Military Justice System, "*Air Force Law Review* 45 (1998): 1–65, especially 29–31.

126. See *United States v. Jacoby*, 29 C.M.R. 244 (1960); UCMJ, Article 51(c); Paragraph 73(b), *Manual for Courts-Martial*.

127. Later judges of the Court of Military Appeals would rely more directly on the Constitution in justifying the rights granted servicemembers, reflecting the trend toward incorporation (of the protections of the Bill of Rights into the Fourteenth Amendment) and the constitutionalization of criminal procedure that accelerated in the 1960s.

128. For judicial descriptions of the inapplicability of the Bill of Rights to servicemembers tried at court-martial, see the Supreme Court opinions *Burns v. Wilson*, 346 U.S. 137 (1953); *United States ex. rel. Toth v. Quarles*, 350 U.S. 1 (1955); and *Reid v. Covert*, 354 U.S. 1 (1957). The debate over the Bill of Rights and courts-martial engaged many military-legal scholars as well as judges; see Gordon D. Henderson, "Courts-Martial and the Constitution: The Original Understanding," *Harvard Law Review* 71 (1957): 293–324; Frederick Bernays Wiener, "Courts-Martial and the Bill of Rights: The Original Practice I," *Harvard Law Review* 72 (1958): 1–49; Frederick Bernays Wiener, "Courts-Martial and the Bill of Rights: The Original Practice II," *Harvard Law Review* 72 (1958): 266–304. See also Joseph W. Bishop, Jr., "Constitutional Rights of Servicemembers before Courts-Martial," *Columbia Law Review* 64 (1964): 127–49.

129. U.S. Constitution, Article I, sec. 8; Article II, secs. 1, 2 and 3; Amendment V. For a concise analysis of the constitutional origins of courts-martial, see William Winthrop, *Military Law and Precedents*, 2nd ed. (Washington, DC: 1920), 15–16.

130. See, e.g., *Mapp v. Ohio*, 367 U.S. 643 (1961) (holding that the Fourth Amendment exclusionary rule applied to the states); *Robinson v. California*, 370 U.S. 660 (1962) (holding the Eighth Amendment's prohibition against cruel and unusual punishment applied to the states); *Gideon v. Wainwright*, 372 U.S. 335 (1963) (holding the Sixth Amendment right to counsel applied to the states); *Miranda v. Arizona*, 384 U.S. 436 (1966) (holding the Fifth Amendment right against self-incrimination applied to the states); *Duncan v. Louisiana*, 391 U.S. 145 (1968) (holding the Sixth Amendment right to jury trial applied to the states).

131. See, e.g., *United States v. Burney*, 21 C.M.R. 98 (1956); *United States v. Cates*, 26 C.M.R. 260 (1958); *United States v. Jacoby*, 29 C.M.R. 244 (1960);

United States v. Culp, 33 C.M.R. 411 (1963); *United States v. McKenzie*, 34 C.M.R. 141 (1964); *United States v. Schalck*, 34 C.M.R. 151 (1964); *United States v. Crawford*, 35 C.M.R. 3 (1964); *United States v. Tempia*, 37 C.M.R. 249 (1967).

132. The "harmless error" doctrine, which prevented a conviction from being reversed in cases of technical error that did not prejudice the substantial rights of an accused servicemember, had long been part of military justice; see Wiener, "Tricentennial," 45.

133. For examples of procedural errors, see Joseph W. Bishop, Jr., "Court-Martial Jurisdiction over Military-Civilian Hybrids: Retired Regulars, Reservists, and Discharged Prisoners," *University of Pennsylvania Law Review* 112 (1964): 317–77, citing "a list of horrible examples" of command influence in particular from congressional hearings held in 1962; Wiener, "Tricentennial," at 40–41, describing seven "worst cases" through 1962 in which the CMA reversed a board of review that had upheld despite a particularly egregious procedural error. Both of these authors drew their examples from the detailed testimony recorded in the 1962 nonjudicial punishment hearings. On shortages of judge advocates, see Siegel, *Origins of the Navy Judge Advocate General's Corps* and *The Army Lawyer: A History of the Judge Advocate General's Corps*.

134. Siegel, *Origins of the Navy Judge Advocate General's Corps*, 631; on the Marine Corps, see Solis, *Trial by Fire*, 11.

135. *United States v. Fisher*, 24 C.M.R. 206 (1957), cited by Siegel, *Origins of the Navy Judge Advocate General's Corps*, 537. The inexperience of military trial lawyers was again a concern in the 1990s armed forces, because of the declining number of courts-martial. See John S. Cooke, "The Twenty-Sixth Annual Kenneth J. Hodson Lecture: Manual for Courts-Martial 20X," *Military Law Review* 156 (1998): 1–51, 13; Transcript of a 1988 interview, at 115, in the Burton Ellis Papers, Senior Officers Oral History Program, Military History Institute, Carlisle Barracks, Carlisle, PA.

136. Siegel, *Origins of the Navy Judge Advocate General's Corps*, 634–36.

137. James L. Spratt, *Military Trial Techniques* (Dallas: American Guild Press, 1956). For another 1950s guide to military law intended for nonspecialists, see Robinson O. Everett, *Military Justice in the Armed Forces* (Harrisburg, PA: Military Service Publishing Co., 1956).

138. Solis, *Trial by Fire*, 51.

139. Siegel, *Origins of the Navy Judge Advocate General's Corps*, 627.

140. See Sherman, "The Civilianization of Military Law," especially 45–59. For an excellent summary of post-UCMJ changes to military criminal law, see Jacobs, "Legal Change."

141. Extensive hearings were held by the House and Senate Armed Services Committees on topics related to military justice in 1962, 1965, 1966, 1968, 1971, and 1972, on topics ranging from the effects of administrative discharges and the proper utilization of female servicemembers to the desertion rate. Each year after 1955 also included a hearing on the number of servicemembers tried in foreign criminal courts under the Status of Forces Agreement (SOFA). The Government Accounting Office (GAO) joined the Department of Defense and the individual branches of service in reporting on perceived shortcomings and inefficiencies of military personnel and disciplinary policies.

142. See, e.g., George William Jernigan, "The Courts of Military Review: Evolution of Judicial Institutions" (Ph.D. diss., Louisiana State University, 1973), 84.

143. See Lurie, *Pursuing Military Justice* for an in-depth analysis of the political and legislative difficulties of making changes during the 1950s and into the 1960s. For a discussion of the changes adopted in 1962, see also Bishop, "Constitutional Rights of Servicemembers before Courts-Martial," 145–48.

144. On the Air Force, see 1962 nonjudicial punishment hearings, 4. Naval leaders echoed this sentiment; see Siegel, *Origins of the Navy Judge Advocate General's Corps*, 629, 12–24n.

145. See *Military Justice Act of 1968, Public Law 90–632, 82 Stat. 1335.* For a summary and analysis of the 1968 reforms, which were advanced by a staunch supporter of military justice reform, North Carolina Senator Samuel Ervin, Jr., see Kenneth Hodson, "The Military Justice Act," *Judge Advocate Journal* 47 (1970): 31–38; Wiener, "Tricentennial," 63–64; Samuel Ervin, "The Military Justice Act of 1968," *Wake Forest Intramural Law Review* 5 (1969): 223–43.

146. See Eugene R. Fidell, "Going on Fifty: Evolution and Devolution in Military Justice," *Wake Forest Law Review* 32 (1997): 1213–34, 1214.

147. See Jacobs, "Legal Change," 409; see also Wiener's discussion of what he terms "insensate antimilitarism" reflected in several proposed, but ultimately rejected, reform bills in "Tricentennial," 68–69.

CHAPTER 2
DISCIPLINING THE COLD WAR ARMED FORCES

1. The Court of Military Appeals recognized this tension, and sometimes upheld convictions despite procedural error at trial. See, e.g, *United States v. Marshall*, 6 C.M.R. 54 (1952), in which the court upheld two privates' convictions for rape and dismissed all of their legal claims—but then remarked that the record of trial was "brief, almost summary," evidence of "the lack of effort on the part of defense counsel and a lack of appreciation for the rights of these accused."

2. See *Selected Manpower Statistics* (Washington, DC: 1967), table P28.2, 151; Allan R. Millett and Peter Maslowski, *For the Common Defense: A Military History of the United States of America*, rev. ed. (New York: Free Press, 1994), 527 and 570.

3. See William C. Westmoreland and George S. Prugh, "Judges in Command: The Judicialized Uniform Code of Military Justice in Combat," *Harvard Journal of Law and Public Policy* 3 (1980): 1–93, 55, 147n, commenting on the volume of general courts held during the Korean War. The authors speculate without offering evidence (in support of their thesis that the UCMJ cannot work during wartime) that many more cases should have been brought to trial during the conflict in Korea but were not because of "the Code provisions or some judicial gloss or interpretation."

4. See appendix B. The total number of courts reported by the Army, Air Force, Navy, and Marine Corps from 1950 to 1954 was 991,328, with 48,110 general courts. This includes some trials that took place before the implementation of the UCMJ on May 31, 1951.

5. See Gary D. Solis, *Marines and Military Law in Vietnam: Trial by Fire* (Wash-

ington, DC: History and Museums Division, Headquarters, U.S. Marine Corps, 1989), 22–24, on the prevalence of "quick draw" cases during Vietnam.

6. For a useful overview and bibliography concerning the effects of Vietnam on the American military, see Millett and Maslowski, *For the Common Defense*, 570–606.

7. Atrocities during the Korean War were publicized in articles carried by newspapers around the country as the fiftieth anniversary of the outbreak of war in Korea passed. For a book-length account, see Charles J. Hanley, Sang-Hun Choe, and Martha Mendoza, *The Bridge at No Gun Ri* (New York: Henry Holt, 2001). See also Christopher D. Booth, "Prosecuting the 'Fog of War?': Examining the Legal Implications of an Alleged Massacre of South Korean Civilians by United States Forces during the Opening Days of the Korean War in the Village of No Gun Ri," *Vanderbilt Journal of Transnational Law* 33 (2000): 933–86. For atrocities during Vietnam, see, e.g., Christian G. Appy, *Working-Class War: American Combat Soldiers and Vietnam* (Chapel Hill: University of North Carolina Press, 1993), 268–72; Michal R. Belknap, *The Vietnam War on Trial: The My Lai Massacre and the Court-Martial of Lieutenant Calley* (Lawrence: University of Kansas Press, 2002); David L. Anderson, ed., *Facing My Lai: Moving beyond the Massacre* (Lawrence: University of Kansas Press, 1998); Michael Bilton and Kevin Sim, *Four Hours in My Lai* (New York: Viking, 1992); Peter Karsten, *Law, Soldiers, and Combat* (Westport, CT: Greenwood, 1978); William George Eckhardt, "My Lai: An American Tragedy," *University of Missouri-Kansas City Law Review* 68 (2000): 671–703; Gary D. Solis, *Son Thang: An American War Crime* (Annapolis: Naval Institute Press, 1997); Roger S. Clark, "Medina: An Essay on the Principles of Criminal Liability for Homicide," *Rutgers-Camden Law Journal* 5 (1973): 59–78. For rape in particular, see Susan Brownmiller, *Against Our Will: Men, Women, and Rape* (New York: Simon and Schuster, 1975), 87–118; and *Vietnam Veterans Against the War: The Winter Soldier Investigation* (Boston: Beacon Press, 1972).

8. Jordan J. Paust, "After My Lai: The Case for War Crime Jurisdiction over Civilians in Federal District Courts," *Texas Law Review* 50 (1971): 6–34; Seymour M. Hersh, *My Lai 4: A Report on the Massacre and Its Aftermath* (New York: Random House, 1970).

9. My Lai was not a completely isolated incident. For another American atrocity prosecuted at court-martial, see Solis, *Son Thang*, which recounts the courts-martial of five Marines for murdering Vietnamese civilians in 1970.

10. *United States v. Calley*, 48 C.M.R. 19 (1973).

11. See Bilton and Sim, *Four Hours in My Lai*, introduction. For a similar comment, see a letter urging commutation of a death sentence for a double murder of German nationals from Mrs. Selwyn R. Mack to Sherman Adams, December 26, 1955, asserting that she and her friends "could not understand how the boy from East Aurora could have become such a hardened criminal in two years in the Army and wondered at Army influences on their boys." See White House Central Files, File OF, Box 102, "Court-Martial Cases," in Folder (3)H, Dwight D. Eisenhower Presidential Library, Abilene, KS.

12. For an analysis of war crimes and military discipline in general, see Mark J. Osiel's trenchant criticism in *Obeying Orders: Atrocity, Military Discipline, and the Law of War* (New Brunswick, NJ: Transaction, 1999). For one of many examples

of public frustration with the military's prosecution of crime during war, see a letter from Ohio state senator Francis D. Sullivan to the president, March 15, 1967, complaining that a soldier who was convicted of premeditated murder "should be treated as a hero," not a criminal. White House Central Files, Folder ND 9-6-1, "Courts-martial," March 22, 1967, Lyndon Baines Johnson Library and Museum, Austin, TX.

13. On the superior orders defense, see James B. Insco, "Defense of Superior Orders before Military Commissions," *Duke Journal of Comparative and International Law* 13 (2003): 389–418; Major Michael L. Smidt, "Yamashita, Medina, and Beyond: Command Responsibility in Contemporary Military Operations," *Military Law Review* 164 (2000): 155–234; Gary D. Solis, "Obedience of Orders and the Law of War: Judicial Application in American Forums," *American University International Law Review* 15 (1999): 481–526. For courts-martial involving defense of superior orders during the Korean War, see the cases of servicemen prosecuted for the murder and mistreatment of a captive at *United States v. Kinder*, 14 C.M.R. 742 (1953) and *United States v. Schreiber*, 18 C.M.R. 226 (1955). This incident (which also implicated an Army corporal named Toth) also led to a Supreme Court precedent restricting court-martial jurisdiction over discharged servicemembers; see *Toth v. Quarles*, 350 U.S. 11 (1955). For such cases during the Vietnam War, see, e.g., *United States v. Griffen*, 39 C.M.R. 586 (A.B.R. 1968), pet. denied, 39 C.M.R. 293 (1968); *United States v. Keenan*, 39 C.M.R. 108 (1969). The leading Supreme Court precedent on the defense of superior orders is *In re Yamashita*, 327 U.S. 1 (1946).

14. *United States v. Calley*, 48 C.M.R. 27.

15. In some cases, courts-martial for crimes of political dissent involved testimony about homosexuality; see, e.g., the discussion of *United States v. Northrup*, 31 C.M.R. 599 (A.F.B.R. 1961) in chapter 3, infra.

16. For an explicit description of the stereotypes of gay men within military culture, see the case of an airman convicted of larceny in Morocco in *United States v. Smith*, 28 C.M.R. 782 (A.F.B.R. 1959). The airman's transfer to a Texas retraining facility was delayed by a fellow prisoner's accusation of sodomy—and by a JAG who noted his "falsetto voice and effeminate manner." See also *United States v. Yeast*, 36 C.M.R. 890 (A.F.B.R. 1966), in which a colonel testified that he could identify a "queer" by his slight build, poor health, effeminate appearance, and mannerisms.

17. The "homosexual menace" was a theme of American political culture during the 1950s, driven by growing awareness of homosexuals and concerns that the character flaws of "sexual perverts" made gays vulnerable to treachery or blackmail. John D'Emilio, *Sexual Politics, Sexual Communities: The Making of a Homosexual Minority in the United States, 1940–1970* (Chicago: University of Chicago Press, 1983), 40–53. See also David K. Johnson, *The Lavender Scare: The Cold War Persecution of Gays and Lesbians in the Federal Government* (Chicago: University of Chicago Press, 2004); William N. Eskridge, Jr., "Privacy Jurisprudence and the Apartheid of the Closet, 1946–1961," *Florida State University Law Review* 24 (1997): 703–83; George Chauncey, Jr., "The Postwar Sex Crime Panic," in William Graebner, ed., *True Stories from The American Past* (New York: McGraw-Hill, 1993). For a journalistic narrative of the 1950s persecution of suspected ho-

mosexuals (including veterans of the armed forces) in Sioux City, Iowa, see Neil Miller, *Sex-Crime Panic: A Journey to the Paranoid Heart of the 1950s* (New York: Alyson Books, 2002).

18. See D'Emilio, *Sexual Politics, Sexual Communities*, 223–39 (1983); *MCM*, Table of Maximum Punishments, 223.

19. See *MCM*, para. 204, 367.

20. *United States v. Parker*, 33 C.M.R. 111, 112–13 (1963). This case is further analyzed in chapter 4, infra.

21. *United States v. Warren*, 20 C.M.R. 135, 137 (1955).

22. *United States v. Bennington*, 31 C.M.R. 151, 152 (1961).

23. *United States v. Parker*, 33 C.M.R. 111, 13 (1963).

24. *United States v. Doherty*, 17 C.M.R. 287, 294 (1954).

25. *United States v. Bennington*, 31 C.M.R. 151, 153, 155, 157 (1961).

26. Consent to sodomy is frequently unclear in the appellate records; disputes of fact and conflicting testimony were common, as in other types of sexual assault cases. Consent could be especially difficult to discern in cases of officer-enlisted sexual relationships. See infra, chapter 6; see also *United States v. Cain*, 3 C.M.R. 260 (A.B.R. 1951); *United States v. Phillips*, 11 C.M.R. 137 (1953) and 9 C.M.R. 186 (A.B.R. 1952); *United States v. Platt*, 44 C.M.R. 70 (1971). Virtually all cases of *non*forcible sodomy that reached the appellate courts involved homosexual contact. However, women and children were the victims of many incidents of forcible sodomy that were prosecuted at court-martial. I analyze these cases in my dissertation, Elizabeth Lutes Hillman, "Cold War Crime and American Military Culture: Courts-Martial in the United States Armed Forces, 1951–1973" (Ph.D. diss., Yale University, 2001), 293–96.

27. In a 1954 opinion, an Army board explicitly recognized the prejudice attached to prosecution for sodomy in reversing the convictions of an Army sergeant and private first class for consensual homosexual acts because of the prejudice introduced by the joint trial. See *United States v. King*, 17 C.M.R. 423 (A.B.R. 1954).

28. *United States v. Goodman*, 33 C.M.R. 195, 202 (1963).

29. *United States v. Jackson*, 12 C.M.R. 403 (A.B.R. 1953). The appellate court overturned Jackson's conviction on the second charge, ruling it was based on uncorroborated, unclear testimony, but upheld the conviction for making improper remarks to an enlisted man.

30. Jackson's statement, according to the charge at court-martial, was "I would like to crawl into the bag with you because you are a cute kid, but I don't think you could hold my '18' inch dick." 12 C.M.R. 403.

31. *United States v. Moore*, 33 C.M.R. 667 (C.G.B.R. 1963).

32. 33 C.M.R. 668.

33. The dissent takes issue with this definition of "indecency," arguing that if mere exposure of Ellis's buttocks could constitute the crime of indecent exposure, then forcibly restraining Ellis and pretending to mark his exposed body must also be a crime of indecency.

34. On the persistence of such rituals in the modern-day military, see Carol Burke, *Camp All-American, Hanoi Jane, and the High-and-Tight: Gender, Folklore, and Changing Military Culture* (Boston: Beacon Press, 2004); Carie Little Hersh,

"Crossing the Line: Sex, Power, Justice, and the U.S. Navy at the Equator," *Duke Journal of Gender, Law, and Policy* 9: 277–322 (2002). Homoerotic "horseplay" was not unique to the armed forces, of course. Other all-male workplaces evidenced similar cultures. The language in these military cases foreshadows the much later prosecution of same-sex sexual harassment in civilian workplaces. See especially Justice Antonin Scalia's opinion for the Supreme Court in *Oncale v. Sundowner Offshore Services, Inc.*, 523 U.S. 75 (1998), and related commentary in John Davidson Miller III, "Same-Sex Sexual Harassment Is Actionable under Title VII of the Civil Rights Act of 1964: Is This the End of Horseplay as We Know it?" *Seton Hall Law Review* 29 (1998): 787–815; Wendy M. Parr, "When Does Male-on-Male Horseplay Become Discrimination Because of Sex? *Oncale v. Sundowner Offshore Servs., Inc.*," *Ohio Northern University Law Review* 25 (1999): 87–99; Richard F. Storrow, "Same-Sex Sexual Harassment Claims after *Oncale*: Defining the Boundaries of Actionable Conduct," *American University Law Review* 47 (1998): 677–745.

35. In 1957, two Army privates were court-martialed for their role in giving a "GI bath" to another private in the latrine (by spraying urine over a man stripped of his clothes) and later, for forcibly sodomizing him. The two men tried to prevent the other participants from testifying against them, to the extent of smuggling threatening messages from the stockade to potential witnesses, revealing the depth of peer pressure among military units to hide this sort of behavior from superior officers. *United States v. Hayes*, 24 C.M.R. 440 (A.B.R. 1957).

36. *United States v. Marcey*, 25 C.M.R. 444 (1958). The members of the court-martial did not agree with this assessment, and sentenced both men to five years confinement and dishonorable discharges. This was not a unique argument; see *United States v. Polak*, 27 C.M.R. 87 (1958), in which two privates defended a charge of consensual sodomy as "horseplay"; both were sentenced to dishonorable discharges and one-year confinements.

37. In the appellate record, Army soldiers predominate in this category of offenders. One Air Force case appears at *United States v. O'Connell*, 18 C.M.R. 881 (A.F.B.R. 1955); other cases of forcible sodomy against men in the Army include *United States v. Williams*, 13 C.M.R. 438 (A.B.R. 1953); *United States v. Jones*, 13 C.M.R. 420 (A.B.R. 1953); *United States v. Morgan*, 24 C.M.R. 151 (1957); *United States v. Bonnell*, 32 C.M.R. 608 (A.B.R. 1962); *United States v. Greene*, 33 C.M.R. 480 (A.B.R. 1963); *United States v. Harrison*, 41 C.M.R. 595 (A.B.R. 1969); *United States v. Lindsey*, 41 C.M.R. 529 (A.B.R. 1969); *United States v. Rockenbach*, 43 C.M.R. 805 (A.C.M.R. 1971); *United States v. O'Neal*, 48 C.M.R. 89 (A.C.M.R. 1973). In addition, a few appellate records do not specify the sex of the victim of the forcible sodomy charge. See *United States v. Farrell*, 24 C.M.R. 118 (1957); *United States v. Davis*, 41 C.M.R. 217 (1970); *United States v. Falls*, 44 C.M.R. 48 (1971) and 44 C.M.R. 748 (N.C.M.R. 1971).

38. See, e.g., the case of an airman who accidentally suffocated a bunkmate, who had passed out from excessive drinking, in the course of forcibly sodomizing him, *United States v. Breeden*, 13 C.M.R. 805 (A.F.B.R. 1953); an airman charged with a sodomitical assault on a sleeping soldier, *United States v. Butts*, 14 C.M.R. 596 (A.F.B.R. 1954); an Army soldier who defended against a charge of premeditated murder by explaining that he shot only after being assaulted in his sleep, *United*

States v. Turner, 18 C.M.R. 69 (1955); a sleeping assault in the bunks onboard a ship, *United States v. Johnson*, 22 C.M.R. 289 (1957); a Navy petty officer who assaulted sailors in their sleep, *United States v. Goodman*, 33 C.M.R. 195 (1963); an airman who allegedly assaulted a sleeping fellow airman, *United States v. Kindler*, 34 C.M.R. 174 (1964); and a Navy commander who apparently assaulted a number of enlisted men in their sleep and was prosecuted in civilian criminal courts, *Silvero v. Chief of Naval Air Basic Training*, 428 F.2d 1009 (C. A. Fla. 1970).

39. See, e.g., *United States v. Holladay*, 36 C.M.R. 598 (A.B.R. 1966).

40. See, e.g., *United States v. Cockram*, 15 C.M.R. 199 (A.B.R. 1952); *United States v. Barker*, 13 C.M.R. 472 (A.B.R. 1953); *United States v. Young*, 18 C.M.R. 729 (A.F.B.R. 1955); *United States v. Martin*, 24 C.M.R. 156 (1957) and 22 C.M.R. 601 (A.B.R. 1956). On homosexuality in military prisons in general, see *United States v. Parrish*, 24 C.M.R. 345 (A.B.R. 1957); *United States v. Smith*, 28 C.M.R. 782 (A.F.B.R. 1959); *United States v. Matthews*, 38 C.M.R. 430 (1968).

41. See, e.g., *United States v. Barker*, 13 C.M.R. 472 (A.B.R. 1953), in which a prisoner thought to be gay was sodomized with the complicity of the prison guard.

42. *United States v. Miasel*, 24 C.M.R. 184 (1957). The other cases were not reported, but were referred to in the court's opinion. See also *United States v. Miasel*, 22 C.M.R. 562 (A.B.R. 1956).

43. *United States v. Miasel*, 24 C.M.R. 184 (1957), C.M.R. 562 (A.B.R. 1956). The victim's testimony corroborated Miasel's story, but also described being sodomized by three of the prisoners who had been part of Miasel's "joke" during a later assault that took place out of Miasel's presence. A board of review reversed Miasel's conviction (and that reversal was confirmed by the Court of Military Appeals) because evidence of this later assault was admitted into evidence at trial, thus prejudicing Miasel's court-martial panel with information irrelevant to his guilt.

44. As a civilian testified at the trial of an Army major for consensual sodomy, attempting to explain why he consented to the major's sexual advances: "Sometimes when I am under the influence of alcohol, I am homosexual myself." *United States v. Chewning*, 9 C.M.R. 528, 530 (A.B.R. 1953).

45. *United States v. Slaughter*, 23 C.M.R. 478 (A.B.R. 1957).

46. *United States v. Holladay*, 36 C.M.R. 598 (A.B.R. 1966); reversed by 36 C.M.R. 529 (1966).

47. Lesbian sexuality was termed "degrading and disgustingly indecent behavior" in *United States v. Chadd*, 32 C.M.R. 438, 444 (1963); see also *United States v. Enzor*, 40 C.M.R. 707, 711 (A.C.M.R. 1969), characterizing "observation of lesbian sexual practices" as deviant.

48. See Leisa D. Meyer, *Creating G.I. Jane: Power and Sexuality in the Women's Army Corps during World War II* (New York: Columbia University Press, 1996), for an astute analysis of this dynamic in World War II.

49. Jean Ebbert and Marie-Beth Hall, *Crossed Currents: Navy Women from WWI to Tailhook* (Washington, DC: Brassey's, 1993), 189.

50. *United States v. Ortega*, 45 C.M.R. 576 (A.C.M.R. 1972). The evidence did not support a charge of sodomy or attempted sodomy; Ortega and the other private were in bed and partially clothed when they were discovered.

51. Citations omitted; 45 C.M.R. 579.

52. In a concurring opinion, the court's chief judge noted the trends in civilian law that made lack of consent a required element of "deviant sexual activity" between consenting adults, citing the *Report by the President's Commission on Law Enforcement and Administration of Justice* (1967), the American Law Institute's 1962 *Model Penal Code*, and the American Bar Association's statement on the subject. 45 C.M.R. 581.

53. See *United States v. Chadd*, 32 C.M.R. 438 (1963). The Army board of review's opinion was not reported; all facts are taken from the Court of Military Appeals opinion.

54. 32 C.M.R. 439.

55. 32 C.M.R. 440.

56. Ibid.

57. 32 C.M.R. 441.

58. Ibid. In some respects, this reversal made little difference; despite his harsh sentence at the first court-martial, Chadd was restored to duty in July 1962 after completing a retraining program. See 32 C.M.R. 439.

59. *MCM*, 291.

60. 32 C.M.R. 442.

61. 32 C.M.R. 443.

62. 32 C.M.R. 444. In particular, the court notes that "another court-martial would view with extreme interest evidence regarding her supposed degrading and disgustingly indecent behavior" rather than the evidence presented of a trusting young girl, quoting the traditional interpretation of rape embraced by the *Manual for Courts-Martial:* "It is true that rape is a most detestable crime. . . . it must [also] be remembered that it is an accusation easy to be made, hard to be proved, but harder to be defended [against] by the party accused, though innocent.'" *MCM*, 355.

63. "Lesbian-baiting" is well documented in the literature written by and about women veterans. See, e.g., Linda Bird Francke, *Ground Zero: The Gender Wars in the Military* (New York: Simon and Schuster, 1997); Margarethe Cammermeyer and Chris Fisher, *Serving in Silence* (New York: Viking Press, 1994); Michelle M. Benecke and Kirstin S. Dodge, "Military Women: Casualties of the Armed Forces' War on Lesbians and Gay Men," in Craig Rimmerman, ed., *Gay Rights, Military Wrongs* (New York: Garland Press, 1996), 71–108.

64. See, e.g., the ruling of a law officer prohibiting such testimony in the court-martial of six female noncommissioned Army officers at Camp Breckinridge, Kentucky, in 1952, *United States v. Long*, 6 C.M.R. 60 (1952). The servicewomen were charged with threatening and beating up a WAC private who had testified against a friend at a previous court-martial. During the trial, counsel for the defense asked the private "whether she had ever been on her bed under blankets with another WAC." 6 C.M.R. 69. The law officer upheld the prosecution's objection to this line of questioning.

65. See, e.g., *United States v. McAdams*, 22 C.M.R. 356 (A.B.R. 1956), the case of an Army private accused of larceny, AWOL, and other minor offenses who claimed that the victim placed the allegedly stolen money in his pocket while making a sexual advance. In another larceny case that reached the appeals court in 1968, a private argued that he stole from another serviceman because he knew him to be

gay. This time, however, both the law officer and appeals court rejected his effort to introduce evidence of the victim's homosexuality at trial. *United States v. Farmer*, 39 C.M.R. 776 (A.B.R. 1968). See also *United States v. Harris*, 1 C.M.R. 348 (A.B.R. 1951), in which two Army privates were convicted of willful disobedience, which one blamed on his bitterness "toward the Army due to indecent proposals made to him by one of a 'clique' of homosexuals in his company" and because he was assigned to a position that did not suit his skills. These men, members of the all African American 24th Infantry, were punished very harshly (one was initially sentenced to thirty-five years, which was reduced to twenty and then fifteen on appeal) for their crimes, consistent with the NAACP's observation that African American men were treated more severely than white soldiers at Korean War courts-martial. See infra, chapter 5, for further discussion of racism at court-martial.

66. For a case of assault, see *United States v. Smith*, 33 C.M.R. 3 (1963), in which a private in the Army was prosecuted for a fight in the latrine, where he said he had to defend himself against indecent assaults. For murder, in addition to the cases cited below, see the case of an Army corporal who accidentally killed a sergeant in a fight after the sergeant had propositioned him, *United States v. Weems*, 13 C.M.R. 25 (1953); an airman who strangled to death a man who made a pass at him while both were drunk, *United States v. Colerick*, 16 C.M.R. 553 (A.F.B.R. 1954), remanded for rehearing because of an insufficient instruction on self-defense; and *United States v. Wilson*, 22 C.M.R. 368 (A.B.R. 1956), in which an Army private first class defended against a murder charge with a self-defense against forcible sodomy claim. In *United States v. Burns*, 19 C.M.R. 3 (1955), the accused was drinking, was solicited by a friend, rejected the advance, and shortly after beat a sleeping soldier who was in charge of quarters with an "iron furnace shaker handle" because of his anger at the solicitation. For an assault motivated by racist hatred as well as a violent response to an alleged homosexual pass, see *United States v. Hite*, 34 C.M.R. 631 (A.B.R. 1964). Hite's conviction for beating up an African American hitchhiker was overturned on appeal because his rights under Article 31 of the UCMJ, which protected servicemembers against self-incrimination, were violated.

67. See, e.g., *United States v. Baker*, 7 C.M.R. 142 (A.B.R. 1952), in which an Army private was convicted of sodomy and attempted murder after he hit his sexual partner, who was discharged for homosexuality himself shortly after the incident, in the head with a rock; *United States v. Hise*, 42 C.M.R. 195 (1970) and 41 C.M.R. 802 (N.B.R. 1969), in which a Navy enlistee convicted of sodomy testified that he had accidentally killed his sexual partner when they fought over whether to have anal sex; and *United States v. Woods*, 46 C.M.R. 503 (N.C.M.R. 1972) and 46 C.M.R. 137 (1973), in which a Marine lance corporal bayoneted a fellow Marine to whom he was losing a fight, an act he defended by claiming that he feared a homosexual assault.

68. See, e.g., *United States v. Parham*, 33 C.M.R. 373 (1963). The sentence in this case—a dishonorable discharge and four years confinement, reduced to one by the convening authority—was overturned and the charges dismissed, however, because of the appellate court's doubt about the proper identification of the accused as the assailant. See also *United States v. Estes*, 22 C.M.R. 432 (A.B.R. 1956), in which two privates robbed and sodomized a German man, and *United States v.*

Dunnahoe, 22 C.M.R. 477 (A.B.R. 1956), in which an Army private was sentenced to death for the brutal murder of a boy, whom he apparently intended to assault sexually.

69. The facts are drawn from *United States v. Mathis,* 34 C.M.R. 543 (A.B.R. 1964), reversed 35 C.M.R. 102 (1964); *United States v. Mathis,* 38 C.M.R. 3 (1967).

70. 34 C.M.R. 545. All quotations in the description of the events at issue are taken from Mathis's testimony, as quoted by the military courts who reviewed his case.

71. Ibid.

72. Ibid.

73. 34 C.M.R. 546.

74. Ibid.

75. 35 C.M.R. 106.

76. 34 C.M.R. 547.

77. The standard for sanity at court-martial during this period was the M'Naghten rule, which turned on whether a mental disorder prevented an accused from realizing the wrongfulness of his or her act. As the *Manual for Courts-Martial* explained the test, an accused could be not guilty by reason of lack of mental responsibility if she or he were not "so far free from mental defect, disease, or derangement as to be able concerning the particular act charged both to distinguish right from wrong and to adhere to the right." *MCM,* 200. The same standard appeared in the 1969 and 1951 manuals. For a history of insanity defenses at courts-martial, see Charles E. Trant, "The American Military Insanity Defense: A Moral, Philosophical, and Legal Dilemma," *Military Law Review* 99 (1983): 1–112.

78. 38 C.M.R. 8.

79. Homosexual tendencies or past experiences appeared in the psychiatric evaluations completed for other courts-martial after *Mathis.* See, e.g, *United States v. Brown,* 44 C.M.R. 308 (A.B.R. 1971); *United States v. Norton,* 46 C.M.R. 213 (1973).

80. 38 C.M.R. 5.

81. Ibid.

82. 38 C.M.R. 8.

83. 38 C.M.R. 6.

84. Ibid.

85. 35 C.M.R. 106.

86. Ibid.

87. Other murders of gay men also exposed the shortcomings of the military's mental health system. In 1962, Private Willie Joe King was sentenced to death for the bizarre murder of a fellow Army private. On appeal, the Army board of review agreed with the trial court that King was sane under the UCMJ but reduced his sentence to confinement for life. King robbed his victim, who was apparently gay, before shooting him to death. At trial, King's long history of mental illness was brought out, including psychiatric treatment in at least three different military hospitals, three suicide attempts (by shooting himself in the abdomen, by taking sleeping pills, and by eating window glass), and bouts of amnesia and repeated refusals to eat or drink. King had been discharged by the Army in 1956 with a diagnosis of

chronic and severe antisocial personality, "manifested by continual maladjustment in almost every facet of life, legal difficulties as a civilian and as a serviceman, maladjustment to the service in terms of duty and authority figures, excessive drinking, and three previous attempts at suicide." He managed to reenlist in November 1961 by changing his name slightly. *United States v. King*, 37 C.M.R. 475 (A.B.R. 1966); 37 C.M.R. 281 (1966).

CHAPTER 3
THREATENING "THE VERY SURVIVAL OF THIS NATION"

1. Whether soldiers in a conscript army consented to these abrogations of their rights is a complex political question. For a wide-ranging analysis of the nature of political consent, including the consent of the soldier, see Elaine Scarry, *The Body in Pain: The Making and Unmaking of the World* (New York: Oxford University Press, 1985), especially 154.

2. On national politics and culture during this period, see, e.g., Margot A. Henriksen, *Dr. Strangelove's America: Society and Culture in the Atomic Age* (Berkeley and Los Angeles: University of California Press, 1997), 38–80; Larry May, ed., *Recasting America: Culture and Politics in the Age of Cold War* (Chicago: University of Chicago Press, 1989); Joanne Meyerowitz, ed., *Not June Cleaver: Women and Gender in Postwar America, 1945–1960* (Philadelphia: Temple University Press, 1994).

3. *United States v. Kauffman*, 34 C.M.R. 842, 844 (A.F.B.R. 1964).

4. On American anticommunism, see, e.g., Stanley I. Kutler, *The American Inquisition: Justice and Injustice in the Cold War* (New York: Hill and Wang, 1982); Ellen Schrecker, *Many Are the Crimes: McCarthyism in America* (Princeton: Princeton University Press, 1998); Victor Navasky, *Naming Names* (New York: Viking Press, 1980); David Caute, *The Great Fear: The Anti-Communist Campaign under Truman and Eisenhower* (New York: Simon and Schuster, 1978). On post–World War II efforts to repress sexual dissent, see also supra, chapter 2.

5. Tom Engelhart, *The End of Victory Culture: Cold War America and the Disillusioning of a Generation* (New York: Basic, 1995), 99.

6. See Richard Primus, "A Brooding Omnipresence: Totalitarianism in Postwar Constitutional Thought," *Yale Law Journal* 106 (1996): 423–57; Morton J. Horwitz, *The Transformation of American Law, 1870–1960: The Crisis of Legal Orthodoxy* (New York: Oxford University Press, 1992), 247–51. For an analysis of the effects of totalitarianism on postwar legal thought, see Carl Landauer, "Deliberating Speed: Totalitarian Anxieties and Postwar Legal Thought," *Yale Journal of Law and the Humanities* 12 (2000): 171–254.

7. See, e.g., Edward F. Sherman, "The Civilianization of Military Law," *Maine Law Review* 22 (1970): 3–103, 91: "[W]hen a commander views a court-martial case as a particular threat to the command, such as cases involving political dissent, alleged homosexual acts, barracks thefts, or any kind of disobedience, the court-martial system seems to provide an unduly attractive opportunity for a commander to influence the trial."

8. For a catalog of these dilemmas, see the case, noted above and discussed further below, of an Air Force captain convicted in a 1962 court-martial for associat-

ing with communist agents after an aggressive investigation unhindered by the usual constraints of modern criminal procedure: *United States v. Kauffman*, 33 C.M.R. 748 (A.F.B.R. 1963); affirmed in part and reversed in part, *United States v. Kauffman*, 34 C.M.R. 63 (1963); on remand, *United States v. Kauffman*, 34 C.M.R. 842 (A.F.B.R. 1964). The Court of Military Appeals declined to hear this case a second time after its second consideration by the Air Force appeals court. Other courts-martial involving officers tried for espionage are discussed infra, chapter 6.

9. See, e.g., part 2 of the unpaginated foreword by Judge Paul W. Brosman of the Court of Military Appeals in Robinson O. Everett, *Military Justice in the Armed Forces* (Harrisburg, PA: Military Service Publishing, 1956).

10. See Raymond B. Lech, *Broken Soldiers* (Chicago: University of Illinois Press, 2000), 212–13 for a list of the servicemen prosecuted. Lech's study reviews 60,000 pages of declassified documents to reconstruct the harrowing experiences of the Korean War POWs. See also Albert G. Biderman, *March to Calumny: The Story of American POWs in the Korean War* (New York: Macmillan, 1963), 36, relying on the data collected by Army general and legal scholar George Prugh in George S. Prugh, Jr., "Prisoners at War: The POW Battleground," *Dickenson Law Review* 60 (1956): 123–38 and "The Code of Conduct for Members of the Armed Forces," *Columbia Law Review* 56 (1956): 678–707. On the politics of the POW situation during and after the war, see Rosemary Foot, *A Substitute for Victory: The Politics of Peacemaking at the Korean Armistice Talks* (Ithaca, NY: Cornell University Press, 1990), especially chapter 5, 108–20; for an overview of the war's origins, see John Lewis Gaddis, *We Now Know: Rethinking Cold War History* (New York: Oxford University Press, 1997), 70–77.

11. For the lone POW court-martial after the Vietnam War, see *United States v. Garwood*, 16 M.J. 863 (N.M.C.M.R. 1983), discussed further below.

12. For an example of POWs in pop culture, consider John Frankenheimer's 1962 film (remade by Jonathan Demme in 2004 for Paramount Pictures) *The Manchurian Candidate*, an unsettling political thriller about mind control and political repression. Adapted from Richard Condon's 1959 novel and starring Frank Sinatra, it drew parallels between the evils of repressive anti-communism and the "brainwashing" allegedly practiced by Chinese communists against prisoners of war. See Cyndy Hendershot, *Anti-communism and Popular Culture in Mid-century America* (Jefferson, NC: McFarland, 2003), 136–43. On the increase in government funding of social science research because of the POWs' experience, see Ron Robin, *The Making of the Cold War Enemy: Culture and Politics in the Military-Intellectual Complex* (Princeton: Princeton University Press, 2001), especially chapters 7 and 8; Ellen Herman, *The Romance of American Psychology: Political Culture in the Age of Experts* (Berkeley and Los Angeles: University of California Press, 1995), 124–52, especially 128. See also Christopher Simpson, *Science of Coercion: Communication Research Psychological Warfare, 1945–1960* (New York: Oxford University Press, 1994), 63–65; John Marks, *The Search for the "Manchurian Candidate": The CIA and Mind Control* (New York: Times Books, 1979), 125–27.

13. See Department of Defense, *POW: The Fight Continues after the Battle: Report of the Secretary of Defense's Advisory Committee on Prisoners of War* (Washing-

ton, DC, August 1955), naming over 2,700 deaths among the POWs at 79–82. Biderman argues convincingly that both the total number of prisoners and the reported death toll were likely underestimates; see Biderman, *March to Calumny*, chapter 7. A more recent investigation into the death rates of the camps, which carefully mines volumes of declassified military records for a more thorough understanding of the experiences and actions of the POWs, estimates 3,000 deaths and puts the death rate at 43 percent. See Lech, *Broken Soldiers*, 1–2.

14. Lech also notes that the only comparable rates of death in modern warfare are the rate of Germans who died after being captured by Russians on the Eastern Front during World War II (45 percent) and the rate of Russians who died in German camps during the same war (60 percent). See Lech, *Broken Soldiers*, 2.

15. Abuses took place on both sides of the 38th parallel; see Foot's *A Substitute for Victory* for discussion of the coercion and poor conditions faced by prisoners of the UN forces in Korea.

16. Lech's study (*Broken Soldiers*) persuasively reconstructs the depth and breadth of prisoner cooperation with Communist indoctrination; see also Marks, *The Search for the "Manchurian Candidate"*, 126–31.

17. See White House Office, Office of the Special Assistant for National Security Affairs, Records, 1952–1961, FBI Series, Box 3, Folder S(1), Dwight D. Eisenhower Presidential Library, Abilene, KS. For a narrative account of the FBI's domestic counterintelligence operations (COINTELPRO), see James Kirkpatrick Davis, *Assault on the Left: The FBI and the Sixties Antiwar Movement* (Westport, CT: Praeger, 1997).

18. See Biderman, *March to Calumny*, 223–26.

19. Seven of the fourteen courts-martial of POWs resulted in extensive appellate records, six of which involved explicit charges of political dissent, including making statements against the interests of the United States and then publishing, broadcasting or otherwise drawing attention to such statements. These cases are *United States v. Gallagher*, 23 C.M.R. 591 (A.B.R. 1957), pet. denied, *United States v. Gallagher*, 24 C.M.R. 311 (table) (1957), 22 C.M.R. 296 (1956); *United States v. Fleming*, 23 C.M.R. 7 (1957), 19 C.M.R. 438 (A.B.R. 1955); *United States v. Olson*, 22 C.M.R. 250 (1957), 20 C.M.R. 461 (A.B.R. 1955); *United States v. Bayes*, 22 C.M.R. 487 (A.B.R. 1956); *United States v. Batchelor*, 22 C.M.R. 144 (1956), 19 C.M.R. 452 (A.B.R. 1955); *United States v. Floyd*, 18 C.M.R. 362 (A.B.R. 1955), pet. denied, 19 C.M.R. 413 (1955); *United States v. Dickenson*, 20 C.M.R. 154 (1955), 17 C.M.R. 438 (A.B.R. 1954). Floyd is the only case that did not include a charge of collaboration with the enemy; see infra, chapter 5 for further discussion.

20. See Department of Defense, *POW*, 81–82. One Marine Corps officer avoided court-martial when he was cleared by a court of inquiry, though the investigation effectively ended his career.

21. See Lech, *Broken Soldiers*, 264–77, for the fate of each court-martialed POW. For a narrative account of Ronald Alley's effort to clear his name, a crusade taken up by his family, several politicians, and a journalist after his death, see Don J. Snyder, *A Soldier's Disgrace* (Dublin, NH: Yankee Books, 1987).

22. On the fear of flying incident, see Vance O. Mitchell, *Air Force Officers: Personnel Policy Development, 1944–1974* (Washington, DC: Air Force History and

Museum Program, 1996), 92–98. See also Snyder, *A Soldier's Disgrace*, which argues that the Air Force regulations and evidence of the collaboration of uncharged POWs was improperly suppressed at the POW trials.

23. The quotation that opens this section is from the closing paragraph of the Court of Military Appeals' decision in *United States v. Batchelor*: "If it be not so at other times, it is necessary in time of serious threat to our form of Government that this country must call upon its men in arms to withstand the horrors of war and prison to prevent an enemy from destroying that which has been our heritage for at least 167 years. It goes without saying that all men cannot stand firm against torture, physical violence, starvation or psychological mistreatment. But in this instance, the record discloses that the accused weakened when others stood fast, and it does not reveal that he was compelled to sacrifice his countrymen because of the use of those influences." *United States v. Batchelor*, 22 C.M.R. 354, 372 (1956).

24. For a list of the name and rank of each soldier court-martialed for their actions in POW camps, see Lech, *Broken Soldiers*, 212–13.

25. On military personnel and training problems during the war, see, e.g., David Rees, *Korea: The Limited War* (New York: St. Martin's, 1964); Ben Shephard, *A War of Nerves: Soldiers and Psychiatrists in the Twentieth Century* (Cambridge: Harvard University Press, 2001), 341–43. See also White House Central Files, File OF, Box 102, Court-Martial Cases, Folder "3-M Court-Martial Cases, B (2)," Eisenhower Library, for a December 8, 1954 letter from Batchelor's parents stating that "Claude was duped by the communists into thinking he was fighting for peace and the common people" and asking for their son's release because he had not been properly trained and would now be a good husband, citizen, and anticommunist.

26. Background information in this paragraph is drawn from Lech, *Broken Soldiers*, 33–37 and the appellate records of *Batchelor* and *Dickenson*.

27. Lech, *Broken Soldiers*, 151.

28. 19 C.M.R. 466. The record focuses in particular on Batchelor's statements about the U.S. practice of germ warfare, right down to details about ants infected with chemical agents. This was a key issue for the Chinese and North Koreans; quite a few Americans were convinced to speak out about American biological warfare.

29. 19 C.M.R. 480.

30. 19 C.M.R. 473–77.

31. See Lech, *Broken Soldiers*, 155–56.

32. The prisoner who Batchelor condemned was not killed; Master Sergeant Wilburn Watson survived to join Dickenson in testifying at Batchelor's court-martial. See Lech, *Broken Soldiers*, 192.

33. Ibid., 242.

34. Ibid., 237. On McCarthy's targeting of the Army, see Schrecker, *Many Are the Crimes*, 260–65; see also Robert Griffith, *The Politics of Fear: Joseph R. McCarthy and the Senate* (Rochelle Park, NJ: Hayden, 1970); David M. Oshinsky, *A Conspiracy So Immense: The World of Joe McCarthy* (New York: Free Press, 1983).

35. See Lech, *Broken Soldiers*, 237–38, recounting public support for Dickenson in particular; see also the court-martial appeal letters in Box 254, General File Series of White House Central Files, Eisenhower Library. On the promises made to the repatriated prisoners, see Lech, *Broken Soldiers*, 238–39; see also White House Central Files, File OF, Box 102, Court-Martial Cases, Folder "3-M Court-

Martial Cases D," files on the Dickenson case, Eisenhower Library, including a letter dated February 6, 1954, written in pencil on lined note paper from Dickenson's sister, Rose Helen Dickinson, from Big Stone Gap, VA. She wrote that her brother "Edward Swanson Dickenson who was the first American that changed his mind and came home after saying he wanted to stay over there. The boys was promised to have a big welcome if they would come home. now look what they have done to him. I know you (IKE) have all power to stop it. Id appreciate very much if you would try to do something about it." Another letter, also in pencil, on similar paper, from Dickenson's father, Van Buren Dickenson, dated February 5, 1954, read "it looks like to me hese had a nuff punishment he was forced to go across the watters to other countrys to fight for freedom back at home and made up his mind to work his way out of hell to get back home the boys was promised freedom welcom and unharmed if they would come back my son was the first to come back now look they have got him locked up in a little room about 8 × 10 . . . may god save the soles of all that is against him in God we trust your truly."

36. 19 C.M.R. 513.

37. 19 C.M.R. 489.

38. For Batchelor's sentence and ultimate punishment after clemency and parole board actions, see Lech, *Broken Soldiers*, 266–68.

39. *United States v. Batchelor*, 22 C.M.R. 144 (1956); 19 C.M.R. 452 (A.B.R.1955); *United States v. Dickenson*, 20 C.M.R. 154 (1955); 17 C.M.R. 438 (A.B.R. 1954).

40. 22 C.M.R. 144.

41. 22 C.M.R. 162.

42. See, e.g., Biderman, *March to Calumny*, 21; Robin, *The Making of the Cold War Enemy*, 169–70; Timothy Melley, *Empire of Conspiracy: The Culture of Paranoia in Postwar America* (Ithaca, NY: Cornell University Press, 2000), vii.

43. I am grateful to Marilyn Young for pointing out the questionable accuracy of Hunter's translation, a linguistic point confirmed in Marks, *"The Manchurian Candidate"*, 125. On the scholarly and popular use of "brainwashing" to describe the POWs' experiences, see Edward Hunter, *Brain-Washing in Red China: The Calculated Destruction of Men's Minds* (New York: Vanguard, 1951); Robert Jay Lifton, *Thought Reform and the Psychology of Totalism: A Study of "Brainwashing" in China* (New York: Norton, 1961), 3. For a discussion of the "brainwashing" gap that the Korean War POWs supposedly exposed, see Alston Chase, *Harvard and the Unabomber: The Education of an American Terrorist* (New York: Norton, 2003), 270–72.

44. For a summary of such practices, see, e.g., Richard Delgado, "Ascription of Criminal States of Mind: Toward a Defense Theory for the Coercively Persuaded ('Brainwashed') Defendant," *Minnesota Law Review* 63 (1978): 1–33. On the consequences, see, e.g., Judith Lewis Herman, *Trauma and Recovery* (New York: BasicBooks, 1992); Robert B. Cialdini, *Influence: How and Why People Agree to Things* (New York: Morrow, 1984), 68–82.

45. 19 C.M.R. 467–68.

46. See White House Office Files, Office of the Special Assistant for National Security Affairs, Records, 1952–61, FBI Series, Box 3, Folder S(1), Eisenhower Library, especially a letter from J. Edgar Hoover to Robert Cutler, administrative

assistant to the president, May 14, 1953, about recent POW repatriates. Hoover writes that the FBI review found "derogatory information" on only a dozen of the repatriates, none of whom were court-martialed.

47. On the blind spot of social scientists regarding race, ethnic, and class divisions among the returning POWs, see Robin, *The Making of the Cold War Enemy*, 181.

48. *United States v. Garwood*, 16 M.J. 863 (N.C.M.R.1983). See also *United States v. Garwood*, 20 M.J. 148 (1985), in which the Court of Military Appeals affirmed the conviction. The Supreme Court denied certiorari at 106 S. Ct. 524 (1985).

49. See Winston Groom and Duncan Spencer, *Conversations with the Enemy: The Story of PFC Robert Garwood* (New York: G. P. Putnam's Sons, 1983).

50. See 16 M.J. 866.

51. On trial tactics and chronology, see Groom and Spencer, *Conversations with the Enemy*, 347–94.

52. See ibid., 340–44, on the selective nature of Garwood's prosecution; for quotation, see 344.

53. For the "turncoat GIs" characterization of some American soldiers, see, e.g., "Notes on Press Conference Briefing," July 6, 1955, Dwight D. Eisenhower Papers, Whitman File, 1953–61, Ann Whitman (ACW) Diary Series, Box 6, Folder ACW Diary July 1955 (6), Eisenhower Library.

54. The opening of Soviet archives in recent years has inspired new research into Cold War espionage. But neither scholarly nor popular accounts of the Americans who spied for communist governments during this period do more than briefly mention spies in the military. They focus instead on civilians in government and private employment. See, e.g., Allen Weinstein and Alexander Vassiliev, *The Haunted Wood: Soviet Espionage in the Stalin Era* (New York: Random House, 1999); Gary May, *Un-American Activities: The Trials of William Remington* (New York: Oxford University Press, 1994); Robert Louis Benson and Michael Warner, eds., *VENONA: Soviet Espionage and the American Response, 1939–1957* (Washington, DC: National Security Agency and Central Intelligence Agency, 1996).

55. On women, gender, and espionage in the twentieth century, see, e.g., Tammy M. Proctor, *Female Intelligence: Women and Espionage in the First World War* (New York: New York University Press, 2003); see also Elizabeth P. McIntosh, *Sisterhood of Spies: The Women of the OSS* (New York: Dell, 1999). Among the best-known American spies of the Cold War was Elizabeth Bentley. Recent studies explore how contemporary and historical assessments of Bentley's significance were colored by negative reactions to her overt sexuality and volatility. See Kathryn S. Olmsted, *Red Spy Queen: A Biography of Elizabeth Bentley* (Chapel Hill: University of North Carolina Press, 2002); see also Lauren Kessler, *Clever Girl: Elizabeth Bentley, the Spy Who Ushered in the McCarthy Era* (New York: HarperCollins, 2004).

56. See infra, chapters 4 and 5.

57. On the United States' use of defectors from communist countries, see, e.g., Engelhardt, *The End of Victory Culture*, 114–15.

58. In addition to the cases cited below, see also *United States v. French*, 27 C.M.R. 245 (1959); *United States v. Svenson*, 35 C.M.R. 645 (A.B.R. 1965).

59. *United States v. Blevens*, 18 C.M.R. 104 (1955); 15 C.M.R. 501 (A.B.R. 1954).

60. See generally Donald P. Steury, ed., *On the Front Lines of the Cold War: Documents on the Intelligence War in Berlin, 1946–1961*, 2nd ed. (Pittsburgh, PA: CIA History Staff, 2000).

61. Like the POW cases, courts-martial of spies and defectors often raised important legal issues. In Blevens's case, for example, a key issue on appeal involved a federal/military law conflict between the terms of the Smith Act, 18 U.S.C. sec. 2385, which governed the criminal prosecution of some forms of treason in federal courts, and the UCMJ. The question involved whether *United States v. Dennis*, 341 U.S. 494 (1951), applied to the Article 134 charge at Blevens's court-martial. In *Dennis*, the Supreme Court established a rule for conviction under the Smith Act that required prosecutors to prove that the accused had intended to accomplish the overthrow of the U.S. Government by means of force and violence. The Court of Military Appeals disregarded the Smith Act jurisprudence of the Supreme Court, holding that the offense was charged under Article 134 of the UCMJ, not the Smith Act, and that all elements of the crime in question were proven at trial.

62. 18 C.M.R. 111.

63. 18 C.M.R. 111–12. This organization was identified as the State Security Service or Staatssicherheitsdienst and referred to by the acronym "SSD" in the record of trial.

64. 18 C.M.R. 112.

65. Ibid.

66. Ibid.

67. Blevens was convicted of charges under Articles 85 (desertion), 95 (escape from confinement), 81 (conspiracy), and 134 (the general article). See 15 C.M.R. 504.

68. 18 C.M.R. 107.

69. 18 C.M.R. 108.

70. 18 C.M.R. 116.

71. 18 C.M.R. 114–16.

72. Jones may not have been the very first soldier to defect, but he was certainly in the first group. His case was later named as the first of its kind by both peace activists and the government. Sweden was the first country to protect American deserters during the Vietnam War. See "Military Deserters," *Hearings before a Subcommittee of the Committee on Armed Services, United States Senate, 90th Cong., 2nd Session, on The Problem of Deserters from Military Service, May 21 and 22, 1968* (Washington, DC: 1968), 57–58 for a description of Jones's case.

73. See generally D. Bruce Bell and Beverly W. Bell, "Desertion and Antiwar Protest: Findings from the Ford Clemency Program," *Armed Forces and Society* 3 (3) (1977): 433–43. See also the report on which this 1977 article was based: D. Bruce Bell and Thomas J. Houston, *The Vietnam Era Deserter: Characteristics of Unconvicted Army Deserters Participating in the Presidential Clemency Board Program* (Arlington, VA: United States Army Research Institute for the Behavioral and Social Sciences, 1976), and G. David Curry, *Sunshine Patriots: Punishment and the Vietnam Offender* (Notre Dame, IN: University of Notre Dame Press, 1985), 79–93.

74. See Bell and Bell, "Desertion and Antiwar Protest," 438.

75. Jones, whose mental health was worsened by the stress of his desertion and the isolation of living in a foreign country, eventually returned to the United States voluntarily and signed a plea agreement with military prosecutors. See "*Army Times* Sparks Return of Defector," *Army Times*, March 20, 1968, 1, 22. See also the case of Sergeant James Henry Grant, a black GI granted asylum in Bavaria in 1970 because the Army refused him permission to marry his German fiancée. See Devi Prasad, *They Love It but Leave It: American Deserters* (London: Farmer and Sons, 1971), 41–42.

76. See Prasad, *They Love It but Leave It* 17–21.

77. Curry, *Sunshine Patriots*, 45; Bell and Bell, "Desertion and Antiwar Protest," 437. See also David Cortright, *Soldiers in Revolt: The American Military Today* (Garden City, NY: Anchor Press/Doubleday, 1975), 10–15.

78. Lawrence M. Baskir and William A. Strauss, *Reconciliation after Vietnam: A Program of Relief for Vietnam Era Draft and Military Offenders* (Notre Dame, IN: University of Notre Dame Press, 1977), 3.

79. See Robert N. Strassfeld, "The Vietnam War on Trial: The Court-Martial of Dr. Howard B. Levy," *Wisconsin Law Review* (1994): 839–963, for a thorough and perceptive account of Levy's trial and appeals, which ended in the Supreme Court in what became a landmark case of judicial deference to the military, *Parker v. Levy*, 417 U.S. 733 (1974).

80. See Strassfeld, "The Vietnam War on Trial," 839–45.

81. *United States v. Kauffman*, 33 C.M.R. 748, 760 (A.F.B.R. 1963); affirmed in part and reversed in part, *United States v. Kauffman*, 34 C.M.R. 63 (1963).

82. 34 C.M.R. 67.

83. Ibid.

84. 34 C.M.R. 844.

85. See Lech, *Broken Soldiers*, 157–58.

86. *United States v. Northrup*, 31 C.M.R. 599 (A.F.B.R. 1961).

87. The long sentence may also have been due to Northrup's high-level security clearance, which gave him access to the documents in the first place and brought with it a special responsibility for protecting classified information. Defense attorneys challenged the composition of the court-martial, arguing that the members were "hand-picked and packed to favor the prosecution" because only those with top security clearances were permitted to serve. 31 C.M.R. 604–05. Servicemembers who were part of the small community entrusted with special access to classified data may have been more likely to resent the weakness of one of their number and therefore more likely to punish such transgressions harshly, but the Air Force board of review summarily rejected the claim of prejudice among the venire. Northup's allegation, however, about the bias inherent in the process by which the court-martial panels were selected, became perhaps the most criticized feature of military criminal procedure under the UCMJ.

88. Reversals for error were common in this area of military law. See, e.g, *United States v. Simms*, 20 C.M.R. 569 (C.G.B.R. 1956); *United States v. Miller*, 21 C.M.R. 149 (1956); *United States v. Walker*, 23 C.M.R. 262 (1957) and 22 C.M.R. 449 (A.B.R. 1956); and *United States v. Kennedy*, 24 C.M.R. 61 (1957).

89. *United States v. Phillips*, 11 C.M.R. 137 (1953).

90. Ibid.

91. See, e.g, the case of Lance Corporal Johnny Mack, a Marine, who was convicted of sodomy (along with his partner in a companion case) and was sentenced to the maximum five-year term but convinced a Navy board to reduce his confinement to a few months. *United States v. Mack*, 31 C.M.R. 387 (N.B.R. 1961). The dissent discusses the critical nature of character instructions at trial. I have criticized the military use of character evidence in "The 'Good Soldier' Defense: Character Evidence and Military Rank at Court-Martial," *Yale Law Journal* 108 (1999): 879–911.

92. *United States v. Stone*, 24 C.M.R. 454, 456 (A.B.R. 1957). In this case, the board dismissed the charges against a sergeant first class who had been convicted of homosexual sodomy on the testimony of a "petty thief."

93. See, e.g., the cases of an Army first lieutenant convicted for lewd acts, *United States v. Massey*, 18 C.M.R. 138 (1955), 16 C.M.R. 316 (A.B.R. 1954); and a Navy supply chief whose conviction was reversed because of the uncorroborated testimony of accusers and his long list of character references, *United States v. Blackwell*, 30 C.M.R. 20 (1960).

94. See *United States v. Warren*, 20 C.M.R. 135 (1955).

95. See, e.g., ibid.; *United States v. Haynes*, 24 C.M.R. 881 (A.F.B.R. 1957) and 27 C.M.R. 60 (1958).

96. *United States v. Marcey*, 25 C.M.R. 444 (1958).

97. 25 C.M.R. 448–49.

98. *United States v. Kindler*, 34 C.M.R. 174 (1964).

99. 34 C.M.R. 177–78.

100. See, e.g., *United States v. Morrison*, 28 C.M.R. 91 (1959); *United States v. Battista*, 33 C.M.R. 282 (1963); *United States v. Whitley*, 39 C.M.R. 20 (1968).

101. *United States v. Hillan*, 26 C.M.R. 771, 779 (N.B.R. 1958).

102. 26 C.M.R. 783.

103. Why gay men continued to frequent the Norfolk Y is not clear; surely word got around that it was not the safest rendezvous. The YMCA's function as a meeting place for gay men was acknowledged during other courts-martial, including *United States v. Grosso*, 23 C.M.R. 30 (1957) and *United States v. Morrison*, 28 C.M.R. 91 (1959). For another example of the Navy's aggressive searches for homosexuals during this period, see *United States v. Adkins*, 18 C.M.R. 116, 119–20 (1955).

104. 26 C.M.R. 782.

105. *United States v. Gandy*, 19 C.M.R. 57, 67 (1955).

106. See the courts' discussion of the admissibility of evidence of homosexuality in *United States v. Worden*, 15 C.M.R. 719 (A.F.B.R. 1954); *United States v. Shotter*, 30 C.M.R. 283 (1961); *United States v. Turner*, 25 C.M.R. 386 (1958); *United States v. Grady*, 32 C.M.R. 242 (1962); *United States v. Blair*, 45 C.M.R. 413 (A.C.M.R. 1972); and *United States v. Hood*, 47 C.M.R. 356 (A.C.M.R. 1973).

107. *United States v. Hudson*, 23 C.M.R. 693, 695 (C.G.B.R. 1957).

108. 23 C.M.R. 696.

109. My analysis in this section relies heavily on the wealth of published material on disaffected Vietnam-era servicemembers. Important works include Gerald Nicosia, *Home to War: A History of the Vietnam Veterans' Movement* (New York:

Crown, 2001); Andrew E. Hunt, *The Turning: A History of Vietnam Veterans against the War* (New York: New York University Press, 1999); Richard Stacewicz, *Winter Soldiers: An Oral History of the Vietnam Veterans against the War* (New York: Twayne, 1997); Richard Moser, *The New Winter Soldiers: GI and Veteran Dissent during the Vietnam Era* (New Brunswick, NJ: Rutgers University Press, 1996); Guenter Lewy, *America in Vietnam* (New York: Oxford University Press, 1980); Cortright, *Soldiers in Revolt*; John Helmer, *Bringing the War Home: The American Soldier in Vietnam and After* (New York: Free Press, 1974); Richard Boyle, *GI Revolts: The Breakdown of the U.S. Army in Vietnam* (San Francisco: United Front Press, 1973); Stewart H. Loory, *Defeated: Inside America's Military Machine* (New York: Random House, 1973); Richard Boyle, *Flower of the Dragon* (San Francisco: Rampart Press, 1972). For a military legal officer's analysis of the problem during the Vietnam, see James H. Granger, "Dissent within the Armed Forces" (Thesis, Judge Advocate Generals School, 1970).

110. On the draft and the military's difficulty recruiting during this period, see George Q. Flynn, *The Draft, 1940–1973* (Lawrence: University of Kansas Press, 1993); John O'Sullivan and Alan M. Mecker, ed., *The Draft and Its Enemies: A Documentary History* (Urbana: University of Illinois Press, 1974); James M. Gerhardt, *The Draft and Public Policy: Issues in Military Manpower Procurement, 1945–1970* (Columbus: Ohio State University Press, 1971).

111. See Moser, *The New Winter Soldiers*, 93.

112. See ibid., 59.

113. See, e.g., Gary D. Solis, *Marines and Military Law in Vietnam: Trial by Fire* (Washington, DC: History and Museums Division, Headquarters, U.S. Marine Corps, 1989), 68, noting rising number of marijuana offenses from 1967 through 1969, when drug use became "virtually out of control" among troops.

114. For a thoughtful discussion of "indiscipline" in Vietnam in particular (from which I borrow this term), see Kurt Lang, "American Military Performance in Vietnam: Background and Analysis," *Journal of Political and Military Sociology* 8 (1980): 269–286.

115. Christian G. Appy, *Working-Class War: American Combat Soldiers and Vietnam* (Chapel Hill: University of North Carolina Press, 1993), quotation at 92; desertion discussed at 95. Young also notes the war crimes and great resistance among troops in Vietnam; Marilyn B. Young, *The Vietnam Wars, 1945–1990* (New York: HarperCollins, 1991), 256.

116. In addition to the works listed above, a few of the many primary sources available on political dissent in the Vietnam-era military include Fred Halstead, *GIs Speak Out against the War: The Case of the Ft. Jackson Eight* (New York: Pathfinder Press, 1970); John Kerry and the Vietnam Veterans against the War, *The New Soldier* (New York: Collier, 1971); Ron Kovic, *Born on the Fourth of July* (New York: Simon and Schuster, 1976); Larry G. Waterhouse and Marrian G. Wizard, *Turning the Guns Around: Notes on the GI Movement* (New York: Praeger, 1971).

117. See, e.g., Cortright, *Soldiers in Revolt*, chapter 3. Cortright's work is both a political tract advocating major reform in military law and policy and a sophisticated analysis of the development of political resistance during the Vietnam War.

118. For the perspective of a senior legal officer on prosecutions for dissent, see

the Wilton B. Persons Papers in the Senior Officers Oral History Program series at the Military History Institute, Carlisle Barracks, PA (1985 interview). Major General Persons's first assigned case as an Army lawyer was that of "Corporal Edward Dickenson, the famous Korean War turncoat," 115 of transcript; 124–56 describes the disciplinary challenges posed by drugs, race riots, and other civil disturbances during and after the Vietnam War.

119. See infra, chapter 5 for discussion of the use of courts-martial in addressing issues of civil rights protests and racial violence.

120. See Moser, *The New Winter Soldiers*, 69–70.

121. *United States v. Bell*, 40 C.M.R. 807 (A.B.R. 1969). On churches that provided sanctuary for AWOL servicemembers, see, e.g., *Bridges v. Davis*, 443 F.2d 970 (9th Cir. 1971), cert. denied, 405 U.S. 919 (1972); *United States v. Beyer*, 426 F.2d 773 (2d. Cir. 1970); Michael Ferber, "A Time to Say No," in David R. Weber, ed., *Civil Disobedience in America: A Documentary History* (Ithaca, NY: Cornell University Press, 1978), 271.

122. 40 C.M.R. 808.

123. Ibid.

124. 40 C.M.R. 814.

125. See, e.g., Curry, *Sunshine Patriots*, 51–52; see generally Charles G. Hoff, "Drug Abuse," (Thesis, Judge Advocate General School, 1970); Barrett S. Haight, "Military Drug Offenses—The Legal Issues" (Thesis, Judge Advocate General School, 1970).

126. Lech, *Broken Soldiers*, 157–58.

127. See William T. Bowers, William M. Hammond, and George L. MacGarrigle, *Black Soldier, White Army: The 24th Infantry Regiment in Korea* (Washington, DC: Center for Military History, U.S. Army, 1996), 53–55 and 264–65, quotation on 265.

128. See White House Office, Office of the Special Assistant for National Security Affairs Records, 1952–61, FBI Series, Box 3; Staff Files, Files of special assistant, administrative assistant, special counsel and deputy assistant to the president (Gerald D. Morgan), Box 19, Folders (1) and (2) on "Narcotics, Interdepartmental Committee on," Eisenhower Library.

129. See Paul Starr, *The Discarded Army: Veterans after Vietnam, The Nader Report on Vietnam Veterans and the Veterans Administration* (New York: Charterhouse, 1973), 121.

130. See Starr, *The Discarded Army*, 113–66. The *Manual for Courts-Martial* addressed the crime of drug use in 1951, but not until the 1969 revision were drug offenses and punishments clarified. See Haight, "Military Drug Offenses," 17–20. See also Engelhardt, *The End of Victory Culture*, 247–48.

131. *United States House of Representatives, "Inquiry into Alleged Drug Abuse in the Armed Forces," Report of a Special Subcommittee of the Armed Services Committee, 92nd Congress, 1st sess., April 23, 1971; U.S. House of Representatives, "The World Heroin Problem," Report of a Special Study Mission by Representatives Morgan F. Murphy of Illinois and Robert H. Steele of Connecticut, Committee on Foreign Affairs, 92nd Congress, 1st sess., May 27, 1971; U.S. Senate, "Staff Report on Drug Abuse in the Military," Report of the Subcommittee on Drug Abuse in the Military, 92nd Cong., 1st sess.; U.S. Senate, "Military Drug Abuse," Hearings before the Sub-*

committee on Alcoholism and Narcotics of the Committee on Labor and Public Welfare, 92nd Congress, 1st sess., June 9 and 22, 1971.

132. See Starr, *The Discarded Army*, 135.

133. Ibid., 137. The best-known amnesty program for military justice offenders was President Ford's conditional amnesty for Vietnam-era deserters. For insight into the complexities of that program, see the extensive holdings related to clemency and pardons in the Gerald R. Ford Presidential Library, Ann Arbor, MI.

134. See Starr, *The Discarded Army* 138–84.

135. See Thomas A. Palmer, "Why We Fight: A Study of Indoctrination Activities in the Armed Forces," in Peter Karsten, ed., *The Military in America: From the Colonial Era to the Present*, rev. ed. (New York: Free Press, 1986), 381–94. David Cortright points out drug abuse was by far the most investigated aspect of Vietnam veterans' experience; see Cortright, *Soldiers in Revolt*, 19–23.

CHAPTER 4
CRIME AND THE MILITARY FAMILY

1. For a study of military folklore, including marching chants, see Carol Burke, *Camp All American, Hanoi Jane, and the High and Tight: Gender, Folklore, and Changing Military Culture* (Boston: Beacon Press, 2004). For discussion of the stresses placed on modern military families, see James A. Martin, Leora N. Rosen, and Linette R. Sparacino, eds., *The Military Family: A Practice Guide for Human Service Providers* (Westport, CT: Praeger, 2000).

2. *United States v. Griffin*, 12 C.M.R. 595, 596 (A.B.R. 1953); see similar comments in *United States v. Bieganowski*, 12 C.M.R. 815 (A.B.R. 1953).

3. See Morris Janowitz, "Civic Consciousness and Military Performance," in Morris Janowitz and Stephen D. Wesbrook, eds., *The Political Education of Soldiers* (Beverly Hills, CA: Sage, 1983), 55–80, 68.

4. "Quit[ ] his unit" is a quotation from Article 85(a)(2), UCMJ; "absents himself" is from Article 86(3).

5. Unauthorized absence was charged at 64 percent of general courts and over 81 percent of special courts. See table VII of Report of the Board of Officers, Roll 24, Frame 96, Col. Charles L. Decker's Collection of Records Relating to Military Justice and the Revision of Military Law, 1948–1956, National Archives at College Park, MD. The report established that the Army held 3,847 general and 20 special courts for desertion along with 2,320 general and 1,192 special courts for AWOL. The percentages were calculated from the reported total of 8,135 general and 1,487 special courts (9,622 total) overall. Forty percent of all courts-martial were for desertion; 36 percent were for AWOL. A 1955 study conducted by the Bureau of Naval Personnel estimated that AWOL offenses cost the combined armed forces over $100 million each year in administrative and personnel expenditures. See W. J. Burke, "Combatting AWOLism," *JAG Journal* 3 (July 1955).

6. See Patrick J. Mackey, "Exploring the Myths of Military Justice: The Judicial System as It Actually Functions" (Thesis for the Judge Advocate General School, April 1975), 18, reporting that AWOL offenses were 65 percent of all special courts held at Fort Bragg from 1971 to 1973 and 90 percent of the special courts held at Fort Knox during the same period; and Bruce M. Burchett, "Race and the AWOL

Offender: The Effect of the Defendant's Race on the Outcome of Courts-Martial Involving Absence Without Leave" (Ph.D. diss., Carleton University, 1983), ii, reporting that 85 percent of all courts-martial held at Fort Meade from 1971 to 1974 were for absence offenses.

7. See, e.g., Frederick Bernays Wiener, "Lament for a Skulker," *Combat Forces Journal* 4 (1954): 33–40. In referring to capital desertion cases in which executions might be delayed until after a war has ended, Wiener writes: "In those circumstances punishment has lost its deterrent effect—which in military life is its principal justification."

8. "To deter personnel from abandoning their duties, absence therefrom is an offense, for without such a deterrent, the strength of such organizations must inevitably disintegrate and disappear." Alfred Avins, *The Law of AWOL* (New York: Oceana Publications, 1957), 33. See also Stanley L. Brodsky, "Crime and Justice in the Military Services," in Stanley L. Brodsky and Norman E. Eggleston, eds., *The Military Prison: Theory, Research, and Practice* (Carbondale: Southern Illinois Press, 1970).

9. See G. David Curry, *Sunshine Patriots: Punishment and the Vietnam Offender* (Notre Dame, IN: University of Notre Dame Press, 1985), 35.

10. See Lawrence J. Morris, "Our Mission, No Future: The Case for Closing the United States Army Disciplinary Barracks," *Kansas Journal of Law and Public Policy* (Fall 1996): 77–121.

11. See generally Major Wayne Anderson, "Unauthorized Absences," *Army Lawyer* (June 1989): 3–17; Frederic Lederer, "Absence Without Leave—The Nature of the Offense," *Army Lawyer* (March 1974): 4–9; and Major Milhizer, "Facts Relevant to Desertion," *Army Lawyer* (June 1991): 30–31. For an example of the powerful effect of civilian criminal jurisprudence on other aspects of military criminal law, consider the Court of Military Appeal's reliance on *Morissette v. United States*, 342 U.S. 246 (1952), termed "a legal phenomenon in military law" in Judge Latimer's concurrence in *Cothern*, 23 C.M.R. 385. Between 1953 and 1957, the Court of Military Appeals repeatedly cites *Morissette* in limiting prosecutorial excess and stressing that the question of intent is a matter for the members of the court-martial to decide. See *United States v. Soccio*, 24 C.M.R. 287 (1957); *Cothern*; *United States v. Miller*, 23 C.M.R. 257 (1957); *United States v. Greenwood*, 19 C.M.R. 335 (1955); *United States v. Rowan*, 16 C.M.R. 4 (1954); *United States v. Rios*, 15 C.M.R. 203 (1954); *United States v. Doyle*, 14 C.M.R. 3 (1954); *United States v. Krull*, 11 C.M.R. 129 (1953); *United States v. Beach*, 7 C.M.R. 48 (1953).

12. See, e.g., Anderson, "Unauthorized Absences," 17.

13. See, for example, a judge advocate's 1965 lecture about court-martial procedure to the officers stationed at Fort Devens, Massachusetts: "Gentlemen, it is not your job as court members to decide that the military justice system is wrong, or that a certain case shouldn't be before your court, or that it is ridiculous to try people for AWOL because they would just be fired in civilian life; the Code of Military Justice says this is a military offense and the *Manual for Courts-Martial* grades the punishment imposable by the length of the absence involved; it is your duty to follow the law, not disregard it, nor to make up rules at your whim." *United States v. Albert*, 36 C.M.R. 267 (1966).

14. Crimes of absence were generally charged under the absence-specific provi-

sions of the UCMJ, though an unauthorized absence often violated other punitive articles of the UCMJ as well. An unauthorized absence might violate Articles 90 ("willfully disobeying officer"), 91 ("insubordinate conduct toward noncommissioned officer"), 92 ("failure to obey"), 94 ("mutiny or sedition"), or 99 ("misbehavior before the enemy"). The 1951 *Manual for Courts-Martial* specified that an AWOL offense could not be charged as a violation of Article 92, "failure to obey an order," despite the fact that a soldier who was absent without authority was frequently disobeying at least an implied order to appear for duty. See *MCM*, "Table of Maximum Punishments," 221, n. 5, which limits the punishment for violations of Article 92 to those instances not covered in other articles of the UCMJ. The 1969 *Manual* included the same provision. See also Anderson, "Unauthorized Absences," 5 and 22n.

15. See Article 85(c); *MCM*, Table of Maximum Punishments, 220.

16. For the range of AWOL offenses and the sentences they provoked, see *MCM*, "Table of Maximum Punishments," Section A, 219–27.

17. See Anderson, "Unauthorized Absences," 6 ("intentional absences are not distinguished from unintentional absences in the UCMJ").

18. See Edward Shils, "A Profile of the Military Deserter," *Armed Forces and Society* 3 (1977): 427–32. Because the Vietnam era attracted so much public and scholarly attention and triggered extensive self-study within the armed forces, the most detailed information about the rank, class, and race of absence offenders is available for the Vietnam War. Two essential data sets are the information collected by the Presidential Clemency Board, which was established by President Ford in 1974, and by the Notre Dame Survey of the Vietnam Generation, conducted in 1975 by two of the key participants in the Clemency Board, Lawrence Baskir and William Strauss. See Lawrence M. Baskir and William A. Strauss, *Reconciliation after Vietnam: A Program of Relief for Vietnam Era Draft and Military Offenders* (Notre Dame, IN: University of Notre Dame Press, 1977); Lawrence M. Baskir and William A. Strauss, *Chance and Circumstance: The Draft, the War, and the Vietnam Generation* (New York: Alfred A. Knopf, 1978); Curry, *Sunshine Patriots*; Presidential Clemency Board, *Report to the President* (Washington, DC, 1975); Mark M. Biegel, *Project STRAY: A Study of Unauthorized Absenteeism and Desertion, Part 1: Deserter Information System* (Washington, DC: Office of the Assistant Secretary of Defense, Manpower, and Reserve Affairs, 1968); John Helmer, *Bringing the War Home: The American Soldier in Vietnam and After* (New York: Free Press, 1974).

19. See Curry, *Sunshine Patriots*, especially 36–37.

20. See Baskir and Strauss, *Chance and Circumstance*, 116.

21. Curry, *Sunshine Patriots*, 24; see also D. Bruce Bell and Thomas J. Houston, *The Vietnam Era Deserter: Characteristics of Unconvicted Army Deserters Participating in the Presidential Clemency Board Program* (Arlington, VA: United States Army Research Institute for the Behavioral and Social Sciences, 1976).

22. See Curry, *Sunshine Patriots*, 23; Baskir and Strauss, *Reconciliation*, 2.

23. See D. Bruce Bell and Beverly W. Bell, "Desertion and Antiwar Protest: Findings from the Ford Clemency Program," *Armed Forces and Society* 3 (1977): 433–43, 435.

24. See ibid., 434. See also Bell and Houston, *The Vietnam Era Deserter*.

25. See Curry, *Sunshine Patriots*, 23; Baskir and Strauss, *Chance and Circumstance*, 120. The percentage of African Americans varied among the services, but remained less than 10 percent even in the most AWOL-prone forces, the Army and Marine Corps, through most of the Vietnam War.

26. Curry, *Sunshine Patriots*, 23.

27. Burchett's study of AWOL offenders at Fort Meade in the early 1970s found that officers were rarely charged, and that higher-ranking personnel with longer records of service were more likely to have their sentence reduced than lower-ranking AWOL offenders. See Burchett, "Race and the AWOL Offender," 184–89.

28. Sec Bell and Bell, "Desertion and Antiwar Protest," 437.

29. See, e.g., Shils, "A Profile of the Military Deserter"; Eugene H. Drucker and Shepard Schwartz, *The Prediction of AWOL, Military Skills, and Leadership Potential* (Alexandria, VA: Human Resources Research Organization, 1973), vi; Roger Little, "Buddy Relations and Combat Performance," in Morris Janowitz, ed., *The New Military: Changing Patterns of Organization* (New York: Russell Sage Foundation, 1970), 195–223.

30. See Baskir and Strauss, *Reconciliation*, 2; Baskir and Strauss, *Chance and Circumstance*, 116 ("Every official analysis of Vietnam-era deserters has found the same thing—that the overwhelming majority were neither conscientious nor cowardly. They were men who decided simply to put their own interests over the day-to-day needs of the military.").

31. See, e.g., Suzanne Clark, *Cold Warriors: Manliness on Trial in the Rhetoric of the West* (Carbondale: Southern Illinois Press, 2000).

32. On the gender norms of this era, see generally Elaine Tyler May, *Homeward Bound: American Families in the Cold War Era* (New York: BasicBooks, 1988); Stephanie Coontz, *The Way We Never Were: American Families and the Nostalgia Trap* (New York: BasicBooks, 1992); Joanne Meyerowitz, ed., *Not June Cleaver: Women and Gender in Postwar America, 1945–1960* (Philadelphia: Temple University Press, 1994).

33. Clark, *Cold Warriors*, 20. See also Robert D. Dean, *Imperial Brotherhood: Gender and the Making of Cold War Foreign Policy* (Amherst: University of Massachusetts Press, 2001); K. A. Cuordileone, "'Politics in an Age of Anxiety': Cold War Political Culture and the Crisis in American Masculinity, 1949–1960," *Journal of American History* 87 (2) (2000): 525–45; Steven Cohan, *Masked Men: Masculinity and the Movies in the Fifties* (Bloomington: Indiana University Press, 1997).

34. See, e.g., Susan Jeffords, *The Remasculinization of America* (Bloomington: Indiana University Press, 1989).

35. In the courts-martial that reached military appellate courts between 1951 and 1973, there are no cases involving servicewomen charged with criminal absence. On the number of servicewomen prosecuted, Baskir and Strauss estimate that about 100 women deserted during Vietnam (compared to 100,000 men), *Chance and Circumstance*, 120. On lower rates of AWOL among servicewomen, see also Linda K. Kerber, "'A Constitutional Right to Be Treated Like . . . Ladies': Women, Civic Obligation, and Military Service," *University of Chicago Law School Round Table* (1993): 95–127, 113, citing E. A. Blacksmith, ed., *Women in the Military* (New York: Wilson, 1992).

36. This section is based on my review of approximately three hundred appel-

late opinions, written between 1951 and 1973, in which women appear in appeals of AWOL or desertion convictions. Many opinions neglect the facts entirely; others provide only the sketchiest of details, so there are of course many other cases in which women were involved in the commission and prosecution of military crime. The sample I rely upon is admittedly small, but considered in the context of other courts-martial, military history, and especially the sociological surveys of absence offenders during this period, which identify personal and family problems as the primary reasons for unauthorized absences, it fairly represents the problems that motivated a majority of criminal absences.

37. *United States v. Colvin*, 46 C.M.R. 1276 (A.F.C.M.R. 1973); *United States v. Miller*, 38 C.M.R. 648 (A.B.R. 1968); *United States v. Sutton*, 36 C.M.R. 29 (1965); *United States v. Charlton*, 34 C.M.R. 660 (A.B.R. 1964).

38. *United States v. Henson*, 47 C.M.R. 696 (A.C.M.R. 1973); *United States v. Erwin*, 46 C.M.R. 1265 (C.G.C.M.R. 1973); *United States v. Cox*, 23 C.M.R. 535 (A.B.R. 1957); *United States v. Bradley*, 18 C.M.R. 494 (A.B.R. 1954).

39. *United States v. Carey*, 29 C.M.R. 259 (1960); *United States v. Bruce*, 26 C.M.R. 809, 813 (C.G.B.R. 1958).

40. *United States v. Cleveland*, 39 C.M.R. 339 (A.B.R. 1968).

41. *United States v. Williams*, 32 C.M.R. 208 (1962).

42. *United States v. Bauman*, 41 C.M.R. 841, 844 (C.G.C.M.R. 1969); *United States v. Robinson*, 7 C.M.R. 618 (A.F.B.R. 1952).

43. *United States v. Nuckols*, 20 C.M.R. 471 (A.B.R. 1955).

44. *United States v. Boone*, 24 C.M.R. 400 (A.B.R. 1957).

45. Female psychiatrists testify in *United States v. Braley*, 47 C.M.R. 46 (C.G.C.M.R. 1973) and *United States v. Wisener*, 46 C.M.R. 1100, 1104 (C.G.C.M.R. 1973).

46. See, e.g., *United States v. Gravley*, 25 C.M.R. 382 (1958).

47. For a case in which an accused Coast Guard member challenged the authority of a female reservist who served as military judge at his court-martial, see *United States v. Patten*, 41 C.M.R. 849, 852 (C.G.C.M.R. 1970).

48. On the ways in which U.S. policy and law have blamed women's inadequacies—as mothers in particular—for the social ills of the twentieth century, see Martha Albertson Fineman, *The Neutered Mother, the Sexual Family, and Other Twentieth Century Tragedies* (New York: Routledge, 1995); Martha Fineman and Isabel Karpin, eds., *Mothers in Law: Feminist Theory and the Legal Regulation of Motherhood* (New York: Columbia University Press, 1995); Dorothy E. Roberts, "Racism and Patriarchy in the Meaning of Motherhood," *American University Journal of Gender and the Law* 1 (1993): 1–38; Nancy Fraser and Linda Gordon, "A Genealogy of Dependency: Tracing a Keyword of the U.S. Welfare State," *Signs* 19 (1994): 309–36; Lee Rainwater and William L. Yancey, *The Moynihan Report and the Politics of Controversy* (Cambridge: MIT Press, 1967).

49. See, e.g., Michael P. Rogin, "Kiss Me Deadly: Communism, Motherhood, and Cold War Movies," in Michael Rogin, ed., *Ronald Reagan, the Movie and Other Episodes in Political Demonology* (Berkeley and Los Angeles: University of California Press, 1987). See Philip Wylie, *Generation of Vipers* (New York: Farrar and Rinehart, 1942) for the derogatory term "Momism," applied to women's purported psychological manipulation of men into helpless dependents. See also the

1962 film *The Manchurian Candidate,* in which Angela Lansbury's evil character is called "smothering" in Roger Ebert's recent review of the film. See Roger Ebert, "Riveting 'Manchurian Candidate' Still a Must," *Chicago Sun Times,* November 29, 2002.

50. *United States v. Deshazo,* 19 C.M.R. 878, 881, 2n (A.B.R. 1955). On blaming women for soldiers' misdeeds, see also *United States v. Jones,* 11 C.M.R. 855 (A.F.B.R. 1953), in which a serviceman's new wife is portrayed as the culprit in the seduction of an inept drunk man.

51. For the former, see *United States v. Packard,* 11 C.M.R. 640, 642 (N.B.R. 1953); for the latter, see *United States v. Robles-Robles,* 14 C.M.R. 250 (A.B.R. 1953); *United States v. Roadcap,* 47 C.M.R. 15, 17 (A.C.M.R. 1973); *United States v. Anderson,* 38 C.M.R. 582 (A.B.R. 1967).

52. *United States v. Qualls,* 22 C.M.R. 450, 451 (A.B.R. 1956); see similar reasoning in *United States v. Roop,* 45 C.M.R. 652 (C.G.C.M.R. 1972) and *United States v. Prather,* 13 C.M.R. 740 (A.B.R. 1953).

53. *United States v. Linerode,* 11 C.M.R. 262, 265 (A.B.R. 1953).

54. *United States v. Ellerbe,* 12 C.M.R. 438, 439 (A.B.R. 1953).

55. *United States v. Looff,* 15 C.M.R. 36 (1954); *United States v. Thrasher,* 4 C.M.R. 350 (A.B.R. 1952). The failure of the government to produce the mother of an accused servicemember as a witness was raised on appeal as well; see *United States v. Ewing,* 44 C.M.R. 738 (N.C.M.R. 1971).

56. *United States v. Wagner,* 33 C.M.R. 853, 854 (A.F.B.R. 1963).

57. In another case, the mother of the private being court-martialed became so distraught at trial that she distracted the military judge. See *United States v. Gibson,* 44 C.M.R. 333, 335 (A.C.M.R. 1971).

58. See, e.g., *United States v. Overton,* 26 C.M.R. 464 (1958); *United States v. Mills,* 44 C.M.R. 460 (A.C.M.R. 1971). But see *United States v. Lenoir,* 40 C.M.R. 99 (1969), in which a mother fraudulently enlisted her sixteen-year-old son using the birth certificate of an older brother. Until 1966, when the age of minimum service was raised to seventeen, male minors who were at least fourteen could be enlisted in naval service with parental consent. In this case, the court upheld the teenager's conviction for desertion. See *Lenoir,* 40 C.M.R. 100.

59. *United States v. Davis,* 46 C.M.R. 241 (1973). The services frequently wrote to servicemen's mothers to ask them to urge their sons to return to duty. See, e.g., *United States v. Burgess,* 44 C.M.R. 67 (1971); *United States v. Shepherd,* 37 C.M.R. 659 (A.B.R. 1967); *United States v. Daniels,* 10 C.M.R. 918 (A.F.B.R. 1953).

60. *United States v. Soccio,* 24 C.M.R. 287 (1957); see also *Patten,* 41 C.M.R. 850; *United States v. Allen,* 25 C.M.R. 8 (1957) (first he tried other means of help, but the Red Cross and Army Emergency Relief had refused him aid and his commanding officer refused his request for furlough); *United States v. Justice,* 14 C.M.R. 669 (A.B.R. 1953); *United States v. Costanza,* 13 C.M.R. 546 (N.B.R. 1953); *United States v. Henry,* 13 C.M.R. 690 (A.F.B.R. 1953); *United States v. Rotski,* 12 C.M.R. 649 (C.G.B.R. 1953); *United States v. Gorringe,* 15 C.M.R. 882 (A.B.R. 1953).

61. *United States v. Hendricksen,* 45 C.M.R. 899 (N.C.M.R. 1972); *United States v. Turpin,* 35 C.M.R. 539 (A.B.R. 1964).

62. *United States v. Mogardo*, 41 C.M.R. 490, 491 (A.B.R. 1969).

63. *United States v. Myatt*, 17 C.M.R. 533 (N.B.R. 1954); *United States v. Walden*, 15 C.M.R. 654 (A.B.R. 1954); *United States v. Rodriguez*, 6 C.M.R. 101 (1952) (involving a Mexican national inducted into U.S. military); *United States v. Knoph*, 6 C.M.R. 108 (1952); *United States v. Johnson*, 6 C.M.R. 810 (A.F.B.R. 1952); *United States v. Wimp*, 4 C.M.R. 509 (C.G.B.R. 1952); *United States v. Gochnour*, 7 C.M.R. 89 (A.B.R. 1952); *United States v. Le Blanc*, 2 C.M.R. 612 (N.B.R. 1952); *United States v. Sturtevant*, 2 C.M.R. 275 (A.B.R. 1951).

64. *United States v. Balagtas*, 48 C.M.R. 339 (N.C.M.R. 1973); *United States v. Temperley*, 47 C.M.R. 235 (1973); *United States v. Anderson*, 43 C.M.R. 960 (A.F.C.M.R. 1971); *United States v. Banner*, 22 C.M.R. 510 (A.B.R. 1956). For servicemen living with a common-law wife, see *United States v. Wilson*, 42 C.M.R. 263 (1970); *United States v. Lowery*, 22 C.M.R. 423 (A.B.R. 1956); *United States v. Stowe*, 12 C.M.R. 657 (A.B.R. 1953); *United States v. Boone*, 3 C.M.R. 115 (1952) (also living with their children).

65. *United States v. LaRue*, 29 C.M.R. 286, 293 (1960); see *United States v. King*, 28 C.M.R. 243; *United States v. Blanton*, 23 C.M.R. 128; and the Supreme Court's analogy between marriage and military service in *United States v. Grimley*, 137 U.S. 147, 151–52 (1890). On the gender politics of consent and contract, see Pamela Haag, *Consent: Sexual Rights and the Transformation of American Liberalism* (Ithaca, NY: Cornell University Press, 1999).

66. *United States v. Haggerty*, 42 C.M.R. 860, 862 (A.C.M.R. 1970).

67. *United States v. Sutton*, 39 C.M.R. 884 (C.G.C.M.R. 1968).

68. *United States v. Larue*, 13 C.M.R. 296 (A.B.R. 1953). For a case in which a serviceman's girlfriend who was pregnant with his child convinced him not to return, see *United States v. Barrett*, 12 C.M.R. 619 (N.B.R. 1953).

69. See, e.g., *United States v. Fleming*, 40 C.M.R. 236 (1969); *United States v. Matheny*, 41 C.M.R. 39 (1969); *United States v. Moore*, 38 C.M.R. 667 (A.B.R. 1968); *United States v. Parker*, see below; *United States v. Rosen*, 25 C.M.R. 437 (1958); *United States v. Tainpeah*, 18 C.M.R. 382 (N.B.R. 1954); *United States v. Gholston*, 15 C.M.R. 435 (A.B.R. 1954); *United States v. Yunque-Burgos*, 13 C.M.R. 54 (1953); *United States v. Griffin*, 12 C.M.R. 595, 596 (A.B.R. 1953); *United States v. Bieganowski*, 12 C.M.R. 815 (A.B.R. 1953); *United States v. Loewen*, 9 C.M.R. 312 (A.B.R. 1953); *United States v. Richardson*, 4 C.M.R. 150 (1952); *United States v. Wilkinson*, 4 C.M.R. 337 (A.B.R. 1952).

70. For servicemen who left to be with their wives, see, e.g., *Anderson*, 43 C.M.R. 966, noting "the accused's destitute wife"; *United States v. Bermudez*, 47 C.M.R. 68, 69 (A.F.C.M.R. 1973); *United States v. Koepnick*, 40 C.M.R. 441 (A.B.R. 1968); *United States v. Albert*, 36 C.M.R. 267 (1966); *United States v. McCarty*, 29 C.M.R. 757 (C.G.B.R. 1960); *United States v. Peterson*, 24 C.M.R. 51 (1957). Although some soldiers who claimed that they left to handle family obligations were not being truthful, see, e.g., *United States v. Taylor*, 4 C.M.R. 450 (N.B.R. 1952), most of these courts-martial involved convincing (if legally irrelevant) testimony about convicted servicemembers' efforts to help their families while absent from duty. For those who left to be with female lovers, see *United States v. Wilson*, 42 C.M.R. 263, 266 (1970); *United States v. Smith*, 31 C.M.R. 367, 367 (A.B.R. 1961); *United States v. Niepoky*, 29 C.M.R. 625 (A.B.R. 1960);

United States v. Peters, 19 C.M.R. 600 (C.G.B.R. 1955); *United States v. Hargrove,* 13 C.M.R. 687 (A.F.B.R. 1953); *United States v. Rushlow,* 10 C.M.R. 139 (1953); *United States v. Oliver,* 10 C.M.R. 111 (1953); *United States v. Stuckey,* 8 C.M.R. 583 (N.B.R. 1953). For more heart-wrenching narratives of soldiers who deserted during Vietnam, see White House Central File, Subject file, Box 1, Folder JL 1, "Amnesties-Clemencies-Pardons, 8/9/74 to 8/31/74," and other folders related to the Clemency Review Board, Gerald R. Ford Library and Museum, Ann Arbor, MI.

71. *United States v. Olsen,* 28 C.M.R. 532, 534–35 (A.B.R. 1959).

72. *Turpin,* 35 C.M.R. 541; *United States v. Boswell,* 22 C.M.R. 461 (A.B.R. 1956); *United States v. Fisher,* 22 C.M.R. 60 (1956); *United States v. Osborne,* 21 C.M.R. 556, 557 (N.B.R. 1956) (explaining his wife and child's situation as near "starvation"). See also *United States v. Gonyo,* 39 C.M.R. 963 (A.F.B.R. 1968); *United States v. Woodruff,* 44 C.M.R. 536 (A.C.M.R. 1971); *United States v. Frasher,* 42 C.M.R. 742 (A.C.M.R. 1970); *United States v. Lawson,* 39 C.M.R. 726, 728 (A.B.R. 1968); *United States v. Morrison,* 33 C.M.R. 899 (A.F.B.R. 1963); *United States v. Welsh,* 33 C.M.R. 502, 503 (A.B.R. 1963); *United States v. Bowen,* 27 C.M.R. 148 (1958); *United States v. Shaughnessy,* 24 C.M.R. 226 (1957); *United States v. Cleckley,* 23 C.M.R. 307 (1957); *United States v. Huff,* 19 C.M.R. 603 (C.G.B.R. 1955) (no wife, and mother deceased, but went home to care for entire family); *United States v. Guthrie,* 12 C.M.R. 299 (A.B.R. 1953); *United States v. Melton,* 12 C.M.R. 221 (A.B.R. 1953); *United States v. Johnsey,* 11 C.M.R. 798 (A.F.B.R. 1953); *United States v. McLean,* 11 C.M.R. 755 (A.F.B.R. 1953); *United States v. Mize,* 11 C.M.R. 587 (N.B.R. 1953); *United States v. Uhland,* 10 C.M.R. 620 (A.F.B.R. 1953); *United States v. Keeton,* 9 C.M.R. 447 (A.B.R. 1953); *United States v. Sparks,* 8 C.M.R. 831 (A.F.B.R. 1953); *United States v. Murillo,* 7 C.M.R. 376 (A.B.R. 1953); *United States v. Affronte,* 7 C.M.R. 815 (A.F.B.R. 1952); *United States v. Hernandez,* 7 C.M.R. 234 (A.B.R. 1952); *United States v. Palmer,* 7 C.M.R. 237 (A.B.R. 1952); *United States v. Show,* 4 C.M.R. 564 (A.F.B.R. 1952); *United States v. Burke,* 2 C.M.R. 753 (A.F.B.R. 1952).

73. *United States v. Smith,* 5 C.M.R. 178, 180 (A.B.R. 1952). See also *United States v. Weems,* 45 C.M.R. 538 (A.C.M.R. 1972); *United States v. Mitchell,* 36 C.M.R. 458 (1966); *United States v. Paul,* 46 C.M.R. 779, 782 (C.G.C.M.R. 1971).

74. *United States v. Wilson,* 25 C.M.R. 788, 789 (A.F.B.R. 1957). See also *United States v. Barnett,* 8 C.M.R. 653 (A.F.B.R. 1953); *United States v. Cliette,* 9 C.M.R. 289 (A.B.R. 1953).

75. *United States v. Kazmorck,* 12 C.M.R. 603, 604 (A.B.R. 1953); *United States v. Morgan,* 23 C.M.R. 776 (A.F.B.R. 1956). See also, for cases in which the travails of the accused mother triggered an unauthorized absence, *United States v. Campbell,* 28 C.M.R. 717 (C.G.B.R. 1959); *United States v. Bowen,* 27 C.M.R. 148 (1958); *United States v. Brown,* 24 C.M.R. 585 (A.F.B.R. 1957); *United States v. Wellman,* 15 C.M.R. 348 (1954); *United States v. Perez,* 13 C.M.R. 593 (C.G.B.R. 1953); *United States v. LaCroix,* 4 C.M.R. 821 (A.F.B.R. 1952).

76. *United States v. Charity,* 11 C.M.R. 621, 623 (N.B.R. 1953). See also *United States v. Shofkom,* 11 C.M.R. 740 (A.F.B.R. 1953); *United States v. Pere-*

grina, 8 C.M.R. 293 (A.B.R. 1953); *United States v. Ibarra*, 7 C.M.R. 232, (A.B.R. 1952); *United States v. Cantu*, 2 C.M.R. 220 (A.B.R. 1951). For a case in which an Army private asserted that he disobeyed an order that would have put him into danger because of his concern for his dependent mother, whose leg had recently been amputated, see *United States v. Young*, 3 C.M.R. 313 (A.B.R. 1952).

77. *United States v. Kim*, 38 C.M.R. 650, 652 (A.B.R. 1967). For other cases in which the actions of the betrayal of wives and female lovers of servicemen led directly to desertion, see *United States v. Victor*, 24 C.M.R. 433, 434 (A.B.R. 1957); *United States v. Norton*, 46 C.M.R. 213, 220 (1973); *United States v. Nelson*, 24 C.M.R. 326, 326 (A.B.R. 1957); *United States v. Reed*, 13 C.M.R. 925, 927 (A.F.B.R. 1953); *United States v. Arocho*, 8 C.M.R. 289 (A.B.R. 1953).

78. *United States v. Wilson*, 28 C.M.R. 844, 847 (A.F.B.R. 1959); see also *United States v. Kirby*, 41 C.M.R. 702, 703 (A.C.M.R., 1970); *United States v. Vance*, 38 C.M.R. 779 (C.G.B.R. 1967); *United States v. Johnson*, 22 C.M.R. 278 (1957); *United States v. Walker*, 20 C.M.R. 931 (A.F.B.R. 1955); *United States v. Dunlap*, 10 C.M.R. 319 (A.B.R. 1953).

79. *United States v. Frazier*, 14 C.M.R. 495, 497 (N.B.R. 1954); see also *United States v. Tisdall*, 28 C.M.R. 119, 120 (1959); *United States v. Johns*, 28 C.M.R. 639, 641 (N.B.R. 1959).

80. *United States v. Moore*, 38 C.M.R. 667, 669 (A.B.R. 1968).

81. See, e.g., *United States v. Roop*, 45 C.M.R. 652, 654 (C.G.C.M.R. 1972); *United States v. Greenwalt*, 20 C.M.R. 285 (1955); *United States v. Charlton*, 16 C.M.R. 384 (N.B.R. 1954).

82. *United States v. Sims*, 22 C.M.R. 591 (A.B.R. 1956); *United States v. Rothman*, 30 C.M.R. 872 (A.F.B.R. 1960); see also *United States v. Clay*, 29 C.M.R. 238 (1960); *United States v. Perry*, 10 C.M.R. 387 (A.B.R. 1953); *United States v. Thomason*, 3 C.M.R. 797 (A.F.B.R. 1952); *United States v. Runner*, 3 C.M.R. 742 (A.F.B.R. 1952); *United States v. Shull*, 2 C.M.R. 83 (1952).

83. See, e.g., *United States v. Peak*, 40 C.M.R. 506, 507 (A.C.M.R. 1969) ("alleged infidelity of wife" contributed to schizophrenic reaction); *United States v. Qualls*, 22 C.M.R. 450, 451 (A.B.R. 1956) (psychiatrist testified that "when his wife threatened to leave him, the accused probably did not have the same freedom of choice as a normal person would have in making a decision as far as placing obligations to his country or to his family in a paramount position"); *United States v. Hunsinger*, 11 C.M.R. 589, 591 (N.B.R. 1953) ("[the accused] considers his mental problems to be the result of his worry over his family, his sexual relations, religious conflicts, a belief that his wife was unfaithful, and heavy drinking.").

84. *United States v. Goodman*, 31 C.M.R. 397, 408 (N.B.R. 1961).

85. *United States v. Batson*, 30 C.M.R. 610, 619 (N.B.R. 1960).

86. 30 C.M.R. 620.

87. Ibid.

88. See *United States v. Carey*, 29 C.M.R. 259 (1960).

89. 29 C.M.R. 261.

90. Ibid.

91. 29 C.M.R. 262.

92. 29 C.M.R. 262–63.

93. 29 C.M.R. 263.

94. 29 C.M.R. 265.

95. 29 C.M.R. 267. He adds: "We live in an age of specialization, and nowhere is particularized knowledge more important than in the area of measuring an individual's mental capacity." 29 C.M.R. 276.

96. Ibid.

97. 29 C.M.R. 271–72.

98. 29 C.M.R. 264.

99. See discussion in *Carey*, 29 C.M.R. 259; see also *MCM*, para. 124.

100. The military's constitutional authority to regulate servicemembers' marriage was upheld by the Court of Military Appeals in *United States v. Wheeler*, 30 C.M.R. 387 (1961) and *United States v. Levinsky*, 30 C.M.R. 541 (1960).

101. See discussion in *United States v. Reese*, 22 C.M.R. 612 (A.B.R. 1956). The regulation of military women's marital status followed a different trajectory. During World War II, regulations that required a servicewoman to resign if she married a military man were relaxed when they proved too costly to enforce. But the demands of military life and the limited support that the government provided to husbands of servicewomen encouraged women to remain single throughout the postwar years.

102. A string of cases reached the appellate courts from the Philippines and concerned junior enlistees in the Navy or Marine Corps who had married without permission while stationed in the Philippines: *United States v. Nation*, 26 C.M.R. 504 (1958); *United States v. Levinsky*, 30 C.M.R. 641 (N.B.R. 1960); *United States v. Wheeler*, 30 C.M.R. 387 (1961); *United States v. Smith*, 31 C.M.R. 150 (1961); *United States v. Mohr*, 45 C.M.R. 134 (1972) (also a black marketeering and stealing government property case). Courts-martial involving marriage regulations were also prosecuted by the Air Force and Army in Germany; see *United States v. Forrest*, 26 C.M.R. 931 (A.F.B.R. 1958) and *United States v. Reese*, 22 C.M.R. 612 (A.B.R. 1956) respectively; and by the Army in Panama, see *United States v. Jordan*, 30 C.M.R. 424 (A.B.R. 1960).

103. See, e.g., *Levinsky, Reese*.

104. See *United States v. Nation*, 26 C.M.R. 504 (1958). The woman is unnamed in the appellate record.

105. 26 C.M.R. 507.

106. Ibid.

107. For evidence from outside the military justice system, see Katharine H. S. Moon, *Sex among Allies: Military Prostitution in U.S.-Korea Relations* (New York: Columbia University Press, 1997), 20–21, for anecdotal evidence of young American enlistees who were involved with Korean prostitutes; for soldier-civilian relationships during the Vietnam War, see, e.g., Gary D. Solis, *Marines and Military Law in Vietnam: Trial by Fire* (Washington, DC: History and Museums Division, Headquarters, U.S. Marine Corps, 1989), 109, for the high number of requests made by Marines who wished to marry Vietnamese women. On race and miscegenation law generally, see Peggy Pascoe, "Miscegenation Law, Court Cases, and Ideologies of 'Race' in Twentieth-Century America," *Journal of American History* 83 (1996): 44–69.

108. The military's pattern of censuring cross-racial intimacy is consistent with the practice in civilian law and policy analyzed in Rachel F. Moran, *Interracial In-*

timacy: The Regulation of Race and Romance (Chicago: University of Chicago Press, 2001).

109. The practice of outlawing interracial marriage ended with the Warren Court's decision in *Loving v. Virginia*, 388 U.S. 1 (1967); for the story of the litigants in that historic case, see Robert A. Pratt, "Crossing the Color Line: A Historical Assessment and Personal Narrative of *Loving v. Virginia*," *Howard Law Journal* 41 (1998): 229–250.

110. Messages about the virility of American men and the sexual availability of foreign women surrounded military bases overseas. For examples of this phenomenon during the Vietnam War, see Tom Engelhart, *The End of Victory Culture: Cold War America and the Disillusioning of a Generation* (New York. Basic, 1995), 190–92.

111. *United States v. Roux*, 3 C.M.R. 232, 234 (A.B.R. 1952). Other soldiers stationed in Korea and Vietnam also went AWOL to marry or pursue relationships that were not approved by their military superiors. See, e.g., *United States v. Faulk*, 48 C.M.R. 185 (A.C.M.R. 1973); *United States v. Pinkston*, 39 C.M.R. 261 (1969); *United States v. Pugh*, 38 C.M.R. 541 (A.B.R. 1967); *United States v. Herring*, 23 C.M.R. 489 (A.B.R. 1957); *United States v. Redenius*, 15 C.M.R. 161 (1954).

112. *United States v. Uzzo*, 13 C.M.R. 119 (1953); *United States v. Greer*, 12 C.M.R. 499 (A.B.R. 1953).

113. Transience and bigamy were not new phenomena in American society or law, however, nor were they confined to military life. Bigamy was a consistent feature of the history of American domestic relations, and men, primarily those from less privileged classes, had frequently been prosecuted for the crime under state statutes. See Nancy F. Cott, *Public Vows: A History of Marriage and the Nation* (Cambridge: Harvard University Press, 2000), 126–27.

114. Lawrence M. Friedman describes bigamy as a crime of mobility in "Crimes of Mobility," *Stanford Law Review* 43 (1991): 637–63, 638. See also Louis Bilionis, "Process, the Constitution, and Substantive Criminal Law," *Michigan Law Review* 96 (1998): 1269–1343.

115. See App. 6c, "Forms and Specifications," Article 134, *MCM*, 489, para. 126.

116. Thirty-nine convictions for bigamy appear in the appellate reports between 1951 and 1974, half of which were prosecuted during the first five years the UCMJ was in operation. See *United States v. Findley*, 1 C.M.R. 731 (A.F.B.R. 1951); *United States v. Graves*, 5 C.M.R. 582 (A.F.B.R. 1952); *United States v. Williams*, 7 C.M.R. 548 (A.F.B.R. 1952); *United States v. Patrick*, 7 C.M.R. 65 (1953) and 10 C.M.R. 319 (A.B.R. 1953); *United States v. Johnson*, 8 C.M.R. 368 (A.B.R. 1952); *United States v. Avery*, 9 C.M.R. 648 (A.F.B.R. 1953); *United States v. Boyles*, 10 C.M.R. 446 (A.B.R. 1953); *United States v. Jones*, 11 C.M.R. 855 (A.F.B.R. 1953); *United States v. Bates*, 12 C.M.R. 395 (A.B.R. 1953); *United States v. Duff*, 12 C.M.R. 802 (A.F.B.R. 1953); *United States v. Weber*, 13 C.M.R. 176 (A.B.R. 1953); *United States v. Williamson*, 14 C.M.R. 676 (A.F.B.R. 1954); *United States v. Smith*, 15 C.M.R. 543 (N.B.R. 1954); *United States v. Brooks*, 17 C.M.R. 467 (N.B.R. 1954); *United States v. McCluskey*, 20 C.M.R. 261 (1955); *United States v. Smith*, 20 C.M.R. 632 (A.F.B.R. 1955); *United States v. Noe*, 22

C.M.R. 198 (1956); *United States v. Matthews*, 23 C.M.R. 790 (A.F.B.R. 1956); *United States v. Guidry*, 22 C.M.R. 615 (A.B.R. 1956); *United States v. Bateman*, 23 C.M.R. 312 (1957); *United States v. Powell*, 24 C.M.R. 835 (A.F.B.R. 1957); *United States v. Geib*, 24 C.M.R. 840 (A.F.B.R. 1957); *United States v. Wille*, 26 C.M.R. 403 (1958); *United States v. Holzhuter*, 27 C.M.R. 448 (1959); *United States v. Wise*, 28 C.M.R. 105 (1959); *United States v. Howell*, 29 C.M.R. 528 (1960); *United States v. Jordan*, 30 C.M.R. 424 (A.B.R. 1960); *United States v. Whitaker*, 31 C.M.R. 333 (A.B.R. 1961); *United States v. McDonald*, 32 C.M.R. 689 (N.B.R. 1962); *United States v. Grogen*, 34 C.M.R. 677 (N.B.R. 1963); *United States v. Politano*, 34 C.M.R. 298 (1964); *United States v. Bradshaw*, 35 C.M.R. 118 (1964); *United States v. Johnson*, 34 C.M.R. 328 (1964); *United States v. Bishop*, 35 C.M.R. 606 (A.B.R. 1965); *United States v. Blackwell*, 36 C.M.R. 835 (A.F.B.R. 1965); *United States v. Pruitt*, 38 C.M.R. 236 (1968); *United States v. Burkhart*, 40 C.M.R. 1009 (A.F.C.M.R. 1969); *United States v. Hadsell*, 42 C.M.R. 766 (A.C.M.R. 1970).

117. Convicted bigamists ranged from an airman basic in the Air Force to a lieutenant colonel in the Army. See *United States v. Williams*, 7 C.M.R. 548 (A.F.B.R. 1952); *United States v. Johnson*, 8 C.M.R. 368 (A.B.R. 1952).

118. The Army and Air Force prosecuted fifteen cases each, the Navy six, and the Marine Corps two. One bizarre—even in the relatively bizarre arena of bigamy crimes—involved both the Army and the Air Force: A sergeant first class in the Army married a woman he had met at a Fort Bliss club in 1957 without realizing that she was already the wife of an Air Force major. When the sergeant realized his error, he reacted with a frenzy of threats and intimidation that resulted in multiple charges at court-martial. *United States v. Wille*, 26 C.M.R. 403 (1958).

119. See *United States v. Burkhart*, 40 C.M.R. 1009 (A.F.C.M.R. 1969) (holding bigamy a service-connected crime under *O'Callahan v. Parker*); *United States v. Hadsell*, 42 C.M.R. 766 (A.C.M.R. 1970) (holding that bigamy was not service connected when a local court in Texas had jurisdiction and there was no proof of fraudulent use of government benefits).

120. *United States v. Guidry*, 22 C.M.R. 615, 617 (A.B.R. 1956).

121. The other case involves a Panamanian woman. See *United States v. Jordan*, 30 C.M.R. 424 (A.B.R. 1960).

122. *United States v. Strand*, 20 C.M.R. 13 (1955).

123. He was sentenced to a dishonorable discharge and one year confinement, but the Court of Military Appeals ruled that the military judge's instructions on sentencing had been improper, and remanded for a rehearing on sentence.

124. See 1951 *MCM*, Table of Maximum Punishments, 224–25.

125. For a discussion of the different "bite" of adultery and bigamy crimes, see Carol M. Rose, "Trust in the Mirror of Betrayal," *Boston University Law Review* 75 (1995): 531–62, 546.

126. *United States v. Leach*, 22 C.M.R. 178 (1956).

127. 22 C.M.R. 191.

128. Only sixteen appear in the appellate record between 1951 and 1974. Counting cohabitation cases is an imprecise task because of the way the military charged persons accused of multiple crimes. Not all of these cases focused on the charge of cohabitation, and other cases were brought where cohabitation could

have been charged but was not. Charging practices were not uniform across different services and commands. See *United States v. Hanna*, 7 C.M.R. 571 (A.F.B.R., 1952); *United States v. Bailey*, 12 C.M.R. 564 (A.B.R. 1953); *United States v. Walters*, 16 C.M.R. 191 (1954) and 11 C.M.R. 355 (A.B.R. 1953); *United States v. James*, 22 C.M.R. 799 (A.F.B.R. 1956); *United States v. Stone*, 24 C.M.R. 356(A.B.R. 1957); *United States v. Melville*, 25 C.M.R. 101 (1958); *United States v. Jones*, 31 C.M.R. 540 (A.F.B.R. 1961); *United States v. Hooten*, 30 C.M.R. 339 (1961); *United States v. Smith*, 35 C.M.R. 662 (A.B.R. 1965); *United States v. Boswell*, 35 C.M.R. 185 (A.B.R. 1965); *United States v. Chancelor*, 36 C.M.R. 453 (1966); *United States v. Westmore*, 38 C.M.R. 204 (1968) and 38 C.M.R. 476 (A.B.R., 1967); *United States v. Rener*, 37 C.M.R 329 (1967); *United States v. Acosta*, 41 C.M.R. 341 (1970); *United States v. Parker*, 46 C.M.R. 737 (A.C.M.R. 1972); *United States v. Mohr*, 45 C.M.R. 134 (1972).

129. Three cases mention non-American women: an Army captain who was living with a Japanese woman, *United States v. Hudson*, 7 C.M.R. 162 (A.B.R. 1952); an Army sergeant living with a Korean woman in *United States v. Case*, 37 C.M.R. 606 (A.B.R. 1966); and an Army captain was court-martialed in the 1960s for cohabiting with a woman who ran a prostitution operation in a hotel in Kaiserslautern, Germany, *United States v. Boswell*, 35 C.M.R. 491 (A.B.R. 1964). The court reversed this last conviction, however, on the grounds that staying frequently at a woman's residence over a period of two months was insufficient evidence for a wrongful cohabitation offense.

130. Domestic cases include the Great Falls case, see *United States v. Hanna*, 7 C.M.R. 571 (A.F.B.R. 1952), as well as *United States v. Bailey*, 12 C.M.R. 564 (A.B.R. 1953); *United States v. Melville*, 25 C.M.R. 101 (1958); *United States v. Jones*, 31 C.M.R. 540 (A.F.B.R., 1961); *United States v. Chancelor*, 36 C.M.R. 453 (1966); *United States v. Smith*, 35 C.M.R. 662 (A.B.R. 1965); *United States v. Rener*, 37 C.M.R. 329 (1967); *United States v. Acosta*, 41 C.M.R. 341 (1970). International cases include *United States v. Walters*, 16 C.M.R. 191 (1954); *United States v. James*, 22 C.M.R. 799 (A.F.B.R. 1956); *United States v. Parker*, 46 C.M.R. 737 (A.C.M.R. 1972). Three cases do not specify location: see *United States v. Stone*, 24 C.M.R. 356(A.B.R. 1957); *United States v. Hooten*, 30 C.M.R. 339 (1961); *United States v. Westmore*, 38 C.M.R. 204 (1968).

131. Among the sixteen cases, eight were Army, five were Air Force, and three were Navy courts-martial.

132. *United States v. Parker*, 46 C.M.R. 737 (A.C.M.R. 1972). For another case involving both wrongful cohabitation and disobedience of orders charges, see *United States v. Mohr*, 45 C.M.R. 134 (1972). For other cohabitation cases that resembled bigamy cases, see *United States v. Andrews*, 9 C.M.R. 667 (A.F.B.R. 1953); *United States v. Hudson*, 7 C.M.R. 162 (A.B.R. 1952); *United States v. Pruitt*, 30 C.M.R. 322 (1961) and 30 C.M.R. 457 (A.B.R. 1960); *United States v. Smith*, 34 C.M.R. 185 (1964); *United States v. Case*, 37 C.M.R. 606 (A.B.R. 1966); *United States v. Acosta*, 41 C.M.R. 341 (1970).

133. See *United States v. Butler*, 5 C.M.R. 213 (1952); *United States v. Perkins*, 17 C.M.R. 702 (A.F.B.R. 1954); *United States v. Frayer*, 29 C.M.R. 416 (1960). Other adultery courts-martial that did take place do not appear in the appellate records because they resulted in acquittal or because the sentences meted out were

slight enough and the legal issues of so little import, they failed to trigger appellate review. Although many recent legal scholars have commented on the armed forces' continued criminalization of adultery in the late-twentieth century, none have explored the incidence of military prosecution of adultery. All, however, note that prosecution has historically been rare despite estimates of relatively high rates of adultery among servicemembers. See, e.g., C. Quince Hopkins, "Rank Matters but Should Marriage? Adultery, Fraternization, and Honor in the Military," *UCLA Women's Law Journal* 9 (1999): 177–266. For an analysis of the post–Cold War law of adultery in the military, see James M. Winner, "Beds with Sheets but No Covers: The Right to Privacy and the Military's Regulation of Adultery," *Loyola of Los Angeles Law Review* 31 (1998): 1073–1111.

134. See App. 6c, "Forms and Specifications," Article 134, *MCM*, 488, para. 118. Treatises on military law did not address adultery before the UCMJ. Colonel Winthrop's thorough nineteenth-century treatise, *Military Law and Precedents*, left it out entirely, as did the Army manuals in effect before 1949. The 1937 Navy manual, *Navy Courts and Boards*, mentioned adultery, fornication, and unlawful cohabitation as punishable offenses (see sec. 127). For a brief military legal history of adultery proscriptions, see *United States v. Hickson*, 22 M.J. 146 (1986).

135. Adultery charges appear twenty-four times in the appellate record, but only five of those prosecutions focused on extramarital sex as the primary offense. Adultery sometimes was charged in conjunction with more serious sex offenses such as carnal knowledge, rape, sodomy, or lewd and lascivious acts. *United States v. Francis*, 12 C.M.R. 695 (A.F.B.R., 1953); *United States v. Radford*, 17 C.M.R. 595 (A.F.B.R., 1954); *United States v. Schuller*, 17 C.M.R. 101 (1954); *United States v. Farrell*, 18 C.M.R. 680 (A.F.B.R. 1954); *United States v. Nastro*, 22 C.M.R. 163 (1956); *United States v. Panchisin*, 30 C.M.R. 921 (A.F.B.R. 1961). It was also added to the list of charges in prosecutions for other crimes of deceit, such as fraud, larceny, or false statements. *United States v. Neville*, 7 C.M.R. 180 (A.B.R. 1952); *United States v. Davis*, 14 C.M.R. 879 (A.F.B.R. 1954); *United States v. Boyd*, 21 C.M.R. 395 (A.B.R. 1956); *United States v. Hogsett*, 25 C.M.R. 185 (1958); *United States v. Walbert*, 33 C.M.R. 246 (1963); *United States v. Carter*, 36 C.M.R. 433 (1966); *United States v. Bricker*, 35 C.M.R. 566 (A.B.R. 1965). Adultery was added to other types of charges as well. See *United States v. Lane*, 12 C.M.R. 347 (A.B.R. 1953); *United States v. Chavers*, 23 C.M.R. 701 (C.G.B.R. 1957); *United States v. Alcantara*, 39 C.M.R. 682 (A.B.R. 1968).

136. See William T. Cavanaugh, Jr., "The United States Military Chaplaincy Program: Another Seam in the Fabric of Our Society?" *Notre Dame Law Review* 59 (1983): 181–231, at 213. See also Andrew Jensen, with Martin Abramson, *The Trial Of Chaplain Jensen* (New York: Arbor House, 1974); Richard G. Hutcheson, Jr., *The Churches and the Chaplaincy* (Atlanta: John Knox, 1975), 124. There is no published opinion for this case because Chaplain Jensen was acquitted.

137. Beginning in the 1950s, an increasing number of legal scholars and prosecutors began to doubt the wisdom of treating adultery as a crime. In 1962, the American Law Institute chose not to specify adultery as a crime in the Model Penal Code, terming its prosecution an unwarranted invasion of privacy. Model Penal Code sec. 213.6; Martin J. Siegel, "For Better or for Worse: Adultery, Crime and the Constitution," *Journal of Family Law* 30 (1991–92): 45–89, 49.

138. *United States v. Butler*, 5 C.M.R. 213 (A.B.R. 1952).

139. See, e.g, *United States v. Miller*, 20 C.M.R. 782 (A.F.B.R. 1955), in which an airman in Seattle was charged with Mann Act violations as well as adultery, larceny, and forgery; and *United States v. Dixon*, 38 C.M.R. 221 (1968), in which an Army captain at Fort Bragg was prosecuted for his adulterous relationship with a married college professor.

140. One case involved an airman basic who slept with the wife of a deployed seaman in 1953: *United States v. Howard*, 12 C.M.R. 916 (A.F.B.R. 1953). Two other servicemen were court-martialed for violating orders by committing adultery: *United States v. Hedgecock*, 30 C.M.R. 624 (N.B.R. 1960); *United States v. Aycock*, 35 C.M.R. 130 (1964) and 31 C.M.R. 874 (A.F.B.R. 1964).

141. *United States v. Parker*, 33 C.M.R. 111 (1963). See also *United States v. Parker*, 32 C.M.R. 482 (A.B.R. 1962).

142. 33 C.M.R. 113.

143. 33 C.M.R. 114.

144. There is no mention of Parker's alleged sexual partner being available as a witness.

145. 33 C.M.R. 116.

146. Paragraph 148e, *MCM*. The 1951 *Manual* adopted the common-law evidentiary privilege, explaining that husband and wife were competent to testify in favor of each other but not against each other, except in cases where the party who would testify has been injured by the crime being tried. The *Manual* listed several offenses in which this exception permitted one spouse to testify against the interests of another, including bigamy, unlawful cohabitation, abandonment or failure to support a wife or children, or violations of the "white slave" act. The military courts added adultery, rape of a biological daughter, and incest to this list. On spousal privilege, see also *United States v. Yzaguirre*, 19 C.M.R. 585 (C.G.B.R. 1955); *United States v. Thrasher*, 4 C.M.R. 350 (A.B.R. 1952).

147. 33 C.M.R. 118.

148. 33 C.M.R. 112–13. The military did not recognize marital rape at this time, nor did civilian criminal jurisdictions. Whether a husband was protected from his wife's testimony about acts of forcible or consensual sodomy against her was not entirely clear; the court in this case raised but declined to answer that question. On the history of marital rape exemptions, see Jill Elaine Hasday, "Contest and Consent: A Legal History of Marital Rape," *California Law Review* 88 (2000): 1373–1463.

149. 33 C.M.R. 119. However, the court upheld the assault conviction on the grounds that evidentiary rules permitted a wife to testify about a husband's assault against her.

150. This case raises echoes of Carson McCullers's homoerotic novel about an Army officer obsessed with a young enlisted man, who is in turn obsessed with the officer's philandering wife. See Carson McCullers, *Reflections in a Golden Eye* (Boston: Houghton Mifflin, 1941).

151. On domestic violence in military society, see, e.g., Peter J. Mercier and Judith D. Mercier, *Battle Cries on the Home Front: Violence in the Military Family* (Springfield, IL: Charles C. Thomas, 2000); Stephen J. Brannen and Elwood R. Hamlin II, "Understanding Spouse Abuse in Military Families," in James A. Mar-

tin, Leora N. Rosen, and Linette R. Sparacino, eds., *The Military Family: A Practice Guide for Human Service Providers* (Westport, CT: Praeger, 2000), 169–83.

152. See, e.g., *United States v. Benavides,* 2 C.M.R. 520 (A.B.R. 1952); *United States v. Kane,* 2 C.M.R. 470 (A.B.R. 1952); *United States v. McKay,* 18 C.M.R. 629 (A.F.B.R. 1954); *United States v. Wheeler,* 27 C.M.R. 981 (A.F.B.R. 1959); *United States v. Erb,* 31 C.M.R. 110 (1961) and 30 C.M.R. 938 (A.F.B.R. 1961); *United States v. Weaver,* 31 C.M.R. 662 (A.F.B.R. 1961).

153. See, e.g., *United States v. Madison,* 34 C.M.R. 435 (1964), in which an Air Force captain claimed he shot his wife to death by accident. Although the court-martial initially sentenced the captain to two years confinement for the killing, the convening authority reduced the sentence to only dismissal (the officers' equivalent of a dishonorable discharge), with no time served, and total forfeitures.

154. For example, in 1966, John James, Jr., a noncommissioned officer in the Army at Fort Leonard Wood, was convicted for the premeditated murder of his wife. According to trial testimony, James sometimes beat his wife, and was drunk and "lightly slapping" his wife early on the day of the fatal assault. Later that day, while James was kicking and beating his wife to death, their five year-old son hid in a closet, coming out only after neighbors arrived at the house. James was sentenced to confinement for life, reduced to twenty-five years by the convening authority. *United States v. James,* 38 C.M.R. 637 (A.B.R. 1967). For another case noting a history of abuse, see *United States v. Judd,* 27 C.M.R. 187 (1959).

155. *United States v. Moore,* 34 C.M.R. 415, 422 (1964).

156. Ibid.

157. Historical statistics on the incidence of domestic violence can only suggest the extent of a problem that was largely ignored until the 1970s. Social work efforts in the nineteenth century brought some attention to intrafamily violence, but only in the 1970s did public discourse about the issue return to prominence. See Elizabeth Pleck, *Domestic Tyranny: The Making of Social Policy against Family Violence from Colonial Times to the Present* (New York: Oxford University Press, 1987), 182, and chapter 10 generally.

158. See Pleck, *Domestic Tyranny,* appendix B, "Changes in the Incidence of Family Murder."

159. The chronological list of nondeadly domestic violence courts-martial includes *United States v. Downard,* 1 C.M.R. 405 (A.B.R. 1951); *United States v. Francis,* 12 C.M.R. 695 (A.F.B.R. 1953); *United States v. St. Clair,* 21 C.M.R. 208 (1956); *United States v. Rowe,* 32 C.M.R. 302 (1962); *United States v. Riska,* 33 C.M.R. 939 (A.F.B.R. 1963); *United States v. Moore,* 34 C.M.R. 415 (1964); *United States v. Burton,* 42 C.M.R. 970 (A.F.C.M.R. 1970). Among the domestic murders were fourteen wives and two girlfriends killed by men, along with two servicemen killed by their wives (for the latter, see the discussion of *Reid v. Covert* below). See *United States v. O'Brien,* 11 C.M.R. 105 (1953) and 9 C.M.R. 201 (A.B.R. 1952); *United States v. Kane,* 2 C.M.R. 470 (A.B.R. 1952); *United States v. McKay,* 18 C.M.R. 629 (A.F.B.R. 1954); *United States v. Wheeler,* 27 C.M.R. 981 (A.F.B.R. 1959) and 28 C.M.R. 212 (1959); *United States v. Judd,* 28 C.M.R. 388 (1960) and 27 C.M.R. 187 (1959); *United States v. Marymont,* 29 C.M.R. 561 (1960) and 28 C.M.R. 904 (A.F.B.R. 1960); *United States v. Erb,* 31 C.M.R. 110 (1961) and 30 C.M.R. 938 (A.F.B.R. 1961); *United States v. Weaver,* 31 C.M.R.

662 (A.F.B.R. 1961); *United States v. Herrington,* 33 C.M.R. 814 (A.F.B.R. 1963); *United States v. Madison,* 34 C.M.R. 435 (1964); *United States v. Smith,* 35 C.M.R. 662 (A.B.R. 1965); *United States v. James,* 38 C.M.R. 637 (A.B.R. 1967); *United States v. Ross,* 41 C.M.R. 51, 52 (1969); *United States v. Wilson,* 40 C.M.R. 112 (1969); *United States v. Fields,* 41 C.M.R. 119 (1969); *United States v. Griggs,* 41 C.M.R. 541 (A.C.M.R. 1969).

160. See *Downard, Rowe,* and *Moore* for public fights; see *Francis* for a wife abuse charge added to other charges of child sexual abuse.

161. *United States v. Downard,* 1 C.M.R. 405 (A.B.R. 1951).

162. 1 C.M.R. 408.

163. For example, consider the case of Adlin D. St. Clair, the wife of an Army captain, who was court-martialed in Stuttgart, Germany, for assault with intent to commit murder after she attacked her husband. She was convicted and sentenced to one year of confinement—a notably lenient sentence given the twenty-year maximum punishment for attempted murder under the UCMJ. *United States v. St. Clair,* 21 C.M.R. 208 (1956); table of Maximum Punishments, *MCM,* 219, spec ifying that the maximum sentence for criminal attempts is the same as that for the completed offense, to a maximum of twenty years (and not including the death penalty). See also *United States v. Griggs,* 41 C.M.R. 541 (A.C.M.R. 1969).

164. For example, a 1969 opinion of the Court of Military Appeals in the case of a sergeant first class in the Army who murdered his wife in a parking lot at Schofield Barracks, Hawaii, does not report the sentence adjudged at trial. *United States v. Fields,* 41 C.M.R. 119 (1969).

165. See, e.g., the case of an Army enlisted man convicted of premeditated murder in the death of his wife; in May 1967 he was sentenced to twenty-five years by a court-martial, but it was reduced to three years for unspecified errors at trial. *United States v. Wilson,* 40 C.M.R. 112 (1969).

166. *United States v. Riska,* 33 C.M.R. 939 (A.F.B.R. 1963). See *Burton* for another attempted murder of wife prosecution.

167. 33 C.M.R. 941.

168. Ibid.

169. For example, an Air Force sergeant who was convicted for killing his wife in Mississippi in January 1961 testified that his "marital troubles were caused by [his wife's] jealousy, false accusations of infidelity, and continuous arguments in which she cursed him and called him foul names." *United States v. Weaver,* 31 C.M.R. 662 (A.F.B.R. 1961).

170. See the trial of an Air Force colonel for a deadly outburst against his family for a lengthy treatment of sanity issues reported at *United States v. Herrington,* 33 C.M.R. 814 (A.F.B.R. 1963).

171. See, e.g., William E. Nelson, "Criminality and Sexual Morality in New York, 1920–1980," *Yale Journal of Law and Humanities* 5 (1992): 265–355, 317–18.

172. See Linda Gordon, *Heroes of Their Own Lives: The Politics and History of Family Violence, Boston, 1880–1960* (New York: Viking, 1988), 282–85.

173. See *United States v. O'Brien,* 11 C.M.R. 105 (1953) and 9 C.M.R. 201 (A.B.R. 1952). O'Brien's death sentence was unique in domestic violence courts-martial, but his modus operandi was not. In 1962, Sergeant First Class David B.

Smith also staged a car accident, this one on a Kentucky state highway, to hide the cause of his wife's death after he had apparently knocked her unconscious with several blows to the head. Smith was trying to escape his marriage so that he might take up with a former WAC, who had already borne his child. Convicted of unpremeditated murder "by means of crushing her with a blunt instrument" and unlawful cohabitation, Smith was sentenced to eight years confinement and dishonorably discharged. But the murder charge was dismissed on appeal when an Army board of review balked at the circumstantial nature of the government's evidence and threw out the murder conviction. *United States v. Smith*, 35 C.M.R. 662 (A.B.R. 1965).

174. See *United States v. Erb*, 31 C.M.R. 110 (1961) and 30 C.M.R. 938 (A.F.B.R. 1961).

175. 31 C.M.R. 113–14.

176. 31 C.M.R. 113.

177. Jurisdiction over civilians was important during this period because of the increasing number of civilian dependents and contractors who lived and worked with servicemembers on critical military projects. Civilian employees posted overseas with the military were occasionally court-martialed for acts of domestic violence similar to those for which servicemen were tried. For example, an Army employee in France was court-martialed for beating his wife to death because he was jealous of her attentions to a cab driver. *United States v. Grisham*, 13 C.M.R. 486 (A.B.R. 1953). On the vulnerability of civilians to court-martial, see also *United States v. Burney*, 21 C.M.R. 98 (1956), upholding the court-martial conviction of a government contractor for killing another civilian government employee in Japan while playing Russian roulette.

178. *United States v. Covert*, 19 C.M.R. 174 (1955); 16 C.M.R. 465 (A.F.B.R. 1954); *Reid v. Covert*, 354 U.S. 1 (1957).

179. The second case decided in *Reid v. Covert* was that of Dorothy K. Smith, who stabbed her colonel husband to death in Tokyo in October 1952. Like Covert, Smith was court-martialed, convicted, and sentenced to life in prison despite doubts about her sanity that were raised at trial. Smith's mental health was brought into question by evidence about her excessive drinking, drug abuse, erratic behavior, and a suicide attempt. See *United States v. Smith*, 10 C.M.R. 350 (A.B.R. 1953); 17 C.M.R. 314 (1954).

180. Frederick Bernays Wiener, "American Military Law in Light of the First Mutiny Act's Tricentennial," *Military Law Review* 126 (1989): 1–88, 50–55.

CHAPTER 5
COMMANDING DISCRETION

1. This brief overview of the military's racial integration relies on the insights of a relatively deep historiography. Among the most important works are Richard M. Dalfiume, *Desegregation of the U.S. Armed Forces: Fighting on Two Fronts, 1939–1953* (Columbia: University of Missouri Press, 1969), an essential account that focuses on the early years of integration and the impact of civil rights leaders; the authoritative work of Bernard C. Nalty and Morris J. MacGregor, Jr., including Nalty's *Strength for the Fight: A History of Black Americans in the Military* (New

York: Free Press, 1986); MacGregor's *Integration of the Armed Forces, 1940–1965* (Washington, DC: Center for Military History, U.S. Army, 1981); and MacGregor and Nalty's multivolume compilation of documents, Bernard C. Nalty and Morris J. MacGregor, Jr., eds., *Blacks in the Military: Essential Documents* (Wilmington, D.E.: Scholarly Resources, 1981). On the Air Force, see Alan L. Gropman, *The Air Force Integrates, 1945–1964*, 2nd ed. (Washington, DC: Smithsonian Institution Press, 1998). Though a journalistic rather than scholarly account, Lee Nichols, *Breakthrough on the Color Front* (New York: Random House, 1954) is a pioneering work. See also Charles C. Moskos and John Sibley Butler, *All That We Can Be: Black Leadership and Racial Integration the Army Way* (New York: Basic Books, 1996); Sherie Mershon and Steven Schlossman, *Foxholes and Color Lines: Desegregating the U.S. Armed Forces* (Baltimore: Johns Hopkins University Press, 1998); Richard O. Hope, *Racial Strife in the U.S. Military: Toward the Elimination of Discrimination* (New York: Praeger, 1979); Jack D. Foner, *Blacks and the Military in American History: A New Perspective* (New York: Praeger, 1974); Leo Bogart, ed., *Social Research and the Desegregation of the U.S. Army: Two Original 1951 Field Reports* (Chicago: Markham, 1969), republished with a new introduction as *Project Clear: Social Research and the Desegregation of the United States Army* (New Brunswick, NJ: Transaction, 1992).

2. For an analysis of the link between racial justice and Cold War politics, see Mary L. Dudziak, *Cold War Civil Rights: Race and the Image of American Democracy* (Princeton: Princeton University Press, 2000).

3. See Nalty, *Strength for the Fight*, 281–85. See also *The President's Commission on Equal Opportunity in the Armed Forces, Initial Report: Equality of Treatment and Opportunity for Negro Military Personnel Stationed within the United States* (Washington, DC: 1963).

4. See Nalty, *Strength for the Fight*, 281–85.

5. For statistics, see ibid., 313.

6. See ibid.; see also MacGregor, *Integration*, 569, noting that in 1969, there were 116 black cadets and midshipmen at the elite service academies, a paltry 1.1 percent of the total enrollment of 10,404.

7. See Paul Stillwell, ed., *The Golden Thirteen: Recollections of the First Black Naval Officers—A Long-Overdue Tribute to the Men Who Desegregated the U.S. Naval Officer Corps* (Annapolis: Naval Institute Press, 1993); MacGregor, *Integration*, chart on 416; *Selected Manpower Statistics* (1967). The Army had commissioned African American officers in the nineteenth century, in contrast to the Navy's policy of exclusion.

8. See, e.g., MacGregor, *Integration*, 612.

9. Between 1953 and 1962, the Army and Air Force counted approximately 10 percent nonwhite recruits among enlistees. The Navy rate of nonwhite enlistments was less than 5 percent, while the Marine Corps' was just over 7. See MacGregor, *Integration*, 522–25.

10. Ibid., charts on 416 and 525.

11. Ibid., 605–8.

12. On the racial and class dimensions of the Vietnam soldier, see Christian G. Appy, *Working-Class War: American Combat Soldiers and Vietnam* (Chapel Hill: University of North Carolina Press, 1993). On excessive death rates among blacks

in Vietnam from 1961 to 1967, and self-conscious reaction by military leaders to correct this, see James E. Westheider, *Fighting on Two Fronts: African Americans and the Vietnam War* (New York: New York University Press, 1997), 12–13.

13. For a description of the racial tension onboard ships in the early 1970s, see Leonard F. Guttridge, *Mutiny: A History of Naval Insurrection* (Annapolis: Naval Institute Press, 1992), 255–84. For examples of race riots, see Gary D. Solis, *Marines and Military Law in Vietnam: Trial by Fire* (Washington, DC: History and Museums Division, Headquarters, U.S. Marine Corps, 1989), 124, describing a riot that left one dead and fourteen wounded at a Camp LeJeune, North Carolina enlisted men's club in July 1969; Gropman, *The Air Force Integrates*, 159–63, describing a four-day riot at Travis Air Force Base in May 1971, with casualties of one dead and thirty injured. See also Westheider, *Fighting on Two Fronts*, especially 1–20.

14. Westheider, *Fighting on Two Fronts*, 45.

15. My conclusions about the extent of racism in military justice are based on my review of reported military justice cases as well as the secondary literature on race and military justice, most of which draws on studies that took place during and after the Vietnam War. Available statistics point out racial disparities at court-martial in the second half of the twentieth century but leave open the question of whether those disparities were a direct result of racial discrimination. See generally Robert J. Stevenson, "The Containment and Expulsion of Wayward Soldiers in the U.S. Military," *Social Science Journal* 25 (2) (1988): 195–210; Daniel A. Lennon, "A Communitarian Army? Status and Role Considerations in the Use of Courts-Martial in the United States Army," *Deviant Behavior* 12 (1) (1991): 31–79; Lawrence J. Morris, "A Closer Look at Army Court-Martial Conviction Rates," *Army Lawyer* (March 1993): 26; Dan Landis and Rick Tallarigo, "Race and the Administration of Non-judicial Punishments in the U.S. Army," *Armed Forces and Society* 24 (1997): 193–220.

16. For an assessment of the dynamic of race at court-martial during the nineteenth century, see the extensive scholarship on the 1881 courts-martial of Army officer Henry Flipper and West Point cadet Johnson Whittaker: Henry O. Flipper, *Black Frontiersman: The Memoirs of Henry O. Flipper, First Black Graduate of West Point* (College Station: Texas A&M University Press, 1997); Charles M. Robinson III, *The Court-Martial of Henry Flipper* (El Paso: Texas Western Press, 1994); John F. Marszalek, Jr., *Court-Martial: A Black Man in America* (New York: Charles Scribner's Sons, 1972); Darryl W. Jackson, Jeffrey H. Smith, Edward H. Sisson, and Helene T. Krasnoff, "Bending toward Justice: The Posthumous Pardon of Lieutenant Henry Ossian Flipper," *Indiana Law Journal* 74 (1999): 1251–96.

17. See, e.g., Howard Ball, *A Defiant Life: Thurgood Marshall and the Persistence of Racism in America* (New York: Crown, 1998), 95–113, recounting NAACP efforts to stop racial brutality and discrimination in the armed forces during World War II and Marshall's heavy caseload of court-martial cases after the war's end.

18. See Robert L. Allen, *The Port Chicago Mutiny* (New York: Amistad, 1993).

19. See Adam Clayton Powell, "The Rape of Justice by Court Martial," reprinted in the 1946 congressional record and cited in Keith M. Harrison, "Be All You Can Be without the Protection of the Constitution," *Harvard Blackletter*

Journal 8 (1991): 221–51, 42n. For a much later invocation of similar rhetoric about a World War II court-martial, see Walter A. Luszki, *A Rape of Justice: MacArthur and the New Guinea Hangings* (Lanham, MD: Madison Books, 1991), a former Army officer's account of the 1944 hanging of six African American GIs in New Guinea for the alleged sexual assault of two white Army nurses.

20. See Records of the NAACP, 1842–1992, especially Series B of Groups II, III, and IV, and the Papers of the NAACP Legal Defense and Educational Fund, 1915–68, both collections in the Manuscript Division, Library of Congress, Washington, DC. The NAACP Legal Defense and Education Fund separated from the NAACP in 1956. The LDEF records are currently closed to researchers because of concerns about protecting attorney-client privilege, but an extensive (though incomplete, since the entire collection has not been processed) finding aid reveals the high number of courts-martial and military justice issues that crowded the civil rights litigators' docket through the mid-1950s. See, e.g., the Subject File, 1929–68, including Box 38, Air Force (correspondence, 1950–59); Boxes 40 through 43, Armed Forces (records of Korean War era courts-martial); Box 99 (records on a Defense Fund for Men in Korea); Boxes 125 and 126 (Navy courts-martial, 1952–56); Box 143 (military correspondence and memoranda, 1953–62); Boxes 145 through 149 ("Soldier troubles" and discharge review cases); Boxes 150 through 157 (court-martial files from the 1950s); Box 162 through 173 (veterans complaints); Box 188 (records of 1948 court-martial on Guam, three capital cases); and the Legal Case File, 1915–67, Boxes 239 through 245 (World War II and Korean War court-martial records).

21. Gilbert eventually served five years of this sentence. On the incident, see William T. Bowers, William M. Hammond, and George L. MacGarrigle, *Black Soldier, White Army: The 24ᵗʰ Infantry Regiment in Korea* (Washington, DC: Center of Military History, U.S. Army, 1996), 185–86.

22. More than three dozen other African American soldiers faced court-martial for the same charge, which was a violation of Article of War 75. Because the UCMJ did not become effective until the summer of 1951, Gilbert and the others were prosecuted under the Army's Articles of War, not the UCMJ. For Gilbert's story, see the draft version of Marshall's article, eventually published in *The Crisis* as "Summary Justice—The Negro GI in Korea" (May 1951), in the Records of the NAACP, 1842–1992, Group II, Series B, Box 100, folder titled "Marshall, Thurgood, General, 1951–55." See also Ball, *A Defiant Life*, 110–13; Michael D. Davis and Hunter R. Clark, *Thurgood Marshall: Warrior at the Bar, Rebel on the Bench* (Secaucus, NJ: Carol Publishing Group, 1992), 120–35; Roger Goldman with David Gallen, *Thurgood Marshall: Justice for All* (New York: Carroll and Graf, 1992), 112–19; and Carl T. Rowan, *Dream Makers, Dream Breakers: The World of Justice Thurgood Marshall* (Boston: Little, Brown, 1993), 159–69.

23. On the disputed facts of Gilbert's retreat, see Blair's discussion of the portrayal of the events by the official Army historian as compared to the accounts of black officers who were on the battlefield in question. Blair, *The Forgotten War*, 161–62. See Bowers, Hammond, and MacGarrigle *Black Soldier*, 172–73, for a chart of general courts-martial in the 24th Infantry from July to October 1950. Although it does not mention Gilbert's case, for a scathing indictment of the treatment of African Americans in the 24th Infantry, see Curtis James Morrow, *What's*

a Commie Ever Done to Black People? A Korean War Memoir of Fighting in the U.S. Army's Last All Negro Unit (Jefferson, NC: McFarland and Co., 1997).

24. Rowan, *Dream Makers*, 167–68.

25. Marshall commented: "Even in Mississippi a Negro gets a trial longer than that if he is brought to trial." Rowan, *Dream Makers*, 167–68. On the response of the Army's Far East Command, and General MacArthur in particular, to Marshall's report, see Bowers, Hammond, and MacGarrigle, *Black Soldier*, 186–88. The Army investigated Marshall's charges, but found reasons for brief trials (the charges were "easy to prove," 187), defended the zeal of the attorneys who represented the accused soldiers, and blamed poor leadership and training for the much-maligned performance of the 24th Infantry. Army leaders also argued that the racism that existed among troops in Korea was no excuse for malingering or otherwise failing to respond appropriately under fire.

26. See, for example, the pamphlet published by the NAACP documenting the complaints of troops stationed in Germany in the late 1960s: NAACP, *The Search for Military Justice: Report of an NAACP Inquiry into the Problems of the Negro Serviceman in West Germany* (New York: NAACP Special Contribution Fund, 1971). See also the memoranda included in the folder "United States Armed Forces, General, 1956–63," in Box 327 of Papers of the NAACP, Group III, Series A, and Box 2, Folder 1, "Correspondence, 1968. October–November, 1 of 2" in the Papers of Robert Lee Carter (1917–) (both documents in the Manuscript Division, Library of Congress), which includes letters related to a 1968 court-martial appeal in which Carter, then general counsel of the NAACP, was interested.

27. See e.g., Jay M. Siegel, *Origins of the Navy Judge Advocate General's Corps: A History of Legal Administration in the United States Navy, 1775–1967* (Washington, DC: 1997), appendix P, "African-American, Hispanic-American and Other Ethnic Minorities in the Navy Judge Advocate General's Corps," A-161 to A-173. The first law specialist in the Navy was Franklin D. Cleckley, commissioned in 1965. Cleckley served for three years and was followed, virtually one at a time, by other African American men for a decade. The Navy's difficulty in retaining young lawyers generally was reflected in the short-term service of these African American lawyers. Not until the late 1970s would the recruiting efforts of a D.C. Superior Court judge and commander in the Naval Reserve JAG Corps, John D. Fauntleroy, combine with the equal opportunity directives of the Department of Defense to create a sizable cohort of African American navy judge advocates. Three African American men served among the four hundred Marine Corps lawyers on duty in Vietnam. See Solis, *Trial by Fire*, 131 and 244.

28. See Westheider, *Fighting on Two Fronts*, 54. The demographics of judge advocates reflected the larger racial portrait of the legal profession in the United States, in which the representation of racial minorities increased only gradually through the 1970s. See Edward J. Littlejohn and Leonard S. Rubinowitz, "Black Enrollment in Law Schools: Forward to the Past?" *Thurgood Marshall Law Review* 12 (1986): 415–55.

29. Department of Defense, *Report of the Task Force on the Administration of Justice within the Armed Forces* (Washington, DC: 1972).

30. See also Westheider, *Fighting on Two Fronts*, 55. But see Solis, *Trial by Fire*,

232, reporting a 1972 poll of servicemembers that demonstrated confidence in military justice across race lines.

31. See *United States v. Floyd*, 18 C.M.R. 362 (A.B.R. 1955). He was sentenced to ten years confinement—reduced from the forty years adjudged at trial—and a dishonorable discharge.

32. See Ron Robin, *The Making of the Cold War Enemy: Culture and Politics in the Military-Intellectual Complex* (Princeton: Princeton University Press, 2001), 173–74, on anecdotal evidence of racial and ethnic tension in an official report—evidence that was disregarded by investigators.

33. On racism in the camps, see generally Robin, *The Making of the Cold War Enemy* and Raymond B. Lech, *Broken Soldiers* (Urbana: University of Illinois Press, 2000).

34. Robin, *The Making of the Cold War Enemy*, 172–73, and chapter 8.

35. Ibid., 165. Robin also points out how the Korean War POWs surfaced in Betty Friedan's *The Feminine Mystique*, which cited their failings as a negative consequence of mothers who were limited by conventional feminine roles. On how Project 100,000 and military psychology results directly influenced the Moynihan Report, see Ellen Herman, *The Romance of American Psychology: Political Culture in the Age of Experts* (Berkeley and Los Angeles: University of California Press, 1995), 200–207.

36. Harold G. Stagg, "Brain-Washing," *Army Times*, August 15, 1953.

37. See Westheider, *Fighting on Two Fronts*, 45–65, on bias within the system and efforts to address it; see also Ned E. Felder, "Civil Rights in the Armed Forces" (Thesis, Judge Advocate Generals School, 1969), 111–12, reprinting a March 1969 memo from the Army Judge Advocate General to all staff judge advocates about the importance of ending any racial discrimination in military justice, including in the imposition of nonjudicial punishment.

38. For a list of racial incidents in 1967 and 1968, see Felder, "Civil Rights in the Armed Forces," 106–11. On African American resistance to military policies, see Wallace Terry, "Black Power in Viet Nam: Racial Tensions in the Military, September 1969," 704–8 (reprinted from *Time*, September 19, 1969) in *Reporting Vietnam: Part One, American Journalism, 1959–1969* (New York: Library of America, 1998).

39. See David Cortright, *Soldiers in Revolt: The American Military Today* (Garden City, NY: Anchor Press/Doubleday, 1975) 47; for more statistics and context about mutiny and insurrection charges, see Richard Moser, *The New Winter Soldiers: GI and Veteran Dissent during the Vietnam Era* (New Brunswick, NJ: Rutgers University Press, 1996), chapter 2.

40. See Stephen D. Wesbrook, "Historical Notes," in Morris Janowitz and Stephen D. Wesbrook, *The Political Education of Soldiers* (Beverly Hills, CA: Sage, 1983): 251–84, 272.

41. See Moser, *The New Winter Soldiers*, 46; see also Charley Trujillo, *Soldados: Chicanos in Vietnam* (San Jose, CA: Chusma House, 1990). Race riots appear in many court-martial records. See *United States v. Peirce*, 42 C.M.R. 390 (A.C.M.R. 1970); *United States v. Daniels*, 42 C.M.R. 131 (1970); *United States v. Holmes*, 43 C.M.R. 430 (A.C.M.R. 1970); *United States v. Taylor*, 46 C.M.R. 461

(A.C.M.R. 1972); *United States v. Favors*, 48 C.M.R. 873 (A.C.M.R. 1974). Dozens of other incidents characterized as "riots," some of which likely involved racial tension, also appear in the appellate record; many took place in brigs and other military jails. For example, black and hispanic Marines rioted at Twentynine Palms in 1971; see *United States v. Rosa*, 46 C.M.R. 480 (N.C.M.R. 1972) and *United States v. Brown*, 45 C.M.R. 911 (N.C.M.R. 1972); a 1969 riot at Camp Lejeune led to *United States v. Hundley*, 45 C.M.R. 94 (1972); see also *United States v. Peirce*, 42 C.M.R. 390 (A.C.M.R. 1970); *United States v. Johnson*, 43 C.M.R. 604 (A.C.M.R. 1970); *United States v. Henderson*, 44 C.M.R. 749 (N.C.M.R. 1971).

42. See Wilton B. Persons Papers in the Senior Officers Oral History Program series at the Military History Institute, Carlisle Barracks, PA (1985 interview), 348–66 on the Darmstadt case. On a 1970 protest by African Americans in Germany, see *United States v. Alexander*, 47 C.M.R. 786 (1973). See generally Byron G. Fineman, Jonathan F. Borus, and M. Duncan Stanton, "Black-White and American-Vietnamese Relations among Soldiers in Vietnam," *Journal of Social Issues* 31 (4) (1975): 39–48.

43. See Moser, *The New Winter Soldiers*, 48; Cortright, *Soldiers in Revolt*, 43–47. For narratives of fragging incidents, see Solis, *Trial by Fire*, 169–70; James Kitfield, *Prodigal Soldiers: How the Generation of Officers Born of Vietnam Revolutionized the American Style of War* (New York: Simon and Schuster, 1995), 121. Courts-martial for fragging appear occasionally in appellate records; see, e.g., *United States v. Johnson*, 3 M.J. 143 (1977).

44. Tom Engelhart, *The End of Victory Culture: Cold War America and the Disillusioning of a Generation* (New York: Basic, 1995), 247–48, describes the situation vividly: "As the 1960s ended, statistics flowing back to Washington about the American war machine pointed toward an unimaginable nightmare. Drug taking was rampant (by 1971, up to 60 percent of returning soldiers admitted to some sort of use); desertions stood at seventy per thousand, a modern high; small-scale mutinies or 'combat refusals' were at critical, if untabulated, levels; incidents of racial conflict had soared; and strife between officers ('lifers') and men was at unprecedented levels (reported 'fraggings'—assassination attempts—against unpopular officers or NCOs rose from 126 in 1969 to 333 in 1971, despite declining troop strength in Vietnam)." See also Thomas E. Ricks, *Making the Corps* (New York: Scribner, 1997), 136.

45. See Wesbrook, "Historical Notes," 273.

46. See Moser, *The New Winter Soldiers*, 74.

47. See Cortright, *Soldiers in Revolt*, 41–43; Moser, *The New Winter Soldiers*, 51–52; Cecil B. Curry, *Long Binh Jail: An Oral History of Vietnam's Notorious U.S. Military Prison* (Washington, DC: Brassey's, 1999).

48. See Fred Gardner, *The Unlawful Concert: An Account of the Presidio Mutiny Case* (New York: Viking, 1970). See also *United States v. Sood*, 42 C.M.R. 635 (A.C.M.R. 1970). For other instances of brig riots with racial overtones and "black militant" leaders, see Solis, *Trial By Fire*, 114, describing 1968 riots in Vietnam.

49. On the Presidio incident, see the polemical account of Robert Sherrill, *Military Justice Is to Justice as Military Music Is to Music* (New York: Harper and Row, 1970), 4–6.

50. On the minimum time required for an AWOL charge, see Alfred Avins, *The Law of AWOL* (New York: Oceana Publications, 1957), 260–64.

51. See, e.g., *United States v. Sims*, 22 C.M.R. 591 (A.B.R. 1956).

52. Unauthorized absences dominated military justice under virtually every regime of military criminal law. See, e.g., Charles Royster, *A Revolutionary People at War: The Continental Army and American Character, 1775–1783* (Chapel Hill: University of North Carolina Press, 1979), 71; Ella Lonn, *Desertion during the Civil War* (Lincoln: University of Nebraska Press, 1998; first published 1928); Mark A. Weitz, *A Higher Duty: Desertion among Civil War Troops during the Civil War* (Lincoln: University of Nebraska Press, 2000); Jack D. Foner, *The United States Soldier between Two Wars* (New York: Humanities, 1970), 223; A. W. Brown, "Administration of Justice in the Army," *Cornell Law Quarterly* 3 (1918): 178–210. During World War II, more than half of Army courts and 80 percent of Navy courts involved unauthorized absences. See Robert L. Patterson, "Military Justice," *Tennessee Law Review* 19 (1945): 12, estimating that over half of all World War II Army crimes were absence offenses, and Avins, *The Law of AWOL*, 34, estimating that 80 percent of Navy courts-martial during World War II involved charges of unauthorized absence. See also Herman L. Goldberg and Frederick A. C. Hoefer, "The Army Parole System," *Journal of Criminal Law and Criminology* 40 (1949), 158–69, 163, on World War II.

53. The quotation is taken from Major Wayne Anderson, "Unauthorized Absences," *Army Lawyer* (June 1989): 3–17, quoting Frederic Lederer, "Absence Without Leave—The Nature of the Offense," *Army Lawyer* (March 1974), 4–9.

54. James H. Hayes, *The Evolution of Armed Forces Enlisted Personnel Management Policies: Executive Summary* (Santa Monica, CA: RAND, 1982), vii.

55. Ibid., 58–59.

56. Ibid.

57. See, Lawrence M. Baskir and William A. Strauss, *Chance and Circumstance: The Draft, the War, and the Vietnam Generation* (New York: Alfred A. Knopf, 1978), 161; see also *United States v. Sims*, 22 C.M.R. 591 (A.B.R. 1956), a case discussing the effects of Army policies that influenced commanders' decisions about whether to send an AWOL offender to court-martial or to an administrative discharge hearing. Policies even changed with respect to absence offenders from prior wars; beginning in 1956, the Army authorized administrative discharges for desertion cases from World War II so long as "extenuating circumstances, such as critical family conditions" had existed at the time of the offense. See *United States v. McCarty*, 29 C.M.R. 757, 760 (C.G.B.R. 1960).

58. See D. Bruce Bell and Beverly W. Bell, "Desertion and Antiwar Protest: Findings from the Ford Clemency Program," *Armed Forces and Society* 3 (3) (1977): 433–43, 439–40, 1n.

59. For a particularly clear set of recommendations advocating this shift, see Arthur F. Lincoln, "The Predictability of AWOL" (Thesis, Judge Advocate Generals School, 1972). See also Eugene H. Drucker and Shepard Schwartz, *The Prediction of AWOL, Military Skills, and Leadership Potential* (Alexandria, VA: Human Resources Research Organization, January 1973).

60. Scholarship on this issue has grown in recent years; see, e.g., Beverly Allen, *Rape Warfare: The Hidden Genocide in Bosnia-Herzegovina and Croatia* (Min-

neapolis: University of Minnesota Press, 1996); Cynthia Enloe, *Bananas, Beaches, and Bases: Making Feminist Sense Out of International Politics* (Berkeley and Los Angenes: University of California Press, 1990); Tamara L. Tompkins, "Prosecuting Rape as a War Crime: Speaking the Unspeakable," *Notre Dame Law Review* 70 (1995): 845–90; Alexandra Stiglmayer, ed., *Mass Rape: The War against Women in Bosnia-Herzegovina* (Lincoln: University of Nebraska Press, 1994); Madeline Morris, "By Force of Arms: Rape, War, and Military Culture," *Duke Law Journal* 45 (1996): 651–781. The concentration of rape prosecutions during wartime is clear in the military appellate court records as well, particularly in the crimes of violence that were prosecuted in Korea from 1950–1953.

61. On the Berlin rapes, see Johannes Steinhoff, Peter Pechel, and Dennis Showalter, *Voices from the Third Reich: An Oral History* (Washington, DC: Regnery Gateway, 1989); Atina Grossman, "A Question of Silence: The Rape of German Women by Occupation Soldiers," in "Special Issue, Berlin, 1945: War and Rape, 'Liberators Take Liberties,'" *October* 72 (1995): 43. On the rape of Nanjing, see Iris Chang, *The Rape of Nanking: The Forgotten Holocaust of World War II* (New York: Basic Books, 1997); John W. Dower, *War without Mercy: Race and Power in the Pacific War* (New York: Pantheon, 1986). Chang's work has been widely read and translated, but some of its conclusions have been questioned. For this criticism as well as a perceptive assessment of the mythic and empirical challenges of writing history about this twentieth century tragedy, see Daqing Yang, "Convergence or Divergence: Recent Historical Writing on the Rape of Nanjing," *American Historical Review* (June 1999): 842–65.

62. On the Civil War, see James M. McPherson, *Battle Cry of Freedom: The Civil War Era* (New York: Oxford University Press, 1988), 497; Reid Mitchell, *The Vacant Chair: The Northern Soldier Leaves Home* (New York: Oxford University Press, 1993), 103–4; Jane E. Schultz, "Mute Fury: Southern Women's Diaries of Sherman's March to the Sea, 1864–1865" in Helen M. Cooper, Adrienne Auslander Munich, and Susan Merrill Squier, eds., *Arms and the Woman: War, Gender and Literary Representation* (Chapel Hill: University of North Carolina Press, 1989), 61–73. For a psychotherapist's study of the sexual harassment and assault of women in the U.S. military during peacetime as well as war, see T. S. Nelson, *For Love of Country: Confronting Rape and Sexual Harassment in the U.S. Military* (New York: Haworth Maltreatment and Trauma Press, 2002).

63. See Chapter 2, supra, for discussion of American war crimes.

64. This phenomenon was not limited to the armed forces; law enforcement in civilian communities had long been guilty of vindictive punishment of African Americans accused of rape. On the historical links between race and rape prosecutions, see, e.g., Gail Bederman, *Manliness and Civilization: A Cultural History of Gender and Race in the United States, 1880–1917* (Chicago: University of Chicago Press, 1995); Peter Bardaglio, "Rape and the Law in the Old South: 'Calculated to Excite Indignation in Every Heart,'" *Journal of Southern History* 60 (1994): 749–72; Elizabeth Iglesias, "Rape, Race, and Representation: The Power of Discourse, Discourses of Power, and the Reconstruction of Heterosexuality," *Vanderbilt Law Review* 49 (1996): 869–992.

65. For example, in the first ten volumes of published military justice opinions, each of the nine reported cases in which the defendant was identified as African

American by the court resulted in sentences ranging from twenty years to life. See *United States v. Lamb*, 1 C.M.R. 440 (A.B.R. 1951), *United States v. Walton*, 2 C.M.R. 194 (A.B.R. 1951), *United States v. Kaulay*, 2 C.M.R. 296 (A.B.R. 1951), *United States v. Nelson*, 3 C.M.R. 165 (A.B.R. 1952), *United States v. Smith*, 3 C.M.R. 383 (A.B.R. 1952), *United States v. Brown*, 4 C.M.R. 342 (A.B.R. 1952), *United States v. Hunter*, 6 C.M.R. 37 (1952), *United States v. Borner*, 8 C.M.R. 483 (A.B.R. 1951), *United States v. Townsend*, 9 C.M.R.348 (A.B.R. 1952). The one rape case that did involve an officer during the early 1950s suggests the extent of differential sentencing based on race and rank. A white Army officer charged with the rape of a fifteen-year-old British girl, whose allegations were corroborated by forensic evidence, was sentenced to dismissal from the service after a court-martial panel rejected the rape charge and reduced the offense to "committing indecent acts with a child under the age of sixteen years" under the "conduct unbecoming an officer and a gentleman" clause of the UCMJ. See *United States v. Barbee*, 1 C.M.R. 314 (A.B.R. 1951). For a few cases of courts-martial for rape in which the race of the accused servicemember and the victim played a role at trial and appeared in the appellate record, see *United States v. Plummer*, 3 C.M.R. 107 (1952); *United States v. Gephart*, 4 C.M.R. 306 (A.B.R. 1952); *United States v. Muse*, 12 C.M.R. 544 (A.B.R. 1953); *United States v. Pugh*, 9 C.M.R. 536 (A.B.R. 1953); *United States v. Copeland*, 21 C.M.R. 838 (A.F.B.R. 1956); *United States v. Hobbs*, 21 C.M.R. 410 (A.B.R. 1956); *United States v. Sanford*, 25 C.M.R. 648 (A.B.R. 1958); *United States v. Steele*, 43 C.M.R. 845 (A.C.M.R. 1971). On race and adultery prosecutions, see Chapter 4, supra.

66. *United States v. Henderson*, 15 C.M.R. 268 (1954). See also *United States v. Pugh*, 9 C.M.R. 536 (A.B.R. 1952). The accused was a "colored" private who received a life sentence for raping a German woman who had a "questionable" sexual past and did not "resist to the maximum of her abilities."

67. See 15 C.M.R. 272. The quotation is unattributed in this opinion, but it is taken from Justice Felix Frankfurter's opinion in *Watts v. Indiana*, 338 U.S. 49, 52 (1949), which reversed the conviction of Robert A. Watts. Watts, charged with murder while attempting to commit rape, had confessed to the crime under extreme duress. Thurgood Marshall and Franklin H. Williams argued on behalf of Watts before the Supreme Court.

68. 15 C.M.R. 273.

69. 15 C.M.R. 272.

70. See cases cited in note 65 above, in which race is made explicit, as well as the hundreds of other sexual assault cases that appear in the military appellate record during this period. Taken as a whole, these cases reveal the legal doctrines and cultural assumptions that guided judge advocates, commanders, and military appellate judges in their handling of rape cases.

71. See Robert J. Lilly and J. Michael Thomson, "Executing United States Soldiers in England, World War II: Command Influence and Sexual Racism," *British Journal of Criminology* 37 (1997): 262–88; J. Robert Lilly, "Dirty Details: Executing United States Soldiers during World War II," *Crime and Delinquency* 42 (1996): 491–516.

72. See Dwight Sullivan, "A Matter of Life and Death: Examining the Military Death Penalty's Fairness," *Federal Lawyer* 45 (June 1998): 38–46; Dwight H. Sul-

livan, "Playing the Numbers: Court-Martial Panel Size and the Military Death Penalty," *Military Law Review* 158 (1998): 1–47; Dwight H. Sullivan, "The Last Line of Defense: Federal Habeas Review of Military Death Penalty Cases," *Military Law Review* 144 (1994): 1–76.

73. See *Burns v. Wilson*, 346 U.S. 137 (1953).

74. The clemency files of the presidential archives reveal the consideration that went into executive decisions in these cases. For example, the Bennett case is discussed in Folder "3-M Court-Martial Cases, B (2)," Box 102, White House Central Files, File OF, Dwight D. Eisenhower Presidential Library, Abilene, KS. Other cases are detailed in these files as well.

75. For a compelling study of both the Bennett case and the racial dimensions of military capital punishment, see Richard A. Serrano, "Private John Bennett Is the Only U.S. Soldier Executed for Rape in Peacetime," *Los Angeles Times Magazine*, September 10, 2000.

76. Servicemen were court-martialed for using and selling illegal drugs, particularly heroin and marijuana, in houses of prostitution throughout this period. See, e.g., *United States v. Durham*, 6 C.M.R. 320 (A.C.M.R. 1952); *United States v. Kellum*, 4 C.M.R. 74, 76 (1952); *United States v. Nabors*, 27 C.M.R. 101 (1958); *United States v. Karo*, 46 C.M.R. 633 (A.C.M.R. 1972); *United States v. Simmons*, 46 C.M.R. 288 (1973). For examples of other serious crimes involving violence, see cases cited below; for minor crimes committed by sex-seeking Army men, see, e.g., *United States v. Corey*, 11 C.M.R. 461, 464 (A.B.R. 1953); *United States v. Jackson*, 40 C.M.R. 355, 356 (A.B.R. 1968); *United States v. Bellamy*, 47 C.M.R. 319, 323 (A.C.M.R. 1973).

77. Occasionally, an accused was charged with a consensual sex act with a prostitute, but most often the charge was added to a list of other offenses; see, e.g., *United States v. Cleveland*, 35 C.M.R. 185 (1965), in which an Army private was accused of larceny, false swearing—and sodomy with a prostitute.

78. See Katharine H. S. Moon, *Sex among Allies: Military Prostitution in United States–Korea Relations* (New York: Columbia University Press, 1997), 37. It is apparent from court-martial records, as well as from both secondary and primary accounts of the American military experience, that many soldiers were customers in the sex industry during this period. For a few of the many appellate opinions that mention soldiers' use of prostitutes in Korea and Japan, see *United States v. Gibson*, 13 C.M.R. 825, 827 (A.F.B.R. 1953); *United States v. Person*, 7 C.M.R. 298, 300 (A.B.R. 1953); *United States v. Harvey*, 22 C.M.R. 415, 417 (A.B.R. 1956); *United States v. Simpson*, 26 C.M.R. 553, 554 (A.B.R. 1958); *United States v. Miller*, 26 C.M.R. 570 (A.B.R. 1958); *United States v. Johnson*, 37 C.M.R. 698, 699 (A.B.R. 1967).

79. See Allan R. Millett and Peter Maslowski, *For the Common Defense: A Military History of the United States of America*, rev. ed. (New York: Free Press, 1994), 571.

80. The comments appear in the court-martial of a private first class who was prosecuted for disloyal statements after he took issue with the general's statement. *United States v. Gray*, 42 C.M.R. 255 (1970). In 1968, a Navy board of review considered the case of a lance corporal in the Marine Corps who had killed a man in a fight outside a house of prostitution. Holding that the marine had not been

prejudiced at trial by evidence that he had frequented a prostitute and been involved in both "fornication and bastardy," the board explained that "an all-male military court in a combat zone" would not consider such acts misconduct, much less crimes. *United States v. Butler*, 39 C.M.R. 824, 829–30 (N.B.R. 1968). See also *United States v. Laffitte*, 41 C.M.R. 746, 747 (N.C.M.R. 1969), in which the court terms "innocuous" the conduct of a Marine who went to a Vietnamese house of prostitution—and was court-martialed because he forgot to bring his M-16 with him.

81. See Cynthia H. Enloe, *Does Khaki Become You? The Militarisation of Women's Lives* (Boston: South End Press, 1983), especially 32–45; Moon's *Sex among Allies*; Saundra Pollock Sturdevant and Brenda Stoltzfus, eds., *Let the Good Times Roll: Prostitution and the United States Military in Asia* (New York: New Press, 1993); Ryan Bishop and Lillian S. Robinson, *Nightmarket: Sexual Cultures and the Thai Economic Miracle* (New York: Routledge, 1998).

82. See Moon, *Sex among Allies*, 28.

83. See ibid., 28–29, for both the term "GI's Kingdom" and a disturbing characterization of it.

84. See Bruce Cumings, "Silent but Deadly: Sexual Subordination in the United States-Korean Relationship," in Sturdevant and Stoltzfus, *Let the Good Times Roll*. Cheap female labor was also exploited by Americans in Vietnam; for a visual depiction, see the photo of "hootchmaids," who cleaned up after American soldiers, in Solis, *Trial by Fire*, 91.

85. Both civilian and military legal systems sought to alleviate the anxieties that accompanied shifting sexual norms. For an analysis of military policy and law on these subjects during the first half of the twentieth century, see Nancy K. Ota, "Flying Buttresses," *DePaul Law Review* 49 (2000): 693–727. Ota's study of military constraints on "interracial, heterosexual, and transnational relationships" points out many of the same dynamics that I found in Cold War courts-martial. On civilian consensual sex crimes in the mid-twentieth century, see William E. Nelson, "Criminality and Sexual Morality in New York, 1920–1980," *Yale Journal of Law and the Humanities* 5 (1993): 265–355; William N. Eskridge, Jr., "Privacy Jurisprudence and the Apartheid of the Closet, 1946–1961," *Florida State University Law Review* 24 (1997): 703–852; see also Lawrence Friedman, *Crime and Punishment in American History* (New York: Basic Books, 1993), especially chapter 15.

86. On the essential service provided to the military by female workers, see Enloe, *Does Khaki Become You?*

87. The cases below document many of these relationships, which provided a ray of hope to many sex workers. For example, Korean prostitutes considered marriage to an American soldier one of the few ways out of their desperate situation. See Moon, *Sex among Allies*, 2 (on the "prize" of marriage to an American). Marriages between prostitutes and servicemen were likely to end in divorce, however; Moon suggests a divorce rate of 80 percent. See ibid., 35.

88. On increasing acceptance of commercial sex, see, e.g., Herbert L. Packer, *The Limits of the Criminal Sanction* (Stanford, CA: Stanford University Press, 1968), 328–31; *The Report of the President's Commission on Obscenity and Pornography* (Washington, DC, 1970). On changing sexual norms, see John D'Emilio and

Estelle B. Freedman, *Intimate Matters: A History of Sexuality in America*, 2nd ed (Chicago: University of Chicago Press, 1997), chapters 13 and 14; see also Beth L. Bailey, *From Front Porch to Back Seat: Courtship in Twentieth-Century America* (Baltimore: Johns Hopkins University Press, 1988).

89. *United States v. Adams*, 40 C.M.R. 22, 24 (1969); see also a companion case, *United States v. Wysingle*, 40 C.M.R. 26 (1969) and 39 C.M.R. 693 (A.B.R. 1968).

90. For off-limits prosecutions, see *United States v. Moss*, 3 C.M.R. 773 (A.F.B.R. 1952); *United States v. Rice*, 14 C.M.R. 316 (A.B.R. 1954); *United States v. Jones*, 23 C.M.R. 444, 447 (A.B.R., 1957); *United States v. Plummer*, 30 C.M.R. 18 (1960); *United States v. Laffitte*, 41 C.M.R. 746 (N.C.M.R., 1969); *United States v. Suggs*, 43 C.M.R. 36 (1970); *United States v. Mason*, 45 C.M.R. 163 (1972).

91. Henry Berry, *Hey Mac, Where Ya Been? Living Memories of the U.S. Marines in the Korean War* (New York: St. Martin's, 1988), 236. Medics at U.S. bases often treated prostitutes for venereal disease (see, e.g., Moon, *Sex among Allies*, 19, for the practice in Korea); on the history of misguided efforts to control venereal disease through the punishment of prostitutes, see Allan M. Brandt, *No Magic Bullet: A Social History of Venereal Disease in the United States since 1880*, expanded ed. (New York: Oxford University Press, 1987).

92. *United States v. Raily*, 35 C.M.R. 595, 600–601 (A.B.R. 1965). Fort Leonard Wood was the site of a series of pandering prosecutions during this period; see also *United States v. Streeter*, 22 C.M.R. 363 (A.B.R. 1956) and *United States v. McGlothlin*, 44 C.M.R. 533 (A.B.R. 1971).

93. See NAACP, *Search for Military Justice*, 18. See also Curtis Daniell, "Trouble Spot for GIs," *Ebony* (August 1968), 125–28.

94. NAACP, *Search for Military Justice*, 25.

95. Berry, *Hey Mac*, 146–56.

96. See Moon, *Sex among Allies*, 20, for a discussion of Korean women's uncertainty and fear regarding the consequences of sex with dark-skinned African American men.

97. See Moon, *Sex among Allies*, 70–74, for a thorough analysis of the race riots and escalating tensions that led up to the violence.

98. If courts-martial did result from the riots, they were either acquittals, resulted in sentences too light to provoke automatic appellate review (less than one year of confinement and no punitive discharge), or were summarily reviewed and not reported by the board of review that examined them. Given the publicity that would have accompanied prosecution for racially motivated violence in 1971, it is unlikely that many, if any, courts-martial triggered by the riots were so low profile, even if held in Korea, that they generated no appellate record at all. The relationship between the United States military and Korean communities was fragile in the early 1970s, as the sex economy faltered in the face of more aggressive regulation of prostitutes by the Korean government and a cleanup campaign around American bases implemented by the Nixon administration. See Moon, *Sex among Allies*, 58, 68–69.

99. However, war, and even the peacetime dangers of military service, provided an opportune means of explaining away deaths that were caused by accident, mis-

take, bad judgment, or even malice by fellow troops. This is not to suggest that cover-ups were necessarily routine among reported deaths, but to point out the distinctive circumstances in which military criminal justice operated.

100. In Korea, see *United States v. Wilson*, 6 C.M.R. 276 (A.B.R. 1952); *United States v. Schaefer*, 11 C.M.R. 405 (A.B.R. 1953); in Japan, see *United States v. Walker*, 10 C.M.R. 773 (A.F.B.R. 1953); for jealous disputes, see *United States v. Moore*, 6 C.M.R. 233 (A.B.R. 1952); *United States v. Porcello*, 10 C.M.R. 509 (A.B.R. 1953); *United States v. Sandoval*, 15 C.M.R. 61 (1954). For a Vietnam War example, see Alan G. Cornett, *Gone Native: An NCO's Story* (New York: Ballantine, 2000), a memoir of a serviceman convicted for murdering an officer because of a conflict over the serviceman's Vietnamese wife.

101. See, e.g., *United States v. Orosco*, 2 C.M.R. 222 (A.B.R. 1951).

102. 37 C.M.R. 818–19.

103. *United States v. Garza*, 37 C.M.R. 814 (A.F.B.R. 1966).

104. Violence may have been more common in the foreign sex trade than in the prostitution that occurred around American bases, but the court-martial record is insufficient to draw such a conclusion.

105. *United States v. Hurt*, 27 C.M.R. 3 (1958); 22 C.M.R. 630 (A.B.R. 1956).

106. See Moon, *Sex among Allies*, 69.

107. *United States v. Shaull*, 10 C.M.R. 241 (A.B.R. 1953).

108. *United States v. England*, 44 C.M.R. 142 (1971). The opinion did not mention the date of the crime or the sentence meted out, and the lower court's opinion was not recorded.

109. *United States v. Waldrop*, 41 C.M.R. 907 (A.F.C.M.R. 1969). For another robbery murder, this time in Germany, see *United States v. Mayberry*, 36 C.M.R. 703 (A.B.R. 1966).

110. See, e.g., *United States v. Jarvis*, 1 C.M.R. 217 (A.B.R. 1951); *United States v. Martin*, 1 C.M.R. 370 (A.B.R. 1951) and a companion case, *United States v. Day*, 1 C.M.R. 376 (A.B.R. 1951); *United States v. Earley*, 1 C.M.R. 268 (A.B.R. 1951); *United States v. Ellison*, 1 C.M.R. 159 (A.B.R. 1951); *United States v. Jarvis*, 3 C.M.R. 102 (1952); *United States v. Cloutier*, 8 C.M.R. 44 (1953); *United States v. Robins*, 7 C.M.R. 314 (A.B.R. 1953); *United States v. Kachougian*, 21 C.M.R. 276 (1956). Other men in a house of prostitution were at risk as well from servicemen; see, e.g, *United States v. Dalhaus*, 12 C.M.R. 712 (A.F.B.R. 1953). For violence against prostitutes, see also *United States v. Newvine*, 48 C.M.R. 188 (A.F.C.M.R. 1974); *United States v. Lowry*, 20 C.M.R. 911 (A.F.B.R. 1955); *United States v. Hypolite*, 39 C.M.R. 830 (N.C.M.R. 1969).

111. For Korean cases, see *United States v. Washington*, 7 C.M.R. 53 (1953) and *United States v. Broomfield*, 16 C.M.R. 306 (A.B.R. 1954); for German cases, see *United States v. Stephens*, 14 C.M.R. 321 (A.B.R. 1954) and *United States v. Brooks*, 31 C.M.R. 9 (1961).

112. *United States v. Robertson*, 38 C.M.R. 402 (1968); see example of the gang rape of Vietnamese women treated as prostitutes at *United States v. Steele*, 43 C.M.R. 845 (A.B.R. 1971). Some servicemen became politically radicalized and joined the antiwar movement after witnessing soldiers' mistreatments of women in Vietnam. See John Helmer, *Bringing the War Home: The American Soldier in Vietnam and After* (New York: Free Press, 1974), especially 752–56.

113. See, e.g., *United States v. Frymeyer*, 1 C.M.R. 124 (A.B.R. 1951); *United States v. Walker*, 10 C.M.R. 773 (A.F.B.R. 1953); *United States v. Burden*, 10 C.M.R. 45 (1953); *United States v. Young*, 5 C.M.R. 276 (A.B.R. 1952); *United States v. Day*, 8 C.M.R. 424 (A.B.R. 1952); and the case that resulted in the most recent execution of a servicemember in the military justice system, *United States v. Bennett*, 21 C.M.R. 223 (1956). See also the prosecution of three African American soldiers for the gang rape of a Korean woman, which resulted in two death sentences, at *United States v. Borner*, 12 C.M.R. 62 (1953), 8 C.M.R. 483 (A.B.R. 1952).

114. *United States v. Short*, 16 C.M.R. 11 (1954); see also *United States v. Smith*, 2 C.M.R. 256 (A.B.R. 1951); *United States v. Borrowman*, 1 C.M.R. 290 (A.B.R. 1951); *United States v. King*, 13 C.M.R. 261 (A.B.R. 1953).

115. *United States v. Jordan*, 44 C.M.R. 44 (1971). As in many of these cases, the lower court's opinion (the Navy Court of Military Review) was not reported. For similar defenses, see *United States v. Goins*, 37 C.M.R. 396 (1967), in which a German "maid in the woods" successfully defended herself against a soldier's assault with a springblade knife that she carried, having been raped before in a similar situation; and *United States v. O'Brien*, 12 C.M.R. 81 (1953), in which an Army private raped and assaulted a German woman whom he assumed to be a prostitute because of where she was walking.

116. See *United States v. Dunnahoe*, 21 C.M.R. 67, 72 (1956).

117. For one academic recitation of the argument that prostitution is a rape "substitute," see Richard Posner, "An Economic Theory of Criminal Law," *Columbia Law Review* 85 (1985): 1193–1231.

118. See *United States v. Brown*, 24 C.M.R. 65 (1957).

119. See *United States v. Wright*, 48 C.M.R. 295, 298 (A.F.C.M.R. 1974).

120. For a chilling anthropological study of gang rape, see Peggy Reeves Sanday, *Fraternity Gang Rape: Sex, Brotherhood, and Privilege on Campus* (New York: New York University Press, 1990).

CHAPTER 6
"GENTLEMEN UNDER ALL CONDITIONS"

1. See UCMJ, Articles 89 and 90.

2. Unlike enlistees, officers could be confined only upon the written, not verbal, orders of a commanding officer and could not be restricted to bread and water if embarked on a vessel. See UCMJ, Article 9(c); see also Articles 4 and 15(c).

3. The Green Beret case was heavily pursued by the media, but was pushed aside in the national spotlight when the My Lai story broke in 1969. For a detailed account of the bizarre situation that led to charges being filed against six Army officers, see Jeff Stein, *A Murder in Wartime: The Untold Spy Story that Changed the Course of the Vietnam War* (New York: St. Martin's Press, 1992).

4. See chapter 2, supra, for discussion of the My Lai massacre.

5. Of course, Calley was not the only officer called to task for his actions in Vietnam. By the end of the Vietnam War, in part because of the recriminations that followed the My Lai cover-up, the Army had prosecuted a handful of officers for negligence in failing to keep sexual torture and gang rapes from occurring under their commands. See, e.g., an Army first lieutenant charged in a gang rape, *United States*

v. Maxfield, 43 C.M.R. 336 (1971) and 42 C.M.R. 650 (A.B.R. 1970), and an Army captain similarly charged in *United States v. Goldman*, 43 C.M.R. 711 (A.B.R. 1970) and 44 C.M.R. 471 (A.B.R. 1970).

6. John C. Stevens III, *Court-Martial at Parris Island: The Ribbon Creek Incident* (Annapolis: Naval Institute Press, 1999).

7. Article 133, UCMJ.

8. See *United States v. Downard*, 1 C.M.R. 405 (A.B. R. 1951) and 3 C.M.R. 80 (1952).

9. The Marine Corps' almost exclusive emphasis on ground troops placed its percentage of officers below 10, while the Air Force, which required that pilots, navigators, and missileers be commissioned officers, reached 15 percent by 1967 and 17 percent by 1974. See table P23.2, *Selected Manpower Statistics, FY 1979*, 72–73.

10. See ibid.

11. Noncommissioned officers were explicitly protected under military law, though not quite in the terms that applied to officers. Article 91 of the UCMJ made "insubordinate conduct toward a non commissioned officer" criminal.

12. For examples of officers charged with these offenses, see *United States v. Barbee*, 1 C.M.R. 314 (A.B.R. 1951) (an Army major convicted for sexually assaulting a minor); *United States v. Herrington*, 33 C.M.R. 814 (A.F.B.R. 1963) (an Air Force colonel who murdered his wife); *United States v. Johnson*, 8 C.M.R.368 (A.B.R. 1952) (an Army lieutenant colonel convicted of bigamy); *United States v. Pitasi*, 44 C.M.R. 31 (1971) (a Navy lieutenant junior grade convicted for homosexual conduct); *United States v. French*, 25 C.M.R. 851 (A.F.B.R. 1958) (an Air Force captain who attempted to sell diagrams of weapons and other documents to the Soviet embassy in Washington, DC); *United States v. Fleming*, 23 C.M.R. 7 (1957) (an Army lieutenant colonel convicted for collaborating as a Korean War POW); *United States v. Calley*, 48 C.M.R. 19 (1973) (an Army lieutenant convicted for "the premeditated murder of 22 infants, children, women, and old men").

13. The officers court-martialed for their conduct included two lieutenant colonels, two majors, and one lieutenant. See Raymond B. Lech, *Broken Soldiers* (Chicago: University of Illinois Press, 2000), 212–13.

14. Lech, *Broken Soldiers*, 29–33.

15. 23 C.M.R. 11.

16. 23 C.M.R. 22; 19 C.M.R. 445. Ronald Alley, another officer prosecuted for collaborating, admitted that he stopped resisting the indoctrination program because he thought it more important to keep his soldiers alive. See Don J. Snyder, *A Soldier's Disgrace* (Dublin, NH: Yankee Books, 1987), 176.

17. *United States v. Fleming*, 23 C.M.R. 7 (1957), 19 C.M.R. 438, 440 (A.B.R. 1955).

18. Robert N. Strassfeld, "The Vietnam War on Trial: The Court-Martial of Dr. Howard B. Levy," *Wisconsin Law Review* (1994): 829–963. See also Terry H. Anderson, "The GI Movement and the Response from the Brass," in Melvin Small and William D. Hoover, eds., *Give Peace a Chance: Exploring the Vietnam Antiwar Movement*, (Syracuse, NY: Syracuse University Press, 1992), 93–115; Charles DeBenedetti, *An American Ordeal: The Antiwar Movement of the Vietnam Era* (Syracuse, NY: Syracuse University Press, 1990).

19. "Dilapidated" is the description of Mitchell Lerner, author of the best scholarly treatment of the Pueblo incident. See Mitchell B. Lerner, *The Pueblo Incident: A Spy Ship and the Failure of U.S Foreign Policy* (Lawrence: University Press of Kansas, 2002), 1; see also Lloyd M. Bucher, *Bucher: My Story* (Garden City, NY: Doubleday, 1970). Bucher and his crew—several of whom were wounded in the attack—were captured and imprisoned under brutal conditions for eleven months. Another Vietnam-era case of alleged misconduct by a Navy skipper is the "Arnheiter affair," in which an officer was nearly court-martialed after his conduct threatened the morale and welfare of his sailors. See Neil Sheehan, *The Arnheiter Affair* (New York: Random House, 1971).

20. For a journalistic account of Captain Kunze's case, see Joseph DiMona, *Great Court-Martial Cases* (New York: Grosset and Dunlap, 1972), chapter 10. On black market offenses more generally, see Gary D. Solis, *Marines and Military Law in Vietnam: Trial by Fire* (Washington, DC: History and Museums Division, Headquarters, U.S. Marine Corps, 1989), 32.

21. See *MCM*, Forms, App. 6c, 493. Pandering was charged as a violation of Article 134, the general article.

22. See the discussions of negative publicity in the newspapers and federal and state police raids on vice districts near Fort Leonard Wood, Missouri, in *United States v. Raily*, 35 C.M.R. 595 (A.B.R. 1965).

23. See, e.g., *United States v. Bohannon*, 20 C.M.R. 870 (A.F.B.R. 1955), in which an Air Force second lieutenant was convicted and sentenced to dismissal and two years of confinement for bringing a fourteen-year-old girl, who was apparently working as a prostitute in Houston, Texas, back to his base for the pleasure of four other lieutenants.

24. *United States v. Snyder*, 4 C.M.R. 15 (1952).

25. *United States v. Brown*, 24 C.M.R. 65 (1957).

26. *United States v. Wright*, 48 C.M.R. 295 (A.F.C.M.R. 1974). Additional pandering prosecution took place in Waco, Texas: see *United States v. Barcomb*, 3 C.M.R. 623 (A.F.B.R. 1952); Fort Benning, Georgia: see *United States v. Gentry*, 23 C.M.R. 238 (1957); and an unspecified Army post in *United States v. Baldwin*, 27 C.M.R. 269 (1959).

27. See, e.g., Robert Buzzanco, *Masters of War: Military Dissent and Politics in the Vietnam Era* (New York: Cambridge University Press, 1996).

28. Ibid.

29. The judicial opinions related to Hooper's court-martial are reported at *Hooper v. Hartman*, 163 F. Supp. 437 (S. Dist. of Cal. 1958); *United States v. Hooper*, 26 C.M.R. 417 (1958); *Hooper v. Hartman*, 274 F.2d 429 (9th Circ. 1959); *United States v. Hooper*, 28 C.M.R. 352 (1960); *Hooper v. United States*, 326 F. 2d 982 (Ct. Cl. 1964); *Hooper v. Laird*, 41 C.M.R. 329 (1970).

30. Perhaps because his case is so singular, Admiral Hooper has received little attention from scholars. Hooper is not mentioned in the main historical treatments of gay servicemembers. His case also escapes mention in the legal scholarship criticizing the "don't ask/don't tell" version of the military's antigay policies and the growing number of more general histories of gay life in the twentieth-century United States.

31. *United States v. Hooper* established the legitimacy of court-martial jurisdic-

tion over military retirees. See, e.g., *Maxwell v. United States*, 1997 WL 643294, *2 (A.F.C.C.A., September 25, 1997); *United States v. Allen*, 31 M.J. 572, 636 (N.M.C.C.A. 1990); Lieutenant Colonel Foote, "Courts-Martial of Military Retirees," *Army Lawyer* (May 1992): 54–60, 15n; Major Holland, "Courts-Martial Jurisdiction over Enlisted Retirees?—Yes, But a Qualified Yes in the Army," *Army Lawyer* (October 1989): 31, 5n; John G. Kester, "Soldiers Who Insult the President: An Uneasy Look at Article 88 of the Uniform Code of Military Justice," *Harvard Law Review* 81 (1968): 1697–1769, 1726 183n; Joseph Bishop, "Court-Martial Jurisdiction over Military-Civilian Hybrids: Retired Regulars, Reservists, and Discharged Prisoners," *University of Pennsylvania Law Review* 112 (1964): 317–77, 340. See Richard E. Blair, "Court-Martial Jurisdiction over Retired Regulars: An Unwarranted Extension of Military Power," *Georgetown Law Journal* 50 (1961): 79–104, for an article inspired by the Hooper case.

32. See table 22.8, *Selected Manpower Statistics* (1967), 103.

33. In the twentieth century, very few American flag officers (generals or admirals) have been court-martialed. Two notable exceptions are the 1925 court-martial of air power advocate Billy Mitchell and the McCarthy-era court-martial of Major General Robert Grow. Charged with making diary entries about military operations that fell into the hands of Soviet intelligence agents, Grow was court-martialed in 1952, just five years before Hooper. See George F. Hofmann, *Cold War Casualty: The Court-Martial of Major General Robert W. Grow* (Kent, OH: Kent State University Press, 1993). On Mitchell, see Michael S. Sherry's discussion in *The Rise of American Air Power: The Creation of Armageddon* (New Haven, CT: Yale University Press, 1987), 22–46; see also Douglas Waller, *A Question of Loyalty: Gen. Billy Mitchell and the Court-Martial that Gripped the Nation* (New York: HarperCollins, 2004).

34. One observer has remarked that Hooper's acts "had achieved considerable notoriety" (Foote, "Courts-Martial of Military Retirees," 56). Because there is no further explanation, and no sources cited in support of this remark, it appears to be based on the author's assumptions about Hooper's situation rather than on any concrete evidence. Hooper's case is not mentioned in the local paper (*San Diego Union-Tribune*), military newspaper (*The Navy Times*), or the California homophile publications (*The Mattachine Review*, *The Ladder*, and *One*), save for brief articles reporting his conviction and the failures of his appeals. See "Retired Admiral Found Guilty of Morals Charges," *San Diego Union-Tribune*, May 8, 1957; see also "Navy Trial Upheld for Retired Officer," *New York Times*, September 27, 1958; "Pensioner's Court-Martial Ruled Valid," *Washington Post and Times-Herald*, September 27, 1958. The many judicial opinions in his case make no mention of public knowledge of Hooper's sexual orientation or activity, nor did any of my interviewees believe that Hooper's sexuality was widely known. Hooper's attorneys also wrote about the covert nature of his sexual exploits in their briefs on appeal ("There is no showing here that plaintiff's activities were known to large numbers of the public," Brief for Plaintiff-Appellant, 17–18). I reviewed the "Cases and Points" volume on *Hooper v. Laird* in the law offices of Victor Rabinowitz, Counsel, at Rabinowitz, Boudin, Standard, Krinsky and Lieberman, 5th Floor, 740 Broadway, New York, on February 1, 1999 (hereinafter the Rabinowitz file).

35. Unless otherwise noted, biographical information about Hooper is taken

from his military personnel record (obtained through Freedom of Information Act requests) or midshipman records at the United States Naval Academy Nimitz Library and Archives, Annapolis, MD. For Hooper's file, see Midshipmen Personnel Records, Microfilm Box No. 29, Class of 1927, Selden G. Hooper, Nimitz Library.

36. I do not know when, or why, Selden's father left the family, but it appears that Selden was not on good terms with his father. In 1922, Selden and his mother petitioned the Superior Court of California in San Francisco to change his name to Selden Gain Hooper. Although Hooper claimed on a 1942 Navy form that his father was dead, on Oct. 20, 1949, "there was passed to Rear Admiral Hooper a message received from the Commandant, TWELFTH Naval District, advising in substance that Rear Admiral Hooper's father had died on 20 October 1949 in San Francisco, by reason of a cardiac condition, and that no funds were available for burial expenses." See Memo from the Chief of Naval Personnel to the Judge Advocate General, comment concerning the General court-martial in the case of Rear Admiral Selden G. HOOPER, USN, Retired, dated October 9, 1957, prepared by K. Craig, Acting Chief of Naval Personnel (hereinafter Personnel Memo), in Hooper's military personnel file.

37. Hooper's 1925 medical examination lists his height at nearly six feet and his weight at 134 pounds. For his extracurricular activities, see *The Lucky Bag: The Annual of the Regiment of Midshipmen* (Rochester, NY: DuBois Press, 1927), 290, 490–92; *Lucky Bag: The Annual of the Regiment of Midshipmen* (Rochester, NY: DuBois Press, 1926), 241–44.

38. *The Lucky Bag* (1927), 290.

39. Even the Judge Advocate General (JAG) officer who reviewed Hooper's court-martial record and recommended no clemency noted that "[h]is performance ratings appear to have been highly satisfactory throughout his active naval service." Personnel Memo in Hooper's military personnel file.

40. In November 1940, he wrote to the Naval Academy requesting a copy of his transcript so that he might apply to work toward a master's degree while at Marquette.

41. "His courage and devotion to duty were in keeping with the highest traditions of the United States Naval Service." See Hooper's military personnel file, Citation accompanying the Silver Star Medal, presented to Captain Selden Gain Hooper by Secretary of the Navy James Forrestal, January 7, 1947. Hooper also received the American Defense medal, two Commendation Ribbons, a Philippine Liberation medal with two Bronze stars, a China Service Occupation, Neutrality Patrol Ribbon with one star, American Theater and Asiatic Pacific Ribbons with two stars, and the Battle of Koumondorski Islands campaign ribbon.

42. Letter from Hooper to the naval personnel office, 1948; see also Memo from the Secretary of the Navy re Hooper's transfer to the retired list, December 8, 1948 ("Having been specially commended by the head of the executive department for your performance of duty in actual combat, you were on 1 December 1948 transferred to the retired list with the rank of Rear Admiral but with the retired pay based on the rank of Captain"). M. E. Andrews, acting secretary of the Navy, wrote the following in his letter granting Hooper's retirement request: "I regret your retirement from active service and take this occasion to extend to you my heartiest congratulations and appreciation for your long and distinguished service

to our Nation. May I wish you continued success and many years of health and happiness." All documents are in Hooper's military personnel file. This end-of-career bump up to flag officer rank made Hooper a "tombstone admiral" in Navy parlance.

43. Letter from Hooper to chief of the Bureau of Naval Personnel, March 22, 1951, Hooper's military personnel file.

44. See Brief for Plaintiff-Appellant, *Hooper v. Laird*, 3–4, in the Rabinowitz file.

45. For the "wayward boys" concerns, see Personnel Memo, Hooper's military personnel file; see also Brief for Plaintiff-Appellant, *Hooper v. Laird*, for the D.C. Court of Appeals, No. 72–1198, in the Rabinowitz file. For the boys' school, see the last entries in Hooper's midshipman file: a letter from Hooper to the Academy, dated August 1949, requesting training manuals, and a note complying with his request, dated September 1949.

46. California was a center of the 1950s homophile movement. By 1953, the Mattachine Society, whose members included some former servicemembers, had expanded beyond its Los Angeles origins and included a San Diego chapter. John D'Emilio, *Sexual Politics, Sexual Communities: The Making of a Homosexual Minority in the United States, 1940–1970* (Chicago: University of Chicago Press, 1983), 71. Although Hooper would have had the opportunity to join the homophile movement, as far as I can tell, he did not. Neither his name nor the circumstances of his prosecution appear in any of the homophile publications, and he is not mentioned in the published histories of the early movement. A friend of the late Hooper, Judge Herb Donaldson of San Francisco, confirmed that Hooper had not been active in homophile organizations or in later gay rights efforts. I am grateful to Judge Donaldson for his insight into Admiral Hooper. Telephone interview with the Honorable Herbert M. Donaldson, retired judge of the State of California Municipal Court, San Francisco District, on April 2, 1999.

47. See Brief for Appellees, 6–11, in the Rabinowitz file.

48. Information regarding the charges against Hooper are taken from the official charge sheet, dated April 12, 1957 (copy in Hooper's military personnel file). Incidentally, the charge sheet misspelled Hooper's first name ("Seldon") as did the Court of Military Appeal's first opinion in his case ("Shelden"), *United States v. Hooper*, 26 C.M.R. 417 (1958).

49. This account of the government's case against Hooper is drawn from the legal documents in the Rabinowitz file, the charge sheet in Hooper's military personnel file, telephone interviews in January 1999 with Dean Kristin Booth Glen, City University of New York School of Law and Victor Rabinowitz, who together represented Hooper during his final appeal, and the sketchy details recounted in judicial opinions.

50. I use "first" and "second" here for narrative purposes, not to indicate the chronological order of government witnesses. I do not know in what order the witnesses took the stand. Although a record of trial from Hooper's court-martial may still exist, I have been unable to find it. In response to repeated Freedom of Information Act requests, Navy officials variously reported the transcript misfiled or checked out and never returned.

51. The ages of these witnesses are not entirely clear in the available records; the government brief that notes their ages in several different paragraphs is inconsis-

tent. They were not younger than eighteen nor older than twenty-two, however, when the court-martial was convened. See Brief for Appellees, Rabinowitz file.

52. The military ranks of the sailors who testified against Hooper were personnelman third class, hospital apprentice, and seaman; they had been in the Navy between two and three years by May 1957. See Charge Sheet, Hooper's military personnel file; Brief for Appellees, Rabinowitz file. The UCMJ required that an accused person be tried, if possible, by a court-martial panel of servicemembers who were at least equal in rank to the accused. Because the record of trial is missing, I do not know the composition of Hooper's court-martial panel, but if enough active-duty or retired flag officers were available, he faced a jury of fellow admirals.

53. Seaman Braddock, twenty-two at the time of the trial, denied the allegation that he was "married" to Hooper, admitting only that the lived with Hooper "on and off" during the preceding two years. Braddock also denied committing sodomy with Hooper, despite the testimony of naval investigators who observed him engaging in sexual foreplay with Hooper. Braddock said that he remembered "sleeping" with Hooper, but could not recall the alleged sodomy. See Brief for the Appellees, Rabinowitz file.

54. This was Hospital Apprentice Michael Alvin McDaniels, son of a Navy lieutenant commander, who appears to have been the prosecution's star witness. See Brief for the Appellees, Rabinowitz file; see also *United States v. Hooper*, 28 C.M.R. 352 (1960) (Ferguson, J., dissenting).

55. See Brief for the Appellees, Rabinowitz file.

56. See Petition for Rehearing Pursuant to Rule 40 of the Federal Rules of Appellate Procedure, Rabinowitz file.

57. See Brief for Appellees, Rabinowitz file.

58. See ibid. Kristin Booth Glen recalled the periscope detail in her 1999 interview.

59. See Brief for Appellees, Rabinowitz file. Because Braddock refused to testify about what happened after the lights went out, this evidence was sufficient to prove only the Article 134 charge of "discrediting" conduct, not to prove a violation of Article 125 for sodomy.

60. See ibid. Again, the agents could corroborate only what happened up to the point that the lights went out. However, since Schmidt testified that he had committed sodomy with Hooper, these events were the basis for Hooper's single-count conviction for violating Article 125.

61. I have criticized the use of the good soldier defense in contemporary courts-martial in Elizabeth Lutes Hillman, "The 'Good Soldier' Defense: Character Evidence and Military Rank at Court-Martial," *Yale Law Journal* 108 (1999): 879–911.

62. *United States v. Kennedy*, 24 C.M.R. 61 (1957).

63. Recall the discussion in Chapter 5, supra, of the Supreme Court's dismissal of Clarice Covert's court-martial conviction for killing her Air Force husband in *Reid v. Covert*, 354 U.S. 1 (1957). See also *United States ex rel. Toth v. Quarles*, 350 U.S. 11 (1955), which held that the extension of court-martial jurisdiction over former servicemembers for crimes committed during their tour of service was unconstitutional; *Kinsella v. United States ex rel Singleton* (1960), holding that a military dependent could not be charged with a noncapital offense at court-martial

(Mrs. Covert's alleged murder was a capital crime under the UCMJ); and *Grisham v. Hagan*, 361 U.S. 278 (1960) and *McElroy v. United States ex rel. Guagliardo*, 361 U.S. 281 (1960), holding that civilian employees of the military could not be tried by court-martial.

64. On the visibility of sexual minorities after World War II, see D'Emilio, *Sexual Politics*; Jonathan Katz, *Gay American History: Lesbians and Gay Men in the U.S.A.* (New York: Harper and Row, 1976), especially 134–307; Robert J. Corber, *In the Name of National Security: Hitchcock, Homophobia, and the Political Construction of Gender in Postwar America* (Durham, NC: Duke University Press, 1993). Some of the proliferating cultural representations of gay life during this period were set in military contexts. See, for example, James Barr, *Quatrefoil: A Modern Novel* (New York: Greenberg, 1950). Set in 1946, it relates the tale of a young aristocratic ensign who faces court-martial for insubordination. The naval officer manages to clear his name with the help of a senior officer who becomes both mentor and lover. Barr's novel was important to the gay community when published. See Anthony Slide, *Lost Gay Novels: A Reference Guide to Fifty Works from the First Half of the Twentieth Century* (New York: Harrington Park, 2003), 6–12.

65. See *United States v. Hillan*, 26 C.M.R. 771, 804 (N.B.R. 1958): "The seduction of our young men in the service by the homosexual is a singularly detestable and reprehensible crime. It is apparently a growing evil, or else it is more noticeable now than before. The evil corrupts; it can destroy those it touches. It should be wiped out." The conviction in this case was overturned on appeal because of an illegal search; see discussion below. See also an official memo reprinted in full at *United States v. Adams*, 21 C.M.R. 733 (A.F.B.R. 1956), concerning the importance of protecting young servicemen from sexual corruption; and in addition to cases cited in the text below, see *United States v. Davisson*, 6 C.M.R. 174 (A.B.R. 1952); *United States v. April*, 23 C.M.R. 58 (1957); *United States v. Phillips*, 32 C.M.R. 501 (A.B.R. 1962).

66. In upholding the conviction of a petty officer for engaging in consensual sodomy and offering to pay sailors for sex, a Coast Guard board of review stressed the age of the parties involved: the petty officer was forty years old, while one of the recruits he solicited was only twenty. See *United States v. Stell*, 4 C.M.R. 490 (C.G.B.R. 1952).

67. See the promises made and pressure applied to potential witnesses by Army investigators in the case of an Army private convicted of sodomy, *United States v. Cash*, 12 C.M.R. 215 (A.B.R. 1953), and the Office of Naval Intelligence agents who coerced the confession of a Marine Corps private to a charge of sodomy, *United States v. Morris*, 25 C.M.R. 299 (1958). See also a case involving an airman whose testimony against a master sergeant wavered and eventually led to his own court-martial for false swearing: *United States v. Clayton*, 38 C.M.R. 46 (1967) and 37 C.M.R. 883 (A.F.B.R. 1967). A soldier accused of homosexuality as well as other crimes could be pressured to plead guilty by prosecutors who threatened to add sex crimes to the other charges if he insisted on going to trial. For example, an Army private tried for larceny testified that he was persuaded to plead guilty in return for prosecutors dropping sodomy charges. He disputed the charges, but the investigators told him that his mother would find out about the sodomy, so he pled guilty anyway. His conviction was overturned on appeal. *United States v. Dicario*,

24 C.M.R. 163 (1957). See also *United States v. Bell*, 25 C.M.R. 519 (A.B.R. 1957).

68. *United States v. Bennington*, 31 C.M.R. 151 (1961).

69. For a similar case in which an officer was charged after an alleged homosexual encounter with an enlisted man, see *United States v. Phillips*, 11 C.M.R. 137 (1953) and 9 C.M.R. 186 (A.B.R. 1952). In this case, a Marine Corps major who was a happily married father of two, with no history of homosexuality, was convicted of sodomy.

70. See, e.g., the case of an Army first lieutenant sentenced to dismissal and one year confinement for consensual sodomy, *United States v. Norton*, 11 C.M.R. 365 (A.B.R. 1953). Convicted on the testimony of his "accomplices," the lieutenant was subjected to an investigation that involved threats against and coercion of witnesses. See also an Army captain convicted for consensual sodomy in *United States v. Chewning*, 9 C.M.R. 528 (A.B.R. 1953).

71. Defamation and criminal libel cases were prosecuted against servicemen who accused others of homosexuality in *United States v. Brown*, 30 C.M.R. 368 (1961); *United States v. Grosso*, 23 C.M.R. 30 (1957); and *United States v. Cox*, 26 C.M.R. 582 (A.B.R. 1958).

72. See the cases below involving violence against allegedly gay men, but see also *United States v. Burnom*, 35 C.M.R. 908, 912–13 (A.F.B.R. 1965), in which an airman accused of theft explained that the owner of the camera in question, another airman, gave it to the accused to keep him quiet after he observed the owner engaged in a homosexual act.

73. *United States v. Gandy*, 19 C.M.R. 57 (1955).

74. See, e.g., *United States v. Berlin*, 13 C.M.R. 364 (A.B.R. 1953), recounting the case of an Army major sentenced to dismissal and five years for coercing sex from enlisted men; *United States v. Taylor*, 13 C.M.R. 201 (A.B.R. 1953), in which an Army captain was sentenced to dismissal and five years for both coerced and consensual sex with enlisted men.

75. *United States v. Yeast*, 36 C.M.R. 890 (A.F.B.R. 1966).

76. *United States v. Warren*, 20 C.M.R. 135 (1955).

77. *United States v. Battista*, 33 C.M.R. 282 (1963).

78. *United States v. Page*, 23 C.M.R. 746 (A.F.B.R. 1956); *United States v. Thacker*, 37 C.M.R. 28 (1966). See also an Army master sergeant sentenced to a dishonorable discharge and seven years for five acts of forcible sodomy against enlisted men in *United States v. Wedge*, 9 C.M.R. 437 (A.B.R. 1953), and, in a less clearly coercive situation but also involving teenagers and young men, a Navy enlistee convicted for his relationship with another enlisted man and a fourteen-year-old boy in Pensacola, Florida, in *United States v. White*, 34 C.M.R. 426 (1964).

79. See Solis, *Trial by Fire*, 124; see also Christian G. Appy, *Working-Class War: American Combat Soldiers and Vietnam* (Chapel Hill: University of North Carolina Press, 1993).

80. See *United States v. Whitley*, 38 C.M.R. 724, 727 (N.B.R. 1967); reversed by the Court of Military Appeals at 39 C.M.R. 20 (1968).

81. 39 C.M.R. 21. Similar antigay violence appears in *United States v. Bell*, 25 C.M.R. 519 (A.B.R. 1957). This case resulted from an incident at Camp Roberts, California, in August 1957, when several Army soldiers decided to "roll" another

soldier whom they thought to be homosexual. One of the assailants engaged in consensual oral sodomy with the victim prior to the robbery.

82. As in many of these cases, the motivations of the men involved is not clear, but it appears that the seamen conspired against Whitley. At trial, they testified that they did not meet until the court-martial started, an apparent lie that Whitley's attorneys tried to capitalize on. During the trial, the members of the court had asked several questions about the enlisted men's relationship, indicating that the issue was important to their decision. They were both mess cooks, lived on the same floor in the barracks, were assigned to the same galley, were seen together at work and socially, and, according to one witness, actually "occupied the same berthing cubicle." 39 C.M.R. 22. Whether they were involved in a homosexual relationship themselves was left unclear at trial, but it is certainly possible, given that one admitted engaging in consensual homosexual acts with Whitley. The sailor who hit Whitley may have been a violent homophobe—or a jealous lover.

83. 39 C.M.R. 20.

84. Ironically, in reversing Whitley's conviction, the court relies on the standard set out in *Chadd*, discussed in chapter 2, supra, in which a rape conviction was dismissed because the victim turned out to be a lesbian.

85. *United States v. Yeast*, 36 C.M.R. 890 (A.F.B.R. 1966). Yeast was convicted for "conduct unbecoming an officer and a gentleman" and failure to obey a lawful order; the disobedience charge was added because one of the gay clubs that Yeast frequented, the Kismet Café, had been declared off-limits by the base commander. The Court of Military Appeals rejected the disobedience charge, however. Apparently Yeast only entered the off-limits bar (it was declared off-limits after he visited with the airmen) for bureaucratic, not social reasons. Yeast was looking for insurance and other papers that belonged to Paul Rawson, the proprietor of the café, who died under circumstances not reported in the record, at the behest of Rawson's mother. Yeast had tried and failed to reach someone at the bar by telephone; eventually he went there in person, despite the order to avoid the premises, to find the papers.

86. 36 C.M.R. 896.

87. 36 C.M.R. 909.

88. The court held that Yeast lacked standing to assert that the search of Rawson's apartment was illegal. See, however, the different outcome in *United States v. Woodard*, 39 C.M.R. 6 (1968), a case in which an Army captain convicted of sodomy successfully challenged the admissibility of "homosexual literature" found in his home.

89. 36 C.M.R. 905.

90. Ibid.

91. See David S. Jonas, "Fraternization: Time for a Rational Defense of a Department of Defense Standard," *Military Law Review* 135 (1992): 37–129, 47.

92. See Wilton B. Persons Papers in the Senior Officers Oral History Program series at the Military History Institute, Carlisle Barracks, PA (1985 interview), 460–64 of the transcript. According to Persons's account, Second Lieutenant Marylou Follett, a nurse stationed in Heidelberg, was living in a Mannheim apartment with Specialist James Johnson, a twenty-year old medical technician whom she supervised. Her living arrangements generated "considerable outrage" in the

hospital, prompting the legal officers to write a policy regarding fraternization. Soon after, Lieutenant Follett resigned.

93. See Paul H. Turney, "Relations among the Ranks: Observations of and Comparisons among the Service Policies and Fraternization Case Law, 1999," *Army Lawyer* (April 2000): 97–107.

94. See *Report of the Secretary of War's Board on Officer-Enlisted Man Relationships to Hon. Robert P. Patterson, the Secretary of War* (Washington, DC: 1946), 1.

95. See Jonas, "Fraternization," 108–11.

96. These cases share other similarities: each involved the prosecution of a junior officer in the Navy or Marine Corps. See *United States v. Free*, 14 C.M.R. 466 (N.B.R. 1953); *United States v. Lovejoy*, 42 C.M.R. 210 (1970); *United States v. Pitasi*, 44 C.M.R. 31 (1971).

97. *United States v. Free*, 14 C.M.R. 466 (1953).

98. 14 C.M.R. 469–71.

99. *United States v. Pitasi*, 44 C.M.R. 31 (1971).

100. 44 C.M.R. 34. Many of the social situations that led to fraternization charges included excessive consumption of alcohol. See, e.g., Jonas, "Fraternization," 45.

101. 44 C.M.R. 34.

102. 44 C.M.R. 35. Pitasi's conviction was overturned for a violation of the "fresh complaint" rule and because of the many inconsistencies in Schultz's testimony against him.

103. *United States v. Lovejoy*, 41 C.M.R. 777 (N.C.M.R. 1969).

104. The board's opinion does not explain why Niebank sought out advice about touring England from Lovejoy when he already had family connections in-country.

105. 41 C.M.R. 781.

106. Ibid.

AFTERWORD

1. On the all-volunteer force, see Robert K. Fullinwider, ed., *Conscripts and Volunteers: Military Requirements, Social Justice, and the All-Volunteer Force* (Totowa, NJ: Rowman and Allanheld, 1983); William Bowman, Roger Little, and G. Thomas Sicilia, eds., *The All-Volunteer Force after a Decade: Retrospect and Prospect* (New York: Pergamon-Brassey's, 1986).

2. See, e.g., Michael S. Foley, *Confronting the War Machine: Draft Resistance during the Vietnam War* (Chapel Hill: University of North Carolina Press, 2003), ix–x; on statistics regarding women in the military, see http://www.womensmemorial.org/PDFs/StatsonWIM.pdf; http://web1.whs.osd.mil/mmid/military/rg0209f.pdf (last visited July 19, 2004).

3. See, e.g, Thomas E. Ricks, *Making the Corps* (New York: Scribner, 1997), 279–97.

4. See, e.g., Kevin J. Barry, "A Face Lift (and Much More) for an Aging Beauty: The Cox Commission Recommendations to Rejuvenate the Uniform Code of Military Justice," *Law Review of Michigan State University Detroit College of Law* (2002): 57–128, 117–18; Richard B. Cole, "Prosecutorial Discretion in the Mili-

tary Justice System: Is It Time for a Change?" *American Journal of Criminal Law* 19 (1992): 395–409.

5. See, e.g., Fredric I. Lederer and Barbara Hundley Zeliff, "Needed: An Independent Judiciary," in Eugene R. Fidell and Dwight H. Sullivan, eds., *Evolving Military Justice* (Annapolis, MD: Naval Institute Press, 2002), 27–59.

6. See, e.g., Christopher W. Behan, "Don't Tug On Superman's Cape: In Defense of Convening Authority Selection and Appointment of Court-Martial Panel Members," *Military Law Review* 176 (2003): 190–308.

7. See, e.g., Major James Kevin Lovejoy, "Abolition of Court Member Sentencing in the Military, *Military Law Review* 142 (1993): 1–62.

8. For assessments of the trends in modern courts-martial, see Major Walter M. Hudson, "Two Senior Judges Look Back and Look Ahead: An Interview with Senior Judge Robinson O. Everett and Senior Judge Walter T. Cox III," *Military Law Review* 142 (2000): 42–96; John S. Cooke, "Manual for Courts-Martial 20X," in Fidell and Sullivan, *Evolving Military Justice*, 173–94.

9. Military Justice Act of 1983, Pub. L. No. 98–209, 97 Stat. 1393 (1983). For background, see Andrew S. Effron, "Supreme Court Review of Decisions by the Court of Military Appeals: The Legislative Background," *Army Lawyer* (January 1985): 59.

10. On the multiple roles of judge advocates in late-twentieth-century conflicts, see Frederic L. Borch, *Judge Advocates in Combat: Army Lawyers in Military Operations from Vietnam to Haiti* (Washington, DC: Office of the Judge Advocate General and Center of Military History, United States Army, 2001).

11. See, e.g., Jonathan Turley, "Pax Militaris: The *Feres* Doctrine and the Retention of Sovereign Immunity in the Military System of Governance," *George Washington Law Review* 1 (2003): 77–81; Diane H. Mazur, "Rehnquist's Vietnam: Constitutional Separatism and the Stealth Advance of Martial Law," *Indiana Law Journal* 77 (2002): 701–91; Jonathan Turley, "Tribunals and Tribulations: The Antithetical Elements of Military Governance in a Madisonian Democracy," *George Washington Law Review* 70 (2002): 649–780.

12. *Toth v. Quarles*, 350 U.S. 11 (1955); *Reid v. Covert*, 354 U.S. 1 (1957); *Kinsella v. Singleton*, 361 U.S. 234 (1960); *McElroy v. Guagliardo*, 361 U.S. 234 (1960); *Grisham v. Hagan*, 361 U.S. 278 (1960); *O'Callahan v. Parker*, 395 U.S. 258 (1969); *Latney v. Ignatius*, 416 F.2d 821 (D.C. Cir. 1969).

13. *Solorio v. United States*, 483 U.S. 435 (1987) overruling *O'Callahan v. Parker*, 395 U.S. 258 (1969); *Parker v. Levy*, 417 U.S. 733 (1974); *Rostker v. Goldberg*, 453 U.S. 57 (1981).

14. On the limited congressional and civilian interest in military justice matters since the Vietnam era, see the Cox Commission Report of 2001, reprinted and analyzed in Barry, "A Face Lift." I served as reporter for this commission.

15. See, e.g., Beth Hillman, "Chains of Command," *Legal Affairs* (May–June 2002): 50–51.

16. See Kenneth J. Hodson, "Military Justice: Abolish or Change?" *Kansas Law Review* 22 (1973): 31–54; Joseph W. Bishop, Jr., *Justice under Fire: A Study of Military Law* (New York: Charterhouse, 1974); Robert Sherrill, *Military Justice Is to Justice as Military Music Is to Music* (New York: Harper and Row, 1970).

17. On civilian involvement in military justice at the end of the twentieth cen-

tury, see Kevin J. Barry, "Modernizing the Manual for Courts-Martial Rule-Making Process: A Work in Progress," *Military Law Review* 165 (2000): 237–76; Barry, "A Face Lift"; Eugene R. Fidell, "Going on Fifty: Evolution and Devolution in Military Justice," *Wake Forest Law Review* 32 (1997): 1213–34; http://www.nimj.org (last visited January 27, 2004).

18. See Barry, "Modernizing the Manual for Courts-Martial Rule-Making Process."

19. See, e.g., Carrie Peterson, "Separation Anxiety and Boot Camp: Why Basic Training Should Remain Gender-Integrated," *Law and Inequality: A Journal of Theory and Practice* 17 (1999): 139–70; C. Quince Hopkins, "Rank Matters but Should Marriage?: Adultery, Fraternization, and Honor in the Military," *UCLA Women's Law Journal* 9 (1999): 177–250; Elizabeth Lutes Hillman, "The 'Good Soldier' Defense: Character Evidence and Military Rank at Courts-Martial," *Yale Law Journal* 108 (1999): 879–911; Martha Chamallas, "The New Gender Panic: Reflections on Sex Scandals and the Military," *Minnesota Law Review* 83 (1998): 305–70; Jean Zimmerman, *Tailspin* (New York: Doubleday, 1995); Yxta Maya Murray, "Sexual Harassment in the Military," *Southern California Review of Law and Women's Studies* 3 (1994): 279–302; J. Richard Chema, "Arresting 'Tailhook': The Prosecution of Sexual Harassment in the Military," *Military Law Review* 140 (1993): 1–63.

20. A 1990 study found more than a third of military women experience harassment; eighty percent of female cadets at the Air Force Academy reported being demeaned on a daily basis; high rates of rape, attempted rape, and domestic violence exist in military communities. See, e.g., Murray, "Sexual Harassment in the Military," 280–83; Hopkins, "Rank Matters," 202–4 and 232–38; Madeline Morris, "By Force of Arms: Rape, War, and Military Culture," *Duke Law Journal* 45 (1999): 651–761. On antigay harassment, see the annual reports of the Servicemembers Legal Defense Network at http://www.sldn.org and the data collected by the Center for the Study of Sexual Minorities in the Military at http://www.gaymilitary.ucsb.edu (last visited March 15, 2004).

21. See, e.g., Richard N. Haass, *Intervention: The Use of American Military Force in the Post–Cold War World* (Washington, DC: Carnegie Endowment for International Peace, 1994) (describing recent cases of American military peacekeeping in the former Yugoslavia, Somalia, and Haiti); James Burk, ed., *The Military in New Times: Adapting Armed Forces to a Turbulent World* (Boulder, CO: Westview Press, 1994).

22. See, e.g., James Surowiecki, "The Financial Page: Army, Inc.," *New Yorker* (January 12, 2004): 27 (criticizing the "outsourcing" trend); Marek Fuchs, "Out of Khaki, into Blue at the Gates of West Point," *New York Times*, January 21, 2004 (describing how West Point replaced the military police who formerly guarded its gates with civilian security personnel); Dan Baum, "Nation Builders for Hire," *New York Times Magazine*, June 27, 2003, 32–27 (chronicling the outsourcing of the American effort to restore Iraqi industry).

23. On October 26, 2000, Congress passed Senate Bill 768, the "Military Extraterritorial Jurisdiction Act of 2000." See 1400 Stat. 2488 (Nov. 22, 2000).

24. 18 U.S.C. sec. 3261.

25. 18 U.S.C. sec. 3261(c).

26. "President Issues Military Order: Detention, Treatment, and Trial of Cer-

tain Non-citizens in the War against Terrorism," www.whitehouse.gov/news/ releases/2001/11/20011113-27.html (Nov. 13, 2001).

27. For arguments in support of the commissions' legitimacy, see Curtis A. Bradley and Jack L. Goldsmith, "The Constitutional Validity of Military Commissions," *Green Bag 2d* 5 (2002): 249–60; Gary D. Solis, "Military Commissions and Terrorists," in Fidell and Sullivan, *Evolving Military Justice,* 195–205; Ruth Wedgwood, "Al Qaeda, Terrorism and Military Commissions," *American Journal of International Law* (2002): 328–39, Viet D. Dinh, "Freedom and Security after September 11," *Harvard Journal of Law and Public Policy* 25 (2002): 399–405; Oren Gross, "Chaos and Rules: Should Responses to Violent Crises Always Be Constitutional?" *Yale Law Journal* 112 (2003): 1011–1134. For arguments critical of the tribunals, see Neal K. Katyal and Laurence H. Tribe, "Waging War, Deciding Guilt: Trying the Military Tribunals," *Yale Law Journal* 111 (2002): 1259–1310; Laura A. Dickinson, "Using Legal Process to Fight Terrorism: Detentions, Military Commissions, International Tribunals, and the Rule of Law," *Southern California Law Review* 75 (2002): 1407–84; Turley, "Tribunals and Tribulations."

28. See Article 18, UCMJ, 10 U.S.C. sec. 818 ("General courts-martial also have jurisdiction to try any person who by the law of war is subject to trial by a military tribunal. . . ."); UCMJ, Article 21, 10 U.S.C. sec. 821 ("The provisions of this chapter conferring jurisdiction upon courts-martial do not deprive military commissions, provost courts, or other military tribunals of concurrent jurisdiction with respect to offenders or offenses that by statute or by the law of war may be tried by military commissions, provost courts, or other military tribunals."). On the use of courts-martial and other types of military tribunals to try terrorists, see Robinson O. Everett and Scott L. Silliman, "Forums for Punishing Offenses against the Law of Nations," *Wake Forest Law Review* 29 (1994): 509–23; Robinson O. Everett, "The Law of War: Military Tribunals and the War on Terrorism," *Federal Lawyer* 48 (Dec. 2001): 20–23.

29. See UCMJ, Article 36, for the president's explicit statutory authority to prescribe the rules for courts-martial. On the rule-making process with respect to military commissions, see Eugene R. Fidell, "Military Commissions and Administrative Law," *Green Bag 2d* 6 (July 2003): 379–89.

30. See, e.g., William H. Rehnquist, *All the Laws But One: Civil Liberties in Wartime* (New York: Alfred A. Knopf, 1998); Michal R. Belknap, "A Putrid Pedigree: The Bush Administration's Military Tribunals in Historical Perspective," *California Western Law Review* 38 (2002): 433–82; Carol Chomsky, "The United States–Dakota War Trials: A Study in Military Justice," *Stanford Law Review* 43 (1990): 13–106.

31. See especially Rehnquist, *All the Laws but One,* 3–169.

32. See, e.g., David J. Danelski, "The Saboteurs' Case," *Journal of Supreme Court History* 1: (1996): 61–82; G. Edward White, "Felix Frankfurter's 'Soliloquy' in *Ex parte Quirin*: Nazi Sabotage and Constitutional Conundrums," *Green Bag 2d* 5 (2002): 423–38; Peter Maguire, *Law and War: An American Story* (New York: Columbia University Press, 2000).

33. For an overview of judge advocates' roles in these conflicts, see Borch, *Judge Advocates in Combat.*

34. See, e.g., Everett and Silliman, "Forums for Punishing Offenses against the Law of Nations."

35. U.S. Constitution, Article I, sec. 8.

36. U.S. Constitution, Article II, sec. 2.

37. *Ex parte Milligan*, 71 U.S. (4 Wall.) 2 (1867).

38. *Ex parte Quirin*, 317 U.S. 1 (1942); David J. Danelski, "The Saboteurs' Case," *Journal of Supreme Court History* 1 (1996): 61–82; G. Edward White, "Felix Frankfurter's 'Soliloquy' in *Ex parte Quirin*: Nazi Sabotage and Constitutional Conundrums," *Green Bag 2d* 5 (2002): 423–38; *In re Yamashita*, 327 U.S. 1 (1946); *Johnson v. Eisentrager*, 339 U.S. 763 (1950).

39. For a detailed, if preliminary, analysis of the rules, see *Military Commissions Instructions Sourcebook* (Washington, DC: National Institute of Military Justice, 2003).

40. *Rasul v. Bush*, 124 S. Ct. 2686 (2004); *Hamdi v. Rumsfeld*, 124 S. Ct. 2633 (2004).

41. *Rumsfeld v. Padilla*, 124 S. Ct. 2711 (2004).

INDEX

POLITICS AND SOCIETY IN TWENTIETH-CENTURY AMERICA

Morning in America: How Ronald Reagan Invented the 1980s
by Gil Troy

Defending America: Military Culture and the Cold War Court-Martial
by Elizabeth Lutes Hillman